Second Language Learning
Contrastive Analysis, Error Analysis, and Related Aspects

Edited by
Betty Wallace Robinett and
Jacquelyn Schachter

D1521842

Ann Arbor
The University of Michigan Press

Library of Congress Cataloging in Publication Data

Main entry under title:

Second language learning.

    Bibliography: p.
    1. Language and languages—Study and teaching—
Addresses, essays, lectures. 2. Contrastive
linguistics—Addresses, essays, lectures. I. Robinett,
P51.S34 1983   407   83-1245
ISBN 0-472-10027-0
ISBN 0-472-08033-4 (pbk.)

Second Language Learning

Preface

This book is intended to serve as a text for a graduate level semester or quarter course. The first two sections provide a survey of the historical underpinnings of second language research in contrastive analysis and error analysis. The remaining section broadens the perspectives on second language learning to include recent developments in this emerging field.

The articles have been carefully chosen to represent various viewpoints and approaches within each section. Included are both theoretical presentations and articles which exhibit application of theory.

Each section contains a set of discussion questions designed to integrate the readings and to facilitate the use of the book as a classroom text. A unique feature of the volume is the presence of data on learner errors in problem format. These problems have been classroom tested and have proved useful in training people to analyze language learner data.

It is our hope that since the volume provides broad coverage of areas related to second language learning, particularly from a linguistic perspective, it will serve the needs of a wide audience, including ESL/EFL teachers and the growing number of students interested in applied linguistics, second language learning, and education. We welcome comments.

Betty Wallace Robinett
Jacquelyn Schachter

Contents

Contrastive Analysis

Introduction

A contrastive analysis (CA) of the structure of two languages is said to enable one to predict problems encountered or to explain errors made by those learning a second language. Wardhaugh applies the terms *strong hypothesis* to the predictive application of CA and *weak hypothesis* to the explanatory. He feels that the weak form of CA is probably used most often, and he questions the validity of the strong version, the predictive ability of CA.

Lado was an early proponent of the predictive use of CA. Reflecting the viewpoint held by Charles C. Fries, he advocates the use of CA as a basis for selecting the content of language teaching materials. He maintains that a careful comparison of the native language of the learner with the language to be learned will result in predictable problems for the learner, which, therefore, should be points of emphasis in instructional materials.

Stockwell and Bowen took the predictive version of CA one step further: they presented a "hierarchy of difficulty" of learning problems based on types of differences between languages. Their approach argues that the greater the difference between languages, where *difference* is defined in terms of the relative freedom of choice the speaker has in specified contexts, the more persistent the predicted errors will be. In commenting on their work later, Stockwell pointed out the following:

> Our hierarchy itself—the ranking of particular problems of pronunciation on a scale from hardest to acquire and most persistently difficult down to virtual nonexistence as problems—is totally empirical in terms of our own experience in some ten years of intensive Spanish teaching. The only thing that was theoretical was our attempt to categorize these errors in terms which seemed to us to provide an explanation of why the facts should be as our experience indicated them to be.[1]

The Lehn and Slager article offers a classical contrastive analysis of the sound systems of English and Egyptian Arabic. The authors provide the familiar contrastive charts of the segmental phonemes of the two languages from which they deduce their predictions of difficulties that Arabic speakers will encounter in learning English. Their conclusions, they point out, "have been supplemented by our own observations made in the teaching of English to Egyptian secondary school and university students."

In another example of the classical predictive approach, Koutsoudas and Koutsoudas introduce a perspective toward sources of difficulty that differs from that of Lado, who claims that the major source of difficulty is the *differences* in the systems: "Those elements that are similar to his native language will be simple for him, and those elements that are different will be difficult" (*Linguistics Across Cultures,* p. 2). Koutsoudas and Koutsoudas, on the other hand, predict interference where there are *similarities:* "We believe that interference will occur whenever the student is presented with a foreign sound which has some perceptual degree of similarity to a phoneme in his native language."

The article by Brière, Campbell, and Soemarmo, and the article by Ritchie both point out the need for caution in the interpretation of contrastive analyses of two phonological systems on the basis of phonemic inventories alone. The evidence provided in the Brière et al. article demonstrates the importance of the syllable in explaining the presence or absence of phonological interference in particular cases. Ritchie points out the possible use of distinctive feature analysis in generative phonology as a means of explaining certain errors and in developing instructional materials to deal with learners' pronunciation errors.

Because of differing attitudes toward the use of CA, an article like that by James is important. He describes his article as "an attempt to examine critically some recurrent strictures on the logical foundation of, and hence continued practice of, CA in language teaching." In it he provides counterarguments to the major criticisms of CA, not in a polemic fashion but as a matter of general information.

The last three articles in this section represent the application of CA to language in a broader sense. They include discussions of the application of CA to the study of lexical contrasts, the part played by the cognitive process as related to languages in contact, and the analysis of cultural contrasts in communication.

Prator, in a 1963 application of CA to an aspect of language other than phonology, examines some lexical items of temperature in English, Chinese, and French to illustrate the necessity of contrasting them in their actual use rather than merely as discrete and isolated linguistic items.

Cowan's interest in CA revolves around the development of a theory of language acquisition based on principles that will predict interlingual interference. His concern is with the cognitive processes by which a learner establishes a correspondence between rules in the first language and those in the language being learned. He cites examples from English as contrasted with Hausa, Farsi, and German to illustrate "the principles that predict the likelihood of an error's occurring once a correspondence has been established." His principles are not meant to account for all interference errors; rather, he poses them as one step along the path toward an explanatory theory of second language acquisition, one aspect of which is the prediction of interference errors.

Weeks documents cultural contrasts in the discourse of Yakima Indian children and non-Indian children. The Indian children in her study, for example, tended to organize discourse into narrative form more often than did the non-Indian children, reflecting a cultural-rhetorical difference in the two groups.

The selections in this section provide a view of CA that reveals a change in emphasis from contrasts of discrete linguistic items to those of language use, culture, and patterns of discourse. Interestingly enough, this broader approach parallels the changes over the years in research in language teaching and language learning.

Note

1. Robert P. Stockwell, "Contrastive Analysis and Lapsed Time," *Report of the Nineteenth Annual Round Table Meeting on Linguistics and Language Studies* (Washington, D.C.: Georgetown University Press, 1968), p. 19.

The Contrastive Analysis Hypothesis

Ronald Wardhaugh

During the course of their reading, students of linguistics encounter a number of very interesting hypotheses concerning different aspects of language and language function. One long-lived hypothesis which has attracted considerable attention from time to time—but more, it must be added, from psychologists and anthropologists than from linguists—is the Sapir-Whorf hypothesis with its claim that the structure of a language subtly influences the cognitive processes of the speakers of that language.

A much more recent hypothesis, and one much more intriguing to linguists today than the Sapir-Whorf hypothesis, is the language-acquisition device hypothesis proposed by the generative-transformationalists. This hypothesis is that infants are innately endowed with the ability to acquire a natural language and all they need to set the process of language acquisition going are natural language data. Only by postulating such a language-acquisition device can a generative-transformationalist account for certain linguistic universals, including, of course, not only one very important universal, the ability to learn a first language with ease, but also, apparently, another universal, the inability to learn a second language after childhood without difficulty. Like the Sapir-Whorf hypothesis, the language-acquisition device hypothesis is extremely intriguing, but it too presents seemingly insurmountable difficulties to anyone seeking to devise a critical test to prove its truth or falsity. A linguist may accept the hypotheses because they usefully and economically explain certain language data that he wants to explain in terms of a set of axioms he can accept; or he may reject the hypotheses because they reek of mentalism or subjectivity, or because he prefers a different set of axioms on which to base his work.

Still a third hypothesis, and the one which is of special interest in this paper, is the contrastive analysis hypothesis, a hypothesis of particular interest to those linguists who are engaged in language teaching and in

Reprinted from *TESOL Quarterly* 4, no. 2 (1970):123–30, copyright 1970 by Teachers of English to Speakers of Other Languages, by permission of the publisher and the author. This paper was presented at the TESOL Convention, March, 1970.

writing language-teaching materials. However, the contrastive analysis hypothesis also raises many difficulties in practice, so many in fact that one may be tempted to ask whether it is really possible to make contrastive analyses. And even if the answer to that question is a more or less hesitant affirmative, then one may well question the value to teachers and curriculum workers of the results of such analyses.

Actually the contrastive analysis hypothesis may be stated in two versions, a *strong* version and a *weak* version. In this paper the claim will be made that the strong version is quite unrealistic and impracticable, even though it is the one on which those who write contrastive analyses usually claim to base their work. On the other hand, the weak version does have certain possibilities for usefulness. However, even the weak version is suspect in some linguistic circles.

It is possible to quote several representative statements of what has just been referred to as the strong version of the contrastive analysis hypothesis. First of all, Lado in the preface to *Linguistics Across Cultures* (1957) writes as follows:

> The plan of the book rests on the assumption that we can predict and describe the patterns that will cause difficulty in learning, and those that will not cause difficulty, by comparing systematically the language and culture to be learned with the native language and culture of the student. [P. vii]

Lado goes on to cite Fries in support of this proposition. Here is the appropriate quotation from Fries's *Teaching and Learning English as a Foreign Language* (1945):

> The most efficient materials are those that are based upon a scientific description of the language to be learned, carefully compared with a parallel description of the native language of the learner. [P. 9]

More recently, in a book edited by Valdman, entitled *Trends in Language Teaching* (1966), Banathy, Trager, and Waddle state the strong version of the contrastive analysis hypothesis as follows:

> . . . the change that has to take place in the language behavior of a foreign language student can be equated with the differences between the structure of the student's native language and culture and that of the target language and culture. The task of the linguist, the

cultural anthropologist, and the sociologist is to identify these differences. The task of the writer of a foreign language teaching program
is to develop materials which will be based on a statement of these
differences; the task of the foreign language teacher is to be aware
of these differences and to be prepared to teach them; the task of
the student is to learn them. [P. 37]

The same idea is presented in each of these three statements, the idea
that it is possible to contrast the system of one language—the grammar,
phonology, and lexicon—with the system of a second language in order to
predict those difficulties which a speaker of the second language will have
in learning the first language and to construct teaching materials to help
him learn that language.

An evaluation of this strong version of the contrastive analysis hypothesis suggests that it makes demands of linguistic theory, and, therefore, of linguists, that they are in no position to meet. At the very least
this version demands of linguists that they have available a set of linguistic universals formulated within a comprehensive linguistic theory which
deals adequately with syntax, semantics, and phonology. Furthermore, it
requires that they have a theory of contrastive linguistics into which they
can plug complete linguistic descriptions of the two languages being contrasted so as to produce the correct set of contrasts between the two
languages. Ideally, linguists should not have to refer at all to speakers of
the two languages under contrast for either confirmation or disconfirma-
tion of the set of contrasts generated by any such theory of contrastive
linguistics. They should actually be able to carry out their contrastive
studies quite far removed from speakers of the two languages, possibly
without even knowing anything about the two languages in question except what is recorded in the grammars they are using. Such seems to be
the procedure which the strong version of the contrastive analysis hypothesis demands of linguists. Stated in this way, the strong version
doubtless sounds quite unrealistic, but it should be emphasized that *most
writers of contrastive analyses try to create the impression that this is the
version of the hypothesis on which they have based their work*—or at least
could base their work if absolutely necessary. Here is yet another instance
of a "pseudoprocedure" in linguistics, a pseudoprocedure being a procedure which linguists claim they could follow in order to achieve definitive
results if only there were enough time.

If one looks specifically at how phonological problems have been
dealt with in this strong version, he can easily find evidence to support
the assertions just made. Many a linguist has presented contrastive state-

ments of the phonemic systems of two languages without asking whether it is possible to contrast the phonemic systems of two languages by procedures which attempt to relate an English *p* to a French *p*, because linguists have chosen to symbolize some not well-defined similarity between the two languages in the same way, in this case by the letter *p*, or because both *p*'s are associated with certain movements of the glottis and lips. The use of the similarity of the symbols is more deceiving than the use of the similarity of phonetic features. The latter may be justified to some extent in terms of what will be referred to later as the weak version of the hypothesis, but statements about a language *lacking* certain phonemes or two languages having the *same* phonemes are possibly even more dangerous than they are naive. Any such statements must ultimately rest on phonetic evidence, and, if they do, the strong version of the hypothesis is being disregarded in favor of the weak version. As Weinreich (1953) points out, phonemes are not commensurable across languages; phones, individual sounds, are much more manageable, because they do have some connection with events in the world, in this case articulatory and acoustic events.

Let us suppose that a linguist contrasts the allophonic variants described in accounts he finds of the phonological system of two languages. Could he then meet the demands of the strong version? Once again the answer must be negative, at least within the present state of linguistic knowledge. Ideally, a linguist interested in making a contrastive analysis would like to be able to take a statement of the allophones of Language A and say for each one exactly what difficulties a speaker of Language B would have in producing that allophone. However, the difficulties in the way of doing this are formidable. Are the phonetic statements the linguist finds sufficiently detailed and of the right kind to be of use: that is, what is the adequacy of the *phonetic theory* and the particular phonetic information at his disposal? Do the descriptions take into account all the phonological variables that should be taken into account, such as segmentation, stress, tone, pitch and juncture, and syllable, morpheme, word and sentence structures: that is, what is the state of the *phonological theory* he is using? Does the linguist have available to him an overall contrastive system within which he can relate the two languages in terms of mergers, splits, zeroes, overdifferentiations, underdifferentiations, reinterpretations, and so on: that is, what is the state of the *contrastive theory* he is employing? In this age of linguistic uncertainty the answer to all of these questions is obvious.

It seems, therefore, not a little strange, given all the problems which the strong version of the contrastive analysis hypothesis creates, that so many linguists claim to use it in their work. None of them has actually conformed to its requirements in such work. However, there have been attempts, some more successful and some less successful, to use what may be called the weak version of the contrastive analysis hypothesis. In this case, one must offer his own definition of the weak version, because the literature contains little or no reference to what linguists have actually done in practice, in contrast to what they have claimed they were doing or could do.

The weak version requires of the linguist only that he use the best linguistic knowledge available to him in order to account for observed difficulties in second language learning. It does not require what the strong version requires, the prediction of those difficulties and, conversely, of those learning points which do not create any difficulties at all. The weak version leads to an approach which makes fewer demands of contrastive theory than does the strong version. It starts with the evidence provided by linguistic interference and uses such evidence to explain the similarities and differences between systems. There should be no mistake about the emphasis on systems. In this version systems *are* important, because there is no regression to any presystemic view of language, nor does the approach result in merely classifying errors in any way that occurs to the investigator. However, the starting point in the contrast is provided by actual evidence from such phenomena as faulty translation, learning difficulties, residual foreign accents, and so on, and reference is made to the two systems only in order to explain actually observed interference phenomena.

A close reading of most of the contrastive analyses which are available shows them to conform to some of the demands made by the weak version of the theory and not at all to the demands of the strong version. Even the two highly regarded texts on English and Spanish by Stockwell and Bowen, *The Sounds of English and Spanish* (1965) and *The Grammatical Structures of English and Spanish* (1965), fall into this category. It appears that Stockwell and Bowen use their linguistic knowledge to explain what they know from experience to be problems English speakers have in learning Spanish. The linguistic theory they use is actually extremely eclectic and contains insights from generative transformational, structural, and paradigmatic grammars; nowhere in the texts is there an obvious attempt to predict errors using an overriding contrastive theory of any power. Even the hierarchy of difficulty which Stockwell and Bowen establish in the second chapter of the *Sounds* volume is based more on their experience and intuition than on an explicit theory for predicting difficulties.

In recent years there have been two still different approaches taken to the problems of contrastive analysis, both resulting from the current enthusiasm for generative transformational theory. One of these approaches dismisses the hypothesis from any consideration at all. This dismissal stems from a strong negative reaction to contrastive analysis, as, for example, in recent articles by Ritchie (1967) and Wolfe (1967) in *Language Learning*. The second approach attempts to use the generative-transformational model in order to provide some of the necessary overriding theory to meet either the demands of prediction in the strong version or of explanation in the weak version.

The case for dismissal may be stated as follows: Languages do not differ from each other without limit in unpredictable ways, statements to the contrary notwithstanding. All natural languages have a great deal in common so that anyone who has learned one language already *knows* a great deal about any other language he must learn. Not only does he know a great deal about that other language even before he begins to learn it, but the deep structures of both languages are very much alike, so that the actual differences between the two languages are really quite superficial. However, to learn the second language—and this is the important point—one must learn the precise way in which that second language relates the deep structures to its surface structures and their phonetic representations. Since this way is unique for each language, contrastive analysis can be of little or no help at all in the learning task because the rules to be internalized are, of course, unique. Even though the form and some of the content of the rules to be acquired might be identical for both languages, the combinations of these for individual languages are quite idiosyncratic so that superficial contrastive statements can in no way help the learner in his task.

Now there is obviously some merit in the above argument. If the underlying vowel system of French is something like the one Schane outlines in *French Phonology and Morphology* (1968), and the underlying vowel system of English is something like the one Chomsky and Halle outline in *The Sound Pattern of English* (1968), and if the speaker of English must somehow internalize the underlying vowel system of French and the fifty or so phonetic realization rules which Schane gives in order to speak acceptable French, then one may easily be tempted to reject the whole notion of contrastive analysis, claiming that it has nothing at all to contribute to an understanding of the learning task that is involved.

Uncertainty is obviously piled upon uncertainty in making contrastive analyses. Such uncertainties arise from inadequacies in existing linguistic theories. As an example of theoretical inadequacy, one may observe that the notion of deep structure itself is extremely uncertain. Chomsky (1968), McCawley (1968), and Fillmore (1968) all mean somewhat different things by it, but all at least agree that it has something to do with meaning. However, for the purposes of contrastive analysis any claim that all languages are very much the same at the level of deep structure seems to be little more than a claim that it is possible to talk about the same things in all languages, which is surely not a very interesting claim, except perhaps in that it seems to contradict the one made by Sapir and Whorf. The preceding statement is not meant to be a criticism of generative transformational theory; it is meant to show how acceptance of that theory can fairly easily lead one to reject the idea that it is possible to make contrastive analyses, or, put less strongly, to reject the idea that generative transformational theory has something to contribute to a theory of contrastive analysis, given the present state of the art.

Many experienced teachers find themselves unable to accept such reasons for rejection of the hypothesis. Their experience tells them that a Frenchman is likely to pronounce English *think* as *sink* and a Russian likely to pronounce it as *tink,* that a Spaniard will almost certainly fail to differentiate English *bit* from *beat,* and that an Englishman learning French will tend to pronounce the French word *plume* as *pleem* or *ploom.* They admit that in each case they must be prepared to teach the whole of the second language to a learner, but also insist that some parts of that second language are easier to learn than others, for no one ever must learn *everything* about the second language. However, many also admit that they do not know in what order learners should try to overcome the various difficulties they are observed to have. Should a Spaniard learning English learn to differentiate *bit* from *beat* and *bet* from *bait* because of the important surface contrasts which he does not make in Spanish? Or should he learn to associate the vowels in such pairs of words as *weep* and *wept, pale* and *pallid, type* and *typical, tone* and *tonic, deduce* and *deduction* so that he can somehow internalize the underlying phonological system of English? The mind boggles at this last possibility! But it is one which descriptions of Spanish and English based on generative transformational theory would seem to hold out for teachers.

Some recent suggestions for using generative transformational theory in contrastive analysis have actually been attempts to bring powerful theoretical insights to bear within the weaker version of the hypothesis in order to explain observed interference phenomena, for example some interesting work by Ritchie (1968) and by Carter (unpublished). In their work, Ritchie and Carter have used distinctive feature hierarchies in attempts to explain such problems as why a Russian is likely to say *tink* and a Frenchman *sink* for English *think*. Such work, using the notions of feature hierarchy, rule cycling, and morpheme and word structure rules, has considerable possibilities. Certainly this kind of work seems more promising than some being done by others in an attempt to show gross similarities between deep structures in an assortment of languages.

In conclusion, it is fair to say that teachers of second or foreign languages are living in very uncertain times. A decade or so ago contrastive analysis was still a fairly new and exciting idea apparently holding great promise for teaching and curriculum construction. Now, one is not so sure—and not solely as a result of the Chomskyan revolution in linguistics. The contrastive analysis hypothesis has not proved to be workable, at least not in the strong version in which it was originally expressed. This version can work only for one who is prepared to be quite naive in linguistic matters. In its weak version, however, it has proved to be helpful and undoubtedly will continue to be so as linguistic theory develops. However, the hypothesis probably will have less influence on second language teaching and on course construction in the next decade than it apparently has had in the last decade. One cannot predict whether that diminishing influence will have a good or bad effect on second language teaching. Today contrastive analysis is only one of many uncertain variables which one must reevaluate in second language teaching. No longer does it seem to be as important as it once was. Perhaps, like the Sapir-Whorf hypothesis, it too is due for a period of quiescence.

References

Banathy, Bela; Trager, Edith Crowell; and Waddle, Carl D. "The Use of Contrastive Data in Foreign Language Course Development." *Trends in Language Teaching,* edited by A. Valdman, pp. 27–56. New York: McGraw-Hill, 1966.

Carter, Richard J. "An Approach to a Theory of Phonetic Difficulties in Second-Language Learning." Bolt Beranek and Newman Inc., Report No. 1575.

Chomsky, Noam. *Language and Mind.* New York: Harcourt, Brace & World, 1968.

Chomsky, Noam, and Halle, Morris. *The Sound Pattern of English.* New York: Harper & Row, 1968.

Fillmore, Charles J. "The Case for Case." *Universals in Linguistic Theory,* edited by E. Bach and R. T. Harms, pp. 1–88. New York: Holt, Rinehart and Winston, 1968.

Fries, Charles C. *Teaching and Learning English as a Foreign Language.* Ann Arbor: University of Michigan Press, 1945.

Lado, Robert. *Linguistics Across Cultures*. Ann Arbor: University of Michigan Press, 1957.

McCawley, James D. "The Role of Semantics in a Grammar." *Universals in Linguistic Theory*, edited by E. Bach and R. T. Harms, pp. 124–69. New York: Holt, Rinehart and Winston, 1968.

Ritchie, William C. "Some Implications of Generative Grammar for the Construction of Courses in English as a Foreign Language." *Language Learning* 17 (1967):45–69, 111–31.

———. "On the Explanation of Phonic Interference." *Language Learning* 18 (1968):183–97.

Schane, Sanford. A. *French Phonology and Morphology*. Cambridge, Mass.: MIT Press, 1968.

Stockwell, Robert P., and Bowen, J. Donald. *The Sounds of English and Spanish*. Chicago: University of Chicago Press, 1965.

Stockwell, Robert P.; Bowen, J. Donald; and Martin, John W. *The Grammatical Structures of English and Spanish*. Chicago: University of Chicago Press, 1965.

Weinreich, Uriel. *Language in Contact: Findings and Problems*. New York: Linguistic Circle of New York, 1953.

Wolfe, David L. "Some Theoretical Aspects of Language Learning and Language Teaching." *Language Learning* 17 (1967):173–88.

Procedures in Comparing Two Grammatical Structures

Robert Lado

General Procedure

We begin with an analysis of the foreign language and compare it structure by structure with the native language. For each structure we need to know if there is a structure in the native language (1) signaled the same way, that is, by the same formal device, (2) having the same meaning, and (3) similarly distributed in the system of that language. Let's illustrate these points. Both English and German have the kind of sentences we call questions. Both English and German use word order as the signal in many questions. So far we have not discovered any structural problem as to (1) formal device or (2) meaning. We note further that English uses the function word *do, does, did* before the subject to achieve the word order signal of that type of question. German does not use that device. We have thus found a problem as to (1) formal signaling device. We may expect a German speaker to say, for example, *Know you where the church is?* as a question instead of *Do you know where the church is?* He will simply be transferring the German pattern *Wissen Sie wo die Kirche ist?* which is similar to the pattern used with the verb *be* in English but not with the verb *know.*

Let's consider an illustration with Spanish as the native language. Both English and Spanish have the type of sentences we call questions. But questions which are signaled in English by means of word order are signaled in Spanish by an intonation contrast. We can expect trouble here since the Spanish speaker has learned to react to the intonation signal and to disregard the order of the words, which in his language is not structurally significant in this particular case. He has to learn to react to a different medium—word order—for the same structure. The German speaker had less of a task since his problem was simply to use a new word, *do,* in a medium—word order—which he already used in his native language to signal a question.

Reprinted from *Linguistics Across Cultures* (Ann Arbor: University of Michigan Press, 1957), pages 66–70, and 72 by permission of the publisher and the author.

More Specific Procedures

In a signaling system less complex than human language, for example in the flag language used at sea, the above general procedure for comparison of two systems would be more than enough. In human language, however, the situation is much more complex, and we need to illustrate the procedure in greater detail.

First step: Locate the best structural description of the languages involved. Both descriptions should contain the form, meaning, and distribution of the structures. If the form, the meaning, or the distribution of a pattern is not described, or not adequately described, an attempt must be made to describe it accurately before proceeding any further.

Second step: Summarize in compact outline form all the structures. If English is one of the languages involved, we would describe the sentence types in it as questions, statements, requests, calls (Fries 1952, chaps. 3, 8). Under questions would be several patterns: questions with the verb *be;* questions with *do, does, did;* questions with *can, may, will,* etc. (function words of group B in Fries's classification [1952, chap. 6]); questions with *when, where, why,* etc., plus reversal of word order; questions with *who, what,* etc., as subject; questions with a mid–high intonation sequence regardless of word order; and other minor types of questions.

For each type, we need to know the inventory of formal signals at the sentence level. For questions with *be,* as for example *Is he a farmer?* the inventory would include (1) the form of *be* preceding the subject, (2) a sentence tie between *be* and the subject (Fries 1952, pp. 144–45), (3) a falling high–low intonation. We also need to know the structural meaning of this pattern, namely, "to elicit verbal responses of the yes-no types (*yes; no; certainly; yes, he is;* etc.)." As to distribution, this sentence occurs as a sequence sentence, that is, after another sentence has been said, in conversational style. We know this because it contains the sequence signal *he.* In situations in which the farmer of the example is in the attention of both speaker and listener, for example in a picture or present in person, *Is he a farmer?* can then also be used as a situation utterance, that is, at the beginning of a conversation. In literature, this same type of sentence may be used at the beginning of a work for a special effect, usually to arouse curiosity as to the identity of the *he.*

Also under sentence types should be described the types occurring as response utterances, that is, in response to a previous one. For example, *Home,* in response to *Where are you going?* or *Now,* in response to *When are you going home?*

In addition to the sentence types we need the parts of speech that constitute the elements of minimal sentences. The traditional eight parts of speech in English are more than can justifiably account for the elements of minimal sentences and too few to account for the variety of expansions of sentences used in English. Fries recognizes four parts of speech, which he labels with the numbers 1, 2, 3, and 4: class 1, *idea, tea, goodness, he,* etc.; class 2, *think, drink, be, enable,* etc.; class 3, *good, thoughtful, critical,* etc; and class 4, *well, thoughtfully, critically,* etc.

The outline should include function words used in expanded sentences. Fries identifies fifteen groups of function words. A few examples are given in italics in the following sentence: *The* small cloud *that the* men saw *on the* horizon *might not* be *a* cloud *but an* island.

The structure of modification, its various patterns, meanings, and distribution, must be included in the description. What is the formal signal that makes *sky blue* a color and *blue sky* the sky in English? Can *sky* as a modifier be used in all modifier positions or is it restricted in any way?

Word elements that are syntactically relevant, that is, part of the signaling apparatus of sentences, should be included. For example, elements that identify parts of speech, as the *-s* plural of *hats,* would be relevant to sentence structure.

Sentence stress, final pauses, tentative pauses, and intonation patterns complete the outline.

A similar compact outline of the other language would conclude the work of the second step.

Third step: Actual comparison of the two language structures, pattern by pattern. If English and Spanish are being compared we would find a question pattern in Spanish illustrated by *¿Es un campesino?,* literally, 'is a farmer?' but actually equatable to English *Is he a farmer?* which usually has a high–low intonation sequence. The inventory of formal signals of the Spanish pattern includes (1) the form of *ser* 'be' and (2) a rising intonation sequence from mid to high or a rise to extra high and a drop to mid or low, or some other sequence which is also an intonation signal for this type of question.

A comparison of the formal features reveals that (1) Spanish does not require the presence of a separate word for *he,* while English does; (2) Spanish does not require a word order contrast with that of a statement, English does; and (3) Spanish requires an intonation signal which contrasts with that of statements, English does not. Problems as to form for a Spanish speaker learning English will then be (1) including a separate word, *he, she,* etc., as subject, (2) placing the verb *be* before the subject *he* to signal question, and (3) using a high–low intonation sequence instead of a rising one or an extra high–low (or mid) sequence as in Spanish.

An English speaker learning Spanish will have as his problems (1) remembering to omit a separate word for *he*, which if included will produce a stilted "foreign" style, but will not by itself change the question to a statement; and (2) using the contrastive mid–high or mid–extra high–low (or mid) intonation pattern which actually signals the question in Spanish.

A comparison of the meanings reveals no major differences. In both languages a verbal response is elicited and the response is of a yes-no type; hence no problems will be expected here.

Comparing the structures as to distribution we find that in English the pattern discussed is restricted to the verb *be* and optionally to *have*. With other verbs the pattern is constituted by the function word *do* tied to the subject and preceding it. In Spanish the pattern discussed extends to all verbs. A Spanish speaker will thus have not only the problems of the form of the pattern as listed above but also the restriction of that pattern to *be* and optionally to *have*. This problem may also be stated as another case in which one pattern in the native language can be equated to two patterns in the foreign language. The problem of the English speaker learning Spanish is less severe since he will be going from two patterns into one.

Regrouping single problem patterns into larger patterns of difficulty. By comparing each pattern in the two language systems we can discover all the learning problems, but often the problem involved in learning one pattern is parallel to or actually the same as the problem in learning another pattern. It will make for economy and neatness to regroup the problems into larger patterns. In questions with *be* we saw that the problems of the Spanish speaker learning English would be: the reversal of word order, the inclusion of a subject pronoun, and the use of a falling, high–low, intonation. Upon analyzing questions with *can, will, may*, etc., we would find that the difficulties would be precisely those connected with *be*. These then are not two problems but one and the same problem applying to two patterns in English.

Analyzing questions with *do* we would find that the problem of the same Spanish speaker learning English would be (1) including the function word *do*, (2) a reversal of word order resulting from the position of *do* at the beginning, (3) the inclusion of the subject pronoun, (4) noninflection of the lexical verb, e.g., *he studies: does he study*, and (5) a falling, high–low, intonation in most instances. We see that part of the problem is the same as with questions with *be* and with *can, will*, etc., namely the reversal of word order, the inclusion of a subject, and the use of a falling intonation.

Proceeding to questions with *when, where,* and *what, who(m), why,* not as subjects, we would find that the problems would parallel those of questions with *do* above except for the intonation, which in this case is also a falling, high–low, intonation in Spanish and would therefore not constitute a problem here. We would still have as problems (1) the inclusion of a function word, *do, can,* etc., (2) the reversal of word order, (3) the inclusion of the subject pronoun, and (4) noninflection of the lexical verb.

We could thus group these question problems into a larger pattern, involving word order and the inclusion of a subject pronoun in all cases. A falling, high–low intonation would be restricted to some patterns, those eliciting a yes-no type of response. The noninflection of the lexical verb would be a problem in all but the pattern of questions with *be.*

Necessity of Validating the Results of the Theoretical Comparative Analysis

The list of problems resulting from the comparison of the foreign language with the native language will be a most significant list for teaching, testing, research, and understanding. Yet it must be considered a list of hypothetical problems until final validation is achieved by checking it against the actual speech of students. This final check will show in some instances that a problem was not adequately analyzed and may be more of a problem than predicted. In this kind of validation we must keep in mind of course that not all the speakers of a language will have exactly the same amount of difficulty with each problem. Dialectal and personal differences rule out such a possibility. The problems will nevertheless prove quite stable and predictable for each language background.

Reference

Fries, Charles C. *The Structure of English.* New York: Harcourt, Brace and Company, 1952.

Sound Systems in Conflict:
A Hierarchy of Difficulty

Robert P. Stockwell and J. Donald Bowen

In attempting to arrive at a reasonable hierarchy of difficulty, we must take into account information from what psychologists have developed as learning theory.[1] There are no doubt many aspects of learning theory from which we might benefit, but one concept in particular seems promising: the notion of transfer—negative transfer, positive transfer, and zero transfer. A student may have some habitual responses which are contrary to the responses required for a new skill which he is trying to master (negative) or which are similar to the new responses (positive), or which have no relation to them (zero). This notion of transfer is applicable throughout the structure of the language: the sound system, the grammar, the vocabulary. Let us use illustrations of transfer based on the relation of pronunciation to spelling.

Suppose, for instance, that a student is trying to learn to pronounce Spanish by using Spanish orthography as a guide. He sees the word *Habana*, spelled (as in English) with an initial *h-*. But the *h-* is "silent" (i.e., represents no phonological reality) in Spanish orthography. The student's literacy habits have conditioned him to produce the initial sound of *have, hold, her, him* when he sees *h-*. These are the conditions of negative transfer—a familiar response to a familiar stimulus is carried over where a new response to the stimulus is wanted. The effect of the old response is negative: he pronounces the Spanish word with an *h-*. On the other hand, to continue with orthographically conditioned transfers, the existence of *ch* in both Spanish and English orthographies with approximately the same sound values is a condition for positive transfer: the familiar *ch* of *church* carries over to *Chile, leche, lechuga* with positive effect. Finally, the symbol *ñ* might lead to zero transfer—but in fact, since the student is familiar with *n* but not with *ñ*, he often ignores the tilde and hence encounters negative transfer. An unarguable instance of zero transfer for the reader of English does not exist in Spanish orthography; we must look instead to a symbol system

Reprinted from *The Sounds of English and Spanish* (Chicago: University of Chicago Press, 1965), pages 7–18 by permission of the publisher and the authors.

like those of Korean or Chinese to find true instances of zero transfer
for him.

The conditions of negative, positive, and zero transfer by themselves
would enable us to set up a reasonable hierarchy of difficulty. We could
safely assume that instances where conditions for positive transfer existed
would lend themselves to mastery more readily than instances where conditions for negative or zero transfer existed. It is probable that we should
have somewhat more difficulty determining whether the instances of negative transfer were more difficult than those of zero transfer: does the
student have more trouble mastering gender concord in Spanish (*el mucha-
cho mejicano,* but *la muchacha mejicana*), an instance of zero transfer, or
with *por–para,* where the phonetic similarity of *por* and English *for* seems
to set up an instance of negative transfer? Indeed, we would have no little
difficulty deciding exactly which instances involved negative transfer and
which ones zero: it is not at all clear, for example, whether *ser–estar* is
difficult because of negative transfer from *is* to *es,* or because of zero
transfer from lack of distinction between such verbs in English to presence
of it in Spanish, or because of both factors together.

It seems that we may get around the difficulties inherent in the
question of types of transfer by focusing our attention on the kinds of
choices that exist at any given point in the two languages. We have
already seen that the pronunciation of a language may be characterized as
a set of choices, plus obligatory consequences, or, as we might say, optional choices and obligatory choices. We can add to these a third set;
zero choices—those which exist in one language but not at all in the
other. An example is the phoneme /ž/—the middle consonant of
pleasure—which exists in English but not in Spanish. We can now set up
the following three-way correspondences between English and Spanish.
(*Op* optional, *Ob* obligatory, Ø zero).

There are eight possible situations, not counting the theoretical
ninth possibility of zero choice in both languages:

	English choice	Spanish choice
1.	Op	Op
2.	Ob	Op
3.	Ø	Op
4.	Op	Ob
5.	Ob	Ob
6.	Ø	Ob
7.	Op	Ø
8.	Ob	Ø

In this method of comparison of sound systems, *optional choice* refers to the possible selection among *phonemes*. For example, the English speaker may begin a word with /p/ or with /b/. *Obligatory choice* refers, for one thing, to the selection of conditioned *allophones*. For example, when the English speaker has /p/ at the beginning of a word, the structure of the language requires the aspirated allophone [pʰ] in that environment. Also, obligatory choice refers to limitations in distribution of phonemes. For example, before /m/ at the beginning of a word, English has only /s/, never /z/. The term "zero choice," which is meaningful only when two languages are being compared, refers to the existence of a certain sound in one language which has no counterpart at all in the other. Let us see what sort of examples might exist for each type.[2]

1. English *Op*, Spanish *Op*. Both languages allow certain consonants to appear at the beginning of a word before a vowel. There are words like *me, knee, tea; mí, ní, tí;* and others. We can symbolize this fact in a general way:

$$\left\{ \begin{array}{c} \text{English} \\ \\ \text{Spanish} \end{array} \right\} C \rightarrow \left\{ \left\{ \begin{array}{c} /m/ \\ /n/ \\ /t/ \\ \\ \cdot \\ \cdot \\ \cdot \end{array} \right\} \text{ in env. } -V \right\}$$

That is, initially before a vowel, English and Spanish share the possibility of choosing such consonants as /m, n, t/. Although this description is obviously incomplete, since the full list of possible consonants is not specified, the mere fact that the two languages share a specifiable list of prevocalic consonantal possibilities is a huge source of positive transfer. One can barely imagine how much more difficult Spanish would be to teach if this set of choices were not held in common.

2. English *Ob*, Spanish *Op*. Examples for this comparison are scarce. If we limit our coverage of English to a particular dialect, however, an example can be found. In the dialect that is sometimes called southwest midland (Oklahoma, Arkansas, southern Missouri, southern Kansas, northwest Texas), the vowels of *pin* and *pen* are identical. That is, speakers of this dialect have no choice between /ɪ/ and /ɛ/ before /n/. They can of course choose other vowels, like those of *pat, pot, bought, beat,* but the only vowel they can choose in the area of /ɛ/ and /ɪ/ is a

vowel which is really neither one of these but more or less midway between. It is a well-known joke that they can distinguish between *pin* and *pen* only by specifying a "stickin' pin" or a "writin' pin." For these speakers it is clear that there is no choice between /ɛ/ and /ɪ/ in the environment: -*n*. Faced with a Spanish item like *lento*, the conditions of negative transfer exist for them: they will regularly produce the only vowel their dialect allows in the general phonetic area of /ɛ/ or /ɪ/, and it is not very similar to the correct vowel.[3]

3. English *Ø*, Spanish *Op*. This correspondence characterizes the classic difficulty the English speaker has with the *erre* of Spanish *perro*, or the *jota* of Spanish *hijo*. In neither instance does the sound exist in English, although both sounds represent optional choices of considerable frequency in Spanish. From the English speaker's point of view, they are new sounds.

4. English *Op*, Spanish *Ob*. This correspondence characterizes one of the more difficult problems of Spanish phonology for the English learner. Take, for example, the pronunciation of items like *dado* and *dedo* in isolation. The *d* at the beginning is pronounced differently from the *d* in the middle. The initial *d* is much like the initial *d* of English *den, doll, door*. (It is not exactly the same, but the difference is irrelevant for this purpose). We will write it with the phonetic symbol [d]. The middle *d* of *dado, dedo*, on the other hand, is conspicuously different—to the English ear—from the initial *d*. It sounds more nearly like the initial *th* of *then, there, those*. We will write it with the phonetic symbol [đ]. *Dado* and *dedo* can now be written phonetically as [dáđo], [déđo]. For the Spanish speaker, the pronunciation of [đ], rather than [d], in the middle of these words is obligatory. He will not ordinarily even be aware that he pronounces two quite different sounds for the *d*'s of *dado* and *dedo*. To use the technical terminology introduced earlier, [d] and [đ] are *allophones* of a single phoneme /d/ in Spanish. Among the consonants of Spanish, /d/ exists as one possible optional choice, which may be symbolized:

$$
\text{Spanish } C \rightarrow \left\{ \left\{ \begin{array}{l} /p/ \\ /t/ \\ /k/ \\ /b/ \\ /d/ \\ /g/ \\ \cdot \\ \cdot \\ \cdot \end{array} \right\} \quad \text{in env. } -V \right\}
$$

There is then a subsidiary rule about /d/ (illustrated, incompletely, below):

$$
/d/\rightarrow \left\{ \begin{array}{l} [d] \text{ in env. } \left\{ \begin{array}{l} /l/ \\ /n/ \\ \# \end{array} \right\} - \\ [\text{d}] \text{ in env. } \quad V \quad - \end{array} \right\}
$$

That is, if /d/ is preceded by silence (a break in utterance continuity symbolized in the formula by #) or an /n/ or /l/, it is pronounced as [d]. If it is preceded by a vowel, it is pronounced as [d]. The phonetic difference between [d] and [d] is conditioned by this rule—a rule which merely describes a set of conditions to which Spanish speakers habitually, and unconsciously, conform. Because of this rule, [d] is for them simply a kind of /d/. But for the English speaker, the conditions are different. For him [d] and [d] are in contrast—that is, they belong to different phonemes, /d/ and /d/. The fact of contrast is proved by pairs such as *dine–thine, dare–there, dough–though.* [d] and [d] exist as two possible choices among the consonants of English:

$$
\text{English C} \rightarrow \left\{ \left\{ \left\{ \begin{array}{l} /p/ \\ /t/ \\ /k/ \\ /b/ \\ /d/ \\ /g/ \\ /v/ \\ /d/ \\ \bullet \\ \bullet \\ \bullet \end{array} \right\} \quad \text{in env. } -V \right\} \right\}
$$

In English, unlike Spanish, /d/ and /d/ are in contrast: they are both optional choices, and their distribution cannot be predicted. Predictability is at the heart of the matter: the occurrence of Spanish [d] and [d] can be predicted by writing merely one symbol, /d/; given this symbol in an environment, it is possible always and infallibly to predict whether it will be pronounced [d] or [d]. The difference between them is obligatory.

This correspondence between English optional choices and Spanish obligatory choices is so important in its consequences that another example may clarify it still further. Suppose we consider the possibilities of nasal consonants ([m] as in *ham*, [n] as in *hen*, [ŋ] as in *hang*) in the environment of following stop consonants ([p] as in *up*, [t] as in *putt*, [k] as in *puck*, [b] as in *tub*, [d] as in *dud*, [g] as in *dug*). The phonetic symbols needed for this discussion are all familiar letters of the alphabet in familiar values, except for [ŋ]. Note that the letters *ng* are used to spell both /ŋ/ and /ŋg/ in English: words like *singer* and *banging* have /ŋ/, whereas words like *finger* and *younger* have /ŋg/.

Certain articulatory facts about these consonants must be briefly explained in order to make the point clear. In terms of the place in the mouth at which the sound is articulated, the nasal and stop consonants fall into three classes: those made at the lips ([m, p, b]); those made by the tip of the tongue at or just behind the upper teeth ([n, t, d]); and those made toward the back of the mouth, with the tongue touching the back part of the roof of the mouth (the velum) ([ŋ, k, g]).

Lips	*Teeth*	*Velum*
m	n	ŋ
p	t	k
b	d	g

It is characteristic of Spanish that in a sequence of nasal consonant plus stop consonant, the point of articulation of both consonants is fixed by the stop consonant. This can be formulated:

$$\text{Spanish N} \rightarrow \begin{cases} \text{[m] in env. } - \begin{Bmatrix} /p/ \\ /b/ \end{Bmatrix} \\[2ex] \text{[n] in env. } - \begin{Bmatrix} /t/ \\ /d/ \end{Bmatrix} \\[2ex] \text{[ŋ] in env. } - \begin{Bmatrix} /k/ \\ /g/ \end{Bmatrix} \end{cases}$$

That is, a nasal (N) can be only [m] if the following consonant is [p] or [b], only [n] if the following consonant is [t] or [d], only [ŋ] if the following consonant is [k] or [g]. This restriction remains valid regardless of word boundaries and spelling: *hombre, un beso; endosar, un día; inglés, un gato*. It is optional whether a nasal be chosen at all; but if one is chosen, it is obligatory that its point of articulation be the same as that of

a following stop consonant. In English, on the other hand, no such restriction exists: [mb] *lumber,* [nb] *unbend,* [ŋb] *kingbird;* [md] *lambda,*
[nd] *under,* [ŋd] *kingdom;* [mg] *Baumgardner,* [ng] *ingrown,* [ŋg] *finger.*
In English, not only is the choice of a nasal consonant optional, as in
Spanish, but so is the choice of a particular nasal, regardless of the
following stop consonant, which is not true in Spanish.

    5. English *Ob,* Spanish *Ob.* It is here that we get maximum positive
transfer. Any English pattern that is obligatory is necessarily one to which
the speaker gives no thought—it is an area where he has no choice. If the
same pattern is obligatory also in Spanish, there should be no problem—
indeed, there will not normally even be any awareness that there might
have been a problem. These instances are more frequent than we realize:
comparison between Japanese and Spanish, on the one hand, and between English and Spanish, on the other, will reveal that the English
speaker is not so bad off for Spanish-like habits as we who are faced with
the student's errors are prone to think. To take a simple instance: given
the consonantal sequence /s/ plus /w/, both languages require that a vowel
be chosen in the next position—*swear, suerte.* This is not a trivial observation: if the consonantal sequence is /p/ followed by /r/, English requires a
vowel, as in *pray,* but Spanish allows /y/ or /w/, for example, *prieto*
/pryéto/, *pruebo* /prwébo/.[4] Thus the fact that the Spanish speaker has a
different range of choice after /pr/ constitutes a problem for the English
speaker, even though the sequence /pr/ itself does not.

    6. English ℚ Spanish *Ob.* This correspondence is the extreme of
the scale. In English, a given habit does not exist at all; in Spanish, it is
obligatory and hence normally outside the speaker's conscious control—it
is a habit which he internalized at an early age and has given no thought
to since. Zero may be viewed as a kind of negative obligation: to say that
a pattern is zero is about the same as saying that it is obligatory that the
speaker not conform to the pattern. We have, as it were, an absolute
negative restriction in the one instance, an absolute positive restriction in
the other. An example is to be found in the middle consonant of Spanish
words like *haba, leva, avance.* Although spelled with *b* or *v,* this sound is
different from anything represented by *b* or *v* in English. The phonetic
symbol we will use for it is [ƀ]. It is articulated by bringing the lower lip
up toward the upper lip, as if for *b,* but without touching, so that the air
produces a friction noise, as if for *v.* In Spanish, the difference between
[b] and [ƀ] is closely parallel to that between [d] and [đ]. The two sounds
are allophones of a single phoneme, predictable from a single symbol in
the following way (this formulation of the rule is illustrative only, not
complete):

$$\text{Spanish } /b/ \rightarrow \left\{ \begin{array}{ll} \text{[b] in env.} & \left\{ \begin{array}{l} /m/ \\ \# \end{array} \right\} - \\ \text{[ƀ] in env.} & V \quad - \end{array} \right\}$$

That is, [ƀ] normally occurs after vowels, [b] elsewhere. The situation of [b]–[ƀ] is different from that of [d]–[đ] in only one significant respect: [ƀ] does not exist in English at all (a zero category), but [đ] does (an optional category). But this is a big difference pedagogically. In the instance of [đ], the English speaker must transfer a familiar sound and redistribute it with respect to other sounds; in the instance of [ƀ], he must learn a new sound as well as a new distribution.

7. English *Op*, Spanish ₡. This particular correspondence is a frequent one in going from English to Spanish pronunciation. English has several vowels, for instance, that are entirely lacking in Spanish. The vowel of American English *grass*, symbolized by [æ], does not exist in Spanish. Partly because of negative transfer from the spelling *a*, words like *gracias* are often pronounced with this vowel in early stages of learning. The problem is merely to reduce the range of choice that the English speaker is accustomed to exercising.

8. English *Ob*, Spanish ₡. An English obligatory pattern of pronunciation can be difficult to get rid of. For instance, it is obligatory in most English dialects that items with *t* or *d* between syllables, where the first syllable is stressed (*butter, shudder, splatter, Betty, patty*), have an allophone of /t/ (or /d/) that is rather like the Spanish *r* of *para, pero*. It is a voiced tongue-tip flap. Faced with Spanish words like *foto, beta, pita*, the English speaker of most dialects will produce the obligatory English flap rather than the fully articulated /t/ of Spanish. Another example also involves allophones of English /t/: in items like *mountain, button, latent*, the English speaker of most dialects has a variety of /t/ for which instead of dropping the tongue tip as he usually does to release a /t/, he maintains the tongue tip in the same position for the following /n/. Such an articulation does not exist under any conditions in any dialect of Spanish. Words like *quitan, meten*, which always have a normally released /t/ and a full vowel, are subject to this kind of transfer.

Having at least an idea, now, of the eight kinds of differences that a comparison can reveal when it is based on the different possibilities of choice in the two languages, we can attempt to rearrange the comparisons in an order which will constitute a hierarchy of difficulty. We must know which kinds of differences will be most difficult to master and which will be easiest, in order to grade our teaching materials, arrange them into an effective sequence, and determine how much drill is needed on each point. The hierarchy suggested below is by no means final; further experience with it may well result in readjustments in the relative position of one category of difficulty or another.

Difficulty		Comparison			Examples (from
Magnitude	Order	English	Spanish	Type	preceding discussion)
I	1	Ø	Ob	6	[ƀ]
	2	Ø	Op	3	erre, jota
	3	Op	Ob	4	[d]/[đ]
II	4	Ob	Op	2	i/e before n
	5	Ob	Ø	8	flap /t/ between vowels
	6	Op	Ø	7	[æ]
III	7	Op	Op	1	list of prevocalic consonants
	8	Ob	Ob	5	sw—plus vowel

Given such a hierarchy, we must examine several other criteria that will enter into the grading and sequencing of materials designed to eliminate these difficulties.

The most important of these is functional load—that is, the extent to which a given sound is used in Spanish to distinguish one word from another, the quantity of distinctive information that it carries. The Spanish ñ belongs in Group I in the hierarchy of difficulty (Ø in English, Optional in Spanish). But its functional load is almost zero. There are about a dozen words in which ñ carries the burden of contrast with the cluster [ny] (spelled -ni-): uñón (big toenail) versus unión and the like.[5] An American can speak Spanish for a long time without ever needing this contrast. For ñ he can substitute [ny], modifying a cluster he controls from his English habits only to the extent of being careful not to make the syllable division between [n] and [y]—that is, he must say [u.nyón] rather than [un.yón]. The ñ would, therefore, in spite of its relatively high rank in the hierarchy of difficulty, be placed very late (indeed, almost last) in a reasonable pedagogical hierarchy.

A less important additional criterion is potential mishearing. Spanish initial [t±]—the variety of /t/ that appears before vowels—provides an example. This sound is very difficult, Group I (ʘ in English, Obligatory in Spanish), in our hierarchy above. But failure to produce it correctly (with the tongue tip against the back side of the upper teeth, without a puff of air) will rarely cause misunderstanding. However, the American who is listening rather than speaking—receiving rather than producing— will often hear a Spanish initial [t⁼] as being a [d]. One good way for him to learn to hear it correctly is for him to produce it correctly. We would therefore place the [t⁼] fairly high in a pedagogically oriented sequence even though when evaluated as to its effect on the production of Spanish, it will only add American accent to the student's pronunciation—not unintelligibility at any point.

The final additional criterion is pattern congruity. The sounds of a language pattern themselves in groups or sets. In Spanish, /b/, /d/, and /g/ constitute a set. /b/ and /d/ are high in difficulty, in functional load, and in potentiality for mishearing. There is no doubt they must appear early in a pedagogical sequence. /g/ is also difficult, but it is considerably lower in functional load and has less potential for mishearing. Because it patterns like /b/ and /d/, we feel it would be incongruous to place it out of sequence with them even though it does not constitute a problem of the same order.

These, then, are the criteria which have determined the sequence of our presentation:

1. Hierarchy of difficulty
2. Functional load
3. Potential mishearing
4. Pattern congruity

Matching these criteria against one another is no easy task, and there is clearly no single "right" or "best" sequence of presentation. Our own procedure has been, in general, to put those things first that were most important in the task of communication, either because mishandling of them could easily result in misunderstanding or because they carried a heavy functional load and would therefore be especially obvious and frequent sources of accent. In order to get similar problems together, however, we have violated the mixed criteria of importance. Our preferred pedagogical sequence is:

1. Basic intonation features and patterns (including stress, pitch, juncture, and rhythm)
2. Weak stressed vowels

3. Strong stressed vowels and diphthongs
4. Voiced stop-spirants
5. Vibrants and liquids
6. Voiceless stops
7. Spirants
8. Nasals and palatals
9. Semivowels
10. Consonant clusters
11. Other intonation features and patterns

Notes

1. For a convenient summary of learning theory as relevant to linguistics, see James J. Jenkins (1954).
2. In the discussion of optional versus obligatory choices on the level of phonology, we are reversing a familiar use of these terms. There is a sense in which nearly all phonological choices are obligatory: if one has in mind, so to speak, a string of words, then the distinctive phonological shape of each word is obligatory; that is, if one wishes to utter the word in English which has the meaning "one plus one" for "four minus two," he must say something which can be written phonetically [tvw], or (in a more detailed phonetic writing) [tʰvu̯]. In other words, the physical shape of the word *two* is established by lexical rule—any other sequence of sounds will presumably be some other word. But if he wishes to say the word which means "dealing with monetary problems" (i.e., *economic), he may say either* [ɛ̀kinámiyk] or [ìykinámiyk]— that is, the first syllable may rhyme either with *Tech* or with *teak*. This is free variation on a specifiable level of analysis—the choice may be considered entirely optional. This usage of the terms *optional* versus *obligatory* is possible—and quite proper—if, and only if, the phonology is viewed within the context of a complete set of rules of sentence formation (i.e., a complete grammar). But in the present situation, where only phonology is under consideration, and where the purpose is to specify the possibilities of combining sounds to produce words—where the words cannot be said to have been selected before the phonological rules—then the usage of optional and obligatory must be reversed, because the matters that are optional are the minimally significant phonological elements, and the matters that are obligatory are the phonetic consequences of choosing one or another combination of these minimal elements.
3. Of the writers, R. P. S. has been plagued by this disability since his first exposure to Spanish. He can testify to its persistence. Even as a trained phonetician, he can avoid the obligatory vowel of his native dialect only with concentrated effort.

4. The semivowels /y/ and /w/ are definitely different from ordinary vowels (even though they are spelled with the same letters), because they are not syllabic.

5. The word *unión* is to be transcribed as [unyón]. In the view of other analysts, it is better transcribed as [unión], which would alter the example. The comparison to be made with English still stands, because in the English pattern the syllable division would obligatorily be [un.yón].

References

Bowen, J. Donald, and Stockwell, Robert P. *Patterns of Spanish Pronunciation.* Chicago: University of Chicago Press, 1960.

Jenkins, James J. "The Learning Theory Approach." In *Psycholinguistics: A Survey of Theory and Research,* ed. Charles E. Osgood. Indiana University Publications in Anthropology and Linguistics, Memoir 10, pp. 20–35, 1954.

A Contrastive Study of Egyptian Arabic and American English: The Segmental Phonemes

Walter Lehn and William R. Slager

It has become widely accepted among linguists that materials to be used in teaching English as a foreign language should be based on a comparison of the native language and the target language, English. Such a comparison, which includes both the phonology and the grammar, is essential because it locates the areas of difficulty for the learner (the Thai does not have the same problems learning English as the Turk), and because it makes possible proper grading. The well-known materials prepared by the English Language Institute of the University of Michigan (specifically, for native speakers of Spanish to English) were guided by this assumption. Fries (1945, p. 9) has expressed the basic concepts as follows:

> The most effective materials are those that are based upon a scientific description of the language to be learned, carefully compared with a parallel description of the native language of the learner.

Lado's book, *Linguistics Across Cultures,* elaborates this assumption, as a glance at the chapter headings will show: "How to Compare Two Sound Systems," "How to Compare Two Grammatical Structures," etc. Hill (1958, p. 4), in his preface to the report on the Ann Arbor Conference on Linguistics and the Teaching of English as a Foreign Language, says:

> There are many statements in the pages of the Conference report on the need for structural comparisons of English and various other languages, and the construction of teaching materials based on such comparisons.

Reprinted from *Language Learning* 9, nos. 1 and 2 (1959): 25–33 by permission of the publisher and the authors.

However, the classroom teacher, the "practitioner" who is often faced with the necessity of preparing teaching materials, searches in vain for the comparisons that he needs.[1] And if he himself wants to make the comparisons, he discovers that there are relatively few analyses available. Further, many of these are so technical that they are not accessible to the nonspecialist.

This paper presents, for the practitioner or nonspecialist, a contrastive[2] study of the segmental phonemes (consonants and vowels) of Egyptian Arabic and American English.[3] The primary materials on which this study is based are: (1) recent analyses of English, chiefly the one that has come to be known as Trager-Smith;[4] (2) the analysis of Arabic by Harrell (1957), and (3) the manual by Twaddell (1956) for Egyptian elementary school teachers of English. All of these have been supplemented by our own observations made in the teaching of English to Egyptian secondary school and university students.

Consonants

In the labial to velar regions, English has twenty-three (or twenty-one, depending on how affricates are analyzed,) consonants. Arabic, in the same regions, has only sixteen. On the other hand, in the postvelar regions Arabic has seven consonants, but English only one. The details are given in the following chart.

			t		k	q		?
	b		d		g			
	f		s	š		x	ħ	
			z	(ž)		ġ	ʕ	
Arabic	m		n					
			l					
			r					
				y	w			h
	p		t	č	k			
	b		d	ǰ	g			
	f	θ	s	š				
English	v	ð	z	ž				
	m		n		ŋ			
			l					
			ɹ	y	w			h

The so-called emphatics of Arabic have been omitted because of the different analyses possible (as additional consonants or as a prosodic feature—the latter in Harrell (1957), and because they do not generally constitute a problem in the learning of English.

In the following discussion, the consonants are grouped according to the point of articulation. At each point the order is: stop, spirant, nasal, lateral, trill, semivowel. Not all of these types, of course, occur at all points: e.g., labials are only stop, spirant, and nasal.

Labials

Arabic	—	b	f	—	m
English	p	b	f	v	m

This table indicates that the speaker of Arabic will have difficulty with English contrasts such as *pan–ban, fan–van, cap–cab, half–have.* In addition, he will also have difficulty with *pan–fan* and *ban–van.* The English *b–v* contrast as in *habit–have it, robing–roving* is further complicated not only because Arabic has no such contrast, but also because Arabic /b/ has a free variant [ƀ] intervocalically. Consonant clusters as in *caps, kept, halves, halved* are not generally a source of difficulty because Arabic /b/ has another free variant [p] before voiceless obstruents, and /f/ has a free variant [v] before voiced obstruents.[5]

Interdentals

Arabic	—	—
English	θ	đ

/θ/ and /đ/ do not occur in Arabic, and Arabic speakers substitute /s/ and /z/ respectively. Hence English contrasts such as *thistle–this'll, ether–either, think–sink, bath–bass, breathe–breeze* are all troublesome. The occurrence of /θ, đ/ in classical Arabic complicates the problem; although the learner has been exposed to these sounds in the study of Arabic, he has usually substituted /s, z/ while laboring under the illusion that he was saying something else. He may also have had teachers of English who identified English /θ, đ/ with classical Arabic /θ, đ/, not realizing that in all probability Arabic speakers regularly substituted /s, z/ for these when reading or speaking classical Arabic.

Dentals

Arabic	t	d	s	z	n	l	r
English	—	—	—	—	—	—	—

Alveolars

Arabic	—	—	—	—	—	—	—
English	t	d	s	z	n	l	ɹ

Arabic /t, d/ etc., are dental and English alveolar. However, this difference does not constitute a major problem in the learning of English, since substitution of the dentals for the alveolars does not materially affect or impair communication in English. The extent to which this difference is a problem varies directly in proportion to the degree of native-like control which is expected or demanded.

Arabic /l/ is "clear" or i-colored and hence the u-colored allophones in English *full, fall, bottle,* etc., are troublesome. Arabic /l/ and /r/ have voiceless allophones prepausally following voiceless obstruents, and the nasals may have voiceless allophones in the same environments, but in practice these differences do not constitute learning problems.

The conventional use of *r* in the transcription of Arabic and English completely obscures the fact that the sounds so symbolized in the two languages are entirely different; in Arabic *r* represents an apical trill, in English a slightly retroflex resonant continuant (a vocoid). To highlight this difference (following IPA) /ɹ/ is here used for English, and /r/ for Arabic. Arabic speakers have difficulty with /ɹ/ in all environments and substitute /r/, which is (probably) least acceptable to speakers of English in items such as *bird, shirt, fur, her.*

Palatals

Arabic	—	—	š	(ž)	y
English	č	ǰ	š	ž	y

Even though Arabic does not have affricates which can be interpreted as structural units, English /č/ causes relatively little difficulty because Arabic has the noninitial sequence /tVš/ which alternates with /tš/.[6] Hence English *watch–wash, watching–washing* are not troublesome, although initial contrasts such as *chin–shin* may be. Arabic /ž/ is statistically very infrequent, and some speakers do not have it at all; its occurrence is limited to a few relatively unassimilated borrowings. The possible sequence /dž/ has not been observed; therefore, as would be expected, Arabic speakers have more difficulty with English /ǰ/ and contrasts such as *chump–jump, version–virgin.*

These statements about difficulties with English /ǰ/ hold for lower Egyptian dialects (roughly, Cairo and vicinity and the Nile Delta); they do not hold for upper Egyptian dialects with an affricate /ǰ/ which patterns as a unit.[7] In these dialects the sequence /tš/ (alternating with /tVš/) also occurs, and, as in the case of lower Egyptian, it cannot be interpreted as a unit. In contrast with English, at this as well as several other points, the Arabic consonant system is markedly asymmetric.

Velars

Arabic	k	g	—	w
English	k	g	ŋ	w

Since Arabic [ŋ] is an allophone of /n/ before velar obstruents, English /ŋ/ in this environment is not difficult. Hence English *sink, sank, finger, longer* are no problem, but contrasts such as *sin–sing, sinner–singer, lawn–long* are. And items such as *sinning, singing* are extremely difficult.[8]

Uvulars, Pharyngeals, Laryngeals

Arabic	q	x	ġ	ħ	ʕ	ʔ	h
English	—	—	—	—	—	—	h

For the speaker of Arabic, English presents no problems at this point. (The problems are all in the other direction!)

Consonant Sequences

Arabic has no sequences of more than two consonants, whether in close transition or with intervening juncture (Harrell 1957). Since English has as many as four consonants in close transition, and as many as six or seven with intervening juncture,[9] the Arabic speaker has obvious difficulty with English consonant sequences and supplies intrusive vowels which act as "cluster breakers."

The details of Arabic and English consonant sequences are summarized in the following table.

	Initial	Medial	Final
Arabic	C	C	C
		CC	CC
English	C	C	C
	CC	CC	CC
	CCC	CCC	CCC
		CCCC	CCCC

Initial here means either after pause or after juncture, and *medial* means intervocalic with no intervening juncture. *Final* means either before pause or before juncture for English, but only before pause for Arabic. Before juncture, Arabic has a maximum of one consonant; utterance final CC is CCV before juncture.

Although the speaker of Arabic does not have initial CC, in practice he has very little difficulty with English CC in this or any other environment. CCC initially is usually reproduced as CVCC, finally as CCVC, and medially as CVCC or CCVC, with an intrusive vowel (predominantly /i/ or /ɨ/) as indicated. CCCC medially is usually reproduced as CCVCC, and finally as CCVCC or, more often, CCCVC, the latter with the point of syllable division after the second consonant. Still longer sequences, as in c*arved st*raight, are similarly "broken up."[10]

Vowels

Simple Nuclei

Arabic			English		
			i	ɨ	u
i		u			
			e	ə	o
	a				
			æ	a	ɔ

The phonemically simple nuclei in Arabic and English are similar in that both sets are phonetically short and lax. The main, and pedagogically most important, difference is the number of contrasts. Since Arabic has fewer contrasts, the range of allophonic variation of each vowel phoneme is much greater than in English; e.g., Arabic /a/ has allophones within the area bounded by [ɛ], [æ], [ɑ], and [ʌ], and hence English contrasts as in *bet–bat, cat–cot, cot–cut, cot–caught* are all difficult. In fact all contiguous pairs on the English vowel chart are troublesome: *bit–bet* and *bet–bat* are, but *bit–bat, fit–foot,* and *foot–fought* are not.

Complex Nuclei

Arabic   English

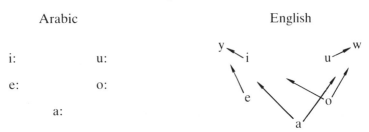

i: u:

e: o:

a:

Arabic has fewer phonemically complex nuclei than English.[11] Further, these nuclei are phonetically long and tense monophthongs. Hence the speaker of Arabic tends to substitute his tense monophthongs for the English diphthongs /iy, ey, uw, ow/. The degree of nativelike control expected determines the extent to which this substitution is a problem. English /ay, aw/ are not difficult, since they are phonetically similar to Arabic (phonemically vowel-consonant) sequences /ay/ and /aw/. Even though he does not have anything similar to English /oy/, this nucleus is relatively easy for the Arabic speaker to learn.

English /i/ and /u/ are (for most speakers) slightly higher than the corresponding Arabic vowels. For this reason, English /i, u/ tend to be identified by speakers of Arabic with their /i:, u:/ and reproduced accordingly; thus contrasts such as *bit–beat* and *could–cooed* are difficult.

Another English contrast which is particularly troublesome is that in *caught–coat, bought–boat*. The Arabic speaker tends to substitute his /o:/ for both.

Summary

The speaker of Arabic has difficulties with the segmental phonemes of English because of (1) differences in the number of contrasts, (2) differences in the permissible sequences, and (3) differences in the phonetic expression of "similar" contrasts. English has many more vowel contrasts, and more consonant contrasts in the labial to velar regions than Arabic. It also permits much longer sequences of consonants initially, medially, and finally in utterances. Both English and Arabic have consonants which are conventionally symbolized /t, d, s, z/. In English, however, these represent alveolars, whereas in Arabic they represent dentals. All of these differences constitute a major (although not the only) source of difficulty for the speaker of Arabic learning English.[12]

Notes

1. A few such comparisons, limited to the segmental phonemes, have been published; see, e.g., David W. Reed, Robert Lado, and Yao Shen 1948.
2. Because the more obvious term *comparative* is already used as a technical term—comparative linguistics, comparative method—it seems unwise to extend its use to cover studies such as this. Hence the term *contrastive* is suggested. Charles F. Hockett's (1948) definition would seem to include this use.
3. Hereafter *Arabic* will mean colloquial Egyptian Arabic and *English* American English.
4. George L. Trager and Henry Lee Smith, Jr. (1951), *An Outline of English Structure*. For a discussion of this and other analyses, and their antecedents, see the review by James Sledd (1955) of Trager and Smith (1951), and Fries (1945).
5. Since Arabic /b/ and /f/ both have voiced and voiceless allophones, and /b/ has stop as well as spirant allophones, the primary contrast here is not voiced/voiceless or stop/spirant, but bilabial/labiodental.
6. For this reason it is advisable to use the symbols /tš/ and /dž/, rather than /č/ and /ǰ/, in English transcriptions for speakers of Arabic. The use of the latter symbols invites gratuitous pronunciation problems.
7. Although historical details are beyond the scope of this paper, it may be relevant to indicate that the upper Eg. /ǰ/ corresponds distributionally to lower Eg. /g/, and upper Eg. /g/ to some occurrences of lower Eg. /ʔ/; e.g., upper Eg. /ǰabal/, /gahwa/, and /saʔal/ are /gabal/, /ʔahwa/, and /saʔal/ (respectively, 'mountain', 'coffee', and 'he asked') in lower Eg.
8. The *n–ŋ* contrast seems to be much more difficult for Arabic speakers than, e.g., *p–b*, although there is no immediately obvious reason why this should be so.
9. Hockett, *Manual of Phonology* (1955, p. 63). For more details as well as examples, see also Archibald A. Hill, *Introduction to Linguistic Structures* (1958).
10. Since in every instance the extent to which a sequence is difficult depends on the constituent consonants and their order, as well as the length of the sequence, a more detailed presentation would require an exhaustive list of

English and Arabic consonant sequences and (almost) individual discussion. Such a list, which unfortunately is based on analyses which disregard juncture in both English and Arabic, has been published for American English and Iraqi Arabic; see Alice Paul Malick, "A Comparative Study of American English and Iraqi Arabic Consonant Clusters," (1956–57).

11. The list of English complex nuclei in the above chart is obviously incomplete. However, it adequately illustrates the differences between the Arabic and English systems.

12. The authors intend, in subsequent papers, to continue with a contrastive study of the suprasegmentals and the grammars of the two languages.

References

Fries, Charles C. *Teaching and Learning English as a Foreign Language.* Ann Arbor: University of Michigan Press, 1945. P. 9.

Harrell, Richard S. *The Phonology of Colloquial Egyptian Arabic.* New York: American Council of Learned Societies, 1957.

Hill, Archibald A. *Introduction to Linguistic Structures.* New York: Harcourt, Brace and World, 1958. Pp. 68–88.

Hockett, Charles F. "Implications of Bloomfield's Algonquian Studies." *Language* 24(1948):119.

Hockett, Charles F. *Manual of Phonology.* Baltimore: Waverly Press, 1955. P. 63.

Language Learning, special issue, June, 1958.

Malick, Alice Paul. "A Comparative Study of American English and Iraqi Arabic Consonant Clusters." *Language Learning* 7, nos. 3–4 (1956–57):65–87.

Reed, David W.; Lado, Robert; and Shen, Yao. "The Importance of the Native Language in Foreign Language Learning." *Language Learning* 1 (1948):17–23.

Sledd, James. Review of Trager and Smith (1951) and Fries (1945) in *Language* 31 (1955):312–45.

Trager, George L., and Smith, Henry Lee. *An Outline of English Structure.* Norman, Okla.: n.p., 1951.

Twaddell, W. Freeman. *Oral Practice in Elementary English Instruction.* Cairo: n.p., 1956.

A Contrastive Analysis of the Segmental Phonemes of Greek and English

Andreas Koutsoudas and Olympia Koutsoudas

Introduction

This paper has a dual purpose: (1) to predict the problems that will arise in teaching English pronunciation to native speakers of Greek and thus to provide a guide for the empirical solution to these and other problems, and (2) to provide an insight as to what will constitute a problem in language learning.

The basis for the prediction of pronunciation problems is a contrastive analysis of the segmental phonemes of Greek and English presented herein.[1] While, as is the common practice, we state the differences between the two languages, we lay special stress on the ways in which *similarities* can *adversely* affect learning the pronunciation of a language. Too often in the past, contrastive analysts have approached their task with the idea that any similarities between the native and the foreign language will facilitate learning, while the obvious differences will be problems simply because they are different. As a consequence, neither the teacher nor the student has been prepared to cope with the problems resulting from native habits of pronunciation which appear to be different from those of the foreign language but which in reality are similar.

The Segmental Phonemes of Greek

Greek has five vowel and nineteen consonant phonemes, which will now be discussed in that order.

Reprinted from *Language Learning* 12, no. 3 (1962):211–30 by permission of the publisher and the authors.
We wish to thank F. W. Householder, Jr., of Indiana University, and H. V. King of the University of Michigan for their helpful comments on this paper.

Vowels: /i, u, e, o, a/

/i/ and /u/ are high tense while /e/ and /o/ are midlax vowels. The members of these two pairs are characterized by a difference in both tongue and lip position: /i/ and /e/ have the tongue at the front of the mouth and the lips neutral; /u/ and /o/ have the tongue at the back of the mouth and the lips rounded. /a/ is a low central vowel.

At the beginning and in the middle of words, vowels are slightly nasalized when followed by a nasal consonant. When unstressed, all vowels are slightly centered. Examples: [pɷ̃·tE›] 'when' /póte/; [É̃·na^] 'one' /éna/; [dzá̰·mi›] 'glass' /dzámi/; [dza̰^mí·] 'mosque' /dzamí/; [lu˅lú·ka^] 'proper name' /lulúka/; [kṵ˅nú·pi›] 'mosquito' /kunúpi/.

In addition, when the high vowels /i/ and /u/ occur unstressed in voiceless surroundings, they may have voiceless allophones, [ɪ] and [ʊ] respectively, which are in free variation with their voiced counterparts; thus we may have [pÉ·zi›] or [pÉ·zI] 'he plays' /pézi/ when /i/ is followed by a voiceless consonant or when it is in utterance final position; and we may also have [ká·pu˅] or [ká·pU˅] 'somewhere' /kápu/ under the same conditions. Voiceless allophones of vowels do not, however, occur in careful speech.

Lastly, /i/ has a glided allophone [i̯] and /e/ has a mid–close front unrounded allophone [e]: [i̯] occurs medially after unstressed vowels and is in free variation with [i] after stressed vowels in word-medial and final position; [e] occurs only when stressed before /i/.[2] Examples: [ma^i̯mú·] 'monkey' /maimú/; [ká·i̯›ka^] or [ká·i›ka^] 'I was burned' /káika/; [řo‹lɷ·i̯›] or [řo‹lɷ·i›] or [řo‹lɷ·I›] 'a watch' /řolói/; [lé·i̯›] or [lé·i›] or [lé·I›] 'he says' /léi/; [cé·i̯›] or [cé·i›] or [cé·I›] 'he burns' /kéi/.

Consonants: /p, t, k, b, d, g, f, θ, s, x, v, ð, z, γ, m, n, l, ř, y/

Stops

/p, t, k/ are voiceless fortis unaspirated, while /b, g, d/ are voiced lenis unaspirated stops. /p, b/ are bilabial /t, d/ are dental, and /k, g/ are velar: /polí/ 'much', /boří/ 'he can', /tóřa/ 'now', /dóřa/ 'Dora', /kóma/ 'comma', and in the Alexandrian dialect /góma/ 'eraser'. /k/ before /i, e, t, s/ is palatal [c] and before /ř, y/ is palato-velar [k̟]; examples: [cɪ›má·mE›] 'I sleep' /kimáme/, [kyá·lya^] 'field glasses' /kyálya/. /g/ before /i, e/ is palatal [ɟ] and before /ř, y/ is palato-velar, [g]; examples: [a̰^ŋɟí·stři›] 'a hook' /angístři/, [a̰^ŋgyó·] 'pottie' /angyó/.

Fricatives

/f, θ, x/ are flat voiceless and /v, ð, γ/ are flat voiced fricatives. /f, v/ are labiodental, /s, z/ are alveolar, /θ, ð/ are interdental, and /x, γ/ are velar: /fáros/ 'lighthouse', /város/ 'weight', /sáli/ 'shawl', /záli/ 'dizziness', /θíos/ 'uncle', /ðío/ 'two', /xámo/ 'on the floor', /γámo/ 'wedding'. /x/ before /i, e, t/ is palatal [ç] and before /ř, y/ is palato-velar [x̱]; examples: [x̱y̱ǫ̇·ni̯] 'snow' /xyóni/, [vřo˘çí·] 'rain' /vřoxí/. /γ/ before /i, e/ is palatal [j] and before /ř/ is palato-velar [γ̱]; examples: [ji̯ꞏnÉ·kaˆ] 'woman' /γinéka/, [γ̱řá·fΩ‹] 'I write' /γřáfo/.

Nasals

/m, n/ are voiced nasals. /m/ is bilabial and /n/ is alveolar: /misí/ 'he despises' /nisí/ 'island'. /m/ before /f, v/ is labiodental [ɱ]: [sι̯>ɱfΩnó·] 'I agree' /simfonó/. /n/ before /t, d, θ, ð/ is dental [n̪] and before /k, g, x, γ/ is velar [ŋ]: [ą́·n̪θΩ<s] 'flower' /ánθos/, [ą́·n̪ðřaˆs] 'man' /ánðras/, [ÉlꞏÊ>ŋxo<s] 'report card' /élenxos/.

Liquids

/l/ is a voiced alveolar lateral, and /ř/ is a voiced alveolar flap: /líγa/ 'few', /říγa/ 'ruler'.

Palatalizing phoneme: /y/

/y/ is a palatal glide phoneme the only function of which is to (nonsimultaneously) palatalize the preceding consonant with which it occurs; examples: /pyós/ 'who' and /pós/ 'how'; /xyóni/ 'snow' and /xóni/ 'he stuffs'; /γála/ 'milk' and /γjála/ 'jar'; /aftá/ 'those' and aftyá/ 'ears'.

Summary

The segmental phonemes of Modern Greek are summarized in the following chart.

Phonemic Chart

A. *Consonants*	Labial	Dental	Alveolar	Palatal	Velar
Stops	p b	t d			k g
Fricatives	f v	θ ð	s z		x γ
Nasals	m		n		
Lateral			1		
Flap			ř		
Palatalizing				y	

B. *Vowels*	Front	Central	Back
High	i		u
Mid	e		o
Low		a	

Distinctions in Greek But Not in English

There are a number of phonemic and allophonic distinctions in Modern Greek which are either absent or have a reverse function in English. The following is a discussion of what we consider to be the most important ones.

Vowel Distinctions

Three general statements can be made regarding vowel distinctions in Greek which are absent in English: statements involving (1) vowel tenseness, (2) length, and (3) neutralization. In articulating Greek vowels, the tongue is generally higher (or more tense) than in articulation of the English approximates; thus, for example, the Greek vowel /e/ is much more tense than its English approximate /e/. On the other hand, the lengthening of vowels under stress in Greek is negligible when compared with the lengthening of stressed vowels followed by voiced consonants or a pause in English. Finally, unstressed vowels are only slightly centered or 'obscured' in Greek, while in English unstressed vowels are always realized as either /ə/, /i/, or /o/. In other words, while in Greek unstressed vowels more or less maintain their full quality (i.e., are not neutralized) vowels in English lose most of their distinctive quality when not stressed (i.e., they are almost completely neutralized).

Consonant Distinctions

There are four classes of consonants exhibiting distinctions peculiar to Greek: (1) the velar fricatives, (2) the lateral, (3) the flap, and (4) the velar nasal.

The Velar Fricatives /x, γ/

When the back of the tongue is held high and toward the velum and the air is allowed to escape, with considerable friction, out of the mouth and over the center of the tongue, the resulting phone (i.e., a particular range of sounds) is a voiceless velar fricative [x]. When, in addition, the vocal folds are set into vibration, the resulting phone is a voiced velar fricative [γ]. The [x̧] (a palato-velar variation of [x]) is sometimes heard in English in words like 'hue', 'humor'; otherwise these two phones do not occur in English. But they do occur in Greek; moreover, they are phonemic in Greek. Examples: /xóma/ 'earth' and /γóma/ 'eraser'; /xáno/ 'I lose' and /káno/ 'I make'; /gařízi/ 'it brays' and /γalízi/ 'he speaks like a Frenchman'.

The Voiced Alveolar Flap /ř/

The flap is a phone resulting from a single very rapid flip of the blade of the tongue against the alveolar ridge. In English the flap occurs at least (the exact conditioning factors are still unknown) between a stressed and unstressed vowel as an allophone of both /t/ and /d/; as for example in 'matter', 'latter', 'sadder', etc. In Modern Greek, however, the flap is phonemic: /élava/ 'I received' and /éřava/ 'I was sewing'; /kséřo/ 'I know' and /kséno/ 'someone else's'; /bóta/ 'boot' and /bóřa/ 'storm'; /kóři/ 'daughter' and /kódi/ 'shot'.

The Voiced Alveolar Lateral /l/

The phone resulting from having the apex of the tongue in close contact with the alveolar ridge and the rest of the tongue in about the position for [ɪ] or [e] while the vocal folds vibrate and the air escapes over the sides of the tongue is the voiced alveolar lateral, [l] or "clear l." This phone occurs in both Greek and English. In Greek it is phonemic: /ř ́ya/ 'ruler'; /lí ́ya/ 'few'; /pí ́ya/ 'I went'; /mí ́ya/ 'fly'. In English, however, [l] is allophonic: it occurs at least (the exact conditioning factors are still unknown) in word initial position and medially after consonants: [líyp] 'leap' /líyp/, [glów] 'glow' /glów/.

The Voiced Velar Nasal [ŋ]

This phone is produced by placing the back of the tongue against the velum and by forcing the air to escape through the nose instead of the mouth. In English [ŋ] contrasts with every other consonant and is therefore phonemic; witness, for example, the minimal pairs [sí·n] 'sing' and [sí·n] 'sin', and [sík] 'sick', [sít] 'sit', [sís] 'sis', etc. In Modern Greek, however, the velar nasal is an allophone of /n/; it occurs only before /k, g, x, γ/; examples; [sfí·ŋcs] 'sphynx' /sfínks/, [spó·ŋgos] 'sponge' /spóngos/, [É>lĘ>ŋçtí·s] 'inspector' /elenxtís/, [É·ŋγřafo<] 'document' /énγřafo/.

Distinctions in English But Not in Greek

As is the case with Greek, there are a number of distinctions which occur in English that either have a different function or do not occur at all in Greek. The major ones are discussed below.

Vowel Distinctions

The vowel distinctions which are unique to English involve the vowels [æ, ə, ɪ, ɛ, ʊ, ɔ].

[æ] *and* [ə]

The low lax front unrounded vowel [æ] and the mid central unrounded vowel [ə] are phonemic in English but do not even occur in Greek. Examples: /bǽt/ 'bat', /hǽd/ 'had'; /bə́t/ 'but', /hə́t/ 'hut'.[3]

[ɪ, ʊ, ɛ, *and* ɔ]

The high lax front unrounded [ɪ], high back rounded [ʊ], and the mid lax front unrounded [ɛ], and mid lax back rounded [ɔ] are phones which occur in English but not in Greek. Furthermore, they are allophones of the English phonemes /i/, /u/, /e/, and /o/, respectively: [ɪ, ʊ, ɛ, ɔ] occur only before consonants. Examples: [bɪ́t] 'bit' /bɪ́t/; [fʊ́t] 'foot' /fʊ́t/; [bɛ́t] 'bet' /bɛ́t/; [fɔ́t] 'fought' /fɔ́t/. (The long allophone of /o/, namely [ɔ:], occurs before a pause.)

Glide Distinctions

These distinctions involve the glides or semivowels /y, w/ and the phenomenon of diphthongization.

/y/ and /w/

There are two semivowels or glides in English: the voiced palatal glide [y] or [i̯], and the voiced labiovelar glide [w] or [u̯]; the latter does not occur in Greek, while the former has a different function in Greek than it has in English (see 2:2.5). These glides are phonemic in English. Examples: /yɛ́s/ 'yes', /tóy/ 'toy'; /wɛ́t/ 'wet', /háw/ 'how', /áwər/ 'hour'.

Diphthongization

Diphthongization, or the occurrence of a glide after another vowel, is phonemic in English but not in Greek. Diphthongization occurs in English whenever a stressed vowel is immediately followed by a glide. Examples: /bów/ 'bow', /fúwd/ 'food', /máyn/ 'mine', /méy/ 'may', /síy/ 'see'.

Consonant Distinctions

The four consonant classes exhibiting distinctions unique to English are: (1) the alveopalatals, (2) /h/, (3) the liquids, and (4) the voiceless stops.

The Alveopalatals

Sounds produced with an alveopalatal point of articulation are phonemic in English but nonexistent in Greek. The four alveopalatals of English are: the voiceless and voiced grooved fricatives /š/ and /ž/ respectively, and the voiceless and voiced affricates /č/ and /ǰ/, respectively. Examples: /šíp/ 'ship'; /méžər/ 'measure'; /číp/ 'chip', /méyǰər/ 'major'.

/h/

The glottal fricative [h] is a phone which occurs only in English and which is phonemic. Examples: /hǽŋ/ 'hang'; /mǽnhùd/ 'manhood'; /hə́riy/ 'hurry'.

[ɫ] *and* [ɚ]

The voiced alveolar velarized lateral consonant [ɫ] and the voiced mid central retroflex vowel [ɚ] are phones which occur in English but not in Greek. The velarized or "dark l" is allophonic, while the retroflex vowel is phonemic in English. The approximate conditioning factors (the exact ones are still not known) of [l] are: it occurs at least before another consonant and in absolute final position. Examples: [mɪɫk] 'milk' /mɪlk/; [hɪɫ] 'hill' /hɪl/; [ɹɛ·d] 'red' /rɛd/; [k̟ʰɚiy] 'carry' /kɛriy/.

Aspiration

Aspiration or the "puff of air" produced after certain consonants is allophonic in English and sporadic in Greek. The consonants exhibiting aspiration in English are the voiceless stops /p, t, k/; in general, aspirated stops occur initially, after pauses, before stressed vowels, and sometimes in final position. Examples: [pʰɛt] 'pet' /pɛt/; [tʰɪpʰ] 'tip' /tɪp/; [kʰɪk] 'kick' /kɪk/; [əpʰáɚt] 'apart' /ə párt/.

Phonotactic Differences between Greek and English

Having specified the phonemic and allophonic distinctions existing in one but not the other language under consideration, we will now state the phonotactic differences; i.e., how the distribution of phonemes differs in these two languages.

In order to make our presentation more useful, we made several exclusions with respect to the clustering of consonant and vowel phonemes. First, we excluded those clusters that occur only (1) in place-names or proper names other than those of the days of the week and months, and (2) in borrowed nonassimilated words; for example, /vl-/, /šn-/, /nw-/, and /bw-/ were not included in our consideration of English clusters, since /vl-/ and /šn-/ occur only in proper names such as Vladivostok, Vladimir, and Schneider; and /nw-/ and /bw-/ occur only in borrowed nonassimilated words such as 'noir' and 'bwana'. Second, of the clusters remaining, all those were eliminated for which at least five *different* words could not be established.[4] (By different words we mean two or more words with no stem in common: 'boy' and 'girl' are thus different words, but 'blame' a noun and 'blame' a verb are the same word, as is the pair 'great, greatly', since the first shares the common stem 'blame' and the second the common stem 'great'.) Examples of clusters excluded from consideration by this second restriction are the initial clusters /θy-/ and /θw-/ in 'thews' and 'thwart', respectively.

Distribution of Single Phonemes

Vowels

While in Greek all vowels occur initially, medially, and finally within a word regardless of stress, in English the distribution of vowels is stated in relation to stress: when stressed, all vowels occur initially and medially, but only /a/, /ə/, and /o/ occur finally; when unstressed, only /ə/, /o/, and /i/ occur: /ə/ in all three positions, /o/ and /i/ in medial and final position.

Consonants

In Greek all consonants except /y/ occur initially and medially; and all consonants except /d, θ, γ, ð, y/ occur finally. It should be noted, however, that /p, t, k, b, g, f, x, v, z, m, l, ř/—twelve out of the possible fourteen finally occurring consonants—occur only in borrowed words and some interjections: /třám/ 'streetcar', /bokséř/ 'boxer', /kodák/ 'kodak', /pikáp/ 'phonograph', /áx/ 'sigh of relief or pity', /úf/ 'expression of annoyance'.

    In English all consonants, including the glides, occur in all three positions, except /h/ which occurs only initially and medially, and /ž/ and /ŋ/ which occur only medially and finally.

Clusters

Vowels

There are no vowel clusters in English. In contrast, there are several types of vowel clusters in Greek. Clusters of two dissimilar vowels can occur in all three positions while clusters of two identical vowels are restricted to /ii/, /ee/, and /oo/ in word-initial and final position, and occur in an extremely limited number of very frequent words; e.g., /kířii/ 'gentlemen', /θeé/ 'God', /ipíkoos/ 'native', /peřiiγitís/ 'tourist', /zóo/ 'animal'.

Consonants

Clusters of two and three dissimilar consonants occur in all three positions within a word in both languages. Although there are numerous consonant clusters occurring finally in English, only /ts, dz, ks, lf, lm, řts, nks/ occur finally in Greek and then only in borrowed words and some interjections; e.g., /tánks/ 'tanks', /sóřts/ 'shorts', /fílm/ 'film'; /příts/ 'fooey'. Clusters of four dissimilar consonants are rare in both languages.

Although clusters containing the glide /w/ are unique to English (i.e., /kw, tw, sw/ and /skw/ occur only in English and only in syllable-initial position), both languages have consonant clusters containing the glide /y/. Of the possible C + /y/ clusters in English only /hy/ does not occur in Greek. All consonants in Greek, except /y/ itself, occur before /y/ (/b, d, g, řř/ + /y/ occur only initially within a word; the others occur both initially and medially). The following are the sequences of *two* consonants + /y/ in Greek: ps, ts, ks, fx, sx, vγ, ft, xn, xl, mb, nd, ng, nγ, nð, řt, řf, řθ, řn + /y/ (of which /sx, vγ, ft + y/ occur initially and medially, while the others occur only medially within a word).

To compare the remaining consonant clusters we depart slightly from the orthodox linguistic methodology in that instead of simply listing clusters and stating their distribution, we list the clusters under the *types* they represent; that is, instead of simply listing, for example, the clusters pt, kt, ks, dz, and stating their distribution, we list the particular sequences of classes these clusters represent: *stop + stop:* pt, kt, and *stop + fricative:* ks, dz. By type, therefore, is meant a particular sequence of classes which is represented by a given cluster.[5]

The types of consonant clusters in Greek and English are compared in the following tables. In these tables, the members of types listed on the left of a slant line are Greek clusters; those to the right of it, English clusters. On the Greek side an underlined cluster occurs both initially and medially, a cluster not underlined occurs only medially, and a capitalized cluster occurs only initially within a *word;* on the English side, an underlined cluster occurs initially and finally, a cluster not underlined occurs finally only, and a cluster capitalized occurs only initially within a *syllable.* Medial clusters of consonants are not indicated for English, since these are assumed to be predictable from the lists of final and initial consonants and consonant clusters.

The list of two-consonant cluster types which occur in both languages is given in table 1. Not included are two types of two-consonant clusters that occur in Greek but not in English (there are no two-consonant cluster types which occur only in English):

(1) stop + nasal: pn, tm (which occur both initially and medially).
(2) nasal + nasal: mn (which occurs both initially and medially).

The seven cluster types which are unique to Greek are given in table 2, and table 3 presents the thirteen types of three-consonant clusters which are unique to English. The remaining three-consonant cluster types occur in both Greek and English; these are shown in table 4.

TABLE 1. Two-Consonant Cluster Types Common to Greek and English

Cluster Type	Greek/English
stop + stop:	p̲t̲/ pt, kt, čt, bd, gd, ǰd
stop +fricative:	p̲s̲, t̲s̲, k̲s̲, d̲z̲, gð/ ps, ts, ks, bz, gz, dz
stop + liquid:	p̲l̲, p̲ř̲, t̲ř̲, k̲l̲, k̲ř̲, b̲l̲, b̲ř̲, d̲ř̲, g̲ř̲/ PL, PR, TR, KL, KR, BL, BR, DR, GR, GL
fricative + fricative:	f̲θ̲, f̲x̲, f̲s̲, x̲θ̲, v̲ð̲, v̲ɣ̲, ɣ̲ð̲, s̲f̲, s̲x̲, z̲v̲, z̲ɣ̲/ SF, fθ, fs, θs, vz, ðz
fricative + stop:	f̲t̲, fk, xp, x̲t̲, s̲p̲, s̲t̲, s̲k̲, ZB/ s̲p̲, s̲t̲, s̲k̲, st, ft, vd, ðd, zd
fricative + nasal:	θm, θn, xm, x̲n̲, vm, ɣm, ɣ̲n̲, z̲m̲/ SN, SM
fricative + liquid:	FL, f̲ř̲, θ̲ř̲, x̲l̲, x̲ř̲, v̲l̲, v̲ř̲, ð̲ř̲, ɣ̲l̲, ɣ̲ř̲/ FL, FR, θR, SL, ŠR
nasal + stop:	mb, nd, ng/ mp, ŋk, nč, md, nǰ, ŋd, nt, nd
nasal + fricative:	mf, nθ, nx, nð/ mz, nθ, ns, nz, ŋz
liquid + liquid:	řl/rl
liquid + stop:	lp, lt, lk, řp, řt, řk, řb/ lp, lt, lk, ld, rp, rt, rk, rč, rb, rd, rǰ
liquid + fricative:	lf, lθ, lv, ls, řf, řθ, řx, řv, rð/ lf, rθ, rs, lθ, ls, rf, lv, lz, rv, rz
liquid + nasal:	lm, řm, řn/ lm, rm, rn

TABLE 2. Three-Consonant Cluster Types Unique to Greek

Cluster Type	
S + S + S:*	kpt
F + F + N:	vɣn
S + S + L:	kpl
S + F + L:	kfř, gðř
F + F + L:	s̲f̲ř̲, x̲θ̲ř̲, sxř
N + S + L:	mbř, ndř
N + F + L:	mvř, nθř, nðř, nɣř

*In tables 2, 3, and 4 the cluster types are abbreviated with the first letter of each class in the type.

TABLE 3. Three-Consonant Cluster Types Unique
to English*

Cluster Type	
S + S + F:	pts, kts
F + S + F:	fts, sts, sps, sks
F + S + S:	spt, skt
F + F + F:	fθs
N + F + S:	nst
N + F + F:	nθs
L + F + S:	lst, rst, lvd, rvd
L + S + S:	lpt, rpt, rčt, lkt, rkt, rbd, rǰd
L + L + S:	rld
L + N + S:	rmd, rnd
L + L + F:	rlz
L + N + F:	lmz, rmz, rnz
L + F + F:	lθs, lvz, rfs, rvz

*If one compares the first two consonants or the last two
with any of the two-consonant cluster types occurring in
both Greek and English, it will be seen that no new
cluster type is introduced within the three-consonant
cluster types, although the individual sequences' position within a word may be different; for example, we
have above, the three-consonant cluster type L + F +
S, the first two members of which—i.e., L + F—and
the last two members of which—i.e., F. + S—occur as
two-consonant cluster types in both Greek and English.

Problems

A meaningful discussion of the problems that will arise in teaching English pronunciation to native speakers of Greek can proceed only after
the following questions have been answered: (1) What do we mean by
learning pronunciation? (2) What is a pronunciation problem? (3) What
causes this problem? (4) Can the problems be ordered in terms of difficulty? and (5) Are all problems important?

Learning pronunciation of a language means two things: (1) acquiring the muscular control necessary to produce sounds in all the environ-

TABLE 4. Three-Consonant Cluster Types Common to Greek and English

Cluster Type	Greek/English
S + F + S:	kst/ pst, kst
N + S + F:	mps, nts, ndz/ mps, nts, ŋkθ, ŋks, ndz
N + S + S:	mpt/ mpt, nčt, ŋkt, nǰd
L + S + F:	lts, řdz/ rps, rts, rks, lps, lts, lks, rbz, rdz, ldz
F + S + L:	s̲p̲l̲, s̲p̲ř̲, s̲t̲ř̲, s̲k̲l̲, s̲k̲ř̲, ftř, xtř/ SPL, SPR, STR, SKR

ments in which they occur, and (2) making the muscular control a habit. (It will help the teacher if he bears this in mind in the classroom.) Of the two aspects of learning pronunciation, the first, it seems to us, is the easier. One can learn to make the correct movements to produce a sound under conscious effort, but it is quite another matter to produce it automatically; that is, the student may with effort learn to perceive and then to produce a sound in all its environments, but he will fail many times to produce this same sound (and it is at these very times that he will substitute his familiar habits) until he has acquired the new habit.

When, after some instruction, a student consistently fails to produce certain sounds, we say that the student has a pronunciation problem with these sounds. But precisely what does this mean with respect to teaching a foreign language?

Some of the student's habits of pronunciation can be transferred to the new system (the foreign language) without producing any conflict within it; other habits, however, when transferred will produce a conflict. This process of transferring to a second language habits acquired through familiarity with the native language is called *interference*. Interference can facilitate learning a foreign language when the particular elements transferred do not structure differently than the corresponding elements in the foreign language—this is called *positive* interference. But when the transferred elements do *not* structure the same as the corresponding foreign elements, or when they produce a perceptual problem to a native speaker of the foreign language, the transference is a hindrance—and we then have what is called *negative* interference. This negative interference, then, is the key to the answer to our question, "What is a pronunciation problem with respect to teaching a foreign language?": any phone that causes negative interference.

Now, can we predict when interference will occur? And in particular, what form will it take (i.e., what items in the native language will be substituted for the foreign sounds)?

We believe that interference will occur whenever the student is presented with a foreign sound which has some perceptual degree of similarity to a phoneme in his native language, the form it will take depends on the degree of articulatory and distributional similarity between the foreign sound and the native phoneme. But what do we mean by this?

When the student hears a foreign sound he will unconsciously associate it with the phonetic common denominator which the native phoneme shares with the foreign sound. (We speak of foreign "sounds" but native "phonemes" because to a student the foreign language is a mass of sounds—i.e., we are speaking in terms of the student's perceptions; once the foreign language takes some form to the student [i.e., once he has learned the phonemic system of the language], then we can speak of foreign phonemes as well as native phonemes.) Thus, for example, when a native speaker of Japanese is presented with English /l/, he will associate it with his /l/ phoneme, even though one member of his /l/ phoneme—namely [r]—has little similarity in articulation to either English or Japanese [l]. For the student, however, there exists an unconscious common denominator for [l] and [r] which enables him to associate his /l/ with the English /l/. In other words, he will transfer the entire phoneme and not only that allophone of it which is most like English /l/; for to him [l] and [r] are the same sound. Moreover, he will substitute this same native phoneme for English /r/ for the same reason. Notice, however, that although the transference of these elements will cause positive interference whenever the distribution of English /r/ and /l/ coincides with the allophonic distribution of /l/, the transference is nevertheless a problem because of the negative interference that results whenever these distributions do *not* coincide.

Now, should a foreign sound occur in a position or positions in which the phonetically most closely associated native phoneme does not, the student will then transfer the native phoneme (if one exists) occurring in that position which has the next degree of closeness or similarity— similarity again in terms of the phonetic common denominator which all the members of the native phoneme share with the foreign sound.

Thus, the more closely associated a foreign sound is with the student's native phoneme, the harder it will be for the student *not* to substitute the native phoneme for the foreign sound.

By examining the number of similarities present and capable of producing interference, we can, it is clear, make an attempt to order the problems that will arise in terms of their difficulty.[6] The general premise is that the greater the number of similarities present between the foreign sound and the native phoneme, in both articulation and distribution, the more difficult the mastery of a particular foreign sound or sequence of sounds will be. In other words, we not only believe that the problem of learning a new set of language habits is much less difficult than that of breaking old habits, but also hold that the greater the number of competing old habits, the greater will be the difficulty of mastering the desired pronunciation.

Finally, before actually discussing the problems, we must consider the question, "Which forms of interference are to be considered important?" or, in other words, "How well do we want our students to master the pronunciation of a given foreign language?" If our goal is to make our students speak the foreign language like natives, then *all* forms of interference are important; if, on the other hand, our goal is to make our students be understood, then those forms of interference are important that prevent maintaining all the contrasts of the foreign language as well as any number of allophonic variations which prove necessary for unambiguous perception of the nonnative's speech by a native speaker of the foreign language.

We can now turn to the problems that we predict will arise in teaching English pronunciation to native speakers of Greek, given the goal of making the student understandable when speaking English. The discussion is divided into two sections: (1) problems concerning the production of individual sounds, and (2) problems arising from differences in the distribution of consonants in clusters. The problems of each section are ordered in terms of difficulty.

Problems Concerning the Production of Individual Sounds

In order of difficulty they are: (1) /w/ and /y/, (2) [ɪ, ə, ʊ, ɔ], (3) /č/ and /ǰ/, (4) /š/ and /ž/, (5) aspirated stops, (6) /ŋ/, and (7) /æ/.

/w/ and /y/

Several factors are present to produce interference with the production of both these phonemes. Let us begin with a discussion of /w/.

While there is no labiovelar glide in Greek, the articulation of the Greek high back rounded vowel /u/ is the same as that of English /w/ with the exception of gliding. In addition, both Greek /u/ and English /w/ have several environments in common: both occur after similar vowels, namely

/a/ and /o/, and both occur before most of the vowels of their respective systems (/u/ does not occur before /u/, however). Thus, it can be expected that although the positions of occurrence within a *word* may not be the same, /u/ will usually be substituted for /w/ in syllable-initial position and the interference will not be negative. Since /u/ never occurs before /u/ in Greek, however, the phoneme that is next closest in articulation to /w/ and that occurs before /u/—namely /γ/ (which is labialized before /u/)— will be substituted for /w/ in this environment only. When /w/ clusters with /u/ and /o/, however, as in English 'two' /túw/ and 'toe' /tów/, it can be expected that the student, because of the close similarity in articulation of the first and second English phoneme (i.e., the glide is so close in articulation to the vowel being glided), will not be able to perceive the gliding and will produce [tú] or [tú·] for /túw/ and [tΏ] or [tΏ·] for /tów/, thus obviating two important contrasts in English: u/uw and o/ow.

As for the palatal glide /y/, again there are several factors present to produce interference: the Greek high front unrounded vowel /i/ and the voiced palatal fricative [j] of Greek /γ/ have exactly the same point of articulation (although they are not glided) as /y/, while /i/ also has the same manner of articulation as /y/; in addition, both /i/ and /γ/ occur in almost exactly the same environments as English /y/. /γ/ will be substituted for /y/ initially before front vowels, while /i/ will be substituted for /y/ in other positions. This interference will be negative, however, only when the student is confronted with /iy/, because the glide is so close to the /i/ in articulation and he will perceive and produce /iy/ as the Greek /i/, with or without length; that is, he will not be able to distinguish or make the distinction between such pairs as /bít/ and /bíyt/ and /fít/ and /fíyt/, and will produce the members of each pair the same—as /bít/ and /fít/, respectively.

[ɪ, ə, ɔ, *and* ʊ]

The production of [ɪ,ɔ,ʊ] involves articulations which are close enough to Greek articulations to cause negative interference: the only major difference between English [ɪ] and Greek /i/ is that the Greek vowel has slightly more tenseness (or closeness of the tongue to the roof of the mouth); the same is true of the difference between Greek [Ω] and English [ɔ], and Greek /u/ and English [ʊ]; that is, in each case the tongue and lip positions for the English and corresponding Greek phones are so close that the student will have much difficulty in learning to make the slight difference in the tongue position so as to produce consistently the proper English phone. English [ʌ] and [ə] are very close in both articulation and distribution to the Greek /a/ and /e/, respectively; therefore, negative interference in the form of /a/ for [ʌ] and /e/ for [ə] will arise with this vowel. The following chart illustrates how serious the negative interference is with English vowels.

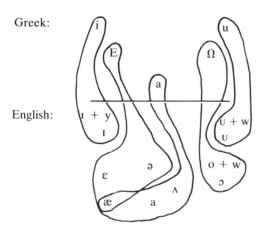

The circled areas show which phones will be produced the same, with the Greek vowel as the norm. From this chart it is clear which English vowel contrasts will not be maintained: iy–i, a–ə, e–ə, uw–u, e or a–æ, ow–o. Examples of the substitutions that will occur are the following: /píts/ for both /píč/ and /píyč/; /dzámp/ for /jə́mp/; /bét/ for /bét/ and /bæt/; /bádzet/ for /bə́jət/; /bót/ for both /bót/ and /bówt/; /bút/ for /búwt/; and /búk/ for /búk/.

/č/ *and* /ǰ/

Phonetically, an affricate is a sequence of two elements—a stop very closely followed by a fricative. In Greek there are two affricates /ts/ and /dz/, the point of articulation being alveolar for both. In English there exists, in addition to these affricates, the pair /č/ and /ǰ/ (phonetically, tš and dž), the fricative members of which have a point of articulation which does not exist in Greek: namely, the alveopalatal. Since (1) the alveopalatal point of articulation is very close to the alveolar and (2) the sequences /ts/ and /dz/ occur frequently in initial and medial position in Greek—positions in which /č/ and /ǰ/ also occur frequently—it can be expected that negative interference will arise in the form of /ts/ for /č/ and /dz/ for /ǰ/ in all positions within a word. Examples of these substitutions are the following: /réts/ for /réč/, /tsék/ for /čék/, /píts/ for both /píč/ and píts; /dzém/ for /jæm/ (and /jem/), /xédz/ for both /héj/ and /hédz/.

/š/ and /ž/

Since these phones have similar counterparts in Greek, they will certainly cause negative interference. There are two possible forms this may take: (1) the voiceless and voiced grooved alveolar fricatives /s/ and /z/ or (2) the palatalized variants of these fricatives namely, /sy/ and /zy/. In the beginning /s/ and /z/ will be substituted for /š/ and /ž/, respectively, since the two pairs have more environments in common than /sy/ and /š/ and /zy/ and /ž/. However, the articulations of /š/ and /ž/ are more similar to /sy/ and /zy/, respectively, than to /s/ and /z/: /š/ and /ž/ are simultaneous palatalizations of the alveolars /s/ and /z/, while /sy/ and /zy/ are nonsimultaneous palatalizations of the alveolars. At a later stage, therefore, /sy/ will be substituted for /š/ and /zy/ for /ž/ in initial and medial position, even though there is less environmental overlap between /sy/ and /š/ and /zy/ and /ž/ than between /š/ and /s/ and /ž/ and /z/.[7] Thus, at the beginning of a course, we can expect to hear, for example, /sú/ for /šúw/ (and /súw/), /só/ for /šów/ (and /sów/), /bés/ for /bæš/; /plézeř/ for /pléžər/, /řúz/ for /rúwž/. Examples of what we can expect to hear at a later stage are /syú/ for /šúw/, /syó/ for /šów/, but again /bés/ for /bæs/, /plézyeř/ for /plézer/, etc.

Aspirated Stops

Although aspiration is a new articulation to a Greek speaker, its production as a release of the voiceless stops /p, t, k/ will produce negative interference, since the articulation of the voiceless stops themselves—bilabial, dental, and velar—is almost identical for both English and Greek. Modification of these stops, therefore, will be difficult for the Greek speaker. It is important, however, that this modification be mastered, for it is difficult for native speakers of English to hear the difference between voiceless unaspirated stops and voiced stops; thus, if the student produces [pín], a native speaker of English would not be sure whether the speaker said [pʰín] or [bín].

The Velar Nasal /ŋ/

The production of the velar nasal before velars will not be a problem for the Greek speaker since this is precisely the position in which it occurs in

Greek. Its production intervocalically and in word-final position, how-ever, will be a problem. Negative interference will arise in those positions because in Greek the velar nasal is an allophone of the voiced alveolar /n/, which like English /ŋ/, occurs both intervocalically and in word-final position (it is [n] that occurs in word-final position in Greek). Thus, the student may substitute either /n/, /ŋk/, or /ŋg/ intervocalically or in word-final position. For example, he may produce /sín/, /síŋk/ or /síŋg/ for /síŋ/; /síneř/, /síŋkeř/, or /síŋgeř/ for síŋər/; and /θín/, /θíŋk/, or θíŋg/ for /θíŋ/.

The Low Front Vowel /æ/

There are two possible forms of negative interference that may occur with /æ/; namely, /e/ or /a/. Both of these are equidistant in articulation from /æ/ and both have distributions similar to that of /æ/. It is possible that the student will substitute sometimes one and sometimes the other Greek vowel for /æ/, until the muscular control necessary to produce /æ/ is habitual. Examples of the substitutions that may occur are /met/ or /mat/ for /mæt/, /at/ or /et/ for /æt/, and /ba/ or /be/ for /bæ/. Since, however, /æ/ is not as close in articulation to either /e/ or /a/ as the other English vowels are to Greek vowels, /æ/ will not cause as much difficulty as the other vowels.

Problems Due to Differences in the Distribution of
Consonants[8]

These problems divide into two equally difficult groups: new clusters that (1) belong to a cluster type common to both languages and (2) are repre-sentative of a new cluster type. It should be noted that, as it turns out, the problems of the first group are restricted to two-consonant clusters, while the majority of the problems of the second group are with three-consonant clusters.

New Clusters Belonging to a Cluster Type
Common to Both Languages

Negative interference will arise with any new two-consonant cluster which has one member in common with a Greek cluster of that type and the other member of which bears certain similarities (such as point and man-ner of articulation and distribution) to the corresponding member of the Greek cluster. The factors that determine which Greek cluster will be substituted for the new cluster, in order of preference, are: same (1) point of articulation, (2) voice (i.e., voiced or voiceless), and (3) manner of articulation (i.e., stop, fricative, etc.).[9] In other words, that Greek cluster will be substituted for the new cluster which has one member in common with it and another member which has either the same point and voice or point and manner of articulation (in that order) rather than the same voice and manner of articulation—provided, always, that the Greek cluster has a distribution similar to that of the English cluster it is replacing. For example, the cluster type stop + liquid is common to both Greek and English and the only new cluster is English /gl/. It would seem that, given this situation and the fact that [g] is phonemic in Greek as well as English, there should be no negative interference with this cluster. There is, however, a cluster in Greek—/γl/—which will frequently be substituted for /gl/ for the following reason: (1) the second member of the Greek and English cluster is the same, (2) both /g/ and /γ/ have the same point of articulation and voice (although a different manner of articulation), and (3) both /gl/ and /γl/ occur initially and medially within a word. By comparing the Greek and English clusters in table 1, while keeping in mind the means for determining whether negative interference will occur, one can decide what new clusters will be a problem for the native speaker of Greek. (It may be, however, that a cluster that ordinarily would cause negative interference will not do so in final position, since Greek consonant clusters generally do not occur in that position.)

New Cluster Types

Included under these problems are the cluster types which occur only in English and those which have many members in English but only one or two in Greek, and which therefore, for practical purposes, must be considered new.

The same conditions are present and potentially liable to produce negative interference with new clusters belonging to new cluster types as with new clusters that belong to a type common to both languages. In the case of new types, however, negative interference will always be in the form of a Greek cluster at least one member of which will differ from the corresponding English cluster only with respect to manner of articulation. Although this form of interference will not occur with native speakers of Greek learning English pronunciation, it may with a native speaker of a different language learning English or some other language.

Negative interference will, however, occur with the new three-consonant cluster types in the form of a Greek cluster at least one member of which will differ from the corresponding member of the English cluster only with respect to voice. This can be explained by the fact that it is possible to view three-consonant clusters as composites of two-consonant clusters; in so doing, it becomes apparent that within the three-consonant cluster types unique to English, no new two-consonant cluster type is introduced (see footnote to table 3). Thus, negative interference that will occur with any new two-consonant cluster (and each belongs to some type common to both languages) will also occur when that cluster occurs as part of a three-consonant cluster. For example, within the new cluster /rld/ (which represents a new cluster type) is the new two-consonant cluster /ld/, which, according to the preceding section, will be produced as /lt/. Now, it seems reasonable to assume that the same interference will occur with /rld/ as with /ld/ and that the student will therefore produce /rlt/ for /rld/ just as he will produce /lt/ for /ld/.

Additional Remarks

Given a Greek word, it is immediately apparent how to pronounce it; i.e., there is no ambiguity in Greek orthography; particular graphemes and sequences of graphemes are always pronounced the same way; e.g., γγ is always pronounced [g]. This is not the case in English, however. For example, that *a* in *hat* is pronounced differently from the *a* in *father* or *fame*. The native speaker of Greek, with his well-entrenched associations between Greek orthography and speech will therefore have trouble when confronted with English orthography for despite any warnings, he may persist in trying to (1) associate a Greek phone with any grapheme that has the same form in both languages and (2) find a consistent association between phones and graphemes. Just how much and precisely what negative interference can be expected from orthography, however, requires a study of the relationship of orthography to speech in both Greek and English, followed by a comparison of the two.

Notes

1. By Greek is meant Modern Athenian Greek and by English is meant that dialect of English spoken in the Ann Arbor and Detroit areas of midwestern America. The description of the segmentals in Greek is based on A. Koutsoudas's *Verb Morphology of Modern Greek: A Descriptive Analysis,* Publication 24 of the Indiana University Research Center in Anthropology, Folklore, and Linguistics, chap. 2 (Bloomington, 1962).
2. A mid close back rounded allophone [o] has been observed for /o/ but its exact conditioning factors are not immediately apparent.

3. These distinctions are based on an analysis of English (see Introduction) in which we posit seven vowels /i, e, æ, ə, a, u, o/, twenty-two consonants /p, t, č, k, b, d, ǰ, g, f, θ, s, š, v, ð, z, ž, h, m, n, ŋ, l, r, and two glides /y, w/; /r/ is not treated as a semivowel since it clusters as a consonant and not as a semivowel.

4. An exception to this rule was made for clusters occurring in what we considered common words.

5. The affricates /č,ǰ/ are included under the stops for this analysis. Notice that by class we mean a group of phonemes classified according to manner of articulation.

6. We are aware that the exact degree of difficulty and precisely what difficulties a person will have with mastering a new language are to a large extent an individual matter, varying from person to person, and depending also on other linguistic (such as lexicon) and extralinguistic factors; we feel, however, that there is such a phenomenon as general problem areas that can be delineated and that such a delineation will have a definite value to a language teacher.

7. Since /s/ is one of the two consonants which occur in word-final position in native Greek words, it is not at all likely that /sy/ would be substituted for /š/ in this position; either the student will continue to produce /s/ finally, or will learn to produce /š/; but we doubt that there will be any transitional stage such as we predict for the word-initial and medial positions.

8. Notice that although the occurrence of consonants, singly or in clusters, in word-final position is common in English but not in Greek, we do not consider learning to produce consonants in this position a problem. Notice, in addition, that any cluster containing a sound considered a problem in the preceding section is not discussed in this section.

9. The ordering of these factors is not arbitrary; the authors feel that in language learning certain oppositions (or contrasts) are more fundamental than others, and it is on this basis that the ordering is made.

A Need for the Syllable in Contrastive Analyses

Eugène J. Brière, Russell N. Campbell, and Soemarmo

In any language-learning situation, the phonological and grammatical categories of the student's native language (N) are partially similar to, and partially different from, the competing linguistic categories of the target language (T) the student is attempting to learn. The partial similarities and partial differences of the competing categories are expected to cause interference in the learning of any second language. Linguists (e.g., Moulton 1962*a*, 1962*b;* Stockwell and Bowen 1965) have assumed that by a contrastive analysis of the N with the T the relevant categories could be defined precisely and, by comparing them, the areas and the degree of interference between the N and the T could be predicted.

Heretofore, in contrastive analyses comparing the N and the T phonological systems, the word has been used as one of the primes of analysis. For example, Lado (1957) and Politzer (1960) posited that the sound /ž/ (as in *leisure* /liyžər/) would be difficult to learn for American-English speakers learning any language in which this sound occurs in word-initial position in the T, since /ž/ never occurs in word-initial position in the N, American English.

However, in a recent experimental investigation of phonological interference (Brière 1966, 1968), the sounds /ž/ and /ŋ/ (as in *ringing* /rɪŋɪŋ/, which, like /ž/, never occurs in word-initial position in English) were presented in a composite language containing French (*jouer* /žue/) and Vietnamese (*ngao* /ŋao/) words, which monolingual American-English speakers attempted to learn. The Ss had difficulty learning /ŋ/ in its new position in the T but displayed perfect positive transfer for /ž/; i.e., all Ss produced /ž/ on *every* trial, thereby indicating that there was no learning problem involved at all.

Brière hypothesized that /ž/ and /ŋ/ have completely different distributions in English and that using the word as a prime of analysis will not reveal this difference. Though both sounds do not occur in word-initial position, it was posited that /ž/ occurs in syllable-initial position but that

Reprinted from the *Journal of Verbal Learning and Verbal Behavior* 7 (1968):384–89 by permission of the publisher and the authors.

/ŋ/ is always syllable-final; e.g., the syllable break in /liyžər/ would be /liy#žər/ but the syllable break in /rɪŋɪŋ/ would be /rɪŋ#ɪŋ/ and never */rɪ#ŋɪŋ/.

It was further posited that any sound which occurred in syllable-initial position in English would be easily learned by American-English speakers in word-initial position in the T, whether the sound occurs in this position or not in the N. In other words, the "accidental" absence of this sound from word initial position in the N is not crucial in predicting interference between the N and the T. However, the absence of a given sound from the syllable-initial position is crucial, and any such sound now occurring in word-initial position in the T will cause interference and present a learning problem.

It was, therefore, posited that using the word as the only prime (above the phoneme) in a contrastive analysis of competing phonological systems is inadequate and that information derived from using the syllable as an additional prime would be necessary for accurate prediction of proactive interference.

The phonological unit called the syllable has been used as a prime in linguistic analyses for some time. Definitions or descriptions of the syllable have been given in terms of the distribution of vowels and consonants (O'Connor and Trim 1953), in terms of acoustic parameters (Lehiste 1960, 1961), in terms of juncture (Harris 1952; Hill 1958), and in terms of physiological correlates (Stetson 1928; Pike 1944). Whatever description of the syllable is used, the enumeration of the number of syllables in a given utterance is usually not a problem. Malmberg (1963, p. 65) says, "even a person without any linguistic training usually has a very clear idea of the number of syllables in a spoken chain." Furthermore, there is general agreement upon the location of the point at which one syllable ends and another begins when certain consonants occur together medially. Thus, Hill (1958) can state with confidence that the syllable boundary in an utterance such as *jackpot* /džækpat/ would fall between the /k/ and /p/ since the consonant cluster /kp/ never occurs initially or finally with a single vocalic nucleus in English. We can, then, accept the generalization which states that the syllable boundary in any polysyllabic utterance will separate all medial consonant sequences which do not adhere to the rules for concatenation of consonant clusters in American English.

However, in spite of the general agreement upon the number of syllables in a given utterance and the location of the syllable boundary between certain consonant sequences, there remains the serious problem of predicting the assignment of single intervocalic consonants to a preceding or following syllable. In an utterance such as *Thomas* /táməs/, all linguists would agree that there are two syllables, but not all would agree whether the medial consonant /m/ should be assigned to the first syllable or to the second syllable. Since /m/ occurs in both initial and final positions in English; e.g., *mom* /mam/, the assignment of /m/ to the first or second syllable cannot be predicted in terms of distribution alone. Furthermore, a specific syllable assignment for /m/ cannot be predicted in terms of acoustic parameters, juncture, or physiological correlates.

In light of the hypothesis, previously stated, that there is a need for using the syllable as a prime in a contrastive analysis of the N with any T, it becomes extremely important to determine which specific consonants can or cannot be assigned to syllable-initial position by the speakers of a given language.

To investigate the manner in which American English speakers actually assign intervocalic consonants to syllable-initial or syllable-final positions, the following experiment was conducted.

Method

Subjects

The Ss (n = 25) were undergraduate students at UCLA. All Ss were monolingual speakers of American English with no bilingual backgrounds in their families. The Ss had a maximum of three years of training in a foreign language. All Ss spoke the standard dialect as heard around Los Angeles and no speakers of other regional dialects were permitted in the study.

Corpus

The corpus consisted of a total of 156 words, 12 monosyllables (e.g., *call*), 42 polysyllables (e.g., *mechanical*), 102 disyllables (e.g., *dozen*). Regardless of the number of syllables in any word, only one intervocalic consonant was being investigated in each word, for example the /p/ in *capacity*. The corpus was divided so that some of the words (80) had primary stress on the syllable immediately preceding and others (67) had primary stress on the syllable immediately following the consonant being investigated. All of the consonantal phonemes in American English were included in the corpus. Where possible each consonantal class was represented by both geminate and nongeminate spellings; e.g., *labor* has a nongeminate "b," stress on first syllable, and *abbot* has a geminate "bb," stress on the first syllable.

Procedure

The Ss were seated at a table with the E. In front of the Ss were placed a microphone, a tape recorder, and a stack of 4 × 6 inch white cards. On each card was printed one word of the corpus in capital letters with equal spacing between the letters. The cards were arranged in random order. An electric metronome was placed nearby and set for 80 beats per minute. The E instructed the Ss as follows: "Please read the words on the cards in front of you. Break the words into parts, if they have parts, and say each part to each beat of the metronome. Allow two beats between each word." The Ss were then given the practice words *nightmare, handful, talk, bedroom, metronome,* and *deep,* to see if they understood the assignment. When the Ss did indeed break *metronome* into three parts, *nightmare, handful,* and *bedroom* into two parts, and *talk* and *deep* into one part, the Ss were told to go ahead and "to allow only one part per beat and to be sure to come to a complete stop after each part. Allow two beats between each word. Ready? Begin." The Ss then turned over the cards in the order presented to them and, where possible, broke the stimulus words into different parts, each part given to one beat of the metronome.

After the entire list had been completed, Ss were then presented a random order of four words from the corpus, chosen to represent utterances of 1, 2, 3, and 4 syllables; e.g., *shoe, ringing, collision,* and *nasality.* The Ss were simply asked to state how many syllables each word contained. The Ss' performances on both tasks were recorded on the tape recorder.

The resulting tapes were judged by the authors. Inventory sheets for each S were kept. The inventory sheets were designed so that the Ss' assignments of each intervocalic consonant being investigated could be scored in one of three columns, "I," "II," or "B." In other words, in the word *minor,* for example, the *n* could have been assigned to the first syllable (I), *min-or,* to the second syllable (II), *mi-nor,* or to both syllables (B), *min-nor* (with or without a clear break in between syllables.)

In addition, all of the Ss' individual pronunciations of all of the utterances were transcribed phonetically on separate charts. All of the individual inventory sheets were then collapsed onto one sheet designed to give the total number of syllable assignments by all Ss for syllables "I," "II," or "B," for every consonant that had been investigated.

A series of chi-square tests were made to see if there was any significant relationship between the syllable assignments made by the Ss and the variables of stress, gemination, and voicing. In addition, chi-square tests were made to determine the relationship between syllable assignments and various phonetic classes such as "stops" versus "sibilants." (Unfortunately, when one is dealing with natural languages, obvious limitations prevent a completely filled matrix which would permit a more sophisticated statistical measure such as an analysis of variance. In American English, for example, there are no words containing /ž/ which have primary stress on the second syllable; there are no words which have a geminate /-kk-/ intervocalically; and all liquids and nasals are phonemically voiced. Thus the variables of stress, gemination, and voice can apply to some, but not all, items in the corpus.)

Results

1. On the second task, counting syllables, Ss agreed 100 percent as to the number of syllables contained in the stimuli.

2. The intervocalic consonants which were investigated were assigned as follows: 141 assignments to I; 2,635 assignments to II; and 824 assignments to B.

3. There was no significant difference in the assignments of intervocalic consonants due to the following variables: (*a*) stress I versus stress II; (*b*) disyllables versus polysyllables; (*c*) geminate versus ageminate spelling; (*d*) consonant groups such as stops versus fricatives; or (*e*) voiced versus voiceless consonants within a given group except as noted below.

4. /ŋ/ was assigned completely differently from all of the other consonants investigated (see table 1).

5. The class of liquids /l, r/ differed significantly in their assignments from the remainder of the consonants (see table 1), $X^2(2) = 63.69$, $p < .001$.

6. The interdentals /θ, ð/ differed significantly in their assignments from the remainder of the consonants (see table 1), $X^2(2) = 37.88$, $p < .001$.

7. When the interactions of gemination and consonant class were analyzed /m/ differed significantly from the remainder of the consonants, $X^2(2) = 43.13$ $p < .001$.

8. When the interactions of stress and consonant class were analyzed /l, r/ differed significantly in their assignments from the remainder of the consonants.

Though the experiment was not designed to investigate the next three results, the observations reported and discussed below are relevant to the study of American English segmentals.

TABLE 1. Actual Assignments of Consonants Converted to Percentages of the Total of a Given Class

Consonant	Syllable I	Syllable II	B(oth) Syllables	Total
/ŋ/	77 (77%)	0 (0%)	23 (23%)	100
/ž/	1 (0.08)	107 (85.6)	17 (13.6)	125
/l, r/	29 (0.07)	143 (33.6)	253 (59.5)	425
/θ, ð/	5 (1.7)	189 (63)	106 (35.3)	300
All other consonants	29 (1.1)	2,196 (82.8)	425 (16.1)	2,650

9. The Ss only produced aspirated allophones of the voiceless stops in syllable initial.

10. Affricates were treated as unit phonemes.

11. "Checked" vowels actually did occur in open syllables.

Discussion

If a particular sound being investigated was assigned to syllable II *after* a break, then that particular sound category occurs *syllable-initial*. On the other hand, if a sound is never assigned to syllable II and is consistently assigned to syllable I before the break, then we say that this sound occurs *syllable-final* only. (The assignments to B (both) was not considered criterial in defining initial or final positions.) On the basis of this definition, all of the consonants which were investigated occur syllable-initial except /ŋ/, and all of the consonants which occur syllable-initial also occur word-initial, except /ž/.

It is important to note that although there were 23 percent of the assignments of /ŋ/ attributed to B, this classification represented a glide rather than an actual break between syllables I and II. In other words, the velar was lengthened at the end of the first syllable but there were no occasions whatsoever of /ŋ/ being produced after a pause.

A glance at table 1 confirms the fact that /ŋ/ is distributed completely differently from the other consonants; i.e., /ŋ/ never occurs syllable-initial, whereas /ž/ is distributed essentially the same as all other American-English consonants in that /ž/ also occurs syllable-initial. This suggests that /ŋ/ will represent a learning problem for American-English speakers who attempt to learn a language which has /ŋ/ in word-initial position but /ž/, since it occurs in syllable-initial position, will not present a learning problem even when it occurs word-initial in the target language. In other words, in the case of /ŋ/ and /ž/, information derived from using the syllable as an encoding unit is necessary in any contrastive analysis of American English with a target language to insure accurate predictions of interference in phonology. ·

The need for using the syllable as one of the units in a contrastive analysis does not, however, mean that the word can be disregarded as a unit. Frequently information that is important in predicting interference in learning a second language can only be gained by considering multiple syllable forms; for example, the distribution of allophones in a language is described in terms of units that are longer than just a single syllable.

In American English, the phoneme /t/ has an unaspirated flap allophone which occurs intervocalically after a stressed syllable; e.g., *city* /sɪɾɪ/, and an aspirated allophone which occurs word initial; e.g., *tin* [tʰɪn]. However, when the Ss were forced to break a word such as *city* into two syllables, they pronounced both syllables with equal stress and they substituted the aspirated allophone for the flap, [sɪ#tʰɪ].

Thus, in general, the allophone which can occur in syllable-initial is the one that occurs in word-initial, except for [ž]. To the extent that the generalization holds true for other languages, in a contrastive analysis of consonants, we should use *word* as a prime to define the distribution of allophones but use *syllable* as a prime to define the distribution of phonemes.

In defining the distribution of vowels in American English, the use of syllables seems to be equally important. Kurath (1964, p. 17) states that "checked vowels . . . /ɪ, ɛ, æ, . . . ʊ/, as in *bid, bed, bad,* . . . *good* . . . do not occur at the end of morphemes; they are always followed by one or two consonants" (table 2).

From our transcriptions of the Ss' responses, however, we were able to make the following observations. When Ss were forced to break words into two or more parts, the so-called checked vowels did, in fact, frequently occur in syllable-final; i.e., in open syllables as unchecked vowels. When the consonant assignment was to syllable II, the Ss produced the "checked" vowels of the first syllable in one of three ways, viz. (*a*) . . . Vʔ#, i.e., checked by a glottal stop (ʔ) before the break (#); (*b*) . . . Vh#, i.e., followed by a devoicing (h) of the vowel; (c) . . . V#, i.e., simply as a completely unchecked vowel in open syllable. For example, for the stimulus word *rapid* /ræpɪd/, all of the following forms were recorded /ræʔ#pɪd/, /ræh#pɪd/, and /ræ#pɪd/.

The above observation that so-called checked vowels can occur in syllable-final suggests that further research should be conducted concerning the distribution of vowels within American English because of the

TABLE 2. "Checked" Vowels in Syllable-Final; Raw Scores and Percentages of the Individual Totals

	Vowel #	Vowel ʔ#	Vowel h#	Total
/ɪ/	12	23	8	43
	27.9%	53.5%	18.6%	
/ɛ/	34	19	37	90
	37.7%	21.1%	41.1%	
/æ/	123	23	14	160
	76.9%	14.4%	8.7%	
/ʊ/	15	6	3	24
	62.5%	25.0%	12.5%	

importance of the theory of contrastive analysis. If a "checked" vowel can occur in syllable-final, then one would predict that when an American English speaker is learning a language in which these vowels occur in open syllables; e.g., French *mais* /mɛ/, then no interference should ensue due to the vowel distribution in the native language.

One interesting result of this experiment, although only of marginal importance to contrastive analysis, was the Ss' treatment of affricates.

The phonemic status of the affricates /č/, as in *chin* /čɪn/, and /ǰ/, as in *gin* /ǰɪn/, has been debated for over 50 years. The problem has been whether to analyze /č/ and /ǰ/ as single-unit phonemes or sequences of the sounds /t/ plus /š/ for the former and /d/ plus /ž/ for the latter. Bloomfield (1933) established /č/ as a single unit phoneme on the basis of the contrastive pair of utterances *white shoes* /hwaitšuz/: *why choose* /hwaɪčuz/. However, some years later, Bloch and Trager (1940) posited that the establishment of /č/ and /ǰ/ as single unit phonemes was unnecessary. They introduced the concept of "plus juncture" (+) into phonological theory and demonstrated that the distinguishing factor in Bloomfield's test pair could be attributed to the placement of the plus juncture rather than to a difference between a single-unit phoneme and a sequence of phonemes; i.e., *white shoes* /hwait + šuz/, and *why choose* /hwai + tšuz/. Since that time, many linguists have disagreed on the way to analyze the affricates, although most American linguists still treat /č/ and /ǰ/ as single-unit phonemes.

In this experiment, Ss were given 346 opportunities to divide words containing the sequences /tš/ and /dž/. There was not one single instance in which any S separated the first and second elements of these sequences. For example, the words *teacher* and *magic* were never divided into the sequences /tiyt + šər/ or /mæd + žɪk/—although /t/, /d/, /š/, and /ž/ are demonstrably permissible syllable-final and syllable-initial phonemes. Out of the 346 occasions the Ss assigned the affricates to syllable I 16 times /tiytš#ər/ and /mædž#ɪk/ and to syllable II 330 /tiy#tšər/ and /mæ#džɪk/.

It might be argued that the only reason Ss treated affricates as single-unit phonemes is that all of the stimulus words in the corpus contained single, intervocalic consonants only. There were no intervocalic consonants clusters which the Ss would naturally break into two distinct parts; e.g., in the word *compare,* the intervocalic cluster would undoubtedly be broken into two parts, *com#pare,* rather than be treated as a single unit assigned to syllable I, *comp#are,* or to syllable II, *co#mpare.*

An additional experiment should be conducted in which the stimulus words contain some single intervocalic consonants, but a majority of intervocalic consonant clusters of the type that would encourage dividing the syllables between the consonants. If Ss continue to treat the affricates as they did in the experiment reported here, then there would seem to be little doubt that, in behavioral terms, /č/ and /ǰ/ are used by speakers of American English (in both syllable-initial and in syllable-final) as single-unit phonemes.

References

Brière, E. J. *A Psycholinguistic Investigation of Phonological Interference.* The Hague: Mouton and Co., 1968.

———. "An investigation of phonological interference." *Language* 42 (1966): 768–96.

Bloch, B., and Trager, G. L. *Outline of Linguistic Analysis.* Baltimore: Linguistic Society of America, 1942.

Bloomfield, L. *Language.* New York: Holt, 1933.

Harris, Z. S. "Discourse Analysis." *Language* 28 (1952):1–30.

Hill, A. A. *Introduction to Linguistic Structure.* New York: Harcourt Brace and Co., 1958.

Kurath, H. *A Phonology and Prosody of Modern English.* Ann Arbor: University of Michigan Press, 1964.

Lado, R. *Linguistics Across Cultures.* Ann Arbor: University of Michigan Press, 1957.

Lehiste, I. "An Acoustic-Phonetic Study of Internal Open Juncture." Supplement to *Phonetica* 5 (1960).

———. "Acoustic Studies of Boundary Signals." *Proceedings of the Fourth International Congress of Phonetic Sciences.* The Hague: Mouton and Co., 1961. Pp. 178–87.

Malmberg, B. *Phonetics*. New York: Dover Publications, 1963.

Moulton, W. G. "Toward a Classification of Pronunciation Errors." *Modern Language Journal* 40, no. 3 (1962a):101–9.

————. *The Sounds of English and German*. Chicago: University of Chicago Press, 1962b.

O'Connor, J. D., and Trim, J. L. M. "Vowel, Consonant and Syllable—a Phonological Definition." *Word* 9 (1953):103–22.

Pike, K. L. *Phonetics*. Ann Arbor: University of Michigan Press, 1944.

Politzer, R. *Teaching French*. New York: Ginn and Company, 1961.

Stetson, R. H. *Motor Phonetics: A Study of Speech Movement in Action*. Amsterdam: North Holland Publishing Co., 1951.

Stockwell, R. P., and Bowen, D. *The Sounds of English and Spanish*. Chicago: University of Chicago Press, 1965.

On the Explanation of Phonic Interference

William C. Ritchie

That the goal of a foreign language (L₂) course is the modification of the learner and his behavior in some way is beyond dispute. A major factor in such modification is the elimination of the influence of the native language (L₁) on L₂ behavior, i.e., the elimination of interference behavior. It follows that we cannot expect to attain maximum success in the teaching of the practical phonology of an L₂ unless we have a clear understanding of what the nature of the influence of the L₁ on L₂ behavior might be—i.e, unless we have an explanation of interference behavior. This paper suggests that certain modes of explanation based on conventional phonemics and conditioning theory are unsatisfactory in the explication of a particular case of interference behavior and that generative phonology in the sense of Halle, Chomsky, et al., shows more promise in this area.

The substitution of different sounds for the interdental fricatives of English by learners from different L₁ backgrounds has been marked by many investigators. Weinreich (1966, p. 20) notes that the majority of French speakers substitute [s] and [z] for English [θ] and [ð], respectively, whereas Russian speakers substitute [t] and [d]. Berger (1951, pp. 47–51) reports the same substitution for Russian speakers as well as the substitution of [s] and [z] among schooled French speakers—[t] and [d] among unschooled. Lado (1957) finds [s] for English [θ] in Japanese speakers, [t] in speakers of Thai and Tagalog. Kohmoto (1965) also reports [s] and [z] for [θ] and [ð] in Japanese speakers. Angus (1937) reports that Turkish speakers fluctuate between [t] and [s] for [θ]. The present discussion will be restricted primarily to the treatment of Russian-based substitution of [t] for [θ] and Japanese-based substitution of [s] for the same sound.

It is generally conceded that one kind of interference behavior, phone substitution, results when a learner unconsciously identifies or categorizes an L₂ sound as being the same as a particular L₁ sound (even though it differs from the L₁ sound in the perceptions of native speakers

Reprinted from *Language Learning* 18, nos. 3 and 4 (1968):183–97 by permission of the publisher and the author.

of the L_2) and substitutes the latter sound for the former in L_2 utterances. The two questions that must be answered by an explanation of phone substitution are: (1) On the basis of what property of the L_2 sound does the learner identify the L_2 sound—i.e., what properties are identified by the learner as being shared by the L_2 sound and the substituted L_1 sound? (2) Why does the learner identify the L_2 sound on the basis of these properties rather than others?

A significant explanation of interference must be based on a phonological analysis which is justified independently of the specific goal of explaining interference. It is possible to construct a phonological analysis specifically for the purpose of explaining interference behavior; but such an analysis would explain nothing, since it would be entirely ad hoc. If our explanation of interference is to be significant, the dimensions we choose in identifying or describing L_1 and L_2 sounds (that is, the answer which we provide for question 1 in a given case of interference) must be motivated within the analyses themselves. For example, we may loosely describe the motivation behind a conventional phonemic analysis as the desire to provide an economical description of contrasting classes of phones (each phone described in articulatory terms), and therefore the dimensions chosen for the conventional description of a sound pattern are those articulatory dimensions (and only those) along which all members of one class are distinguished from all members of each other class. Conventional phonemics, then, provides such dimensions as manner and point of articulation, voicedness in the case of consonants, and height and degree of frontness-backness in the case of vowels; if we are to explain phonic interference in terms of conventional phonemics, we must answer question 1 in terms of these dimensions.

A plausible answer to question 2 would be that the learner identifies the L_2 sound on the basis of those of its properties which are distinctive or phonemic in the L_1, although the obvious subsidiary question arises: On the basis of which of its distinctive features is the sound identified? A phonological analysis of a specific language (and the general theory of phonology from which the specific analysis derives) can be considered as an appropriate basis for the explanation of interference behavior if (*a*) it attributes distinctiveness to that property upon which the learner who speaks the specific language in question bases his identification of the L_2 sound or (*b*) in the cases where the learner chooses one from a *set* of distinctive properties, the analysis provides grounds for explaining this choice (for example, on the basis that some distinctive properties are more important than others in the categorization of sounds).

In the initial stages of L_2 acquisition a learner may fluctuate considerably in the L_1 segment he substitutes for a given L_2 sound. Berger (1951, p. 47) reports that Russian speakers learning English substitute [ds], [tθ], [dð], [s], and [z] for the interdentals before they settle, for the most part, on [t] and [d]. Van Teslaar (1966) has noted that learners who pronounce well in a learning situation may revert to interference behavior under the strain of conversational conditions. In general we can expect the learner's L_1 to influence his performance more deeply under the conditions found in conversation than under those in a learning situation where the learner may be allowed to concentrate on the careful, correct articulation or comprehension of isolated sounds or sound sequences. For these reasons, the study of interference in conversational performance is likely to be more revealing than that of interference in learning performance. An additional reason for studying and attempting to explain conversational rather than learning performance is the obvious practical one that conversational performance is precisely what we wish a course in an L_2 to modify—a course which does not succeed in the specific task of modifying conversational performance must be considered a failure. What is to be explained, then, is the learner's performance in conversation.

Conventional Phonemics and Contrastive Analysis

Most attempts to explain interference in general have been couched in terms of contrastive analysis based on conventional or classical phonemics. It is thus important to ascertain the answers conventional phonemics can provide for the questions formulated earlier.

Phonetic Properties in Conventional Phonemic Analysis

Although the strictly articulatory or physiological description of speech sounds involves, from a narrowly linguistic point of view, an arbitrary system of classification, it has been found that the sound patterns of languages can be described in terms of a limited number of dimensions, usually expressed in articulatory terminology (as in Bloomfield 1933, chap. 6 on "Practical phonetics"; Jakobson, Halle, and Fant 1952; and de Saussure 1959, pp. 38–64 on "Phonologie"). Basic dimensions are (1) consonantal versus vocalic, (2) point of articulation among consonants, and frontness-backness among vowels, (3) manner of articulation among consonants, and height among vowels, and (4) voiced versus voiceless among consonants. Since we will be dealing only with voiceless consonants here, we can ignore the consonantal-vocalic and voiced-voiceless dimensions. In the consonant system, the dimensions point and manner of articulation have several well-known values ("bilabial," "dental," "alveolar," etc., for the point dimension and "stop," "spirant," "nasal," etc., for the manner dimension). The presence in a given segment of one of these values on each dimension implies the absence from that segment of all others on that dimension so that, for our purposes, a voiceless consonant segment is fully determined within the sound pattern by its manner and place of articulation.

Assuming that the usual designations "stop," "alveolar," have universal validity—i.e., that these values have the same meaning from one phonemic description to another—we have some basis for comparison among sound patterns. In these terms the variants of English /θ/ and the variants of Japanese /s/ share the value "spirant" on the dimension "manner of articulation" and differ on the dimension of "point of articulation" in that /θ/ is interdental and Japanese /s/ is alveolar (Bloch 1950, p. 343). Japanese /t/ is dental and therefore "phonetically closer" to /θ/ than is /s/ with respect to the point of articulation dimension although, of course, it differs from /θ/ on the manner dimension in being a stop rather than a spirant.

Trofimov and Jones (1923, p. 96) describe "normal" Russian /t/ as a voiceless dental plosive although one of its chief subsidiary members is alveolar. Russian /s/ is described by the same authors (p. 138) as a breathed blade-alveolar fricative.

Except that Russian /t/ has an alveolar allophone and Japanese does not, the variants of the dental stops and alveolar fricatives do not differ basically between Russian and Japanese.

Conventional Explanation of Substitutions for English /θ/

Phonetic Considerations

As noted above, the articulatory properties of the allophones of Russian /t/ and those of Japanese /t/ are quite similar, as are those of Russian /s/ and Japanese /s/. It seems improbable, then, that the substitutions of different sounds for English [θ] by Russian and Japanese speakers can be explained on purely articulatory grounds.

We might seek to explain the learners' behavior in terms of their respective histories of reinforcement. However, the form of behavior which must have been reinforced in the learner in order for him to exhibit the observed interference behavior—that is, production of [s] and [t] in echoic response to [θ]—is highly improbable since it would require a situation in which Russian- and Japanese-speaking adults produce [θ] and require their children to imitate them with [t] and [s], respectively.

It is possible that a Japanese adult who has a lisp history might identify English [θ] with his earlier attempts to produce [s] and therefore substitute specifically [s] and [θ] but the acceptance of this as a general explanation is excluded on obvious grounds.

The hypothesis that Japanese and Russian children must in general be trained to substitute [t] for earlier [θ] is not in keeping with what is known about child acquisition of phonology: In Lewis's compilation of 310 cases of phone substitution in French-, German-, and English-speaking children there are no cases of the substitution of the interdentals for other segments (Lewis 1951, pp. 310–31).

The characterization of a sound pattern as a three- or four-dimensional matrix in conventional phonemics is apparently motivated on the grounds that this arrangement is convenient either for organizing fieldwork or for publication purposes. While the categories that arise from this motivation may offer the investigator a useful framework, they do not necessarily match the way in which the speaker-hearer tacitly categorizes the same segments. In order to be relevant to an investigation of interference behavior, a linguistic description must make the claim that those categories which it posits are, in fact, the categories in terms of which a native speaker-hearer of the language categorizes or interprets speech utterances. Whether or not the native speaker-hearer unconsciously categorizes, e.g., consonantal sounds in accordance with their point and manner of articulation or in terms of some other set of dimensions and values, is an empirical question and a very basic one for the explanation of interference behavior.

Distinctiveness in Conventional Phonemics

Although conventional phonemicists have not always agreed in detail among themselves as to the basis for phonological analysis, the crucial distinction in phonemic analysis is clearly that between contrastive and noncontrastive distribution of phonetically similar segments. For example, Bloch (1948) finds the set of dental stops in Japanese to be in contrast with (and therefore phonemically distinct from) the set of dental (or denti-alveolar) affricates on the grounds of such pairs as [mats.to] 'if one waits' and [mat.te] 'waiting'.

Bloch finds, on the basis of conventional criteria, that the phonetic difference between the dental and alveolar point of articulation is not distinctive but is predictable on the basis of manner of articulation—stops are dental, spirants alveolar. It might be hypothesized that the possible substitution in Japanese speakers of [t] for [θ] does not actually occur because the basis for such a substitution—that is, the greater proximity of [t] to [θ] than of [s] to [θ] with respect to point of articulation—is undermined by the lack of contrast between dental and alveolar point of articulation in Japanese.

However, the same explanation does not hold for Russian. Apparently, the same relationship between dental stop and alveolar fricative holds in Russian (i.e., dental versus alveolar point of articulation is nondistinctive) since Russian /t/ has alveolar allophones. Thus, according to the hypothesis given above, we would expect the Russian, like the Japanese, to substitute [s] for [θ] whereas he actually substitutes [t].

Although the above treatment of interference behavior in terms of conventional phonemics does not exhaust the possibilities, a satisfactory explanation of interference in these terms is difficult, if not impossible.

Generative Phonology

A generative phonology, as a part of a full generative grammar, describes an aspect of the speaker-hearer's linguistic competence. That is, an empirically adequate generative phonology characterizes that information upon which the native speaker-hearer's categorization or interpretation of speech sounds and sound sequences is based (though its relation to actual categorization performance may be quite indirect). In other words, it makes precisely the claim that a linguistic description must make if it is to be relevant to the explanation of interference behavior.

Phonological Properties in a Generative Phonology

There are two sets of dimensions or features in a generative phonology: (1) classificatory features, which are two-valued, and (2) phonetic features, which may have more than two values (Chomsky 1964). The first set is a modification of the Jakobsonian features. It serves to categorize segment types in the underlying representations of morphemes from which the phonetic representations (in terms of phonetic features) are derived by the rules of the phonology (Chomsky 1964; Halle 1964a, 1964b; McCawley 1965). The underlying representations of morphemes, then, are matrices with segments as columns and features as rows. Except for certain cases which will be noted immediately, each segment is designated within the matrix as having a value with respect to a given classificatory feature. However, if the designation of the value of a particular segment with respect to a particular feature is predictable by the rules of the phonology, either from the values of other features in the segment or from the values of features in neighboring segments, then that feature designation is left unspecified in the underlying form of the morpheme. Such designations will be supplied by the rules. For example, McCawley (1965) finds that the affricateness and length of [ts.] in, e.g., the Japanese form [mats.to] 'if one waits' is predictable by two general rules. The first (rule 25, p. 136) states that when *u* occurs between two voiceless obstruents in underlying representations, it is represented phonetically by its voiceless counterpart [u] and the second (rule 26, p. 137) that all dental stops that precede nonconsonantal, diffuse, grave segments (including [u] are phonetically affricate. (Apparently, Bloch interpreted McCawley's phonetic sequence [tsu] as phonetically [ts.].) Thus affrication need not be represented in the underlying forms of morphemes containing phonetic affricates before underlying *u* since this feature will be supplied by the rules of the grammar.

Part of the problem of explaining a particular instance of phone substitution is establishing what interpretation the learner has imposed on the context in which the substitution occurs. This task is a highly complex one and we shall not attempt to perform it for the particular case of interference under discussion here. Instead we will limit the domain of our explanation of substitution for English interdentals to a phonetic environment which can be assumed to have minimal contextual influence on the learner's interpretation of the consonants in question.

Pause is, perforce, always identifiable by the learner as a boundary in L_2 utterances; we assume that true vowels in L_2 utterances are more easily identified as such than, say, glides are as glides; initial consonant clusters, if they exist in the L_1 at all, are likely to exhibit interdependencies among their constituent segments which may influence the learner's identification of initial clusters in L_2 utterances. With these factors in mind, we choose to limit our explanation to substitutions in the position between pause and a true vowel.

Assuming a direct relationship between the substantive universal classificatory features (that is, "stridency," "continuity," "compactness," etc.; e.g., Halle 1964*a*) and their phonetic correlates, we may evaluate English [θ], Japanese [t] and [s], and Russian [t] and [s] as consonantal, nonvocalic, diffuse (versus compact), acute (versus grave), and voiceless. Japanese and Russian [t] are discontinuous and mellow; [s] in both languages is continuous and strident. The facts to be explained, then, are that the Russian speaker categorizes [θ] as primarily mellow (as like his [t]) whereas the Japanese categorizes it as primarily continuous (like his [s]).

Explanation in Terms of Generative Phonology

Distinctiveness in a Generative Phonology

In a generative phonology a property of a particular segment may be said to be distinctive or phonemic in that segment if it is not predictable by a phonological rule. If it is predictable then it is nondistinctive. Bloch found the segment sequences [ts.] and [t.] to be in contrast on the basis of such forms as [mats.to] 'if one waits' and [mat.te] 'waiting'. In terms of a generative phonology, on the other hand, these two segment sequences are not distinct since the affricateness (or, in Jakobsonian terms, the stridency) of [ts.] is predictable. In this example, the value strident (versus mellow) of the segment [ts.] is predictable from the segment's position before *u* in underlying representations. The value of a particular segment with respect to a given feature may also be predictable on the basis of the values which that segment alone has with respect to other features. For example, the fact that Japanese [s] is strident (rather than mellow) is predictable from the fact that it is "distinctively" obstruent, grave, continuous, and nonsharp (rule 23, McCawley 1965, p. 136).

Halle (1959) imposes on the inventory of underlying segments the condition that the maximum number of feature specifications in underlying segments be rendered predictable by phonological rule. He states (p. 34) that this condition is equivalent to the requirement that the inventory of segments be determined or described by a decision tree (more specifically the *simplest* decision tree) in which each node represents a feature and each branch from a node represents a value (+ or −) of the feature. The first (top) node divides all segments into two classes (those which are [+ consonantal] and those which are [− consonantal]), the second node divides each of these further into two classes ([+ vocalic] and [− vocalic]) and so on. Each path through the tree represents a distinct segment. That is, each segment is identified by answering a sequence of questions about it—Is it consonantal? Is it vocalic? diffuse?, etc. However, the process of identification of any one segment is generally more efficient for a given language if the questions are asked in one order than if they are asked in another. Thus, as a consequence of representing the structure of the segment inventory as the simplest decision tree, a hierarchy is established among the features. Halle writes (1959, p. 34): "The hierarchy of features seems to provide an explanation for the intuition that not all features are equally central to a given phonological system."

Although a generative phonology makes no direct claims about the perception of utterances, we might hypothesize a rather simple relationship between the phonological code and speech perception with respect to centrality of features within a system. This is namely that the information represented by the feature hierarchy on the decision tree is, all things being equal, reflected in perception by a "hierarchy of cue preference" (Bruner, Goodnow, and Austin 1956, pp. 31, 35). The phonetic correlates of a feature which is high in the phonological decision tree will have greater importance in perception or, to use the term of Bruner et al. (p. 31), a higher "degree of criteriality" in the classification of speech sounds by native speakers than that of a lower-placed feature.

Explanation

The value of any segment with respect to the stridency feature is predictable in Japanese (morpheme-structure rule 7, p. 129; phonological rules 23 and 26, pp. 136–37 [McCawley 1965]). On the other hand, the value of continuity is predictable only in very limited contexts. Although McCawley does not impose Halle's simplicity criterion on the inventory of underlying segments in his analysis of Japanese, the complete predictability of stridency values and the incomplete predictability of continuity values would be represented in tree-diagram form by the placement of continuity above stridency in the feature hierarchy. We would thus predict that a Japanese speaker, all things being equal, will "attend to" the phonetic correlates of continuity in speech utterances and ignore the correlates of stridency. This would explain his production of [s] for [θ] since these two segments share the same continuity value though they differ with respect to stridency.

The Russian situation presents a slightly more subtle problem since both continuity and stridency are distinctive. However, the description of the sound pattern of Russian as a whole is simpler if the stridency feature is placed above the continuity feature in the underlying decision tree than if the order is reversed (Halle 1959, p. 46). The Russian speaker will thus attach a higher degree of criteriality to the stridency dimension than to the continuity dimension. He thus groups [θ] with [t] on the basis of shared mellowness. A general rule in Russian states that all mellow non-nasal consonants are stops (Halle 1959, rule P 5a, p. 65). Having categorized [θ] as mellow, the Russian speaker derives the information that it is also a stop and produces [t] instead.

Explanations of the other cases of phone substitution enumerated above may be attempted with the reservation that the structure of the underlying segment inventory of a language cannot be known with any degree of certainty without a set of explicit rules which relate underlying

forms of their phonetic consequences—that is, without a generative phonology. Since treatments of Thai, Tagalog, and French from this point of
view are not available (Lees [1960] provides a generative phonology of
Turkish), we must rely on distinctive feature analyses of conventional
phoneme inventories for our explication of interference in these cases.

From what has preceded, it should be clear that an explanation of
phone substitution for [θ] of the sort offered above for Japanese and
Russian speakers is based on the independence of the stridency and continuity features. If a language has only strident continuants and mellow
stops among its obstruents then we cannot explain the substitution of,
e.g., [t] for [θ] by speakers of that language on the basis of the higher
position of stridency (over continuity) in the hierarchy of features since
stridency and continuity are combined in the same feature. French (Jakobson and Lotz 1949), Turkish (Lees 1960), Tagalog (Bloomfield 1917),
and Thai (Abramson 1962) all have coalesced continuity and stridency.
Turkish and French speakers exhibit fluctuations between [s] and [t] as
might be expected on the grounds of coalescence of stridency and continuity. On the other hand, the explanation of Thai- and Tagalog-based
substitution of [t] for [θ] is not possible in this way. We might conjecture
that, although there is no independent formal reason to differentiate
between continuity and stridency in these languages and no way to establish whether the distinctive phonetic correlates upon which categorization
of sounds is based are those of stridency or those of continuity, the
feature in question is, in fact, stridency, since this would explain the
categorization of mellow [θ] with mellow [t] by speakers of these languages. However, in the absence of independent evidence for this conjecture the explanation is ad hoc.

Pedagogical Implications

Phonological systems are notoriously well entrenched in adults. Halle
(1964b, p. 344) conjectures that ". . . changes in later life are restricted
to the addition of a few rules in the grammar and that the elimination of
rules and hence a wholesale restructuring of his grammar is beyond the
capabilities of the average adult." Although this conjecture is made specifically with respect to changes in the native-language grammar of an
adult its implications for L2 learning are clear; in fact, if the conjecture is
extended to changes in the conceptual structures underlying speech perception in general (including the perception of L2 utterances by learners)
then, as is well known, considerable evidence can be adduced from the
study of L2 learning to support it. In some cases, though, learners do gain

a strong intuition for an L_2, and it is well to inquire how we may increase the probability that a course in an L_2 will produce such learners.

It would be clear that the observed cases of interference in Japanese- and Russian-based articulations of English interdentals cannot be explained simply as the failure of the Russian speaker to "discriminate the stimuli [θ] and [t]" or of the Japanese speaker to "differentiate the responses [θ] and [s]." These problems apparently lie in the identification of an unfamiliar event-type (the sound [θ] in English utterances) in terms of a highly-structured cognitive system (the phonology of the L_1) which is not appropriate to the task of identifying the event-type in question. The solution to these problems lies not in the modification of the superficial, particular consequences of the underlying general system, but in a basic alteration of the underlying general system itself.

One way in which we might proceed to alter the linguistic cognitions of learners of English as an L_2 is by assigning the task of learning to read aloud systematic phonemic (or perhaps more abstract) representations of English utterances. Since the phonology of a language is a set of rules which relate syntactic representations of utterances to their phonetic realizations, the ability to "read" the syntactic representation of an utterance can be considered as equivalent to a tacit knowledge of the phonology of the language. The tacit application of phonological rules in the reading of an abstract transcription demands that segment-letters be categorized by the reader in accordance with the classificatory-feature complexes which characterize their corresponding segments (since the rules are formulated in terms of these features). For this reason, a major goal of phonological instruction is the learner's acquisition of the ability to categorize segments accordingly.

Various simple techniques for accomplishing this task come to mind: for example, in order to teach the consonant system, we might simply present the learner with single-syllable utterances composed of a consonant of the L_2 followed by the optimal vowel [a] and ask him to assign the syllables to categories, reinforcing him positively when he groups them in accordance with the compactness value of the initial consonant and negatively when he does not. Then present him with the same syllables (or perhaps only with syllables that have consonants of the same compactness value) and ask him to categorize them in accordance with their gravity values; similarly with stridency, continuity, etc. This method has several drawbacks. First of all, it is virtually certain to be more time consuming than its effects warrant. Second, it may be confusing for the learner to find (at least in this way) that one categorization places two given segments in different classes and another categorization places the same two segments in the same class. It is conceivable that, if features and their categories are presented in this way, the learner will resort to the completely meaningless and ad hoc memorization of features and the segment categories that they determine.

Phonetic features (as opposed to classifactory features) represent the intrinsic physical properties of sounds; the categories which they determine may therefore be termed formal in the sense of Bruner et al. (1956, pp. 5–6). The method of teaching classificatory features and categories suggested earlier is based on the supposition that classificatory categories might fruitfully be learned formally in terms of the intrinsic physical properties of the sounds which correlate with the segments categorized. However, the role of classificatory features and categories in a phonology is functional or relational rather than formal in that they represent the relationships among segments in the sound pattern and the way in which segments enter into the applicability of phonological rules or the way in which segments "pattern." These facts suggest that the representation of particular segments in terms of classificatory features might best be learned simply as one aspect of learning the rules in which they appear. For example, the choice of the phonemic form of the regular plural and possessive of nouns, and the third person singular of verbs depends upon categorizing correctly the final segments of noun and verb stems— first with respect to gravity and stridency (since stems with final non-grave, strident consonants take the form [+z]), and second with respect to voiced-voiceless (since, of the stems that do not come under the above rule, those that end in voiced segments take [z] and those that end in voiceless segments take [s]). The Japanese speaker's problems distinguishing [θ] from [s] may thus be subsumed under the general problems of first, distinguishing strident continuants from mellow continuants and second, choosing the correct ending for regular noun plurals and possessives, and for third singular verbs. In this case the acquisition of the ability to categorize segments correctly with respect to the stridency feature takes on a functional significance which is lacking in the learning procedure suggested earlier. In fact, the ability to form correctly novel regular noun plurals and possessives, etc., under conversational conditions is strong (if not conclusive) evidence that the learner has acquired the classificatory categories of strident and mellow regardless of whether the learner "differentiates the responses" [θ] and [s].

Similarly, we might make the Russian's mastery of the continuant-discontinuant distinction a part of his acquisition of the rule (noted by Sapir, 1925) that certain noun stems which end in voiceless continuants have corresponding stem-final voiced continuants in their pluralization (for example, [nayf]–[nayvz], [bæθ]–[bæðz], [haws]–[hawz+z], etc. This rule will in no case apply to nouns with stem-final stops. Thus, we might expect a new formation [feyðz] (meaning "religious denominations") as the plural of [feyθ] or *[kʌbz] related to [kʌp]. In learning this rule, then, the Russian speaker must learn to intuit the systematic distinction between continuants and stops and, as a consequence, the functional distinction between [θ] and [t].

It should be clear that the remarks above are only suggestive and that the construction of a maximally effective course in the practical phonology of an L_2 is an intricate task into which all kinds of factors enter. I do not claim that Japanese speakers will suddenly distinguish [θ] from [s] upon learning to pluralize nouns—only that systematic factors are of basic importance in the construction of courses in L_2's and that we cannot hope to maximize the effectiveness of L_2-phonology instruction without giving them central consideration.

Note

The work reported here was done pursuant to Contract No. OEC-3-6-961784-0508. U.S. Office of Education. This paper first appeared in Catford, J. C., ed., *Studies in Language and Language Behavior, VI.* February 1, 1968, Center for Research on Language and Language Behavior, University of Michigan. I wish to thank David P. McNeill, Ronald Wardhaugh, David Michaels, and George D. Allen for reading earlier drafts of this paper and making many helpful suggestions. Any errors are the author's.

References

Abramson, A. S. "The Vowel and Tones of Standard Thai: Acoustical Measurements and Experiments." Supplement to *International Journal of American Linguistics* 28, no. 2 (1962): pt. 3.

Angus, W. "The Turk's Characteristic Difficulties in Learning English Pronunciation." *Quarterly Journal of Speech* 23 (1937):238–43.

Berger, M. D. *The American English Pronunciation of Russian Immigrants.* Ph.D. Dissertation, No. 51–3872. Columbia University. Ann Arbor, Michigan: University Microfilms, 1951.

Bloch, B. "Studies in Colloquial Japanese IV: Phonemics." *Language* 26 (1950):86–125. Reprinted in M. Joos, ed., *Readings in Linguistics I.* 4th ed. Chicago: University of Chicago Press, 1966.

Bloomfield L. *Tagalog Texts with Grammatical Analysis.* Urbana: University of Illinois Press, 1917.

————. *Language.* New York: Holt, 1933.

Bruner, J. S.; Goodnow, J. J.; and Austin, G. A. *A Study of Thinking.* New York: Wiley, 1956.

Chomsky, N. "Current Issues in Linguistic Theory." In *The Structure of Language; Readings in the Philosophy of Language,* edited by J. A. Fodor and J. J. Katz, pp. 50–118. Englewood Cliffs, N.J.: Prentice-Hall, 1964.

Halle, M. *The Sound Pattern of Russian.* The Hague: Mouton & Co., 1959.

————. "On the Bases of Phonology." In *The Structure of Language; Readings in the Philosophy of Language,* edited by J. A. Fodor and J. J. Katz, pp. 324–33. Englewood Cliffs, N.J.: Prentice-Hall, 1964a.

————. "Phonology in a Generative Grammar." In *The Structure of Language; Readings in the Philosophy of Language,* edited by J. A. Fodor and J. J. Katz, pp. 334–52. Englewood Cliffs, N.J.: Prentice-Hall, 1964b.

Jakobson, R.; Fant, G.; and Halle, M. *Preliminaries to Speech Analysis,* Cambridge, Mass.: MIT Press, 1952.

Jakobson, R., and Lotz, J. "Notes on the French Phonemic Pattern." *Word 5* (1949):151–58.

Kohmoto, S. *Applied English Phonology: Teaching of English Pronunciation to the Native Japanese Speaker.* Tokyo: Tanaka Press, 1965.

Lado, R. *Linguistics Across Cultures.* Ann Arbor, Michigan: University of Michigan Press, 1957.

Lees, R. B. *Phonology of Modern Standard Turkish.* Bloomington: Indiana University Press, 1960.

Lewis, H. M. *Infant Speech; a Study of the Beginnings of Language.* 2d ed. London: Routledge & Kegan Paul, 1951.

McCawley, J. D. *The Accentual System of Standard Japanese.* Ph.D. dissertation, MIT. Cambridge, Mass.: MIT Libraries, 1965.

Sapir, E. "Sound Patterns in Language." *Language* 1 (1925):37–51.

de Saussure, F. *Course in General Linguistics.* Translated by Wade Baskin. New York: Philosophical Library, 1959.

van Teslaar, A. P. "Learning New Sound Systems: Problems and Prospects." *International Review of Applied Linguistics* 3, no. 2 (1965):19–93.

Trofimov, M. V., and Jones, D. *The Pronunciation of Russian.* Cambridge: At the University Press, 1923.

Weinreich, U. *Languages in Contact; Findings and Problems.* The Hague: Mouton and Co., 1966.

The Exculpation of Contrastive Linguistics

Carl James

Applied linguistics, like any science, advances along the dialectical path of thesis and antithesis; the syntheses are dilatory. Currently, many serious statements are challenging some cherished tenets of audiolingualism, one of which is that contrastive analysis (CA) is of great value to foreign language teaching. CA has of late been revitalized under the influence of generative-transformational grammar and the psycholinguistic theories associated with it. It is ironical that these very revitalizing forces have engendered criticism of CA, criticism not of those embellishments that CA had added to its superstructure from the new grammar, but more radical criticism, which threatens the foundations of CA.

Besides the new criticism there is the old, which has sporadically appeared in the journals—only, seemingly, to fall on deaf ears. The old criticism may be hackneyed, but it is potentially valid until it is refuted: adherents to CA should not overlook it. This seems to have been the case on the occasion of the recent Georgetown Round Table Meeting (cf. *Georgetown Monograph No. 21,* 1968) which was wholly devoted to discussions of CA. Once again, the critics were unanswered, though they reiterated the old charges, which those scholars known to be proponents of CA chose to disregard, giving their attention to none but the most peripheral (to CA) issues.

This article is an attempt to open the CA debate, so that solutions to some problems may be sought. Although I shall attempt to refute the arguments of those who have raised criticism of CA, no disparagement of the scholarship of those individuals is intended: indeed, they earn respect for their stimulating strictures, and may themselves feel relief that they have at last been heard.

The arguments against CA will be taken in a succession which is not altogether random, though it has the disadvantages of itemization. Cross references will be made wherever it is deemed appropriate.

Reprinted from *Papers in Contrastive Analysis,* edited by Gerhard Nickel (Cambridge: At the University Press, 1971), pages 53–68, by permission of the publisher and the author.

Arguments and Counterarguments

1. *Interference from the L_2 is not the sole source of error in L_2 learning. There are other sources, which CA fails to predict. Even the unsophisticated teacher who knows no linguistics is conscious of more errors than CA can predict.* This rather weak criticism has been voiced recently by a number of scholars. S. Pit Corder (1967, p. 162) says:

> Teachers have not always been very impressed by this contribution from the linguist for the reason that their practical experience has usually already shown them where these difficulties lie and they have not felt that the contribution of the linguist has provided them with any significantly new information. They noted, for example, that many of the errors with which they were familiar were not predicted by the linguist anyway.

Wilkins (1968) restates Upshur (1962) by posing a rhetorical question: "Yet is it true that by listing the areas of differences between languages we are listing all the linguistic difficulties that will occur? This is surely an oversimplified view." He then goes on to say that overgeneralization within the L_2 will also cause the learner to make errors, a fact which Pit Corder finds interesting as an extra indicator of transitional competence in the L_2. As if to strengthen his argument, Wilkins adds that many errors even are "not linguistic in origin" but rather psychological and pedagogical. Lee (1968) echoes Wilkins by observing that interference will emanate not only from the L_1, but also from newly absorbed L_2 material: ". . . the learner . . . will tend to notice and produce, by false analogy, wrong patterns of that language as well as patterns of his own" (language). Dušková's valuable paper (1969) lists separately interference errors and false analogies, and reaches the sober conclusion: "To sum up what has been found about the source of large groups of errors, we may say that while interference from the mother tongue plays a role, it is not the only interfering factor."

   The most obvious way to answer this criticism is to point out that CA has never claimed that L_1 interference is the sole source of error. As Lado put it: "These differences are the chief source of difficulty in learning a second language," and, "The most important factor determining ease and difficulty in learning the patterns of a foreign language is their similarity to or difference from the patterns of the native language" (Lado 1964, pp. 21 and 91). "Chief source" and "most important" imply that L_1 interference is not conceived to be the only source.

Implicit in the criticisms quoted is the suggestion that there is a separate alternative to CA, namely error analysis. This is a strange type of alternative, since the two are so different in their approaches: a priori versus a posteriori detection of error. It is like the alternative: give up smoking or have the tumor removed by surgery. Pit Corder and Dušková do not hold the view that CA and error analysis are simply alternatives for achieving the same end: They rightly realize that error analysis can only become fully *explanatory* if errors coming from L₁ interference are taken into account. CA is a necessary component complementing error analysis, if errors other than false analogies are to be taken into account. Stockwell's view (1968) is slightly different in that he does not see CA and error analysis as merely complementary. For him, there are two kinds of CA, a predictive variety typified by classical CA, and a diagnostic variety which is used in the analysis of students' errors. The relevant passage is:

> This task—comparison in search of sources of interference, commonly called contrastive analysis—can obviously be approached in either of two ways: by collecting lists of errors students have made, and then trying to describe the conflicts between the systems that give rise to such errors (not all the errors can be traced to this source, of course), or by setting up a systematic comparison which scans the differences in structure in search of sources of interference, and predicting that such-and-such errors will occur from such-and-such conflicts. [Pp. 18–19]

Dušková's work employs the first type: she tabulates the errors of Czechs learning English, then attempts to see which are explicable in terms of interference from the L₁.

The point of all this citation is to force a reasonable definition of error analysis. Anyone may eventually ascertain through observation which errors are recurrent in students' L₂, but that is not enough; as Hamp (1968) points out, mere enumeration of errors is taxonomic, and simply not an analysis; analysis, to be meaningful, demands an explanation of the nature and ultimate cause of observed errors. Admittedly, many of them will be explicable (or analyzable) in terms of overgeneralization within the L₂, just as many will be traceable to improper training methods. But as long as some errors are plausibly explained in terms of influence of the L₁ (Dušková establishes that many are), then CA will continue to be valid, whether it be exercised in its prognostic or its diagnostic form. A further point, made by Hamp, is that we wish to be able to make statements about potential as well as actual errors: "We want instead to develop a theory adequate to explain cases not in our corpus. . . . We want, if you like, some kind of competence model here." The present writer would argue that CA is a necessary component of a L_2-learning model which reliably forecasts that the speaker of an arbitrary L_1 is liable to produce grammatically deviant L_2 sentences, the structural descriptions of which will resemble those of analogous L_1 sentences.

As to the criticism that CA fails to predict those errors whose causes are nonlinguistic in nature, it is not to be taken seriously. CA, as a branch of applied linguistics, has been concerned only with *linguistic* sources of error, so the criticism is no more cogent than criticizing a lawn mower on the grounds that it is useless as a combine harvester.

A simple, though nontrivial, point in reply to those proposing error taxonomies as a better alternative than CA has recently been made in a published account of the cruder contrasts of Spanish and American Negro dialect with Standard American. The authors "again found that there is a particular dearth of materials dealing with the actual English speech of Mexican-Americans or Puerto Ricans" (Politzer and Bartley 1969, p. 2). Those observant teachers who know so much about errors have been dilatory in publishing the facts: CA has been more energetic.

Finally, it will probably turn out that many of the errors which are now not traceable to the L_1, and are therefore attributed to L_2 overgeneralization, will, as linguistic knowledge of deep structure develops, be recognized as errors of interference. This will be found to be particularly true for those errors which must now be attributed to L_2 overgeneralization, being "categories non-existent in the mother tongue" (Dušková, p. 18, no. 3.22). Thus while Dušková finds it possible to say that there are no articles in Czech, James (1969) has suggested that such categories do exist in the Slavic languages, but at a deeper level than their Germanic counterparts.

2. *The predictions of student errors in L_2 made by CA are not reliable.* Baird (1967) points out that in some Indian languages there is a dental [ṭ] and a retroflex [ṭ], either of which, in terms of CA, could be substituted for the English /t/ phoneme. What happens, though, is that the retroflex usually substitutes for /t/, while the dental, with aspiration added, stands in for English /θ/. Baird adds: "It is unlikely that a contrastive study of the phonology of Hindi or Urdu and English would have enabled the teacher [sic!] to predict this choice with any certainty." Lee (1968) misses the point of CA by citing this in criticism of CA: the choice is made for

nonlinguistic reasons (as Lee says) and CA is linguistically based (q.v.) so cannot be expected to have taken into account sociocultural conventions. Furthermore, it is very likely that the choice of [t] for /t/ and [t] for /θ/ *is* linguistically determined, but linguistic analysis has not yet discovered the rules governing the choice: applied linguistics is bound by the limitations of linguistic knowledge. So Baird's and Lee's contention does not constitute a valid criticism of CA.

A similar criticism is cited by Wilkins; it concerns "unpredictable alternation between two potential substitutions," a case in point being (Lado 1957) French speakers' propensity to substitute either French /s/, /z/ or /t/, /d/ for English /θ/, /ð/. As it stands, the CA prediction is valid: but the strict veracity of CA is being criticized. As in the preceding Indian example, it is likely that it is the paucity of linguistic knowledge that prevents CA from predicting which and when. Either that, or this is a case of interlingual free variation. As long as linguists choose to make ample use of this concept, it is not surprising that CA should be satisfied with it.

The most regrettable feature of such criticism is that it imputes to CA claims that have never been made for it: CA has never claimed to be able to predict all errors, nor has it claimed linguistic omniscience about which choices speakers will make. Lado (1968, p. 125) claims no more than ability to predict "behavior that is likely to occur with greater than random frequency."

3. *CA is based on, and perpetuates, a naive view of language structure.* Lee (p. 192) informs the reader that "a language is not a collection of separable and self-sufficient parts. The parts are mutually dependent and mutually determinative." Newmark and Reibel (1968, p. 161) go a little farther, suggesting that CA is committed to a piecemeal theory of learning: "to learn a new language . . . one bit at a time." Recent work in generative grammar has shown that what seem to be bits of isolated language fall together at deeper levels of structure. CA is as cognizant of these findings as are the writers just quoted; we need only skim the work of Stockwell et al. (1965), Nickel and Wagner (1968), James (1969), and the PAKS Reports to see that this is so. There is another answer to the criticism: that it is the conventions for stating points of interlingual difference which give the erroneous impression that CA endorses an atomistic view of language. It is impossible to describe in a way accessible to the layman, how any two systems conform or contrast, without first itemizing the systems. Furthermore, since CAs are destined for eventual pedagogic use, whether in textbook or taped form, certain principles of sequencing

and grading must be observed: obviously, an undifferentiated and mono-
lithic entity like a language must be broken down into discrete entities for
pedagogic use. It is ironic that Lee himself uses the term "parts" in
remarks about the unity of language. This is a logical constraint on expo-
sition, not valid criticism of CA.

4. *There are no established criteria for comparability.* Hamp (1968, p.
143) implies that CA has inadequately solved the problem of comparability: "i.e., of establishing what is to be juxtaposed." He further implies
that the only serious attempt is that of Halliday, McIntosh, and Strevens
(1964), who proposed the criterion of translational equivalence. While it
is true that translation is still widely used, it is not true that that has been
the only serious attempt to define the criterion. Nor was Hamp's proposal
for a new criterion, namely "form and placement of rules in a grammar,"
new, even in 1968. Working in the T-G framework that Hamp's proposal
assumes, Klima (1962) and Stockwell et al. (1965, though drafted by
1962) employed just that criterion. Subsequent CA work in the T-G
framework has attempted to elaborate this approach, while there have
been significant attempts to integrate the translation criterion explicitly
with the T-G approach, proposing such factors as congruence and equivalence (cf. Krzeszowski 1967 and Marton 1968). The criticism of criteria
proposed cannot be valid criticism of CA in itself.

5. *CA endorses a teacher-centered rather than a learner-centered approach
to foreign language learning.* An example of such criticism is: "The excessive preoccupation with the contribution of the teacher has then dis-
tracted the theorists from considering the role of the learner as anything
but a generator of interference" (Newmark and Reibel, 1968, p. 149).
This instance of criticism is a reflex of its authors' insistence that the
student's natural language-learning capacity will ensure success, provided
he has sufficient exposure to the target language, ". . . if particular,
whole instances of the language are modeled for him and if his own
particular acts using the language are selectively reinforced" (p. 149). It is
difficult to see why Newmark and Reibel should have gained the impression that CA precludes the teacher's modeling of whole instances of the
languages; they seem to think that teachers will model only the bits that
contrast with bits of the L_1, leaving the rest to chance. Teachers do model
whole instances, in order to provide context for the bits that they assume
will be troublesome. The fact that the context (or, better, Halliday's
"co-texts") varies does not mean that it is considered unimportant: Any
linguist knows that an item's co-text is part and parcel of the definition of

that item. The reason why teachers proceed in this way is that they believe that the learner's "particular acts" stand a better chance of being reinforceable if they are elicited under conditions conducive to success. CA holds the view that such conditions should be built into the teaching strategy. None of this detracts from the dignity of the learner, and adherents of CA would agree that in the last analysis it is the student who learns: the teacher cannot learn for him, but he can provide optimal conditions for learning, as Horace Mann observed in his report of 1838:

> Though much must be done by others to aid, yet the effective labour must be performed by the learner himself. . . . It is the duty of the teacher to bring knowledge within arm's length of the learner; and he breaks down its masses into portions so minute that they can be taken up and appropriated one by one; but the final appropriating act must be the learner's.

To abandon teaching in favor of random exposure to that which needs to be taught is to reject the foundations of educational philosophy.

Hadlich (1965) suggests that CA is so teacher-centred that it concocts problems for the learner. This is a very serious accusation. He is concerned with lexis, and claims that problem pairs like Spanish *salir–dejar* are nonnative: with this we concur. "The relation between the members of each pair is extraneous to the language being studied . . . imposed on the foreign language from without." We are told that Spaniards don't find the pair *salir–dejar* difficult; nor does the Englishman stumble over *do–make:* they are not even pairs for the native. Of course they are not. But the learner of Spanish is "extraneous" to Spanish, or he would not need to learn it, and CA is interested in language contact, not in languages in isolation. If CA could assume that a L_2 could be learned in isolation, as the L_1 is learned, then Hadlich's strictures would be valid: such an assumption seems untenable, however. Hadlich ascribes the problem-making effect of CA to translation. We have shown above that translation is a criterion for comparability in CA, but it is certainly not a teaching technique, as Hadlich thinks. All traces of translation are erased from a CA, long before the textbook based on that CA reaches the classroom. It has been explicitly stated for CA that translation is a hindrance to fluency (James 1969, p. 91). It must be stated quite categorically that CA is *not* a method, and such a phrase as Hadlich's "taught contrastively" (p. 429, col. I) is a misnomer. Either that, or Hadlich is using contrastive in a different sense from that normal in CA. That such is the case is clear from his examples; he uses *sali de casa* and *dejé el sombrero* to illustrate the contrast (i.e., CA-type contrast) between the two verbs, but he then goes on to warn of the danger of "erroneous substitution" (p. 427), as if there were two-minimal pair-phrases in Spanish in which *salir* and *dejar* were contrastively (in his sense) interchangeable. Since there is no such minimal pair in Spanish, the problem pair is not a lexical one, in which case CA would take the distributional constraints into account; so CA and Hadlich would be doing the same thing.

One point implicit in Hadlich's minatory remark that "awareness of the possibility of erroneous substitution fosters in itself the substitution it is designed to forestall" is partly true and interesting. It concerns the possibility of overcompensation, a good example being that of Haugen (1956), who reports that Spanish speakers learning English *some, sun, sung,* will at first identify all the sounds as /n/, because of the L_1. CA would predict this as a perception blind spot. With teaching they will learn to distinguish the sounds, but through anxiety they overcompensate, producing /sʌŋ/ for *sun,* although final /n/ exists in Spanish and so should present no difficulty. Notice that it is not the "very substitution" that is made (Hadlich) but the inverse substitution. It is interesting that this involves backward interference, from the L_2 to the speaker's transitional competence (cf. Pit Corder 1967) of the L_2. Language learning then seems, at times, to be a *tri*lingual process, the three languages being: L_1– Transitional L_2–L_2 model. The same phenomenon occurs in dialect situations, and its effects are termed *hyperurbanisms*. The Yorkshireman, embarrassed by his dialectally inelegant /ʊ/ in *butter,* substitutes the more respectable [ə] for RP /ʌ/, whereupon he overcompensates on the /ʊ/ → /ə/ ~ /ʌ/ rule to produce /kəd/, /kəʃn/ for *could, cushion.* The parallelism with the Spanish example can be shown thus:

L_1 Spanish inventory	Transitional competence	Target inventory (English)
/-n/ only	/-ŋ/ only	/-n/ and /-ŋ/
/ʊ/ only	/ʌ/ (/ə/) only	/ʊ/ and /ʌ/
Yorkshire inventory	Transitional competence	Target inventory (RP)

This suggests that L_1:L_2 conflict produces an intermediary language form, for which "transitional competence" is a good label. The proposal that this *third* language could be provisionally set up as a bridge between L_1

and L_2 has been made in James (1969, p. 91) in an article on CA. One additional point to the Yorkshire example is that such erroneous substitution occurs in a natural unscripted language-learning setting, so it cannot be blamed on CA in that case.

6. The example quoted provides a part answer to a common criticism of interference theory: *CA only conceives of interference in one direction, from L_1 to L_2.*

CA has emphasized this direction of interference, and rightly so, since it is the form most prevalent in L_2 learning, and after all, CA is interested in teaching the L_2, not the L_1. References to backward interference are not hard to find in the literature. Jakobovits (1969) has described the general principles of transfer, including the case where the relationship between the two languages (RL_1-L_2) has a particular value, as with related languages: the L_1 will be influenced by the L_2. Such influence he vividly terms *backlash* interference and adds (p. 70) that it "is expected to be strongest at later stages of L_2 learning and to be minimal at the beginning." Usually, the cognitive effects of L_2 learning are stressed (e.g., Macnamara 1966), but Jakobovits is explicit on the linguistic effects: "Upon learning a second language, the individual may come to adopt new cognitive, attitudinal, *as well as linguistic modes of functioning*" (emphasis added). Teachers frequently notice that the L_2 interferes with their students' L_1, when they write *schul* and *telefon* under the influence of German and Spanish. When translating orally from German, they let stand such words as *deutsch* or *damit;* that is, they adopt them into the L_1, or into the transitional L_2. In writing English, the present author frequently writes *wend, tob* for 'went' and 'top' as if under the spell of *Auslautverhärtung*. As Dodson points out in his remarkable and seemingly underread book (1967, p. 90): "It is only possible to teach a second language by direct-method techniques [such as Newmark and Reibel 1968 are in essence promoting] at the expense of the first language and it is sheer hypocrisy to claim that the final aim of such teaching philosophies is bilingualism." Add to this the common experience of trying to learn a third language: unless the L_2 is almost as well known as the L_1, it is unable to resist interference (backward) from the L_3, and is quite rapidly ousted by it. Nor do the L_2 and L_3 need to be resemblant: the writer has experienced the effect when learning Spanish on top of Polish. Notice that such effects occur whilst learning, so they do not fall under the category mislabeled interference, which should more properly be termed forgetting (a category conceded by Newmark and Reibel).

7. Having turned our attention to L_3 learning situations, we can deal with another argument advanced to discredit interference theory. It runs something like this: *We expect the strongest habits to exert most interference, so why is it that the weaker L_2 habits interfere more with the L_3 than L_1 habits?*

The answer is possibly that the L_2 exerts high level influence on the L_3, affecting such high level features as phonotactics, allophonics, and lexis. The interference from L_1 remains, and affects low level features, to which, however, less attention has been paid than to the high level ones. They are in a sense less startling than the latter, superficial deviations. Another answer involves the notion of psychological *set:* the learner realizes that success in foreign language performance involves excluding the L_1, as far as he is consciously able to, and feels that anything is better for foreign language performance than L_1 material. He is successful in excluding the L_1 on the psychomotor level, but not on the cognitive level. This is probably the explanation of Lee's difficulty with Spanish and Italian, though his anecdote was meant to prove a different point, which we now turn to.

8. *The degree of typological difference between L_1 and L_2 is not proportional to the interference strength.* The traditional CA standpoint is stated by Barrutia (1967, p. 24):

> It was not an unexpected discovery to find that these interferences are considerably less between languages of the same immediate origin and increase in relative proportion as the more distant languages mesh in a common but far-removed source language such as proto Indo-European.

In other words, it will be more difficult for a Spanish speaker to learn Chinese than Italian, since these two languages are at the opposite extremes of isomorphism with his L_1, so he needs to transfer less and learn more when he learns Chinese, and can transfer more and learn less when Italian is his target. That some languages are harder to learn than others, given a certain L_1 as a starting point, is generally accepted. Cleveland et al. (1960), speaking for English L_1 students, point out that French, German, Rumanian, Spanish, and Italian are learned in two-thirds of the time needed to achieve the same proficiency in Russian, Greek, Finnish, and in half the time needed for Chinese, Japanese, and Vietnamese. Since it seems that some languages are not intrinsically more difficult than others, especially if the Japanese speaker learns Vietnamese more quickly than German, we must conclude that the L_1 is the crux of the matter. The explanation can hardly be that the hard languages are hard because they are taught less well than the easy ones, for we do not attest relativity of success among the languages that are traditionally taught in Europe, say. British teachers are not aware, that is, that Spanish is taught better than German, or the German teachers would have learned by now the secrets of the success of their Spanish-teaching colleagues. Those who attack CA, wishing to use random exposure methods, would share the view that the reason for the relative ease of learning one language over another is not to be found in the teaching, since they want to abandon teaching altogether, it seems.

The evidence available confirms the assumption of CA that it is the L_1 which determines whether any particular L_2 will be hard or easy. But Lee is adamant, insisting that learning Chinese lifted him into a new orbit of noninterference, and although he admits that "it would probably be absurd to suggest that this ever happens," he nevertheless suggests it. One wonders where Lee stands in the field of language-learning theory: between the two stools of innate ideas and a L_2 *tabula rasa*, evidently. We would reply in this way: When the Italian learns Spanish, he has a lot in his L_1 to fall back on, but in learning Chinese he has nothing. If he wishes to learn the L_2 he must at all costs perform in that language, and as soon as he starts to perform he will fall back on the L_1: there is no free will for him. His falling back jeopardizes his L_2 performance more when it is Chinese than when it is Spanish: this is interference.[1] A possible counter-argument to my suggestion is: learn the L_2 through the L_2 only. This implies keeping out the L_1 for some reason or other: the only reason I can discover is—to avert interference. So we come back full circle to interference, which was the reason for starting the argument. Implicit in the "stay within L_2" argument is a naive view of language, moreover. It might be just possible to avert interference by learning all L_2 material parrot-wise, or, as H. E. Palmer (1917, p. 103) put it, as *primary* matter. Now, since the number of possible sentences in a language is infinite, reliance on primary matter, learned atomistically, is not a feasible way to learn a language, since the human life span is too short. So the learner must learn to produce his own *secondary* matter from the small amount of primary matter that he can memorize, "by some process of substitution, transformation, or other combination" (Politzer 1965). This applies *a fortiori* where an L_2 *tabula rasa* is posited. In the newer T-G theory of CA, it is the routes by which one proceeds from primary to secondary matter which determine the degree of L_1 interference. The Italian will have more success in following L_1 routes to produce L_2 secondary matter if the L_2 is Spanish than if it is Chinese:

interference will be greater in the second case. CA-based teaching materials are designed to ensure that L_1 routes to L_2 secondary matter are followed only where the results will be good.

The foregoing argument is of particular topical pertinence to the work being undertaken in the United States and in Britain (by Le Page at York) on dialect expansion: speakers of a nonstandard dialect of English (D_1) are being taught a standard dialect (D_2) as a means to economic and social betterment. For two language forms to qualify as dialects of the same language, they must share many features. If Lee's contention (q.v.) were valid, it would be harder to learn another dialect of one's own language than to learn a foreign language; but this is not the case, as people learn new dialects all the time. Those involved in planning dialect-expansion in the United States are preparing CAs of D_1 and D_2. These CAs seem to be motivated academically and linguistically rather than pedagogically, but this author has heard the claim made[2] that CA is probably more relevant to dialect teaching than to language teaching. This seems to be overstating the case, and is a reflection of the zeal with which dialect linguists are working to establish for the D_1 parity of linguistic status with the Standard. Yet in one sense at least a dialect CA *can* contribute more than a L_1–L_2 CA, but prepedagogically. That is, the first type of CA can do much by discovering the (minor) ways in which the dialects differ, so that the rest, which is also the most, can be left out of the teaching. Thus, it will determine the matter to be taught, not strategies for teaching, as is the case in language CA. In all events, dialect comparison, when compared itself to language comparison, adds another linguistic theoretical dimension to CA as we presently know it.

9. *Interference is an otiose idea: ignorance is the real cause of error.* By far the most valuable criticism of interference theory—and therefore of CA—to date is that of Newmark and Reibel (1968): valuable because, unlike the other strictures here examined, it offers an alternative explanation of errors made in L_2 learning. Newmark and Reibel insist that errors are caused by inadequate knowledge of the target language: when the learner is "induced to perform" in the L_2 "there are many things he has not yet learned to do . . . What can he do other than use what he already knows to make up for what he does not know?" While this explanation is made with reference to "the phenomenon of foreign accent," which is manifest at the psychomotor level of performance (cf. Carroll 1968), it is presumably intended to embrace all interference, even at the cognitive level. It is also presumably meant to apply to both productive and receptive interference; but it is rather more acceptable for the former than the latter. That is, it

seems plausible to suggest that if I fail to hear a certain L_2 sound, i.e., if I have a "perception blind spot" (Lado 1957), then I will assume I have heard the nearest L_1 equivalent: so I have indeed filled a L_2 lacuna with L_1 material. But to extend the analogy, to productive filling-in, is not easy, since it would require the learner-speaker to "define" his own L_2 goals, and then fall short of these goals in his performance. The objection is: if he can define the goal, he is, properly speaking, not ignorant of the L_2.

The ignorance theory is vulnerable on another count: what is meant by knowledge of a target language? Surely analytic knowledge of L_2 rules, etc., is not what is meant, but rather skills or manipulative knowledge. Newmark and Reibel (1968) are ambivalent on this issue: they speak of ". . . things . . . he has not learned to do" (p. 159) (= skill?) and in the next breath of "what he does not know" (= analytic?). Now it is widely accepted that having analytic knowledge of a L_2 will not produce the required behavior equatable with such knowledge: "English speaking students know that the Spanish word is [teléfono] from their first encounter with it, but English stress interference will still produce many a [telefóno] and require numerous corrections before the proper habit sets in" (Barrutia 1967, p. 26). We presume that Newmark and Reibel intend by knowledge the unformulated consciousness of linguistic rules which determine acceptable performance, namely *competence*. So they are saying that learners' performance is bad because their competence is bad: nobody would disagree.

Ignorance theory is only ostensibly an alternative to interference theory. If we provisionally accept interference, for the sake of argument, we will concede that at a given stage of L_2 learning, certain L_2 items need to be learned, i.e., the learner is ignorant of those L_2 items. Suppose we now do not explicitly introduce one of those L_2 items, yet insist that the learner perform a repertoire including that L_2 item: "faute de mieux" he will use the closest L_1 item. So far, the competing theories agree: they differ only as to whether using the L_1 item is attributable to ignorance of the L_2 or to the influence of the L_1—the argument is otiose, like which came first: chicken or egg?

No language-learning or language-teaching theory has ever envisaged the state of affairs where the learner is asked to perform before he has had some chance to gain "knowledge" of the L_2 target item. All theories, even those promulgated by the theorists whom Newmark and Reibel disparage, presuppose that the L_2 item shall be introduced—the vague term *introduce* is selected intentionally, to allow for conflicting theories of introduction, whether it be effected by exposure to or by explanation of L_2 items. The fact is that teachers have discovered that with equal amounts of introduction, the learner gains knowledge of some items more easily and quickly than others. This variable can only be attributed—if such others as teaching skill, motivation, etc., are kept constant—to the L_1, whether or not the L_2 item is in some amenable form present in the L_1. If extrapolation from the L_1 is disastrous, one can say that the learner is ignorant (L_1-wise) of the L_2 form required. One can equally well say that his failure to produce an acceptable L_2 form is the result of his L_1 having led him up a blind alley: this is usually termed *interference*. Thus, ignorance and interference become synonymous. Where extrapolation from the L_1 is successful, there is no interference, and apparently no ignorance either: yet L_2-wise, the learner is equally ignorant of the L_2 form, whether his performance be successful or calamitous.

We can emphasize the point just made by reference to the distinction already made in section 8 between easy and hard languages. If the ignorance theory were legitimate, we would have to concede that the Italian learner's ignorance of Chinese and Spanish were at the outset equal. This being the case, why should he find acceptable performance in the one more easily attainable than in the other? One would have to say that he combats his ignorance more easily in one case than the other. Since Chinese is inherently no harder than Spanish, it can hardly be the case that L_2-internal analogizing is consistently more reliable in Spanish than in Chinese: this would be tantamount to saying that some languages are more systematic and logical than others—which is anathema in modern linguistics! We have no choice but to bring in the L_1, and with the L_1 comes interference.

This paper has been an attempt to examine critically some recurrent strictures on the logical foundation of, and hence the continued practice of, CA in language teaching. It is possible that the counterarguments voiced here have often been made, and in turn themselves been refuted in the ivory towers of our discipline: but the present writer is unaware of any document which sets the arguments out in a form rendering them available to the wider public of applied linguistics. This paper is not meant to be provocative, though it is to be hoped that it will stimulate discussion of the topic in hand.

Notes

This paper was prepared during 1969–70 while I was supported by a Graduate School Research Award to the Department of Language Laboratories, Faculty of

Letters, University of Wisconsin, Milwaukee. I wish to acknowledge the generosity of all concerned, particularly Professor Robert F. Roeming, who always found time to discuss problems of applied linguistics with me, and from whose erudition I learned much. The errors of this article are solely my own.

1. Lado's view on this is clear. On the subject of learning a new alphabet, he writes: "Between English and Korean there will be no major negative transfer such as would result if some symbols were similar but represented different sounds. *And there will be no positive transfer* as when similar symbols represent similar sounds" (Lado 1957, p. 106, italics supplied).
2. Robert O. H. Petersen, Director of the Hilo Language Development Project (Hawaii), would claim this (personal communication).

References

Baird, A. "Contrastive Studies and the Language Teacher." *English Language Teaching* 21 (1967).

Barrutia, R. "Dispelling the Myth." *Modern Language Journal* 51, no. 1 (1967).

Carroll, J. B. "Contrastive Linguistics and Interference Theory." *Georgetown Monograph no. 21*. Washington, D.C.: Georgetown University Press, 1968.

Cleveland, H.; Mangone, G. J; and Adams, J. C. *The Overseas Americans*. New York: McGraw Hill, 1960.

Corder, S. Pit. "The Significance of Learners' Errors." *IRAL* 5, no. 4 (1967).

Dodson, C. J. *Language Teaching and the Bilingual Method*. London: Pittman, 1967.

Dušková, L. "On Sources of Errors in Foreign Language Learning." *IRAL* 7, no. 1 (1969).

Hadlich, R. L. "Lexical Contrastive Analysis." *Modern Language Journal* 49, no. 7 (1965).

Halliday, M. A. K.; McIntosh, A.; and Strevens, P. D. *The Linguistic Sciences and Language Teaching*. Bloomington: Indiana University Press, 1964.

Hamp. E. P. "What a Contrastive Grammar Is Not, If It Is." *Georgetown Monograph no. 21*. Washington, D.C.: Georgetown University Press, 1968.

Haugen, E. *Bilingualism in the Americas*. American Dialect Society, 1956.

Jakobovits, L. A. "Second Language Learning and Transfer Theory: a Theoretical Assessment." *Language Learning* 19, nos. 1 and 2 (1969):55–86.

James, Carl "Deeper Contrastive Study." *IRAL* 7, no. 2 (1969).

Klima, E. S. "Correspondence at the Grammatical Level." MIT Research Laboratory of Electronics no. 24, *Mechanical Translation*. Cambridge, Mass.: MIT, 1962.

Krzeszowski, T. "Fundamental Principles of Structural Contrastive Studies." *Glottodidactica* 2 (1967).

Lado, R. *Linguistics across Cultures.* Ann Arbor: University of Michigan Press, 1957.

———. *Language Teaching: A Scientific Approach.* New York: McGraw Hill, 1964.

———. "Contrastive Linguistics in a Mentalistic Theory of Language Learning." In *Georgetown Monograph no. 21.* Washington, D.C.: Georgetown University Press, 1968.

Lee, W. R. "Thoughts on Contrastive Linguistics in the Context of Language Teaching." *Georgetown Monograph no. 21.* Washington, D.C.: Georgetown University Press, 1968.

Macnamara, John. *Bilingualism and Primary Education: A Study of Irish Experience.* Edinburgh: At the University Press, 1966.

Mann, Horace "Report on Massachusetts Schools." Quoted in H. Diack, *In Spite of the Alphabet.* London: Chatto and Windus, 1965. Pp. 50–52.

Marton, W. "Equivalence and Congruence in Transformational Contrastive Studies." *Studia-Anglica Poznaniensia* 1 (1968).

Newmark, L., and Reibel, D. A. "Necessity and Sufficiency in Language Learning." *IRAL* 7, no. 3 (1968).

Nickel, G., and Wagner, K. H. "Contrastive Linguistics and Language Learning." *IRAL* 7, no. 3 (1968).

PAKS Reports: Projekt für Angewandte Kontrastive Sprachwissenschaft, G. Nickel, Director.

Palmer, H. E. *The Scientific Study and Teaching of Languages.* London: Harrap, 1917.

Politzer, R. L. "Some Reflections on Transfer of Training in Foreign Language Learning." *IRAL* 3, no. 3 (1965).

Politzer, R. L., and Bartley, D. E. *Standard English and Nonstandard Dialects: Elements of Syntax.* Research Memorandum No. 54. Stanford: Stanford University, School of Education, 1969.

Stockwell, R. P. "Contrastive Analysis and Lapsed Time." In *Georgetown Monograph no. 21.* Washington, D.C.: Georgetown University Press, 1968.

Stockwell, R. P.; Bowen, J. D.; and Martin, J. W. *The Grammatical Structures of English and Spanish.* Chicago: University of Chicago Press, 1965.

Upshur, J. A. "Language Proficiency Testing and the Contrastive Analysis Dilemma," *Language Learning* 12, no. 2 (1962).

Wilkins, D. A. "Review of A. Valdman, ed., *Trends in Language Teaching.*" *IRAL* 6, no. 1 (1968).

Adjectives of Temperature

Clifford H. Prator

A fuller title for this study would be "Some Temperature Words in English and in Several Other Languages." It deals with the four adjectives which we ordinarily use to describe temperature, their relationships to one another, and the way in which their meanings combine to cover a given area of experience. It then points out that certain other languages cover the same area of experience in quite different ways. Even so limited an exercise in contrastive linguistic analysis gives evidence in support of certain conclusions regarding language instruction, conclusions which have often been formulated but which have by no means been universally accepted.

The four adjectives in question are *cold, cool, warm,* and *hot.* In an article recently published in *Language Learning,* Yao Shen (1960) argues that the meanings of all four are essentially parallel, that in any particular season and locality *cool* represents a higher range of temperature than *cold, warm* a higher one than *cool,* and *hot* one still higher.

> In Ann Arbor, *warm* can be said to have a higher temperature than *cool.* Between the two poles of *hot* and *cold, warm* is closer to *hot* and *cool* is closer to *cold,* regardless of . . . whether the temperature is moving from *hot* toward *cold* (getting cooler or colder) or from *cold* toward *hot* (getting warm). [Yao Shen 1960, p. 2]

She contrasts the use of the four items in English with that of the four terms which cover the same total area of meaning in Chinese: *rè, nwǎnhwo, lyǎngkwai,* and *lěng.* When one speaks of the weather in Chinese, the two intermediate terms are experienced differently. "From *rè* (hot) to *lěng* (cold), the state of warm = cooler is *lyǎngkwai.* From *lěng* (cold) to *rè* (hot), the state of cool = warmer is *nwǎnhwo*" (Yao Shen 1960, pp. 2–3). If we are to accept this analysis, then, the four English terms are simply successive points in a reversible sequence, whereas in Chinese there are two separate sequences, one for rising temperatures and one for falling, each of which includes only three of the four terms.

Reprinted with permission from *English Language Teaching Journal* 17 (1963):158–64, published by Oxford University Press and the British Council.

When a large number of examples are studied, little evidence can be found to support this classification of English temperature words, whether the speaker is referring to the weather, to inanimate objects, or to living creatures. We might state on a day when the thermometer stood high, "It's *hot.*" As the temperature fell, however, we would hardly say: "Now it's *warm,*" "Now it's *cool,*" "Now it's *cold.*" Conversely, on a winter day, though we might declare that we ourselves were cold, we would surely not consider it a logical progression to say as the thermometer rose: "I'm *cold,*" "I'm *cool,*" "I'm *warm,*" "I'm *hot.*" Instead, a normal falling sequence would be: "It's (or I'm) *hot,*" "It's getting *cool,*" "It's *cold*"—omitting *warm.* And a natural rising progression would be: "I'm (or it's) *cold,*" "I'm *warming up,*" "I'm *hot*"—leaving out *cool.*

It would seem, then, that Yao Shen's arrangement of the four Chinese words into two separate sequences of three words each applies equally well to English. *Warm* is a term that we use on the way from *cold* to *hot,* and *cool* fits into a series which begins with *hot* and moves toward *cold.* "It's getting *warm*" always indicates a rising temperature, and "It's getting *cool*" always means that the thermometer is falling. *Warm* and *cool* are alike in that they indicate a change from a generally opposite temperature. The two-word verbs we use to describe a rise or fall in temperature are *warm up* and *cool off,* and no comparable verbs are formed with *hot* and *cold.*

The entire picture, however, is certainly much more complicated than that. Each of the four English adjectives of temperature may be used with the verb *to be* to describe the weather, an inanimate object, or a living creature. We can say "It's *cold* today," "The iron is *cold,*" or "I'm *cold*"; and *cool, warm,* or *hot* can be substituted for *cold* in any of the three sentences. But in describing living creatures English is ambiguous. Even if we leave aside possible figurative meanings, "You're *cold*" may signify either that you are externally cold when someone else touches you—cold in the sense that an inanimate object is cold—or that you feel cold to yourself internally. There appears to be no way to remove the ambiguity short of using an explanatory phrase; "You *feel cold*" still has two possible literal meanings. As we shall see, some other languages are not ambiguous on this point.

Under most circumstances *cold* and *hot* have disagreeable connotations in English, but *cool* and *warm* are agreeable. In so far as *cold* is a disagreeable term, then, its antonym is *warm,* not *hot.* And in a situation where *hot* is disagreeable its opposite is *cool* rather than *cold.* Looking out through the window on a wintry day, we would never turn to our companion in the room and say: "My, it's *cold* outside! Are you *cool* enough?", or "Are you *hot* enough?" It would always be, "Are you *warm* enough?" After strenuous exercise outside on a hot summer's day, we might declare: "It's too *hot* out here; let's go inside where it's *cool*," but never, "Let's go inside where it's *cold*," or "Let's go inside where it's *warm*." *Warm* means pleasantly comfortable against a *cold* background, whereas *cool* means pleasantly comfortable against a *hot* background.

This partial analysis omits consideration of the various figurative and idiomatic uses of *hot, warm, cool, cold* (for example, "a *hot*-blooded man" but a "*warm*-blooded animal"). Even so, it is obvious that the problem of a foreign student of English is much more complex than merely to learn to use the four adjectives to indicate appropriate ranges in a single temperature scale.

Our insight into the nature of that student's difficulties can, of course, be increased by a knowledge of the way in which his mother tongue expresses the area of meaning covered by *cold, cool*, etc., in English.

Even a language as closely related to English as French provides a very substantial amount of interference in this area. In French there appear to be only three commonly used adjectives whose central meaning has to do with temperature: *froid, frais*, and *chaud*—two words for the lower temperatures, one for the higher. One is inevitably tempted, in passing, to wonder if there is any connection between the rather cool French climate and the fact that the vocabulary, when compared with that of English, seems unbalanced in the direction of coolness. To be sure, there is another word, *doux*, which might be equated with the English *warm*, but *doux* is used much less frequently to describe temperature than the other three terms and refers most often to qualities of mildness, softness, or gentleness. To some extent *chaud* must carry alone the burden which in English is divided between *hot* and *warm*. Therefore the native speaker of French will have difficulty learning to distinguish between *hot* and *warm*.

We have already noted that the four English adjectives may be used in the same construction, with the verb *to be*, in referring to either the weather, inanimate objects, or living creatures. French requires an entirely different construction for each of the three types of reference.

In speaking of the weather, *froid, frais, doux*, and *chaud* are all used with the verb *faire* (*to make* or *to do*): "Il fait *froid*" (It's *cold*), etc. In this construction the four words are invariable in form and would traditionally be labelled as nouns rather than adjectives. To indicate a rising temperature, the progression would be from *froid*, through *doux* (or perhaps more commonly *moins froid* [less cold]), to *chaud*, omitting *frais.* In the opposite direction the series would be *chaud, frais, froid,* with *doux* omitted.

Referring to inanimate objects, *doux* is never employed to indicate temperature, but only *froid, chaud,* and—with certain nouns—*frais.* In this type of reference the verb *être,* equivalent to the English *to be,* is used, and the three descriptive terms are certainly adjectives marked by appropriate endings for gender and number: "Le fer est *froid*" (The iron is *cold*), "Les assiettes sont *froids*" (the plates are *cold*).

The same construction is occasionally heard in reference to living creatures: "Vous êtes *chaud*" (You are hot). In this case the meaning would be that you are externally hot to the touch rather than that you feel hot to yourself internally. In order to express the latter meaning, it would be necessary to use the verb *avoir* (*to have*) and the nominal form of the descriptive term: "Vous avez *chaud*" (You are *hot*). French can thus avoid the ambiguity of the English "You are *hot.*" Neither *doux* nor *frais* is applicable to living creatures as an indication of temperature, which leaves only *froid* and *chaud,* the terms at the two ends of the scale. The student of English with a French background will thus have to learn, in speaking of persons, to split his single concept, *chaud,* into two concepts, *warm* and *hot,* and the same will be true of *froid* in relation to *cool* and *cold.*

As we might expect, the agreeable or disagreeable connotation of the French temperature world depends on the general background and on what is being described. *Chaud* in particular may be unlike its nearest English counterpart, *hot,* in connotation. On a cold day it may be pleasant for a person to be *chaud,* though it is certainly not agreeable for him to be *hot.* On the other hand, weather described as *chaud* or *hot* is always unpleasant.

It is perhaps worthy of note, in passing, that there is another fairly common French word which would usually be translated as *warm: chaleureux.* The latter, however, seems to be restricted to figurative uses: *une recommendation chaleureuse* (a warm recommendation). The learner's difficulty here would be in moving from English to French, splitting a meaning, rather than in moving from French to English, in which case the two meanings are coalesced.

The native speaker of Spanish would share most of the Frenchman's problems in learning to describe temperature reactions in English, since the two Romance languages use mostly cognate terms and constructions in covering this particular area of meaning. Spanish even has a special word, *caluroso,* which corresponds to *chaleureux* in that it is employed only in cases when the warmth is figurative. There is one quite striking difference, however. From the point of view of the Spanish speaker, both French and English are ambiguous in describing inanimate objects. By his choice of verb, *ser* or *estar,* the speaker of Spanish indicates whether the coldness or warmth is an inherent, permanent quality of the object or merely a temporary state: "El hielo es *frío*" (Ice is cold), "El agua está *fría*" (The water is cold). In French or English this type of distinction would often necessitate a periphrasis.

In order to round out this brief analysis of temperature terms, it is instructive to examine a non-Indo-European language. Yao Shen (1960, p. 3) mentions the national language of the Phillippines, Tagalog, in her study. However, she merely lists the two terms *maginaw* and *mainit,* equating the former with *cold* and *cool,* the latter with *warm* and *hot.* The implication is that Tagalog covers this area of meaning in a very simple fashion, without complications of the sort noted in English and Chinese. As might be expected, upon closer examination such does not turn out to be the case.

There are in Tagalog at least three temperature terms which one very commonly employs in speaking of the weather: *maginaw, mainit,* and also *malamig.* Like *maginaw, malamig* means cold, and both indicate coolness to approximately the same degree. The only difference in meaning between the two appears to be that *malamig* is somewhat more objective, a word which one might use upon reading the thermometer. On the other hand, *maginaw,* even when used in reference to the weather, indicates that the speaker is also feeling the coldness. *Maginaw* is not used in describing inanimate objects, but only *malamig* and *mainit.* In the Phillippines, then, in a climate which is distinctly and characteristically hot, we find the vocabulary unbalanced in the direction of coldness, just as was the case in France; the temptation to try to associate climate with the way in which temperature words are used vanishes.

In Tagalog the temperature words enter into constructions which differ greatly from those of English or French, and the interference which thus arises is certainly a major source of difficulty for the Filipino student of either Indo-European language. The construction used in speaking of the weather includes neither verb nor subject pronoun: "*Mainit* ngayon" (literally, "*Hot* now"). To describe an inanimate object, one can place either adjective or noun first, but the two must be linked by a particle which varies in shape: "*Mainit* na palantas" or "Palantsang *mainit*" (hot iron). People may be described as though they were inanimate objects: "*Mainit* ka" (You are *hot*). The meaning is then that the person is externally hot to the touch. To indicate that the person feels internally hot, a verbal affix is substituted for the adjectival affix *ma-*: "*Naiinitan* ka" (You are *hot*).

In Tagalog the matter of pleasant and unpleasant connotations is handled by the use of very typical Malayo-Polynesian linguistic devices, repetition and reduplication. If the temperature adjective is repeated and the particle *na* is interposed, the connotation is generally unpleasant: "*mainit na mainit*" (very, very hot). If the root is reduplicated, the connotation is pleasant: "*mainit-init*" (nicely warm).

By using these derivative forms of the adjectives, one can obtain two separate sequences of expressions, similar to those in English, for indicating temperature changes. The rising sequence is *malamig, mainit-init, mainit, mainit na mainit*. The falling sequence is *mainit, malamig-lamig, malamig, malamig na malamig*.

The writer realizes that in the course of these comments he has mixed linguistic levels—lexical and grammatical—in a manner which would be inexcusable in a serious analytical study of a single language. The fact seems to be, however, that what is vocabulary in one language may be grammar in another. As linguists try to extend their contrastive analyses into the lexical area—something which has rarely been attempted up to now—they will almost certainly find that it is impossible to treat vocabulary and grammar as discrete entities, just as it is usually impossible to compare the grammatical structures of two languages while keeping morphology and syntax in strictly separate compartments.

It is hoped that this study will serve to underscore and to illustrate once again certain facts about the teaching of English as a second language. The latter is a job which can be done with full effectiveness only by one who has a considerable analytical knowledge of English and insights into the way the student's native tongue interferes with his learning of the new language. The usual freshman composition instructor is simply not equipped to do the work, to say nothing of the person whose only qualification is that he speaks English as his mother tongue.

The teaching of English as a second language is a perfectly respectable academic field which offers immense opportunities for serious research. It is a discipline which desperately needs more practitioners who will devote their entire career to it and not regard it as a mere temporary way of winning one's bread while preparing to teach courses in linguistics or literature. It is definitely not a job which some university departments of English can continue with impunity to wish off on the most recently hired and most defenseless members of the teaching staff.

Reference

Shen, Yao. *Language Learning* 10, nos. 1 and 2 (1960):1–13.

Toward a Psychological Theory of Interference in Second Language Learning

J Ronayne Cowan

During the past decade, the major thrust of psycholinguistic research has been the investigation of how children acquire their native language. Now it would appear that researchers are gradually becoming interested in exploring the cognitive processes recruited by adults engaged in learning second languages. The data relevant to researching this topic are the errors made by the learner in his attempts at meaningful communication in the second language (Weinreich 1953; Corder 1967; Selinker 1972). There are numerous precedents for using this type of data. Speech errors committed in the native language have provided some of the most useful evidence for formulating hypotheses regarding the nature of the mechanisms underlying speech production (Lashley 1951; Hockett 1967; Boomer and Laver 1968; Laver 1969; MacKay 1970; Nooteboom 1969), the psychological reality of theoretical linguistic concepts (Fromkin 1971) and the perceptual strategies brought to bear in the comprehension of linguistically complex structures (Blumenthal 1967; Bever 1970).

Obviously, no single mechanism can be the source of all speech errors made by second language learners. A number of causes have been recognized: interference from native language, the application of general learning strategies similar to those manifested in first language acquisition, such as overgeneralization of linguistic rules (Richards 1971, 1975), the context of the learning situations (cf. Selinker's [1972] "transfer of training" errors), and emotional factors connected with the pressure of communicating, e.g., the "strategies of communication" suggested by Selinker. In addition, it has been suggested that certain untestable "avoidance strategies," (cf. Schachter 1974) shape the learner's output.

The second of the causal mechanisms mentioned above—general learning strategies similar to the processes at work in native-language acquisition—has enjoyed the greatest amount of attention in the litera-

This is a revised version of a paper first published in *TESL Studies 2* (1977):51–63. Reprinted by permission of the publisher and the author.

ture on second language learning. Unfortunately, much of the evidence cited in support of this mechanism is far from unequivocal, which raises the disturbing possibility that nativelike learning strategies may be invoked to account for any error which is not a totally unambiguous example of one of the other processes. This paper is concerned with the most widely documented source of error in adult second language learning: the intrusion of the native language. The discussion will be confined to the type of interference one frequently encounters in the speech of adult language learners: the application of a grammatical relation of the native language to the morphemes in the second language (cf. Weinreich 1953, p. 30). As a first step toward the formulation of a psychological theory of interlingual interference, I will propose two principles which predict the occurrence of production errors, and illustrate how they account for semantic errors which arise as a result of the learner's false equation of a native language structure with a structure in the target language. Next, I will compare this psychological explanation of one kind of interlingual interference with an alternative account which utilizes linguistic universals as an explanatory device. The purpose of this comparison is to draw a distinction between causal and noncausal explanations.

To be of any interest, a theory of interlingual interference must satisfy two requirements. First, it must provide an explicit specification of the criteria by which the learner pairs elements of the native language—phonological, lexical, syntactic, semantic, or rhetorical—with elements in the target language. Failure to satisfy this requirement markedly reduces the explanatory power of a theory, since the underlying causes of interference are then excluded from empirical investigation. Interlingual interference is generally understood to mean the systematic influence of the native language on the learner's attempts to use (produce and perceive) the target language. This most frequently takes the form of native language intrusions, but whether or not these intrusions are direct importations of native language elements, or whether they take on some form that lies between the native language and the target language is irrelevant. The fact remains that unless interference is to be viewed as totally unsystematic, specific conditions which lead to the learner's associating native language elements with corresponding elements in the native language which will come under the influence of the former must exist. It seems intuitively obvious that the bases for establishing correspondences could differ depending on the nature of the elements. Thus, the grounds for phonological interference may be accoustic and/or articulatory, whereas lexical interference might result from pairing that has an accoustic or graphic basis. There is, however, no reason to exclude the possibility that a single principle for establishing correspondence could apply to a number of different kinds of interference.

The second requirement that a theory of interlingual interference must satisfy is that it contain principles which predict the likelihood of an error occurring once a correspondence has been established. These principles should be formulated with sufficient precision to permit their extension to new cases in different languages.

In seeking to formulate psycholinguistic principles which satisfy the above-mentioned requirements for a theory of syntactic interference, we must proceed from the assumption that speech is rule-governed behavior, and these rules are reflected in cognition. This being the case, the most natural and general principle for specifying the process by which a syntactic construction in the native language is seen as analogous to a syntactic construction in the target language is shown in 1:

1. Principle 1: If the learner views the output of a rule x in the second language to be functionally equivalent to the output structure of a rule y in the native language, then rule y will tend to be applied in contexts where the learner deems x structures appropriate.

I will define functional equivalence as the recognition that the two utterances are equatable in terms of their illocutionary function, i.e., that they both negate, question, modify, express a specific proposition such as existence, predication, etc., or a combination of these functions.

The principle formulated in 2 states the optimal conditions for the occurrence of interference due to applying the native language rules.

2. Principle 2: When the learner employs Principle 1, the maximum possibility of errors occurring exists when the formal properties of rules x and y are antithetical.

By formal properties, I mean the set of conditions imposed upon the manner in which a rule operates. The following example demonstrates that these conditions reflect the mental reality of the rule for the speaker, and that they frequently shape the strategies he employs for communicating in the second language.

Both English and Hausa, a Chadic language spoken primarily in Nigeria, but also as a lingua franca along the coast of West Africa, possess positive and negative questions of the type shown in 3.

3. *a*) Is your father here? (positive question)
   b) Isn't your father here? (negative question)

However, Hausa, like Japanese, Hindi, and other languages, employs a different set of answers for negative questions than English. The alternatives for English and Hausa are shown in 4.

4. *English*
   Q: Isn't your father here?
   A: *a*) No. (He is not here.)
      b) Yes. (He is, in fact, here.)

   Hausa
   Q: Babu   tsōhonkā̀   à nân?
      [Is not father you   here?]
   A: *c*) I, babu.
           [Yes, he is not (here).]
      d) A̅ʔ ā̀, àkwai.
           [No, he is (here).]

Pope (1973) has argued that 3 and 4 provide evidence for two types of question-answering systems. She designates the system in English a positive-negative system, whereby an answer is negative if it contains sentential negation in the highest clause, and positive if it does not. Hence, a *no* answer to 3*a* and 4*a* expresses negative disagreement and agreement, respectively; and a *yes* answer to the same two questions expresses positive agreement and disagreement, respectively. In contrast, Hausa is seen as an agreement-disagreement system: an answer agrees if it matches the question with respect to negativity and disagrees if it does not. Thus, answer 4*c* is an expression of negative agreement, and 4*d* expresses positive disagreement.

   Pope's distinction obscures a basic generalization about yes-no questions which is apparently true for all languages: that they request an affirmation or denial of the truth value of the proposition being questioned. As a result, her description fails to capture the psychological reality of the linguistic structures in both languages. In fact, the only difference between English yes-no questions and their Hausa counterparts is that both negative and positive yes-no in English request an affirmation or denial of a positive proposition. This condition also holds for Hausa positive yes-no questions; however, negative yes-no questions in Hausa request affirmation or denial of a negative proposition. If we let Q_E and Q_H represent positive questions in English and Hausa, respectively, and p stand for proposition, then the formal differences between the two systems can be symbolized as follows:

5. *a)* $Q_E, \sim Q_E = \{p\}$
   b) $Q_H = \{p\}$
   c) $\sim Q_H = \{\sim p\}$

Since negative questions have the same basic functional range in both languages, i.e., they are both used to request information, native speakers of English, in accordance with Principle 1, set up the equation $\sim Q_E = \sim Q_H$ when learning Hausa. (I am purposely ignoring the more restricted functions of English negative questions—that of expressing annoyance, disagreement, e.g., "Aren't you ashamed of yourself?" = "You really ought to be ashamed of yourself!" or disbelief: "Didn't someone call last night?" = "Oh, come on! Admit that someone called last night!" Since this discussion is confined to the more common use of negative questions—requesting information—these other uses are not germane. Note also that, when used in these restricted capacities, English negative questions have distinctly different intonation contours.) However, 5 shows that the formal properties of the rules in each language are diametrically opposed. The result, predictable from Principle 2, is maximal interference, whereby the learner employs his native language answers in response to the Hausa questions. Learners can only correct this error through understanding the mental image of the Hausa structure. It is not sufficient to instruct the student to reverse the questions he would normally employ for the equivalent English structure. He must grasp the notion that the negative question in 6*a* has the formal properties shown in 6*b*.

6. *a)* Wannàn ba   zàbo   ba   nè?
      [that   neg.   guinea fowl   neg.   is
      "Isn't that a guinea fowl?"]
   b) Is it the case [p = that isn't a guinea fowl]?

It is worth noting that this example constitutes one of the rare cases where one could safely predict that second language learning mirrors, to some extent, the sequence that takes place in child language acquisition. This follows because the Hausa child has a more semantically complex system than the English-speaking child. (For a discussion of how one might intuitively define complexity in child language, and how it may affect acquisition, see Slobin 1973, p. 188). Since positive questions are more frequent than negative questions, we would expect the child to master the equation in 5*b* first. Confronted with examples of negative questions, he will first employ the answers to positive questions and only later acquire the additional system shown in 5*c*. Bilingual children may initially have great difficulty with the two systems. A study of the development of yes-no questions in English-speaking, Japanese-speaking, and English-Japanese bilingual children by Akiyama (1977) supports these hypotheses.

An alternative explanation of the semantic errors which arise when English speakers attempt to learn the Hausa yes-no question answering system is provided by Eckman's (1977) "markedness differential hypothesis." Under this proposal, the learner's errors are accounted for and predicted by making reference to a typology of markedness. According to Eckman, those areas of the target language which differ from the native language and are more marked in terms of linguistic universals will be more difficult, giving rise to predictable errors. However, those areas of the target language which are different from the native language but are not more marked will not prove difficult. To apply the markedness differential hypothesis to our previous example, we must first assume the existence of a universal hierarchy of yes-no questions where, using Pope's designations, agreement-disagreement systems are more marked than positive-negative systems. The difference between English and Hausa yes-no question systems is thus reflected in the universal hierarchy and allows only one possible prediction, i.e., errors will arise when English speakers attempt to learn how to manipulate the more marked system, Hausa, but not vice versa. Note also that the markedness differential hypothesis can also lay claim to the aforementioned prediction about the development of yes-no questions in the speech of Hausa children by simply stating that the less-marked system is acquired first.

How are we to decide which of these two explanations, both of which make correct predictions concerning the example under discussion, is to be preferred? Eckman conveniently provides grounds for rejecting the explanatory power of the markedness differential hypothesis. He states that "it would be possible to falsify the MDH if it could be shown that the areas of difficulty that a given language learner has are not those areas of the target language which are different from and more marked than the native language." (Eckman 1977, p. 327). One of the most widely documented causes of errors which fulfills this condition is the false cognate. It is difficult to see how one could relate cognate forms to linguistic universals, but even if one were to construct some universal or typological hierarchy where languages with no cognates are more highly ranked (less marked) than languages which contain many cognate forms, one would still be left with the task of explaining why cognates are both a source of positive, facilitative transfer as well as negative, retroactive interference. What is needed is an explanation of the mechanism underlying these two concepts.

Interestingly enough, just such an explanation was discovered a little over thirty years ago. In summarizing the experimental research in transfer and retroactive interference in verbal learning, Osgood (1949) developed a three-dimensional model which has been confirmed by several tests, e.g., Bugelski and Cadwallader (1956), Dallet (1962), and Wimer (1964). In Osgood's model, when the stimuli are similar but the responses different, interference invariably occurs. If, on the other hand, both responses and stimuli are the same, positive transfer occurs. In the neutral case, where neither transfer nor interference takes place, the stimuli are different (Young and Underwood 1954). Osgood's model provides an explanation of the mechanisms underlying lexical transfer and interference in second language learning. Whenever the learner pairs two words that are highly similar in both languages, e.g., French *coin*, 'corner', and English *coin*, but have different meanings, we have a case of interference due to false cognates. Conversely, true cognates will facilitate learning, since they have the same meaning. Noncognate items cannot be paired since no basis, i.e., similarity, for this exists, so neither transfer nor interference effects will be observed.

The two principles developed earlier represent an attempt to refine the psychological concept "interference," in such a way that it may be meaningfully applied to explain cases of syntactic and semantic errors in second language learning. My claim is that these principles have far more explanatory power than alternative accounts of interlingual interference like the markedness differential hypothesis, because they are rooted in the mechanisms of perception and cognition rather than in a classificatory device such as linguistic universals. It is quite erroneous to assign linguistic universals a causal status in the rather cavalier fashion employed by Eckman. To maintain that universals are "a reflection of human cognition" (Eckman 1978, p. 329) simply sidesteps the more complex issue of how they explain why learners make errors. If, for example, we grant that there are certain universal phonetic tendencies which result from the physiology of the human vocal tract and central nervous system, we are still faced with the task of explaining how these universal tendencies constitute a causal explanation of phonological interference in second language learning. Suppose we observe that a native speaker of English attempting to learn Farsi first produces the postvelar stop /q/ as a voiced alveolar tap, but later shifts to substituting a /g/ for that phoneme whenever he must produce it. We may observe that the markedness differential hypothesis correctly predicts that an error will occur, since Farsi /q/ differs from the phonemic inventory of English and is also more marked, i.e., occupies a lower position in a universal hierarchy of phonetic segments. But even though an error is correctly predicted, it turns out to be more complex than a single substitution, and nothing resembling a causal explanation of both errors has been provided. In fact, the underlying mechanism which results in the English speaker's initial erroneous production must surely involve his pairing the sound he thought he perceived with the one in his own inventory which seemed most accoustically similar to it. (A sophisticated language learner with phonetics training might attempt to substitute a retroflexed flap, which is even closer.) When the true nature of the sound is made clear to the learner, he may nevertheless not be able to produce it with perfect accuracy, at times substituting the phoneme in his native language which is most similar in terms of articulation, and later some interlanguage variant that is neither in the native or the target language. This example, which is taken from the author's personal experience as a language learner, clearly shows that the causal mechanisms underlying phonological interference can only be explained by a theory which employs comparisons that are part of the analytical component incorporated in models of speech recognition, e.g., Stevens and Halle (1967), and production.

It is perhaps overly ambitious to expect that a single set of psychological principles like those proposed in this paper could account for interlingual perception errors as well as production errors, given the difference between these two processes. Nevertheless, in Cowan (1976), I cited some perception errors that are accounted for by Principle 2. The first of these had to do with reading comprehension errors which occur when native speakers of English assign an SVO interpretation to an initial Noun-Verb-Noun sequence in learning to read German. Because German frequently employs an antithetical order, OVS, for this surface structure pattern, incorrect interpretations which involve switching the subject and object can occur if grammatical clues such as case and subject-verb agreement are neutralized. My second example illustrated how reading confusion can occur when the language learner relies on a native-language strategy embodied by one syntactic process (pronominalization), which is opposed by an antithetical process (deletion) in the second language. Native speakers of English come to rely on pronominal signals to establish basic anaphoric relationships that enable them to read with comprehension. Hindi, however, establishes these same anaphoric relationships by deleting the very pronominal signals which are so crucial for the English reader. The comprehension breakdowns that result when English speakers search in vain for the coreference signals they are used to follows naturally from Principle 2. It is interesting to note that production errors made by English speakers learning Hindi also testify to the importance of this opposition in syntactic processes. Learners frequently insert subject pronouns where the native speaker omits them, thereby producing an overly-formal style of spoken Hindi.

To summarize, in this paper I have argued that a psychological theory of interlingual interference must satisfy two requirements implied by the notion "interference": it must specify how elements in the target language are associated with corresponding elements in the native language and stipulate the likelihood of errors resulting from such associations. Two principles which meet these requirements were proposed to account for semantic interference errors. A subsequent comparison of these principles with an alternative account of the error phenomena was carried out to demonstrate the distinction between explanations which are causal and those which are predictive but noncausal. It was suggested that a causal theory of interference would make use of mechanisms characteristic of a broader theory of perception and cognition.

References

Akiyama, M. M. "The Development of the Yes-No Question Answering System in Young Children." Ph.D. dissertation, University of Illinois at Urbana-Champaign, 1977.

Bever, T. G. "The Cognitive Basis of Linguistic Structures." In *Cognition and the Development of Language,* edited by John R. Hayes, New York: John Wiley and Sons, 1970.

Blumenthal, A. L. "Prompted Recall of Sentences." *Journal of Verbal Learning and Verbal Behavior* 6 (1967):203–6.

Boomer, D. S., and Laver, J. D. M. "Slips of the Tongue." *British Journal of Disorders of Communication* 3 (1968):1–2.

Bugelski, B. R., and Cadwallader, T. J. "A Reappraisal of Transfer and Retroactive Surface." *Journal of Experimental Psychology* 52 (1956):360–66.

Corder, S. P. "The Significance of Learners' Errors." *International Review of Applied Linguistics* 5 (1967):161–70.

Cowan, J R. "Reading, Perceptual Strategies, and Contrastive Analysis." *Language Learning* 26, no. 1 (1976):95–109.

Dallet, K. M. "The Transfer Surface Re-examined." *Journal of Verbal Learning and Verbal Behavior* 1 (1962):91–94.

Eckman, F. R. "Markedness and the Contrastive Analysis Hypothesis." *Language Learning* 72, no. 2 (1977):315–30.

Fromkin, V. A. "The Non-anomalous Nature of Anomalous Utterances." *Language* 47 (1971):27–52.

Hays, John R., ed. *Cognition and the Development of Language.* New York: John Wiley and Sons, 1970.

Hockett, Charles F. "Where the Tongue Slips, There Slip I." In *To Honor Roman Jakobson,* vol. 2, pp. 910–36. Janua Linguarum Series Major 32. The Hague: Mouton and Co., 1967.

Jain, M. "Error Analysis of an Indian English Corpus." Ms., University of Edinburgh, 1969.

Jeffries, L. H., ed. *Cerebral Mechanisms in Behavior.* New York: John Wiley and Sons, 1951.

Lashley, K. S. "The Problem of Serial Order in Behavior." In *Cerebral Mechanisms in Behavior,* edited by L. H. Jeffries. New York: John Wiley and Sons, 1951.

Laver, John. "The Detection and Correction of Slips of the Tongue." Work in Progress no. 3, pp. 1–3. Department of Phonetics and Linguistics, Edinburgh University, 1969.

MacKay, D. G. "Spoonerisms: the Anatomy of Errors in the Serial Order of Speech." *Neuropsychologia,* 8 (1970):315–22.

Nooteboom, S. G. "The Tongue Slips Into Patterns." In *Nomen: Leyden Studies in Linguistics and Phonetics,* edited by A. G. Sciarone, et al., pp. 114–32. The Hague: Mouton and Co., 1969.

Osgood, C. E. "The Similarity Paradox in Human Learning: A Resolution." *Psychology Review* 56 (1949):132–43.

Pope, Emily. "Question-Answering Systems." In *Papers from the Ninth Regional Meeting of the Chicago Linguistic Society,* pp. 482–92. Chicago: Chicago Linguistic Society, 1973.

Richards, J. C. "A Non-Contrastive Approach to Error Analysis." *English Language Teaching* 25, no. 3 (1971):204–19.

———. "Simplification: A Strategy in the Adult Acquisition of a Foreign Language: An Example From Indonesian-Malaysian." *Language Learning* 25, no. 1 (1975):115–26.

Schachter, J. "An Error in Error Analysis." *Language Learning* 24, no. 2 (1974):205–14.

Sciarone, A. G., et al., eds. *Nomen: Leyden Studies in Linguistics and Phonetics.* The Hague: Mouton and Co., 1969.

Selinker, L. "Interlanguage." *International Review of Applied Linguistics* 10, no. 3 (1972):219–31.

Slobin, D. I. "Cognitive Prerequisites for the Development of Grammar." In *Studies of Child Language Development,* edited by C. A. Ferguson and D. I. Slobin, pp. 183–86. New York: Holt, Rinehart and Winston, 1973.

Stevens, K. N., and Halle, M. "Remarks on Analysis by Synthesis and Distinctive Features." In *Models for the Perception of Speech and Visual Form*, edited by Walter Dunn, pp. 88–102. Cambridge, Mass.: MIT Press, 1967.

Weinreich, Uriel. *Languages in Contact.* New York: Publication of the Linguistic Circle of New York, 1953.

Wimer, R. "Osgood's Transfer Surface: Extension and Test." *Journal of Verbal Learning and Verbal Behavior* 47 (1964):337–60.

Young, R. K., and Underwood, B. J. "Transfer in Verbal Materials with Dissimilar Stimuli and Response Similarity Varied." *Journal of Experimental Psychology* 47 (1954):153–59.

Discourse, Culture, and Instruction

Thelma E. Weeks

It would not be surprising to find cultural differences between the language usage of an English-speaking American Indian child who was reared on an Indian Reservation and an Anglo child, but what would the differences be?

Ever since I started working with the Indians on the Yakima Indian Reservation (located in central Washington) in 1968, I have been hearing reports from school principals and teachers about the Yakima children's "language problems." While the language problems were never well specified, one complaint was that the children couldn't answer questions—couldn't talk in class. I have commented on some aspects of the problem elsewhere (Weeks 1975; Weeks and Weeks 1975), but in this study, I wish to examine certain aspects of the skills of the Yakima children in verbal discourse.

Home Language

The native language of Yakima Indian children is English. While Sahaptin, the language of the Yakima Indians, was the mother tongue for the grandparents and for most of the parents, only a few older Yakimas are monolingual Sahaptin speakers. The middle generation cannot be easily characterized regarding bilingualism. Some speak Sahaptin fluently in appropriate situations, while others appear to have only minimal passive competence and little, if any, active competence in Sahaptin. When I have asked for translations for words and phrases, some members of this generation have told me that they were punished so severely in Bureau of Indian Affairs schools for using their native language that they are unable to recall anything but the most commonly used expressions in Sahaptin. They seem to have unanimously resolved to speak nothing but English to their children in order to help the children avoid such problems in school. However, many traces of the native Indian language as well as the native culture can be seen in the language behavior of the children.

120

Description of Research

Subjects

I tape-recorded conversations with 12 Yakima children;[1] however, only 9 of them were suitable for the analysis discussed here. I also recorded conversations with 4 Anglo children who lived on the Yakima Reservation and attended the same preschool program that the Yakima children attended. Another 5 Anglo children whose conversations were recorded lived in the Palo Alto, California, area. The children ranged in age from 3 years 10 months to 5 years 11 months.

Recording Sessions

The preschool program where tape recording was done was conducted by Yakima Indian adults, both men and women, and sponsored by the Yakima Indian Tribal Council. A private room (though not quiet) was provided for the research.

Recording time for the conversations with each child varied from about 20 minutes to 40 minutes, depending on other activities, such as recess and lunch time. No recording session was ever cut short because the child tired of it. The Yakima children in particular loved talking and several requested second and third sessions when their original session could not be extended.

Conversation Topics

As a means of offering topics for conversations, I had a stack of colored pictures from which the children chose some to talk about.

There are several ways in which discourse that is stimulated by pictures chosen by a child may differ from most conversations between an adult and a child.

1. The child largely controls the topics to be discussed. When the children finished talking about the picture directly, they often went on to discuss personal experiences suggested by the picture. In adult-child conversations, it is usually the case that the adult asks questions that he thinks are suitable and controls the conversation topics to a large degree even though he may never choose a topic the child is interested in.

2. The child may readily change the topic by selecting another picture. In other child-adult conversations, the child is more likely than the adult to have difficulty in introducing new topics.

3. Because the picture remains where both the child and the adult can see it, the child uses more demonstrative and personal pronouns than he would otherwise. When considering new and given information in a conversation, it is only the given information—that which has been previously mentioned in the conversation—that can properly be represented anaphorically. In this case, information represented in the picture had to be considered as given, resulting in what sounded (when analyzing the transcription of audio-only tapes) as though a number of inappropriate pronouns had been used. An analysis of children's discourse often examines the appropriate use of anaphoric pronouns, but for the reason just given, I didn't consider it appropriate here.

Discourse Features Examined

Answering Questions

Since teachers of the Yakima children had mentioned specifically that they did not seem to be able to answer questions, I looked most intently at this aspect of the conversations with the Yakima children.

Mishler (1975a) is one of many who has noted that questions demand answers. He maintains that questions not only need answers, they need confirmation:

> In more "open" natural conversation the question-answer exchange seems totally inapplicable as a basic unit of conversation; a question not only "demands" a response, but the response demands a further "response" from the questioner. In brief, an answer to a question does not terminate an exchange in any meaningful social sense. It is terminated by a "sign" on the part of the questioner that his question has received a response, adequate or inadequate, appropriate or inappropriate.

Mishler suggests that Question-Response-Confirmation constitutes the usual pattern in conversation.

Philips (1976) suggests, however, that this may be culture-specific. She observes that "for Anglos, answers to questions are close to obligatory, even if they take the form of 'I can't answer that right now', or a brief shake of the head," but that for the Warm Springs Indians, answers to questions are not obligatory. Questions may be answered at a later time, or possibly not at all, but acknowledgment of the question need not be made, since it may be assumed that the listener was indeed listening. "In Indian interaction." says Philips, "the speaker may be certain of attention from hearers."

It appears that the confirmation requirement, referred to by Mishler, serves the purpose of assuring the listener that he has heard the response to his question. Would there be any reason for the Sahaptin-speaking Indians to observe this practice? The Sahaptin-speaking Indians (or those descended from the Sahaptin-speakers) at Warm Springs are closely related to the Yakima Indians, and the cultural patterns are very similar. What might conversational patterns be then among Yakima Indians and, in particular, with Yakima children?

At the Child Language Research Forum at Stanford University in April, 1976, Philip Dale remarked that children are very reluctant to answer with "I don't know." That rang true to the child language researchers present. I scanned the transcriptions of my conversations with the 5 children whose language development I follow regularly and found a few occasions when the 2 girls responded with "I don't know," but could not find even one instance of the 3 boys saying it. The 2 boys who were firstborn in their respective families would go to almost any extreme to avoid it, often using devious methods. The third boy usually avoided the dreaded phrase by stating simply "Let's not talk about that."

In the matter of guessing, I have observed that school teachers are inclined to encourage guessing in cases where a child is uncertain of an answer. I have also noted in conversation with Yakima adults that they are not at all inclined to guess. They feel they would lose face if they gave an answer that turned out to be wrong.

I was interested, then, in whether or not the Yakima children would fail to respond to questions, respond with "I don't know," guess, or change the subject.

Asking Questions

While it is usually thought that asking questions is an indication of brightness in a child, conversations between an adult and a child are usually initiated and controlled by questions from the adult. Mishler (1975*b*) suggests that even when children ask an adult a question, the adult regains control of the conversation by responding with a question.

I considered it a matter of interest to see whether or not the Yakima children would play an active or passive role in conversation regarding question asking. Also, if they asked questions, would they confirm the responses that were given?

Interruptions

Philips (1976) has pointed out regarding the Warm Springs Indians that
"The pauses between two different speakers' turns at talk are frequently
longer than is the case in Anglo interactions. There is tolerance for silences—silences that Anglos often rush into and fill. Indian speakers
rarely, if ever, begin to speak at the same time and rarely interrupt one
another." The situation with the Warm Springs Indians, according to
Philips, and with the Yakimas, by my experience, is that they listen and
appear to wait until the speaker is through talking before formulating
their own response, if any. This contrasts with the mainstream culture in
the United States where the listener often appears to be formulating his
own response long before the speaker is through, and often responds
instantaneously when the speaker finishes, or before.

What would the pattern of interruptions and pauses be with the
Yakima children?

Organization of Material

Chafe (1976) has suggested that there are cultural differences in the way a
person organizes the content of his material when reporting an event in
conversation. He suggests that in our culture we are most apt to start out
by summarizing the event and then expanding on it, e.g., "I'm going to tell
you about my trip to Denver," and then proceeding to report events
chronologically. The Japanese, by comparison, he points out, generally
seem to build up through a series of details to a final conclusion, so that the
summary is at the end rather than at the beginning. He noted also that
there are ways other than chronological ordering to organize material.

The fourth general question regarding conversational skill in the
Yakima children is how they would organize material when reporting
events.

Results and Discussion

The number of children involved in this study was small and the individual differences were great; I have therefore resisted taking totals and
averages of discourse features. Individual differences in conversational
style appear to be normal, in child or adult populations. Some children,
both Indian and Anglo, were far more talkative than others. The number
of turns in conversation ranged from 21 to 80. Some talked briefly during
each turn, averaging about 2 utterances per turn, while others were more

talkative during each turn. The girl who took only 21 turns spoke 14 utterances during one turn, and seldom limited herself to only 1 utterance. Some children chose 7 or 8 pictures and talked briefly about a number of topics, while others chose only 2 or 3 pictures and expanded at length on each one.

One overall pattern that emerged, however, was that the Yakima children were much more inclined to use the pictures as a point of departure and discuss personal experiences. Their conversations were more "conversationlike" than those with the Anglo children, who tended to itemize what they saw in the picture or describe the action, and then choose another picture. One Anglo girl who lived on the Yakima Reservation asked, after I suggested she pick out some pictures she would like to talk about, "What do I have to say?" This was a typical attitude on the part of the Anglo children. They assumed there was something specific that was expected of them and they must determine the rules and follow them. They seemed to be assuming different roles—the Anglos assuming a student role and the Yakimas the role of a friend.

Answering Questions

The Yakima children appeared to be more eager to converse, to have a turn talking into the microphone, than the Anglo children, and exhibited more pleasure in the process. They did, however, leave more questions unanswered.

One problem may have been my own very brief pauses in waiting for an answer. With adult Yakimas, I deliberately waited for a longer period for an answer, but, not wanting to embarrass the child in case he or she couldn't answer, I filled what probably should have been waiting time with another question or remark. However, when I judged the child was pondering the question, I waited as long as 16 seconds, in one instance, but more often not more than 10 seconds, before continuing the conversation. It was not unusual for me to ask 4 or 5 questions before getting a response, but my usual pause was from 3 to 4 seconds. For example, 1 Yakima girl told me she had gone to a war dance, and had been telling me that they had pop and things to eat there. She continued with "and . . ." After 10 seconds I asked "And what does the war dance look like?" No answer. "I've never seen anybody do a war dance. What do they do?" After 6 seconds she said, "Uh . . ." and at 14 seconds I asked, "Do they wear pretty costumes?" She answered obliquely, "I have them in purple and some stuff that's on the ground."

There were no such series of unanswered questions with the Anglo children, but there were unanswered questions that resulted in topic-changing; a child would appear not to hear my question while he chose a new picture. This happened several times with the Anglo children but not at all with the Yakimas.

Oblique answers, or responses that acknowledged that they had heard my question but were not answering it directly, were not unusual with the Yakima children.

There were also a number of instances in which the Yakima children continued the topic of conversation, but appeared to be continuing their own train of thoughts rather than answering my questions. For example, a Yakima girl was telling about going sledding on a sled so big that 12 people could get on it. I said, "That's a big sled! What did you call it—a toboggan or a bobsled?" She answered, "I can't remember when we done that—when 12 got on that big one." She continued reminiscing about the experience. It could be that she didn't know the answer and sidestepped it, or she may have just been continuing her previous train of thought, just as other Yakima children had done several times. However, she paid attention to most of my remarks, and immediately after her recounting her experience, I said that I used to do that when I was a little girl, and she asked, "Did it tickle your tummy?"

I asked all of the children rhetorical questions of the variety, "There are lots of people who like to go to the rodeo, aren't there?" The Anglo children generally acknowledged such questions minimally with "Um hum," "Yeah," or by nodding or shaking their heads. There was just one instance of a Yakima child acknowledging such a question. We were looking at a picture that included several varieties of flowers. This girl had guessed that one lavender flower was a lilac. I asked what the yellow flowers might be, and she answered, "Might be xxx. (The x's represent unintelligible speech.) They must be eatin' it." I remarked, "They look like they might be daisies. Anyway, they're pretty, aren't they?" And she answered, "They're pretty." The answer was appropriate, but such repetition is not usual.

I found two examples of what might have been guessing on the part of Yakima children after I prodded. On the other hand, my "prodding" may have served as clarification of the question, making it possible for the children to answer without guessing. One girl chose a picture of 2 children throwing a ball. The sun was at the horizon in the background. I asked "What time of day do you suppose it is?" No answer. "Do you think it's in the afternoon or the morning?" She ventured, "Morning." I confirmed, "Morning. It looks like the sun's just come up, doesn't it?"

Several times guessing took the form of asking whether or not the reply was correct by the use of rising intonation. One girl chose a picture of a typical middle-class girl's bedroom full of toys, etc. She began to itemize things in the room, always naming the item with a question intonation, and pausing, looking toward me and waiting for agreement before continuing, e.g., "Basket?" "Right. That's a basket." "Playbooks?" "Uh huh." "Doll?" "Right." Etc.

There is a qualitative difference, of course, in guessing with a rising intonation that clearly says, "I'm guessing. Am I right?" and guessing that prosodically suggests full knowledge, as the Anglo children often did, sometimes resulting in incorrect answers.

An instance where the child might have been able to guess the correct answer but wouldn't try follows: a Yakima boy had chosen a picture of sail boats at a marina. I asked, "Do you know what it is he's climbing?" No answer. "What are those things called?" I asked, pointing to the mast. He said, "Mmmmm. What are they?" His lengthened *m* may represent a guess at the initial sound, or may not.

While this boy didn't reply "I don't know," his response was the equivalent. Other Yakima children replied, "I forgot," "I don't know," or simply "What?" on an average of about once during the conversation. I found only one instance of an Anglo child replying, "No, what?" although I answered "I don't know" to their questions quite often.

There were many exchanges such as: "What do you think these 2 girls are doing?" No answer. Was it the case that the child didn't comprehend the question, or that they needed more time than I gave them to ponder the question, or was it that they didn't know the answer for sure and wouldn't guess? It is likely that the Yakima children had had less experience dealing with pictures than the Anglo children, and some responses indicate this. For example, in the example mentioned above of the picture of 2 children playing ball, I asked "Where do you suppose they are?" and the child answered, pointing, "Right there and right there." Another child, cited above, when asked the same question about the same picture, had failed to answer until I asked if it looked like a playground, at which she replied, "Park." Pictures, as opposed to reality, may be somewhat confusing in a culture where books, magazines, and pictures in general (other than TV) are not very common.

Changing the subject when they were unable to answer a question was by far the most usual ruse for the Anglo children to use. The pile of pictures in front of them made it a simple procedure. I found only 1 example of a Yakima child[2] deliberately changing the subject, and this seemed to be because he was embarrassed (at 3:10 he was the youngest child I interviewed). He had explained to me that someone was "one of our brother longs." He ended the sentence with a rising intonation, as though he were either not sure of what he was saying or he thought I wouldn't know. I asked, "He's what?" "He's one of our brother longs." (rising intonation again). "One of your brother longs?" I repeated. He agreed, then started making some sounds, "Um hum. WRRR . . . WRRRRR. Can't see me!" He hid behind the picture. "Peek-a-boo!" he said as he looked around it. The man he was referring to may have been a brother-in-law in the family. I allowed the subject to drop.

In summary, the only examples here of Anglo children not answering questions, with guesses or otherwise, were cases where they ignored the question while they chose another picture (changed the subject). The Yakima children failed to respond to many questions. They did occasionally guess, principally guessing that was in the nature of questioning (ending with a rising intonation). Because of the small sample of children, no conclusions can be drawn about the admission of lack of knowledge, but the Yakima children were more inclined to reply with "I don't know" or equivalents than the Anglo children.

Asking Questions

Bright children are supposed to ask a lot of questions, but it also appears that question asking is role-related. Children, particularly in traditional classrooms, often assume it is the teacher's role to ask questions and their role to answer them. I found that Anglo children were much more inclined to call me "teacher" and to answer every question I asked, even if they answered incorrectly, and not to ask me any questions, than the Yakima children. Some of the Yakima children, on the other hand, took virtual control of the conversation by asking me questions. Out of 51 turns in conversation, the girl who asked me if sledding tickled my tummy, also asked me 22 other questions. One didn't ask me any questions, but most of the Yakimas were in between, usually asking questions for further information about some of the pictures. They could not be characterized as passive participants in the conversation.

None of the questions asked by Anglo children were of a personal nature. They asked questions about the pictures: "Where's the haystack at?" "What kind are these truck?" "How do they make it go?" etc. The Yakima children asked many questions of this sort, but they also asked questions of a more personal nature: "Now whata you gonna do?" "What's your name?" "How did you know my name?" "Didn't you fall?" and "Could I hold that?" (the microphone).

The Yakima children also asked questions requesting clarification: I asked, "What kind of fish do you catch when you go fishing?" and the child asked, "Uh . . . you mean what color" I answered, "Oh, what color, or what kind." No response. "What do you call the fish when you catch fish?" No response. "Have you ever been fishing?" She answered, "We got . . . once my Daddy . . . he caught a fish . . . he caught a whale, too." My response to her request for clarification would have been more help if I had suggested 2 or 3 varieties of fish, such as trout or salmon, which I assume she would have been familiar with.

With regard to asking for clarification or correcting false impressions, I should mention that the Anglo children regularly corrected me if I misunderstood them. They would repeat a word 2 or 3 times if necessary to make me understand. Yakima children did not. One Yakima girl who was very hard to understand had been talking about going camping in the mountains with her grandmother. I asked what they liked to cook when they went to the mountains. She answered "Anything" /initiŋ/ with very high front, tense vowels, and I thought she said "Indian things." So I asked, "What would Indian things be?" She answered, "Well, Grandma cooks mush. Or initing." This time I guessed, "Indian tea?" and she agreed, "She makes tea." She made no move to correct me. I had no inkling of this while I was talking to her, but when I transcribed the tape, I understood instantly what she was talking about, and was amazed at her patience with me. There were several such examples of the Yakima children failing to correct my misconceptions.

It was not always easy to determine the purpose of some questions: A Yakima boy, looking at a picture of some mountains, said, "I think it's a bear! Is there a bear?" "Well, I don't see one, do you?" "Yeah," he answered. "Well," I conceded, "there might be. Because there are big trees, and it's out in the mountains. There might be bears." "There're some bears up there. Up there. Go get 'em! Jump! I probably fall down and jump off." He was fantasizing as he had done other times.

It is interesting that the 4 Anglo children I talked to at Yakima were like the Anglo children recorded in California, not like the Yakima Indian children with whom they played 5 days a week. The Yakima children answered fewer questions and asked more.

In examining the transcriptions for confirmations, I found that Mishler (1975*a*) was correct insofar as my conversation was concerned. There was no instance in which I did not offer confirmation of some kind when a child answered my question. However, I found only 1 case in which a Yakima child confirmed my response to a question. We had been discussing people who were having a picnic on a beach. I said, "They spread out a blanket." She answered, "It look like it. They like to be on beaches? He like to fish, doesn't he?" "Yes, I expect so." She replied, "He likes fish." It may not have been intended as a confirmation, but may have been a continuation of her thoughts about what was happening on the beach, for her next statement was "Because he's a little bit big."

Indications were that the Yakima children were interpreting the situation as a friendly visit, not as a teacher-student interview, and, therefore, might fit into a scheme where confirmation would be required. However, the children did not offer confirmation after a response to their questions. On the other hand, indications were that the Anglo children were interpreting the situation as teacher-student interview, in which case a confirmation was not required. They did not offer them.

Interruptions

As would be predicted from Philips (1976), the Yakima children did not interrupt me in conversation even once. I have not analyzed taped conversations between Yakima children (child-child as opposed to child-adult), but I would not expect it to be different. Of the 5 children whose language development I regularly follow, all interrupt me from time to time, and one does it quite often. The Anglo children at Yakima also broke in while I was speaking. For example, a boy had chosen a picture of a rodeo and I asked, "You ever see . . ." and he interrupted, "Yeah, I was watching them, too . . ." Interruptions usually accompanied excited speech, but not always.

The Yakima children practiced the opposite of interruptions—long pauses.

Organization of Material

In this discussion of the reporting of events in the course of conversation, *events* will refer either to happenings in the lives of the children themselves or events as depicted in the pictures or imagined by the children.

I have commented elsewhere (Weeks 1975) on the preference in our culture for a brief, summarizing report of events that does not use many, if any, direct quotations. The style "Then I says to her and she says to me" is equated with lower socioeconomic class. The approved method involves summarizing.

While it could not be said that the Anglo children briefly summarized the events depicted in a picture, there did emerge definite differences in the style of the 2 groups. The Anglo children usually described what they saw as one might read a grocery list. While the Yakima children usually picked up a picture and waited for me to say something ("What's happening here?" was my usual question), the Anglo children often picked up a picture and started talking instantaneously: "This one. Lots of horses are down on the ground and some people. Tap at the window and horses be mean to it. Putting their head down under. Here." In each case I would follow with comments or questions or both, and they would always respond, but they seemed to be describing the picture as fully as they could with their first turn.

The Anglo children used a discourse (i.e., conversational) register[3] whether they were describing an event depicted in the picture or something that had happened to themselves. For example, one girl chose a picture of a child with a cat. "I like that picture. I had a baby cat like that." "You did?" I asked. "But Mommy . . . it was a baby cat and it was lost and I uh didn't know who it belonged to and I was going to keep it but Mommy started the next morning to keep it but Daddy took it and threw it down and it went away because he never like my Daddy." Not one Anglo child included verbatim conversation in the events they reported.

On the other hand, the Yakima children made frequent use of a narrative (or storytelling) register. They presented material as one might tell a story, using direct quotations and a wider range in intonation patterns. A Yakima girl and I were discussing boats: I asked, "You ever been on a boat?" She answered, "We have a boat at home. Tommy . . . we were out in the wood and there was lots of water there and we used to clean fish." "Oh. You like fish?" "Grandma said, "Tommy's going to get that boat and take us a ride on there. Waaay out there." "Where?" "Waaaay out there." "Where's that?" "Across Hood River." *Way* was lengthened considerably.

It should be noted here that Jacobs (1931, p. 271) comments regarding Sahaptin:

> In quotes and direct discourse, remarks are often treated as a sentence-object of the verb. Not only are remarks turned into object clauses, but Sahaptin may throw into object clauses any statements of sensory or ideational activity. Thus, for "He saw them coming," Sahaptin says, "He saw 'now they are coming.' " Also, "He didn't know where he was going" would become "He did not know 'where am I going?' "

A language tradition of this kind increases the probability that English speakers with a Sahaptin background would use direct quotations in discourse. It was found in an earlier study (Weeks and Weeks 1975) that

Yakima children used significantly more direct quotations than Anglo children in a storytelling task and somewhat more in conversation.

The use of abundant direct quotations is considered appropriate in our culture for storytelling purposes, and we find individuals who enjoy relating experiences in their best narrative register, varying pitch, volume, speed, using other dialects when appropriate, and using direct quotations. Probably every culture has such a register available, but the question is how many individuals use it, and for what occasions.

What appeared to be happening here was that the Yakima children were interpreting the conversation with an adult as an appropriate situation in which to use such a narrative register, whereas the Anglo children did not. The same had been true in the story retelling task (Weeks and Weeks 1975): even though some of the Anglo children were known to have a well developed narrative register, they did not use it in the story retelling task, whereas all of the Yakima children made some style changes in retelling the story.

All of the children organized events, by and large, in a chronological order, where time was involved. None of the children "summarized" material in the way an adult might, though there were differences in the extent to which details were either omitted or included. If one interprets a situation as calling for a narrative style, one will include details and devise ways of making the reported event entertaining that one would not use in a reporting style.

In this instance, the Yakima children interpreted the situation more as I had hoped than the Anglo children did. Other researchers have reported that children from nursery school age can call any new adult in their room "teacher," and this was my experience both in Palo Alto and at Yakima, where the Anglos were concerned. None of the 12 Yakima children called me "teacher." They simply did not address me. When they wanted my attention, they took my hand, caught my eye, or got my attention in some other way. I believe that the interpretation of the situation as a teacher-student relationship on the part of the Anglo children caused some of the differences between their performance and that of the Yakima children.

One important difference between the 2 groups of children, then, involves the matter of what is chosen to report. The Yakima children more often reported extraneous matter—the child's speculations about what might happen as opposed to restricting themselves to what was actually seen in the picture, as the Anglo children did. Second, the Yakima children reported in a more colorful manner, switching from a discourse register (which they used part of the time) to a narrative register for reporting plotlike activities. Where the picture did not indicate a plot, they often invented one (the children will fall into the seal pond as a result of their trying to touch the seals, and their father will jump in to save them; there are bears in the mountains, and if I try to climb a tree to get one, I will fall out of the tree, etc.). Their narrative register as well as their discourse (conversational) register included the use of some direct quotations, whereas the Anglo children used none.

Summary

There were differences between 2 small groups of children, Yakima and Anglo, in language usage that should be categorized as cultural. Differences exhibited in conversation between myself and the children included the following aspects of language usage.

1. The Yakima children were more eager to converse, more eager to extend conversational time, and displayed more pleasure in the process of conversation than the Anglo children.
2. The Yakima children left more questions directed to them unanswered than the Anglo children.
3. The Yakima children guessed at answers less often than the Anglo children and admitted they did not know answers more often.
4. Yakima children paused before answering and never interrupted, while the Anglo children paused more briefly or interrupted before I finished speaking.
5. Yakima children asked more questions, some of them of a personal nature, than the Anglo children, who asked no personal questions.
6. The Yakima children failed to correct my misconceptions or misunderstanding of them in every case, while the Anglo children did not hesitate to correct me.
7. Yakima children tended to reorganize material into a narrative form, selecting different kinds of events to report than the Anglo children, who reported events more simply in a discourse (conversational) register.

I expected to find that the Yakima children would fail to confirm responses to their own questions, inasmuch as Yakimas feel confident of the listener's attention (Philips 1976). I also expected (in view of the Mishler 1975*a* study) that the Anglo children would offer such confirmations. I found only rare examples in either group, but the lack of it may derive from different causes. Evidence suggests that differences in assumed roles on the part of the Yakima and Anglo children could be a determining factor, but more research is needed.

It remains to be determined why some of these differences, particularly in answering questions, exist. Are there important differences in experience that accentuate the inherent cultural differences? For example, do the Yakima children have noticeably less opportunity to converse with adults and to be confronted by questions than the Anglo children? It is an area that needs to be investigated more thoroughly. Nevertheless, the Yakima children were active participants in the conversations by any standards, contributing their full share to the activity. The differences found between their performance and that of the Anglo children need to be recognized by teachers and school officials for what they are—cultural differences—not language deficiencies.

Notes

This is a revised version of a symposium paper presented at the American Educational Research Association Convention in San Francisco, April 21, 1976. Reprinted by permission of the author.

1. The Yakima children attending this program may be thought of as coming from less traditional homes in that their mothers work; in the more traditional homes, mothers do not work outside the home. Children from more traditional homes with whom I have talked offer an even greater contrast in language usage to the Anglo children than those recorded here.
2. This boy's mother was a Yakima and his father a Native American, but not Yakima.
3. *Register* is defined as a variety of language differing at any or all levels of form from other varieties of the same language, "distinguished according to use" (Halliday, McIntosh, and Strevens, 1964).

References

Chafe, Wallace L. "Preliminaries to a Model of Discourse." Paper presented at the American Educational Research Association Convention, San Francisco, April 21, 1976.

Halliday, M. A. K.; McIntosh, A.; and Strevens, P. *The Linguistic Sciences and Language Teaching*. Bloomington: University of Indiana Press, 1964.

Jacobs, Melville. "A Sketch of Northern Sahaptin Grammar." *University of Washington Publications in Anthropology* 4, no. 2 (1931):85–292.

Mishler, Elliot G. "Studies in Dialogue and Discourse: An Exponential Law of Successive Questioning." *Language in Society* 4 (1975*a*):31–51.

Mishler, Elliot G. "Studies in Dialogue and Discourse: II. Types of Discourse Initiated by and Sustained through Questioning." *Journal of Psycholinguistic Research* 4 (1975*b*):99–121.

Philips, Susan U. "Some Sources of Cultural Variability in the Regulation of Talk." *Language in Society* 5 (1976):81–95.

Weeks, Thelma E. "The Speech of Indian Children: Paralinguistic and Registral Aspects of the Yakima Dialect." Paper presented at the National Council of Teachers of English Convention, San Diego, November, 28, 1975.

Weeks, Thelma E., and Weeks, John R. "Some Measures of the Relation Between Linguistic and Cognitive Skills in Young Yakima Indian and Non-Indian Children." *Occasional Papers of the Center for Cross-Cultural Research*, 1, 1975.

Questions

1. Lado says that any list of problems predicted by a comparison of two language systems will be hypothetical until substantiated by actual student speech. Brière et al. and Ritchie point out reasons why a list based on a comparison of phonemic inventories of two languages, such as those in the Lehn and Slager article, is not sufficient to predict problems. Do you have examples of problems predicted by CA which have not appeared in the actual speech of students? How might you account for this?

2. Does Stockwell and Bowen's approach toward the question of difficulty in language learning problems agree more closely with that of Lado or with that of Koutsoudas and Koutsoudas?

3. Which of the criticisms of CA that James is attempting to refute do you think to be the most serious? Why?

4. Weeks describes differences found in comparing the oral discourse of Indian children and Anglo children using English. If you have worked with specific groups of students from another culture who are learning English, have you noticed any differences between them and native English speakers in their use of oral and/or written discourse?

Problems

A. Tagalog Morphology*

English	Tagalog
I (first, sing.)	akó (first, sing.)
you (second, sing. or pl.)	ikáw (second, sing., familiar, before verb)
he (third, sing., masc.)	ka (second, sing., familiar, after verb)
she (third, sing., fem.)	kayó (second, sing. or pl., formal)
it (third, sing., neut.)	siyá (third, sing., masc. or fem.)
we (first, pl.)	(no third sing., neut. form)
they (third, pl.)	tayo (first, pl. inclusive)
	kamí (first, pl. exclusive)
	silá (third, pl.)

Note: In English pronouns of the *I*-class are the only ones used to express the actor in a sentence like "I wrote this." In Tagalog the same relationship may be expressed by pronouns of the *akó*-class or by two other types of pronouns: those of the *ko*-class or the *aking*-class, which are not included in the above list. Thus "I wrote this" can be rendered as "Akó'y sumulat nitó," "Sinulat ko itó," or "Aking sinulat itó."

1. Determine which English pronouns would be most difficult for a speaker of Tagalog to master. Establish the hierarchy of difficulty among Tagalog forms by using (*a*) the method based on differences in form, meaning, and distribution (see table 1), and (*b*) the method based on numerical correspondences (see table 2).

2. Which method seems to give the most helpful insights? Why?

3. Using the numerical-correspondence method, determine which Tagalog forms would be most difficult for a speaker of English to learn.

4. If you were teaching the English pronouns to a class of Tagalog speakers, how would you distribute the drill time among the different forms?

---

*Material for this problem was generously provided by Clifford H. Prator, Professor Emeritus, University of California, Los Angeles.

137

TABLE 1. Hierarchy of Difficulty Determined by Comparing Form (F), Meaning (M), and Distribution (D)

Number of Differences	Nature of Similarities and Differences		Lexical examples from English (E), Spanish (S), and Arabic (A)	Degree of Difficulty (least to most)
0	Similar in every way	M = M F = F D = D	(E) secretary (A) sikirtera	1
1	Similar in M	M = M F = F D ≠ D	(E) papaya (S) papaya	2
		M = M D = D F ≠ F	(E) hat (S) sombrero	
2		M = M F ≠ F D ≠ D	(E) water (S) agua	3
1	Similar in F, giving rise to false assumptions	F = F M = M D ≠ D	(E) hoosegow (S) juzgado	4
		F = F D = D M ≠ M	(E) direction (S) dirección	
2		F = F M ≠ M D ≠ D	(E) cypher (A) sifr	5

TABLE 2. Hierarchy of Difficulty Determined by Numerical Correspondences between Mother Tongue (M) and Target Language (T)

Category and Subcategory	Correspondence M	Correspondence T	Grammatical Examples with Arabic (A) or Spanish (S) as M, and English (E) as T	Task of Student	Degree of Difficulty (least to most)
I. Equivalent					
1. Parallel	1	1	(S) *cuando* (E) *when*	Recognize parallelism between two forms	1
2. Reinterpreted	1	1	(S) first person pronoun *yo* (E) pronoun *I*	Realize parallelism is deceptive	4
II. Underdifferentiated					
1. Absent	1	0	(A) vocative particle *ya* (E) no equivalent	Learn to get along without a form	3
2. Coalesced	2(+)	1	(A) *nabih* and *nabiha* (E) *intelligent*	Learn to equate two or more forms with one	2
III. Overdifferentiated					
1. New	0	1	(S) usually no equivalent (E) pronoun *it*	Learn meaning and function of new form(s)	5
2. Split	1	2(+)	(A) demonstrative *di* (and *da*) (E) *this* and *that*	Learn to divide the functions of a familiar form between two or more new ones	6

B. Czech Phonology*

(An asterisk is used as is traditional in linguistics to indicate an "ungram-matical" form.)

Czech

lev	[lef]	* [lev]
mraz	[mras]	* [mraz]
hrad	[hrat]	* [hrad]
muz	[mus]	* [muz]
dub	[dup]	* [dub]
zeg	[zek]	* [zeg]

English

	Abe	[eib]		ape	[eip]
	leave	[liv]		leaf	[lif]
	his	[hɪz]		hiss	[hɪs]
	mud	[məd]		mutt	[mət]
(v)	house	[hauz]	(n)	house	[haus]

1. On the basis of the differences between Czech and English what predictions would you make about (1) the errors the Czech speaker might make in English and (2) the errors that the English speaker might make in Czech?

2. Why would (1) the Czech speaker and (2) the English speaker make their respective errors? That is, what must each speaker learn to do that they aren't doing? If you were the teacher what would you teach the Czech student and the English student?

Now consider the following additional data:

Czech		English	
zpivat	[spivat]	eggs	[ɛgz]
divka	[difka]	words	[wərdz]
lečba	[lejba]	clasps	[klæsps]
kdo	[gdo]	reads	[ridz]
všedni	[fšedni]	heats	[hits]
sbirka	[zbirka]	gagged	[gægd]
k Brnu	[gbrnu]	walked	[wɔkt]

*Adapted from data provided by Marya Donch, as a graduate student in the Department of Linguistics, University of Minnesota.

3. On the basis of the data, both Czech and English have a similar rule. State this rule and state the difference in the direction in which it applies in each language.

4. What mistakes would you expect English speakers to make? Why? What mistakes would you expect Czech speakers to make? Why?

C. Egyptian Arabic Consonant Clusters*

1.	katab	he wrote
2.	katab gawaab	he wrote a letter
3.	makatabš	he didn't write
4.	makatabšigawaab	he didn't write a letter
5.	katabt	I wrote
6.	makatabtiš	I didn't write
7.	katabtigawaab	I wrote a letter
8.	fasl	class
9.	faslikbiir	large class
10.	kitaab	book
11.	kitaab kibiir	large book
	*katabigawaab	*faslkbiir
	*katabtgawaab	*makatabiš
	*makatabts	*kitaabikbiir
	*fasil	*kitaabkbiir

Arabic Errors in English (marked ** to symbolize learner errors)

**handiball	handball
**transilation	translation
**ispilendid	splendid
**askiBill	ask Bill
**askid	asked
**cardiboard	cardboard
**iksitrinzik	extrinsic

1. What simple phonological rule will account for the well formed consonant clusters in Egyptian Arabic, as well as the Arabic errors in English?

*Data provided by Mushira Eid, as a graduate student in the Department of Linguistics, University of Minnesota.

Error Analysis

Introduction

The collecting of errors made by second language learners is not new. Experienced classroom teachers have long used student errors to guide their teaching emphasis; and we all have our favorite anecdotes about student errors. Lee went one step further. He advocated both systematic and global collections of errors ("mistakes" as he refers to them) from different student populations, arguing that the more teachers know about the problems their learners face the more effectively they can guide them over the rough spots. His article was a precursor to many current claims on the efficacy of error collection and classification for classroom use.

Lee's underlying assumptions about why students make errors are based squarely within the CA paradigm. (As he points out, a certain teaching point may be a mountain for speakers of some languages and a molehill for speakers of other languages.) Yet he does not advocate contrastive analysis. On the contrary, he argues that the most important factor is not the comparison of two languages with its consequent predictions, but rather close observation of students and their learning problems as evidenced by their errors. His goal is to use actual student production difficulties as a basis for planning the time and emphasis to be placed on particular teaching points, as well as their sequencing.

The short excerpt by George comes from a book which ought to be better known among language teachers. It was written long before the field of error analysis (EA) was conceived of and yet contains many ideas current today. Here, for example, we have his development of the "black box" concept, as it applies to second language learners, in which he lays out some of the reasons why input to the learner should not be expected to be the same as output from the learner, i.e., that we should expect errors to occur. His claim that errors arise from the same internal processes as nonerrors is discussed at great length in the Corder and Selinker articles, although from a different perspective.

Corder's interest in error production stems from his proposal to extend the Chomskyan innateness hypothesis regarding first language learning by children to second language learning by adults. No one, he points out, has provided evidence that these are fundamentally different processes. And just as errors in first language production provide evidence for the development of that language in the child, so also should such errors in the second language production of the adult. Corder also offers two terminological clarifications of importance: the mistake/error distinction and the input/intake distinction.

Selinker, in contrast to Corder, claims that the majority of second language learners activate a latent psychological structure which is quite independent of the innate mechanisms activated by children to acquire their first language and which, furthermore, is quite likely to resemble other intellectual (but nonlanguage) psychological structures. He claims that five central processes exist in this latent psychological structure: language transfer, transfer of training, strategies of second language learning, strategies of second language communication, overgeneralization. These together influence the provisional grammar of the learner (which he calls *interlanguage*) and are the source of fossilized errors in the learners' production.

Complementing the three previous highly theoretical articles, Richards presents a large number of errors typically produced by learners from many linguistic backgrounds, grouped into classes on the basis of form and grammatical category. He claims that these errors cannot be attributed to interlingual confusions and discusses them in terms of four intralingual error categories. An experienced teacher will recognize many of these errors instantly. They provide convincing evidence that learner reorganization of the target language input is significant.

The next two articles provide illuminating illustrations of the usefulness of error analysis of specific groups. Each of them includes a wealth of information about learners of English: in the Dušková study, Czech learners; and in the Gatbonton, French learners. These studies are far from being duplicates of one another, however. Dušková, for example, focuses on grammatical and lexical errors in writing. Gatbonton is concerned with transitional stages through which learners progress, with a focus on phonetic variability and how it is to be accounted for. Gatbonton reports error frequencies as functions of total use, providing information on how the production of a specific error fits into the period of acquisition of the construction in which it occurs. Dušková, in addition, presents some discussion of the problems in the analysis and interpretation of errors that is of particular value to those wishing to evaluate other EAs or to attempt an EA themselves.

This section closes not with a cautionary tale but certainly with two cautionary articles, both of which stress problems involved in error analysis. The Stenson article presents sets of errors which appear with some frequency in the classroom but do not fall into the categories so far discussed in the literature. Clearly, these *induced* errors provide challenges to the classroom teacher, but just as clearly, they provide problems in analysis for the researcher. Schachter and Celce-Murcia take a critical look at the field of error analysis, pointing out what they think are the major problems in the current body of error analysis literature.

While none of these authors has advocated abandoning EA, certainly their message is clear: an error analysis, if it is to be of lasting value to the profession, must be carried out with all possible rigor and its results interpreted with due caution.

The Linguistic Context of Language Teaching

W. R. Lee

No language is ever studied in a linguistic vacuum. The environment of learning includes at least that same language or another, and may include several languages, audible and perhaps visible on every side. When a second language is attempted, it is usually in an environment of the learner's first language, acquired as a child, so that all around him are linguistic patterns whose tyranny he is struggling to escape. And even in a community using the second language he needs, a learner has his home-language habits to combat.

D. Y. Morgan, in a recent article (*English Language Teaching* 10, no. 3 [1956]), divided English language teaching into the three categories of presentation, practice, and remedial work, and argued that the last of these can be well planned only by basing it on an inquiry into pupils' mistakes. He is undoubtedly right on the latter point, and has shown too that diagnosis of this kind can be readily made. The merit of such an approach is that we get down to the pupils' level and see some of the difficulties through their eyes. So doing, we are constantly reminded that it is not simple English we teach, but English to Spaniards, English to Chinese, English to Poles, to Nigerians, to Pakistanis, to Brazilians, to Finns, as well, of course, as to pupils of various ages, attitudes, and capacities. It is clear that English, quite apart from the local features which characterize it in different parts of the English-speaking world, appears variously against various linguistic backgrounds. Certain characteristics are thrown into relief in some countries, and other characteristics in others, and this because of contrast with the first language, that which the pupils speak at home. For speakers of Serbo-Croat or Czech, English is a language of several past tenses and puzzling article usage; but these are not a headache to Spanish or Hungarian pupils. Among the problems facing Turkish learners are the English word order patterns, so different from their own; yet word order is much less of a stumbling block to the Italians or Dutch. Speakers of tone languages, such as Chinese, have to

Reprinted with permission from *English Language Teaching Journal* 11 (1957): 77–85, published by Oxford University Press and the British Council.

pay special attention to the very different English use of voice pitch, while some nationalities lose sleep over rhythmic patterns. And although certain features of English are no doubt everywhere fairly easy or fairly hard to acquire, the difficulty of each of these also has, in accordance with the pupils' home language, its varying degrees. In fact, one country's linguistic mountain, to be patiently climbed, is another's molehill, to be lightly skipped over. Mistakes analyses based on adequate material show clearly what is most troublesome for the learners concerned and thus where they most need support.

However, it is not only remedial work which can be guided thus, but the whole of a language course, and at every stage. Writing is the obvious basis for analysis, but mistakes in speaking can be noted too, especially by a trained phonetician and with the help of a tape recorder. A broadly based and representative collection of spoken and written errors, sufficiently classified, may help to determine several things—the scope and nature of pronunciation teaching, the time given to practice with certain structures, the time given to practice with certain expressions and words, and even the order in which these structures, expressions, and words are introduced.

Let us look first at the problem of pronunciation teaching. It is important during early language lessons not to let the temperature of interest drop too low. "More haste, less speed" is a good enough motto up to a point, but we must also remember that a snail's pace can lead to boredom. Interest is a strong driving force at any stage: its value at the beginning is enormous. It is necessary to push on, to get somewhere and to let the pupils see they have got somewhere. They should be able to answer and ask simple questions, using the present continuous tense, and deal with simple requests and commands, before the initial impetus is exhausted. A new current will then carry them along, arising from interest and pride in their linguistic acquirement. To begin with, however, there is or should be an orderly presentation of commonly used words in commonly used structures. But if an oral method is used, the majority of the basic sounds of the language will occur within the first two or three lessons. Progress in the meaningful use of sentences in situations real or contrived cannot safely be delayed for a high polish to be put on pronunciation. It will necessarily be a little awkward and rough in places, and the risk of minor faults becoming a habit has courageously to be taken. This does not at all mean that pronunciation cannot methodically be dealt with.[1] Words and structures which have already been introduced furnish the material for short, regular, and intensive practices involving isolation and comparison not only of sounds, but of rhythmic and intonation patterns, juncture patterns, and in fact of any devices capable of changing the meaning of what is said. At least five minutes of a forty-minute period can be regularly spared for speech work of this kind, over and above incidental correction. A comprehensive review of the phonetic material is unnecessary and indeed digressive. Attention should be focused on the difficult points, and those which cause little bother may be left, more or less, to look after themselves. And this is where mistakes analyses come in. For if these analyses are based on the speech of enough learners, and of a sufficient variety of learners, of the same linguistic background, they enable a teacher to prophesy. Forewarned is forearmed. Mistakes can, of course, be dealt with as a course proceeds, without the prior help of any analysis; but it is preferable to know beforehand what is likely to happen and so to be prepared for the necessity of coping with it. If English [oː] is going to be made too much like English [ou], for instance, as when *George saw Nora at the ball* resembles [dʒoudʒ sou nourə ət ðə boul] (a common mispronunciation among Russians), the obvious thing is to be ready to make it more like [aː], and to make in advance its occurrence in texts used. If learners are likely to want to put the stress and pitch-fall too early in sentences demanding a stressed pitch-fall near their end, such as I *shan't go oftener than* ⭨ *necessary* (where ⭨ *oftener than necessary* would be an unusual pattern), the error can be held at arm's length if the teacher is aware of this tendency and prepared to impose the suitable pattern, perhaps by exaggerating it in some way, on the learners' melodic ear. If, again, it is known that glottal stops may be added to syllables which should begin smoothly with a vowel sound, more trouble can be taken to demonstrate the fact of "linking," and additional phrases to impress the point can be prepared. There are many ways in which a teacher's knowledge of the language strains under which his pupils labor and of the kind of mistakes they are liable to make during a course or even a single lesson can influence his attitude and teaching plans. It is chiefly a matter of knowing the pupils better beforehand, at least in one respect, so that less time and energy have to be spent on getting to know them at the moment of instruction. Instead of discovering at the last minute their tendencies to err, and so in a sense following in the pupils' tracks, we are ahead of the pupils and thus able to lead them better.

Teaching Prague University students English just after the war, and having then an elementary acquaintance with Czech, I noted down and grouped over twenty-five typical errors in their pronunciation.[2] Weekly contact with about three hundred students enabled me to make this collection at odd moments as we went along. The grouping was somewhat rough-and-ready too, yet it could form the basis of a program of ear and speech-organ training, one essential means to the improvement of language-hearing and language-speaking skill.[3]

As with pronunciation, so with other aspects of the language. Once an adequate analysis of errors has been made, this can and indeed must influence the whole course. About eleven years ago I compiled a record of two thousand mistakes occurring in Czechoslovak students' essays. The essay themes were various and of their own choosing, the students (about seventy on this occasion) from whose work the mistakes were gathered were picked out haphazard, and all the mistakes they made were included. Wishing to apply the result of this inquiry at once, I hurriedly grouped them into a few categories, e.g., wrong punctuation (14.4 percent of all errors), misuse or omission of articles (13.6 percent), misspellings (13.5 percent), non-English constructions and wrong word order (11 percent), wrong use of tenses (3.4 percent), and so on. In the light of further language study, I should probably make a somewhat different analysis of this material today and enlarge the collection of mistakes, basing it on a greater number of learners. Nevertheless the immediate purpose was served: I was in a better position to decide how teaching time should be spent. There is no need, of course, to act upon the results of such investigation slavishly. Many would treat punctuation and spelling mistakes in the way I did, as on the whole less serious than mistakes with, for instance, articles and prepositions. But at least one gets a fairly clear picture of what the major difficulties are. It may be that with some classes of (say) French or German pupils, literal translations from the home language, such as *We are here since two hours* (= We have been here since two o'clock) are not one of the commonest types of mistake: there is no need, therefore, to prepare for extensive demonstrations or repeated practice of the correct pattern. An analysis of mistakes made by some West African learners would probably show a need for ample practice of word order in direct and indirect speech, while Turkish learners' mistakes reveal that word order in general required particular attention. With Slavonic pupils, weaknesses on the articles and some relative clauses, as well as on comma usage, would all be shown up in their degree of importance by mistakes analyses, and so the teacher is the better prepared for teaching the points involved to other pupils speaking the same first language.

The behavior of words, and of invariable or slightly variable expressions, in so far as it can be separated from the behavior involved in the chief syntactic patterns, is still another aspect of language. What has been said about the analysis of other types of error applies here too. The frequency with which a word occurs in English is not the only thing of importance about it: there may be no word in the learners' language more than roughly corresponding, or this word may associate with others in a manner quite different from the English word. Choice of vocabulary with which to "operate" the basic patterns, however, is commonly determined more by frequency or by thoughts of its immediate use in classroom situations than by considerations such as these, at least in a printed course meant for use anywhere. Study of the mistakes made by speakers of any other language in using common English words will suggest the inclinations they have to fight against. To take a simple instance, Czechs are liable to say *The news are good* and *Christmas are coming*—the Czech words for "news" and "Christmas" go with a verbal form commonly felt to be plural. Knowing this, a teacher of English to Czechs will be ready to give these words special treatment, and may perhaps postpone using them.[4] Word-mistake study helps a teacher to see which English words are best suited for the "operation" of patterns: possibly those which give difficulty may be avoided for a time.

Thus mistakes analyses may influence the order in which vocabulary is introduced. Can they also help to determine the similar ordering of structures? This may seem unlikely. It is mainly a question of the usefulness of those structures, dependent in part on their frequency of occurrence in English and in part on their capacity for accretion.[5] It is necessary to keep dissimilar structures apart: that is to say, not to introduce them to the pupils simultaneously nor until those already taught have had a chance to establish themselves in the learner's newly acquired speech habits. The word order patterns of *This is a chair, Is this a chair?*, and *What is this?* are an example.[6] If we teach these question types too soon, there is a risk of muddle, resulting perhaps in *What this is?*, a pattern which may be hard to get rid of. Nevertheless the risk is slight where in the learners' language there are similar very commonly used patterns, with the equivalents of *This is* and *Is this* interchangeable in the same way. This change in English is then no problem. In German, for instance, there is *Das ist ein Stuhl, Ist das ein Stuhl?*, and *Was ist das?*, and in Spanish *(Esto) es una silla, ¿Es esto una silla?, and ¿Qué es esto?*. On the other hand, in Czech there is *To je stůl* and *Je to stůl?*, but commonly *Co to je?*. Czech learners of English thus tend to say *What it is?*, but this mistake is much less usual among Spanish and German learners. With the latter we need not, therefore, so carefully space out these patterns to avoid confusion. Again, learners from some countries will readily take to the tense change in converting direct to indirect speech (He said, "*I am coming*"—*He said he was coming*), while elsewhere this will call for cautiously graded treatment. Nevertheless, on the whole it is not so much the sequence in which structures are taught that mistake analyses are likely to influence as the speed with which some of them are taught.

Mistakes in the use of sounds, words, and structures may thus be usefully collected and examined, and mistakes analyses at each of these levels can be applied to language teaching. We are also concerned, however, with stages of achievement in learning the language. On what stage should a mistake analysis be based? Do we require to know only the errors which the class we are teaching is likely to make? Or is it helpful to have an analysis of more advanced learners' errors as well?

It is plain that a whole series of analyses, based on various stages of achievement from elementary to advanced, is desirable. Light shed on the immediate task in hand is of prime interest, and the teacher will look firstly for an analysis of errors made by pupils like his own. Analyses made at more advanced stages, however, can also help, showing as they do what types of error tend to persist and which therefore demand skillful avoiding action or remedial treatment.

Such analyses are of use to both inexperienced and experienced teachers. Previous experience with similar pupils may have given a teacher some of the knowledge a particular analysis yields; but few have had experience so broad as to be able to forecast the errors of any type of class, even in a single language area. Mistakes analyses, especially valuable to the inexperienced, can also be a great help to those faced with a grade of pupil they have not taught before, or pupils speaking a different first language. Even a teacher of great experience, or one to whom a particular type of class is not new, may welcome a systematic statement of difficulties, well illustrated by examples. It is a valuable guide when planning a course of lessons. Without it a teacher is less aware of the task which confronts him, and so plans less effectively.

Through an examination of learners' mistakes a teacher may enter more fully into the environment of teaching and put on, as it were, his pupil's linguistic spectacles. This should enable him to see his way more clearly. An obvious question to ask, however, is whether there is not a more effective manner of looking at things from the learners' viewpoint. As we have already noticed, many learners' difficulties reflect features of the home language. Would a knowledge of this language not be a better pair of spectacles to put on? Are we perhaps not doing things by halves in examining mistakes only? The question can at once be restated, since in most parts of the world the majority of those teaching English will already speak the home language of their pupils. The problem for them, on the contrary, is whether to bother about mistakes analyses. However, a substantial minority of teachers do not speak the learners' language, and have to ask themselves if they can manage well enough without it.

At first sight it would appear that they can. What concerns us chiefly, after all, is the encounter between the two languages. Attention should be focused, it seems, on the struggle of second language usages against those of the first. If knowledge of the learners' language enables one only to forecast mistakes, why bother to acquire it? Those who speak it, on the other hand, would seem to gain something from a study of mistakes, for this involves direct concentration on what is relevant and the reduction of guesswork to a minimum.

To guess at probable types of error from a knowledge of the first language only is, without doubt, to take a somewhat far-off view of teaching problems. Thus if a first language has no final [ŋ], as in *laughing,* it is a good guess that another nasal may be substituted, as in ['la:fin]. But this is not at all the same thing as seeing that it *is* substituted, and in what positions. If a language has no vowel sound close to that in *bet* or that in *bat,* but only a sound lying somewhere between the two, it is likely that [e] will often be pronounced too open and [a] too close. Yet it is surely more helpful to see what happens in practice, for other factors may be influential too, such as frequency of occurrence and the nature of the other first language vowels. All such factors could perhaps, in forecasting error types, be taken into consideration, but the forecaster's task would be extremely complicated if they were. Study of the mistakes themselves seems to be a short cut.

There is much to be said on the other side, however. Learners' mistakes must inevitably mean more to those who know something of the learners' language than to those who are ignorant of it. Using mistakes analyses, the latter have a good close-in view of what may go wrong, but can only guess at the underlying causes. Unless these are understood, the teacher is less aware of the connection between one mistake and another, and is thus less well equipped for systematic treatment. Without some knowledge of the learners' language, moreover, it is sometimes hard to see what is meant. Take, for instance, "They have arrived there are three days," a sentence that would never be perpetrated by anyone properly taught. Could it mean "They have arrived and are staying three days"? Nobody would think so who knew a little French, although an extensive context alone might suffice to give the meaning: "They arrived three days ago." Or take a Czech learner's "I don't know already," almost incomprehensible without a knowledge of Czech, which makes it clear that the speaker wanted to say, "I no longer know." Lastly, a teacher ignorant of the home language cannot use features of it as starting points in instruction. It is an advantage to be proficient at making the sounds, for some of them may be modifiable into English sounds. At other levels too it is desirable to know what there is or is not to work from. Teaching English tense usage to learners whose language has only one past tense form is apt to perplex a teacher unaware of the fact, but errors in several tenses are seen to be linked by one who is so aware. Translation may be excluded from the teaching method: nevertheless it is wise to look closely at the use of single past tense forms in varying contexts, if only to discover that there is little support in the learners' language for what one is trying to teach. Again, at word level there can be a chance similarity between the English and a first language word of different meaning, as with *cigar* and Turkish *sigara* (cigarette), *clinic* and Czech *klinika* (teaching hospital), *station* and Spanish *estación* (season); if the teacher knows such things he can guard the better against misunderstanding.

Knowledge of the learners' language is of practical teaching use in many ways, of which a few only have been illustrated. Yet there is a broader and possibly more powerful argument in favor of acquiring such knowledge, for the evident possession of it awakens the pupils' sympathies and reassures them that the teacher is "on their side." Few learners are not pleased at the accurate, if occasional, use by the teacher of their own tongue; and a little goes a long way. It suggests at least that he is trying to see things from their viewpoint. It makes clear that the learners' language is not looked down upon or regarded as an irrelevant nuisance.

Both procedures are thus to be recommended, a study of the first language and also of characteristic mistakes in learning the second. Advanced knowledge of a language is not necessarily accompanied, of course, by the ability to analyze it. Unfortunately there are many English-speaking teachers who assume that because they speak English they are well qualified to teach it: their ideas on the phonetic and grammatical makeup of English are sometimes extremely naïve. Non-English-speaking teachers may have some similarly crude notions of their own language. They in particular, since most of them are permanently occupied with English teaching in one language area, should make as careful an analytical study of that language as of the one they teach. Otherwise the comparisons they try to draw between the two languages will be hesitant and often invalid.

What cooperation can there be between the "local" teacher, possibly born and brought up among the kind of pupils he teaches, and the teacher from an English-speaking country, born and brought up among those who speak English alone? Each has his strong suit—the former an expert acquaintance with the first language, the latter, a special knowledge of the second. The most obvious form of mutual assistance they can give is to improve each other's grasp of their own language. If both have had a measure of linguistic training, they can usefully cooperate also in the collection and analysis of learners' mistakes. By referring the learners' speech or writing to his own ideas on acceptable English, the one discovers and describes these mistakes. The other looks at the mistakes and, referring them to his experience of the learners' home language, describes them, if possible, in terms of failure to resist the attraction of its phonetic, lexical, syntactic, or other forms. Every mistake is thus seen from two angles, and the resulting account of major types of mistake will show clearly, in the context of any language area, what is most difficult in English for the learners and what in the home language for the teachers. An English-speaking teacher can himself, of course, excavate in the home language to uncover the causes of mistakes; but the "local" teacher seems the better qualified to do so. Similarly the "local" teacher may be able adequately to list and describe the mistakes themselves; but on the whole this appears to be the Englishman's job. Overlapping of the two activities is nevertheless essential if both parties are to get the maximum benefit from this work. Such a project for joint research is likely to have a practical outcome and to be worth doing anywhere, but especially where the rivalry between "local" and "English" teachers is more obvious than the cooperation.

Notes

1. Nor does it mean that attempts at grading the course phonetically are valueless. Certainly some of the more awkward successions of sounds can be postponed, and intonations other than the simplest can also wait (as they do in A. S. Hornby's *Oxford Progressive English* [London: University Press, 1954], for example). However, it is primarily words and structures which are graded.
2. This sounds a large number but, even so, little enough account was taken of rhythm and intonation, perhaps more important for intelligibility than "sounds." On the other hand, several minor mistakes were included.
3. To classify many of the vowel mispronunciations I made use of Professor Jones's cardinal vowel diagram. It can easily be carried in the mind's eye, and the relationship between the tongue positions of the vowels one is concerned with, i.e., the vowel one is trying to teach, the nearest vowel in the learner's language, and the learner's attempt, can be readily pictured. It seems to me a most serviceable tool in an English teacher's equipment. However, a good tool calls for a trained user. (Lip position is also important for some vowel sounds, but can easily be observed.)

4. D. Abercrombie (*English Language Teaching* 3, no. 7 [1949]:171) points out the undesirability of introducing *head* and *hand* very early in a course intended for Greeks: "the words sound to him identical—and his resentment is increased by discovering an unexpected problem of meaning in the word *hand.*"

5. See W. F. Mackey's "What to Look for in a Method: (II) Grading," *English Language Teaching* 8, no. 2 [1954]:48.

6. The same intonation pattern *can*, of course, be used in each.

A Model of Error Production

H. V. George

When a recurring unwanted form appears in a learner's production of spoken or written English, we may assume that it is the result of a process or processes. In other words, the error has been learned, and its presence, therefore, is explainable on the same grounds as the presence of wanted forms.

A learner is exposed to the experience of English from his teacher and from his course book: this is the input to the learner. The learner produces spoken or written English: this is the output from the learner. An error has been defined as "an unwanted form." If the unwanted form has appeared as an independent part of the learner's experience, e.g., in the English of other teachers or of local speakers, there is no difficulty of explanation of its presence. However, this is a return to a double standard. It is when the learner's output includes an unwanted form which was not part of the input that we may usefully speak of an error. When this happens, we have to be interested in intermediate processes and intermediate mechanisms for them. These processes and mechanisms, not being themselves observable, are only indirectly available to investigation. It is by observation of the differences between input and output that we deduce their nature and manner of functioning.

For many years, electronic engineers have used just such sets of observations to deduce the characteristics of a device. By altering and measuring input and output voltage and current parameters, the engineer can determine the nature and efficiency of the device. Since the device does not itself undergo physical examination, it is, from this point of view a "black box," and is so called.

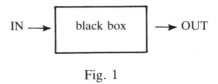

IN → black box → OUT

Fig. 1

This simplified diagram represents a useful model for the study of errors.

Reprinted from *Common Errors in Language Learning* (Rowley, Mass.: Newbury House, 1972), pages 4–8, by permission of the publisher and the author.

What must there be in the black box, i.e., the learner's brain? Since there is a time gap between input and output, there must be storage of information, or memory. However, simple observation tells us that the black box does not store the total input: features are selected for storage. If the learner's selection of input features is erratic or misguided, e.g., through intermittent attention, we can expect a defective output. But if selection of input, without being particularly erratic, does not conform to the expectation of the course designer, the consequence is an output which was unpredicted and probably unwanted. Storage implies storage procedures, and storage procedures themselves must affect selection. If information presented for admission as input appears likely to be easy to store according to established procedures, it will be more acceptable than information which gives the impression of being likely to prove difficult to store.

If storage procedures are inadequate, or if there is muddled classification or organization of material for storage, we may thus expect an imperfect output in two ways, indirectly through impaired selection, and directly.

Information is usually stored provisionally. If there is no, or only slight subsequent call for it, it fades.[1]

Though information may be stored, inefficient search techniques may make access difficult, so that persistence seems uneconomical and, in order that some output is achieved under time pressure, items are substituted for others in a makeshift manner.

Finally, output mechanisms themselves work with variable efficiency.

Figure 1 can be developed (see fig. 2). The input to the learner's black box is the output from other black boxes, in particular, the course designer's and the teacher's. Let us make things convenient by considering these to be one person. Black box 2 then represents the learner's black box and black box 1 the course designer/teacher's, whose output is the course. The input to black box 1 may be called "the English language." Obviously, selection and organization are functions of black box 1, and if procedures here are inadequate the output from the course designer will not be the optimum input to the learner. Here is the developed diagram:

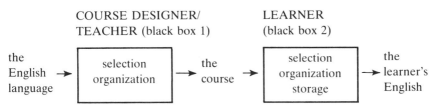

Fig. 2

To the model shown in figure 2, further additions can be made.

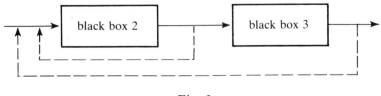

Fig. 3

In figure 3, black box 2 is the learner's, and black box 3 is that of any person reacting to the output of black box 2, i.e., to the learner's written or spoken English. This figure shows that an output from one black box may be an input, to itself as well as to other black boxes. That part of the output which is received as an input gives information which may cause the black box to make changes in its further selection, storage, or search procedures. The perceived effect of an output on another person may also lead to changes in these procedures. Such changes are, of course, "correction," self-correction, and correction prompted by the reactions of others. All correction may be thought of as the result of feedback of information about an output.

Figure 3 shows black box 3 effecting feedback of information to the learner (black box 2). However, the teacher/course designer may himself use the learner's output as a source of information leading to modification of his own output to the learner—or to subsequent learners. To show this, still another addition to figure 2 is needed (see fig. 4).

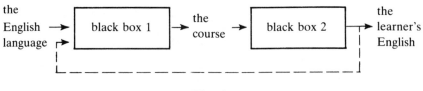

Fig. 4

When the learner's English is different from "the English languages," when the learner's output includes unwanted forms, one assumes that selection and organization processes are responsible.

Responsibility may lie in either black box. Many course designers and teachers take great care over their selection and organization of the teaching material, then assume that their work substitutes for selection and organization on the part of the learner, that is to say, that no further selection and organization will take place. They attribute to the learner only the simplest learning processes. When unwanted forms occur, having confidence in their own selection and organization, they then attribute the learner's "errors" to inadequate registration of the wanted forms, and prescribe "remedial drills."

If, on the other hand, we accept the possibility that the learner's selection and organization may be responsible for the appearance of unwanted forms, we must admit failure on the part of the course designer to predict the appearance of these forms, and in so doing admit that his selection and organization were in this respect themselves defective. Treated as feedback information (fig. 4), the occurrence of an unwanted form should lead to a modification of the course designer's selection and organization of his material.

Comparison of learners' input and output gives the impression of a general tendency to simplify the input. This impression might seem to confirm the assumption of a selection means and procedure. However, an additional assumption is needed, namely, that the black box is by nature an efficiency-seeking organism. Otherwise, selection might reduce the input without necessarily simplifying it, for selection itself could, of course, be random.

It seems reasonable to suppose that black box selection is in terms of significance to the learner. Significance itself must initially be related to regularity in repetition: occurrences showing no pattern of repetition are, in effect, random occurrences. Efficiency seeking implies, too, a tendency to match degree of attention and effort to learn with likelihood of opportunity for use of what is being offered for learning. That is, an efficiency-seeking organism uses past experience of good or poor return for effort to set up patterns of selection, so that further input is actively scanned for significance according to previous experience of effort and reward. In this way, though regularity in repetition remains an essential criterion for selection, previous patterns of acceptance and rejection intervene strongly to determine at each moment what is accepted as significant or rejected as insignificant.

This first elaboration of the observation that selection operates to simplify input explains generally how one reaches a concept of efficiency seeking which accounts both for the native learner's eventual acceptance of features of the mother tongue and for the foreign learner's nonacceptance of the same features. For a more detailed explanation, one must turn to communication theory.

Note

1. For a reasonable contemporary model, see R. M. Shiffrin and R. C. Atkinson, "Storage and Retrieval Processes in Long Term Memory," *Psychological Review* 76, no. 2 (March, 1969).

The Significance of Learners' Errors

S. P. Corder

When one studies the standard works on the teaching of modern languages it comes as a surprise to find how cursorily the authors deal with the question of learners' errors and their correction. It almost seems as if they are dismissed as a matter of no particular importance, as possible annoying, distracting, but inevitable by-products of the process of learning a language about which the teacher should make as little fuss as possible. It is of course true that the application of linguistic and psychological theory to the study of language learning added a new dimension to the discussion of errors; people now believed they had a principled means for accounting for these errors, namely that they were the result of interference in the learning of a second language from the habits of the first language. The major contribution of the linguist to language teaching was seen as an intensive contrastive study of the systems of the second language and the mother tongue of the learner; out of this would come an inventory of the areas of difficulty which the learner would encounter and the value of this inventory would be to direct the teacher's attention to these areas so that he might devote special care and emphasis in his teaching to the overcoming, or even avoiding, of these predicted difficulties. Teachers have not always been very impressed by this contribution from the linguist for the reason that their practical experience has usually already shown them where these difficulties lie and they have not felt that the contribution of the linguist has provided them with any significantly new information. They noted for example that many of the errors with which they were familiar were not predicted by the linguist anyway. The teacher has been on the whole, therefore, more concerned with *how* to deal with these areas of difficulty than with the simple identification of them, and here has reasonably felt that the linguist has had little to say to him.

In the field of methodology there have been two schools of thought in respect of learners' errors. Firstly the school which maintains that if we were to achieve a perfect teaching method the errors would never be

First published in *IRAL* 5, no. 4 (1967):161–70. Reprinted by permission of the publisher and the author.

committed in the first place, and therefore the occurrence of errors is merely a sign of the present inadequacy of our teaching techniques. The philosophy of the second school is that we live in an imperfect world and consequently errors will always occur in spite of our best efforts. Our ingenuity should be concentrated on techniques for dealing with errors after they have occurred.

Both these points of view are compatible with the same theoretical standpoint about language and language learning, psychologically behaviorist and linguistically taxonomic. Their application to language teaching is known as the audiolingual or fundamental skills method.

Both linguistics and psychology are in a state at the present time of what Chomsky has called "flux and agitation" (Chomsky 1966). What seemed to be well-established doctrine a few years ago is now the subject of extensive debate. The consequence of this for language teaching is likely to be far reaching and we are perhaps only now beginning to feel its effects. One effect has been perhaps to shift the emphasis away from a preoccupation with *teaching* toward a study of *learning*. In the first instance this has shown itself as a renewed attack upon the problem of the acquisition of the mother tongue. This has inevitably led to a consideration of the question whether there are any parallels between the processes of acquiring the mother tongue and the learning of a second language. The usefulness of the distinction between acquisition and learning has been emphasised by Lambert (1966) and the possibility that the latter may benefit from a study of the former has been suggested by Carroll (1966).

The differences between the two are obvious but not for that reason easy to explain: that the learning of the mother tongue is inevitable, whereas, alas, we all know that there is no such inevitability about the learning of a second language; that the learning of the mother tongue is part of the whole maturational process of the child, whilst learning a second language normally begins only after the maturational process is largely complete; that the infant starts with no overt language behavior, while in the case of the second language learner such behavior, of course, exists; that the motivation (if we can properly use the term in the context) for learning a first language is quite different from that for learning a second language.

On examination it becomes clear that these obvious differences imply nothing about the *processes* that take place in the learning of first and second language. Indeed the most widespread hypothesis about how languages are learned, which I have called behaviorist, is assumed to apply in both circumstances. These hypotheses are well enough known not to require detailing here, and so are the objections to them. If then these hypotheses about language learning are being questioned and new hypotheses being set up to account for the process of child language acquisition, it would seem reasonable to see how far they might also apply to the learning of a second language.

Within this new context the study of errors takes on a new importance and will I believe contribute to a verification or rejection of the new hypothesis.

This hypothesis states that a human infant is born with an innate predisposition to acquire language; that he must be exposed to language for the acquisition process to start; that he possesses an internal mechanism of unknown nature which enables him from the limited data available to him to construct a grammar of a particular language. How he does this is largely unknown and is the field of intensive study at the present time by linguists and psychologists. Miller (1964) has pointed out that if we wished to create an automaton to replicate a childs performance, the order in which it tested various aspects of the grammar could only be decided after careful analysis of the successive stages of language acquisition by human children. The first steps therefore in such a study are seen to be a longitudinal description of a child's language throughout the course of its development. From such a description it is eventually hoped to develop a picture of the procedures adopted by the child to acquire language (McNeill 1966).

The application of this hypothesis to second language learning is not new and is essentially that proposed fifty years ago by H. E. Palmer (1917). Palmer maintained that we were all endowed by nature with the capacity for assimilating language and that this capacity remained available to us in a latent state after acquistion of a primary language. The adult was seen as capable as the child of acquiring a foreign language. Recent work (Lenneberg 1966) suggests that the child who fails for any reason, i.e., deafness, to acquire a primary language before the age of twelve thereafter rapidly loses the capacity to acquire language behavior at all. This finding does not of course carry with it the implication that the language learning capacity of those who have successfully learned a primary language also atrophies in the same way. It still remains to be shown that the process of learning a second language is of a fundamentally different nature from the process of primary acquisition.

If we postulate the same mechanism, then we may also postulate that the procedures or strategies adopted by the learner of the second language are fundamentally the same. The principal feature that then differentiates the two operations is the presence or absence of motivation.

If the acquisition of the first language is a fulfillment of the predisposition to develop language behavior, then the learning of the second language involves the replacement of the predisposition of the infant by some other force. What this consists of is in the context of this paper irrelevant.

Let us say therefore that, *given motivation,* it is inevitable that a human being will learn a second language if he is exposed to the language data. Study of language aptitude does in some measure support such a view since motivation and intelligence appear to be the two principal factors which correlate significantly with achievement in a second language.

I propose therefore as a working hypothesis that some at least of the *strategies* adopted by the learner of a second language are substantially the same as those by which a first language is acquired. Such a proposal does not imply that the course or *sequence* of learning is the same in both cases.

We can now return to the consideration of errors made by learners. When a two-year-old child produces an utterance such as "This mummy chair" we do not normally call this deviant, ill-formed, faulty, incorrect, or whatever. We do not regard it as an error in any sense at all, but rather as a normal childlike communication which provides evidence of the state of his linguistic development at that moment. Our response to that behavior has certain of the characteristics of what would be called "correction" in a classroom situation. Adults have a very strong tendency to repeat and expand the child's utterance in an adult version; something like "Yes, dear, that's Mummy's chair."

No one expects a child learning his mother tongue to produce from the earliest stages only forms which in adult terms are correct or non-deviant. We interpret his "incorrect" utterances as being evidence that he is in the process of acquiring language and indeed, for those who attempt to describe his knowledge of the language at any point in its development, it is the "errors" which provide the important evidence. As Brown and Fraser (1964) point out, the best evidence that a child possesses construction rules is the occurrence of systematic errors, since, when the child speaks correctly, it is quite possible that he is only repeating something that he has heard. Since we do not know what the total input has been we cannot rule out this possibility. It is by reducing the language to a simpler system than it is that the child reveals his tendency to induce rules.

In the case of the second language learner it might be supposed that we *do* have some knowledge of what the input has been, since this is largely within the control of the teacher. Nevertheless it would be wise to introduce a qualification here about the control of input (which is of course what we call the syllabus). The simple fact of presenting a certain linguistic form to a learner in the classroom does not necessarily qualify it for the status of input, for the reason that input is "what goes in" not what is *available* for going in, and we may reasonably suppose that it is the learner who controls this input, or more properly his intake. This may well be determined by the characteristics of his language acquisition mechanism and not by those of the syllabus. After all, in the mother tongue learning situation the data available as input is relatively vast, but it is the child who selects what shall be the input.

Ferguson (1966) has recently made the point that our syllabuses have been based at best upon impressionistic judgements and vaguely conceived theoretical principles where they have had any considered foundations at all. The suggestion that we should take more account of the learner's needs in planning our syllabuses is not new, but has not apparently led to any investigations, perhaps because of the methodological difficulties of determining what the learner's needs might actually be. Carroll (1955) made such a proposal when he suggested it might be worth creating a problem-solving situation for the learner in which he must find, by enquiring either of the teacher or a dictionary appropriate verbal responses for solving the problem. He pointed out that such a hypothesis contained certain features of what was believed to occur in the process of language acquisition by the child.

A similar proposal actually leading to an experiment was made by Mager but not in connection with language teaching (Mager 1961, pp. 405–13); it is nevertheless worth quoting his own words.

> Whatever sequencing criterion is used it is one which the user calls a "logical" sequence. But although there are several schemes by which sequencing can be accomplished and, although it is generally agreed that an effective sequence is one which is meaningful to the learner, the information sequence to be assimilated by the learner is traditionally dictated entirely by the instructor. We generally fail to consult the learner in the matter except to ask him to maximize the effectiveness of whatever sequence we have already decided upon.

He points out as the conclusions he draws from his small scale experiment that the next step would be to determine whether the learner-generated sequence, or, as we might call it, his *built-in syllabus*, is in some way more efficient than the instructor-generated sequence. It seems entirely plausible that it would be so. The problem is to determine whether there exists such a built-in syllabus and to describe it. It is in such an investigation that the study of learners' errors would assume the role it already plays in the study of child language acquisition, since, as has been pointed out, the key concept in both cases is that the learner is using a definite system of language at every point in his development, although it is not the adult system in the one case, nor that of the second language in the other. The learner's errors are evidence of this system and are themselves systematic.

The use of the term systematic in this context implies, of course, that there may be errors which are random, or, more properly, the systematic nature of which cannot be readily discerned. The opposition between systematic and nonsystematic errors is important. We are all aware that in normal adult speech in our native language we are continually committing errors of one sort or another. These, as we have been so often reminded recently, are due to memory lapses, physical states such as tiredness, and psychological conditions such as strong emotion. These are adventitious artifacts of linguist performance and do not reflect a defect in our knowledge of our own language. We are normally immediately aware of them when they occur and can correct them with more or less complete assurance. It would be quite unreasonable to expect the learner of a second language not to exhibit such slips of the tongue (or pen), since he is subject to similar external and internal conditions when performing in his first or second language. We must therefore make a distinction between those errors which are the product of such chance circumstances and those which reveal his underlying knowledge of the language to date, or, as we may call it, his *transitional competence*. The errors of performance will characteristically be unsystematic and the errors of competence, systematic. It will be useful therefore hereafter to refer to errors of performance as *mistakes,* reserving the term *error* to refer to the systematic errors of the learner from which we are able to reconstruct his knowledge of the language to date, i.e., his *transitional competence.*

Mistakes are of no significance to the process of language learning. However the problem of determining what is a learner's mistake and what a learner's error is one of some difficulty and involves a much more sophisticated study and analysis of errors than is usually accorded them.

A learner's errors, then, provide evidence of the system of the language that he is using (i.e., has learned) at a particular point in the course (and it must be repeated that he is using some system, although it is not yet the right system). They are significant in three different ways. First to the teacher, in that they tell him, if he undertakes a systematic analysis, how far towards the goal the learner has progressed and, consequently, what remains for him to learn. Second, they provide to the researcher evidence of how language is learned or acquired, what strategies or procedures the learner is employing in his discovery of the language. Thirdly (and in a sense this is their most important aspect) they are indispensible to the learner himself, because we can regard the making of errors as a device the learner uses in order to learn. It is a way the learner has of testing his hypotheses about the nature of the language he is learning. The making of errors then is a strategy employed both by children acquiring their mother tongue and by those learning a second language.

Although the following dialogue was recorded during the study of child language acquisition (Van Buren 1967) it bears unmistakable similarities to dialogues which are a daily experience in the second language teaching classroom:

Mother: Did Billy have his egg cut up for him at breakfast?
Child: Yes, I showeds him.
Mother: You what?
Child: I showed him.
Mother: You showed him?
Child: I seed him.
Mother: Ah, you saw him.
Child: Yes, I saw him.

Here the child, within a short exchange appears to have tested three hypotheses: one relating to the concord of subject and verb in a past tense, another about the meaning of *show* and *see* and a third about the form of the irregular past tense of *see*. It only remains to be pointed out that if the child had answered *I saw him* immediately, we would have no means of knowing whether he had merely repeated a model sentence or had already learned the three rules just mentioned. Only a longitudinal study of the child's development could answer such a question. It is also interesting to observe the techniques used by the mother to "correct" the child. Only in the case of one error did she provide the correct form herself: *You saw him.* In both the other cases, it was sufficient for her to query the child's utterance in such a form as: *You what?* or *You showed him?* Simple provision of the correct form may not always be the only, or indeed the most effective, form of correction since it bars the way to the learner testing alternative hypotheses. Making a learner try to discover the right form could often be more instructive to both learner and teacher. This is the import of Carroll's proposal already referred to.

We may note here that the utterance of a correct form cannot be taken as proof that the learner has learned the systems which would generate that form in a native speaker, since he may be merely repeating a heard utterance, in which case we should class such behavior, not as language, but in Spolsky's term (Spolsky 1966) "language-like behavior." Nor must we overlook the fact that an utterance which is superficially nondeviant is not evidence of a mastery of the language systems which would generate it in a native speaker since such an utterance must be semantically related to the situational context. The learner who produced "I want to know the English" might have been uttering an unexceptionable sentiment, but it is more likely that he was expressing the wish to know the English language. Only the situational context could show whether his utterance was an error or not.

Although it has been suggested that the strategies of learning a first and second language may be the same, it is nevertheless necessary at this point to posit a distinction between the two. Whilst one may suppose that the first language learner has an unlimited number of hypotheses about the nature of the language he is learning which must be tested (although strong reasons have been put forward for doubting this) we may certainly take it that the task of the second language learner is a simpler one: that the only hypotheses he needs to test are: "Are the systems of the new language the same or different from those of the language I know?" "And if different, what is their nature?" Evidence for this is that a large number, but by no means all, of his errors, are related to the systems of his mother tongue. These are ascribed to interference from the habits of the mother tongue, as it is sometimes expressed. In the light of the new hypotheses they are best not regarded as the persistence of old habits, but rather as signs that the learner is investigating the systems of the new language. Saporta (1966) makes this point clear.

> The internal structure of the [language acquisition] device, i.e., the learner, has gone relatively unexplored except to point out that one of its components is a grammar of the learner's native language. It has generally been assumed that the effect of this component has been inhibitory rather than facilitative. [P. 91]

It will be evident that the position taken here is that the learner's possession of his native language is facilitative and that errors are not to be regarded as signs of inhibition, but simply as evidence of his strategies of learning.

We have been reminded recently of Von Humboldt's statement that we cannot really teach language, we can only create conditions in which it will develop spontaneously in the mind in its own way. We shall never improve our ability to create such favorable conditions until we learn more about the way a learner learns and what his built-in syllabus is. When we do know this (and the learner's errors will, if systematically studied, tell us something about this) we may begin to be more critical of our cherished notions. We may be able to allow the learner's innate strategies to dictate our practice and determine our syllabus; we may learn to adapt ourselves to *his* needs rather than impose upon him *our* preconceptions of *how* he ought to learn, *what* he ought to learn, and *when* he ought to learn it.

References

Brown, R. W., and Fraser, C. "The Acquisition of Syntax." In *The Acquisition of Language Monograph of the Society for Research in Child Development,* edited by Ursula Bellugi and Roger Brown, 29, no. 1 (1964).

Carroll, J. B. *The Study of Language.* Cambridge, Mass.: Harvard University Press, 1955.

————. "Research in Foreign Language Teaching: The Last Five Years." In *Language Teaching: Broader Contexts,* Report of the Northeast Conference on the Teaching of Foreign Languages. 1966.

Chomsky, N. "Linguistics and Philosophy." In *Language Teaching: Broader Contexts,* Report of the Northeast Conference on the Teaching of Foreign Languages. 1966.

Ferguson, C. A. "Research on Language Learning. Applied Linguistics." In *Language Teaching: Broader Contexts,* Report of the Northeast Conference on the Teaching of Foreign Languages. 1966.

Lambert, W. A. "Some Observations on First Language Acquisition and Second Language Learning." Mimeograph, 1966.

Lenneberg, E. H. "The Natural History of Language." In *The Genesis of Language,* edited by F. Smith and G. A. Miller. Cambridge, Mass.: MIT Press, 1966.

McNeill, D. "Developmental Psycholinguistics." In *The Genesis of Language,* edited by F. Smith and G. A. Miller. Cambridge, Mass.: MIT Press, 1966.

Mager, R. F. "On the Sequencing of Instructional Content." *Psychological Reports* 9 (1961):405–12.

Miller, G. A. "Language and Psychology." In *New Directions in the Study of Language,* edited by E. H. Lenneberg. Cambridge, Mass.: MIT Press, 1964.

Palmer, H. E. *The Principles of Language Study.* 1917. Reprinted in *Language and Language Learning,* edited by A. Marckwardt. London: Oxgord University Press, 1964.

Saporta, S. "Applied Linguistics and Generative Grammar." In *Trends in Modern Language Teaching,* edited by A. Valdman. New York: McGraw-Hill, 1966.

Spolsky, B. "A Psycholinguistic Critique of Programmed Foreign Language Instruction." *IRAL* 4, no. 2 (1950):119–29.

Van Buren, P. Personal communication.

Interlanguage

Larry Selinker

Introduction

This article discusses some theoretical preliminaries for researchers concerned with the linguistic aspects of the psychology of second language learning.[1] These theoretical preliminaries are important because without them it is virtually impossible to decide what data are relevant to a psycholinguistic theory of second language learning.

It is also important to distinguish between a teaching perspective and a learning one. As regards the teaching perspective, one might very well write a methodology paper which would relate desired output to known input in a principled way, prescribing what has to be done by the teacher in order to help the learner achieve learning. As regards the learning perspective, one might very well write a paper describing the process of attempted learning of a second language, successful or not: teaching, textbooks, and other external aids would constitute one, but only one, important set of relevant variables. In distinguishing the two perspectives,[2] claims about the internal structures and processes of the learning organism take on a very secondary character in the teaching perspective; such claims may not even be desirable here. But such claims do provide the raison d'être for viewing second language learning from the learning perspective. This paper is written from the learning perspective, regardless of one's failure or success in the attempted learning of a second language.

In the learning perspective, what would constitute the psychologically relevant data of second language learning?[3] My own position is that such data would be those behavioral events which would lead to an understanding of the psycholinguistic structures and processes underlying attempted meaningful performance in a second language. The term *meaningful performance situation* will be used here to refer to the situation

First published in *IRAL* 10, no. 3 (1972):209–31. Reprinted in *Studies in Descriptive Linguistics*, vol. 2, no. 1, *Studies in Contrastive Linguistics and Error Analysis, The Theoretical Background,* edited by D. Nehls, pp. 55–77. Heidelberg: Julius Groos, 1979. Reprinted by permission of the publisher and the author.

where an adult[4] attempts to express meanings, which he may already have, in a language which he is in the process of learning. Since performance of drills in a second language classroom is, by definition, not meaningful performance, it follows that from a learning perspective, such performance is, in the long run, of minor interest. Also, behavior which occurs in experiments using nonsense syllables fits into the same category and for the same reason. Thus, data resulting from these latter behavioral situations are of doubtful relevancy to meaningful performance situations, and thus to a theory of second language learning.

It has long seemed to me that one of our greatest difficulties in establishing a psychology of second language learning which is relevant to the way people actually learn second languages, has been our inability to identify unambiguously the phenomena we wish to study. Out of the great conglomeration of second language behavioral events, what criteria and constructs should be used to establish the class of those events which are to count as relevant in theory construction? One set of these behavioral events which has elicited considerable interest is the regular reappearance in second language performance of linguistic phenomena which were thought to be eradicated in the performance of the learner. A correct understanding of this phenomenon leads to the postulation of certain theoretical constructs, many of which have been set up to deal with other problems in the field. But they also help clarify the phenomenon under discussion. These constructs, in turn, give us a framework within which we can begin to isolate the psychologically relevant data of second language learning. The new perspective which an examination of this phenomenon gives us is thus very helpful both in an identification of relevant data and in the formulation of a psycholinguistic theory of second language learning. The main motivation for this article is the belief that it is particularly in this area that progress can be made at this time.

"Interlanguage" and Latent Structures

Relevant behavioral events in a psychology of second language learning should be made identifiable with the aid of theoretical constructs which assume the major features of the psychological structure of an adult whenever he attempts to understand second language sentences or to produce them. If, in a psychology of second language learning, our goal is explanation of some important aspects of this psychological structure, then it seems to me that we are concerned in large part with how bilinguals make what Weinreich (1953, p. 7) has called "interlingual identifications." In his book *Languages in Contact*, Weinreich discusses—though briefly—the

practical need for assuming in studies of bilingualism that such identifications as that of a phoneme in two languages, or that of a grammatical
relationship in two languages, or that of a semantic feature in two languages, have been made by the individual in question in a language
contact situation. Although Weinreich takes up many linguistic and some
psychological questions, he leaves completely open questions regarding
the psychological structure within which we assume "interlingual identifications" exist; we assume that there is such a psychological structure and
that it is latent in the brain, activated when one attempts to learn a
second language.

The closest thing in the literature to the concept *latent psychological
structure* is the concept of *latent language structure* (Lenneberg 1967, especially pp. 374–79) which, according to Lenneberg, (*a*) is an already
formulated arrangement in the brain, (*b*) is the biological counterpart to
universal grammar, and (*c*) is transformed by the infant into the *realized
structure* of a particular grammar in accordance with certain maturational
stages. For the purposes of this article, I will assume the existence of the
latent language structure described by Lenneberg; I shall further assume
that there exists in the brain an already formulated arrangement which
for most people is different from and exists in addition to Lenneberg's
latent language structure. It is important to state that with the latent
structure described in this paper as compared to Lenneberg's, there is no
genetic time table;[5] there is no direct counterpart to any grammatical
concept such as universal grammar; there is no guarantee that this latent
structure will be activated at all; there is no guarantee that the latent
structure will be realized into the actual structure of any natural language
(i.e., there is no guarantee that attempted learning will prove successful),
and there is every possibility that an overlapping exists between this
latent language acquisition structure and other intellectual structures.

The crucial assumption we are making here is that those adults who
succeed in learning a second language so that they achieve native speaker
competence have somehow reactivated the latent language structure
which Lenneberg describes. This absolute success in a second language
affects, as we know from observation, a small percentage of learners—
perhaps a mere 5 percent. It follows from this assumption that this 5
percent go through very different psycholinguistic processes than do most
second language learners and that these successful learners may be safely
ignored—in a counterfactual sense[6]—for the purposes of establishing the
constructs which point to the psychologically relevant data pertinent to
most second language learners. Regarding the study of the latter group of
learners (i.e., the vast majority of second language learners who fail to

achieve native speaker competence), the notion of attempted learning is independent of and logically prior to the notion of successful learning. In this paper, we will focus on attempted learning by this group of learners, successful or not, and will assume that they activate a different, though still genetically determined structure (referred to here as the latent psychological structure) whenever they attempt to produce a sentence in the second language, that is whenever they attempt to express meanings, which they may already have, in a language which they are in the process of learning.

This series of assumptions must be made, I think, because the second language learner who actually achieves native speaker competence cannot possibly have been taught this competence, since linguists are daily—in almost every generative study—discovering new and fundamental facts about particular languages. Successful learners, in order to achieve this native speaker competence, must have acquired these facts (and most probably important principles of language organization) *without* having explicitly been taught them.[7]

Regarding the ideal second language learner who will *not* succeed (in the absolute sense described above) and who is thus representative of the vast majority of second language learners, we can idealize that from the beginning of his study of a second language, he has his attention focused upon one norm of the language whose sentences he is attempting to produce. With this statement, we have idealized the picture we wish to sketch in the following ways:[8] the generally accepted notion *target language* (TL), i.e., the second language the learner is attempting to learn, is here restricted to mean that there is only one norm of one dialect within the interlingual focus of attention of the learner. Furthermore, we focus our analytical attention upon *the only observable data to which we can relate theoretical predictions:*[9] the utterances which are produced when the learner attempts to say sentences of a TL. This set of utterances for most learners of a second language is not identical to the hypothesized corresponding set of utterances which would have been produced by a native speaker of the TL had he attempted to express the same meaning as the learner. Since we can observe that these two sets of utterances are not identical, then in the making of constructs relevant to a theory of second language learning, one would be completely justified in hypothesizing, perhaps even compelled to hypothesize, the existence of a separate linguistic system[10] based on the observable output which results from a learner's attempted production of a TL norm. This linguistic system we will call *interlanguage* (IL).[11] One of the main points of this article is the assumption that predictions of behavioral events in a theory of second language learning should be primarily concerned with the linguistic shapes of the utterances produced in ILs. Successful predictions of such behavioral events in meaningful performance situations will add credence to the theoretical constructs related to the latent psychological structure discussed in this paper.

It follows from the above that the only observable data from meaningful performance situations we can establish as relevant to interlingual identifications are: (1) utterances in the learner's native language (NL) produced by the learner; (2) IL utterances produced by the learner; and (3) TL utterances produced by native speakers of that TL. These three sets of utterances or behavioral events are, then, in this framework, the psychologically relevant data of second language learning, and theoretical predictions in a relevant psychology of second language learning will be the surface structures of IL sentences.

By setting up these three sets of utterances within one theoretical framework, and by gathering as data utterances related to specific linguistic structures in each of these three systems, (under the same experimental conditions, if possible) the investigator in the psychology of second language learning can begin to study the psycholinguistic processes which establish the knowledge which underlies IL behavior. I would like to suggest that there are five central processes (and perhaps some additional minor ones), and that they exist in the latent psychological structure referred to above. I consider the following to be processes central to second language learning: first, *language transfer;* second, *transfer of training;* third, *strategies of second language learning;* fourth, *strategies of second language communication;* and fifth, *overgeneralization of TL linguistic material.* Each of the analyst's predictions as to the shape of IL utterances should be associated with one or more of these, or other, processes.

Fossilization

Before briefly describing these psycholinguistic processes, another notion I wish to introduce for the reader's consideration is the concept of *fossilization,* a mechanism which is assumed also to exist in the latent psychological structure described above. Fossilizable linguistic phenomena are linguistic items, rules, and subsystems which speakers of a particular NL will tend to keep in their IL relative to a particular TL, no matter what the age of the learner or amount of explanation and instruction he receives in the TL.[12] I have in mind such fossilizable structures as the well-known "errors": French uvular /r/ in their English IL, American

English retroflex /r/ in their French IL, English rhythm in the IL relative to Spanish, German *time-place* order after the verb in the English IL of German speakers, and so on. I also have in mind less well known "non-errors" such as Spanish monophthong vowels in the IL of Spanish speakers relative to Hebrew, and Hebrew *object-time* surface order after the verb in the IL of Hebrew speakers relative to English. Finally, there are fossilizable structures that are much harder to classify such as some features of the Thai tone system in the IL of Thai speakers relative to English. It is important to note that fossilizable structures tend to remain as potential performance, reemerging[13] in the productive performance of an IL even when seemingly eradicated. Many of these phenomena reappear in IL performance when the learner's attention is focused upon new and difficult intellectual subject matter or when he is in a state of anxiety or other excitement, and strangely enough, sometimes when he is in a state of extreme relaxation. Note that the claim is made here that, whatever the cause, the well-observed phenomenon of backsliding by second language learners from a TL norm is not, as has been generally believed, either random or toward the speaker's NL, but toward an IL norm.[14]

A crucial fact, perhaps the most crucial fact, which any adequate theory of second language learning will have to explain is this regular reappearance or reemergence in IL productive performance of linguistic structures which were thought to be eradicated. This behavioral reappearance is what has led me to postulate the reality of fossilization and ILs. It should be made clear that the reappearance of such behavior is not limited to the phonetic level. For example, some of the subtlest input information that a learner of a second language has to master regards subcategorization notions of verbal complementation. Indian English as an IL with regard to English[15] seems to fossilize the *that* complement or *V that* construction for all verbs that take sentential complements. Even when the correct form has been learned by the Indian speaker of English, this type of knowledge is the first he seems to lose when his attention is diverted to new intellectual subject matter or when he has not spoken the TL for even a short time. Under conditions such as these, there is a regular reappearance of the *that* complement in IL performance for all sentential complements.

Five Central Processes

It is my contention that the most interesting phenomena in IL performance are those items, rules, and subsystems which are fossilizable in terms of the five processes listed above. If it can be experimentally demonstrated that fossilizable items, rules, and subsystems which occur in IL performance are a result of the NL, then we are dealing with the process of *language transfer;* if these fossilizable items, rules, and subsystems are a result of identifiable items in training procedures, then we are dealing with the process known as the *transfer of training;* if they are a result of an identifiable approach by the learner to the material to be learned, then we are dealing with *strategies of second language learning;* if they are a result of an identifiable approach by the learner to communication with native speakers of the TL, then we are dealing with *strategies of second language communication;* and, finally, if they are a result of a clear over-generalization of TL rules and semantic features, then we are dealing with the *overgeneralization of TL linguistic material.* I would like to hy-pothesize that these five processes are processes which are *central* to second language learning, and that each process forces fossilizable mate-rial upon surface IL utterances, controlling to a very large extent the surface structures of these utterances.

Combinations of these processes produce what we might term en-tirely fossilized IL competences. Coulter (1968) presents convincing data to demonstrate not only language transfer but also a strategy of communi-cation common to many second language learners. This strategy of com-munication dictates to them, internally as it were, that they know enough of the TL in order to communicate. And they stop learning.[16] Whether they stop learning entirely or go on to learn in a minor way, e.g., adding vocabulary as experience demands [Jain (1969) insists they must] is, it seems to me, a moot point. If these individuals do not also learn the syntactic information that goes with lexical items, then adding a few new lexical items, say on space travel, is, I would argue, of little consequence. The important thing to note with regard to the evidence presented in Coulter (1968) and Jain (1969) is that not only can entire IL competences be fossilized in individual learners performing in their own interlingual situation,[17] but also in whole groups of individuals, resulting in the emer-gence of a new dialect (here Indian English), where fossilized IL compe-tences may be the normal situation.

We will now provide examples of these processes. The examples presented in the last section are almost certainly the result of the process of language transfer. A few examples relating to the other processes should suffice for this paper.

Overgeneralization of TL rules is a phenomenon well-known to language teachers. Speakers of many languages could produce a sentence of the following kind in their English IL:

    1. What did he intended to say?[18]

where the past tense morpheme *-ed* is extended to an environment in which, to the learner, it could logically apply, but just does not. The Indian speaker of English who produces the collocation *drive a bicycle* in his IL performance, as in 2:

    2. After thinking little I decided to start on the *bicycle* as slowly as I
       could as it was not possible to *drive* fast.

is most probably overgeneralizing the use of *drive* to all vehicles (Jain 1969, pp. 22 and 24; but see note 26 here). Most learners of English quickly learn the English rule of contraction which forms things like *the concert's* from *the concert is*, but then these learners may overgeneralize this rule to produce sentences like:

    3. Max is happier than Sam's these days.

in their English IL. Though this sentence is hypothetical, it illustrates an earlier point. The learner of English who produces contractions correctly in all environments must have learned the following constraint without explanation and instruction, since this constraint was discovered only recently: "contraction of auxiliaries . . . cannot occur when a constituent immediately following the auxiliary to be contracted has been deleted," e.g., *happy* in (3) (Lakoff, 1971). Dozens of examples of overgeneralization of TL rules are provided in Richards (1970).

The transfer of training is a process which is quite different from language transfer (see Selinker 1969) and from overgeneralization of TL rules. It underlies the source of a difficulty which Serbo-Croatian speakers at all levels of English proficiency regularly have with the *he/she* distinction, producing in their English IL *he* on almost every occasion wherever *he* or *she* would be called for according to any norm of English. There is no language transfer effect here since, with regard to animateness, the distinction between *he* and *she* is the same in Serbo-Croation as it is in English.[19] According to a standard contrastive analysis then there should be no trouble. It seems to be the case that the resultant IL form, in the first instance, is due directly to the transfer of training; textbooks and teachers in this interlingual situation almost always present drills with *he* and never with *she*. The extent of this fossilization can be seen with respect to speakers of this IL over the age of eighteen, who even though they are consciously aware of the distinction and of their recurrent error, in fact, regularly produce *he* for both *he* and *she,* stating that they feel they do not need to make this distinction in order to communicate.[20] In this case, then, the fossilizable error is due originally to a type of transfer of training and later to a particular strategy of second language communication.

Concerning the notion *strategy* little is known in psychology about what constitutes a strategy; and a viable definition of it does not seem possible at present. Even less is known about strategies which learners of a second language use in their attempt to master a TL and express meanings in it. It has been pointed out[21] that learner strategies are probably culture bound to some extent. For example, in many traditional cultures, chanting is used as a learning device, clearly relating to what is learned in these situations. Crucially, it has been argued[22] that strategies for handling TL material evolve whenever the learner realizes, either consciously or subconsciously, that he has no linguistic competence with regard to some aspect of the TL. It cannot be doubted that various internal strategies[23] on the part of the second language learner affect to a large extent the surface structures of sentences underlying IL utterances. But exactly what these strategies might be and how they might work is at present pure conjecture. Thus, one can only roughly attribute the source of the examples presented herein to one or another strategy.

One example of a strategy of second language learning that is widespread in many interlingual situations is a tendency on the part of learners to reduce the TL to a simpler system. According to Jain (1969, pp. 3 and 4), the results of this strategy are manifested at all levels of syntax in the IL of Indian speakers of English. For example, if the learner has adopted the strategy that all verbs are either transitive or intransitive, he may produce IL forms such as:

4. I am feeling thirsty.

or

5. Don't worry, I'm hearing him.

and in producing them seems to have adopted the further strategy that the realization of the category *aspect* in its progressive form on the surface is always with *-ing* marking (for further discussion, see Jain 1969, p. 3ff.).

Coulter (1968) reports systematic errors occurring in the English IL performance of two elderly Russian speakers of English, due to another strategy which seems also to be widespread in many interlingual situations: a tendency on the part of second language learners to avoid grammatical formatives such as articles (6), plural forms (7), and past tense forms (8):

> 6. It was Ø nice, nice trailer, Ø big one. (Coulter 1968, p. 22)
> 7. I have many hundred *carpenter* my own. (Coulter 1968, p. 29)
> 8. I *was* in Frankfort when I *fill* application. (Coulter 1968, p. 36)

This tendency could be the result of a learning strategy of simplification, but Coulter (1968, p. 7 ff.) attributes it to a communication strategy due to the past experience of the speaker which has shown him that if he thinks about grammatical processes while attempting to express in English meanings which he already has, then his speech will be hesitant and disconnected, leading native speakers to be impatient with him. Also, Coulter claims that this strategy of second language communication seemed to dictate to these speakers that a form such as the English plural "was not necessary for the kind of communicating they used" (Coulter 1968, p. 30).

Not all of these strategies, it must be pointed out, are conscious. A subconscious strategy of second language learning called *cue-copying* has been experimented with by Crothers and Suppes (1967, p. 211) on Americans learning Russian morphological concepts. This *copy the cue* strategy is most probably due to what they call *probability matching,* where the chance that the learner will select an alternative morphological ending related to the cue noun is not random. Crothers and Suppes do not provide examples of the result of this strategy in meaningful performance situations; an example would be the *r* at the end of words like *California* and *saw* which foreign students of English who have had teachers from the Boston area regularly reproduce in their English IL.

To conclude this section, it should be pointed out that beyond the five so-called central processes, there exist many other processes which account to some degree for the surface form of IL utterances. One might mention spelling pronunciations, e.g., speakers of many languages pronounce final -*er* on English words as [ɛ] plus some form of *r;* cognate pronunciation, e.g., English *athlete* pronounced as [atlit] by many Frenchmen whether or not they can produce [θ] in other English words;[24] holophrase learning (Jain 1969), e.g., for *half-an-hour* the Indian learner of English may produce *one and half-an-hour;* hypercorrection, e.g., the

Israeli who in attempting to get rid of his uvular fricative for English retroflex [r] produces [w] before front vowels, "a vocalization too far forward";[25] and most assuredly others such as long exposure to signs and headlines which according to Jain (1969) affect by themselves the shape of English IL utterances of Indians, or at least reinforce more important processes such as language transfer.

Problems with This Perspective

There are certainly many questions one might wish to ask regarding the perspective presented so far in this article; I shall attempt to deal with five. The reader should bear in mind that we are here calling for the discovery, description and experimental testing of fossilizable items, rules and subsystems in interlanguages and the relating of these to the above-mentioned processes—especially to the central ones. What seems to be most promising for study is the observation concerning fossilization. Many IL linguistic structures are *never* really eradicated for most second language learners; manifestations of these structures regularly reappear in IL productive performance, especially under conditions of anxiety, shifting attention, and second language performance on subject matter which is new to the learner. It is this observation which allows us to claim that these psycholinguistic structures, even when seemingly eradicated, are still somehow present in the brain, stored by a fossilization mechanism (primarily through one of these five processes) in an IL. We further hypothesize that interlingual identifications, uniting the three linguistic systems (NL, IL, and TL) psychologically, are activated in a latent psychological structure whenever an individual attempts to produce TL sentences.

The first problem we wish to deal with is: can we always unambiguously identify which of these processes our observable data is to be attributable to? Most probably not. It has been frequently pointed out that this situation is quite common in psychology. In studies on memory, for example, one often does not know whether one is in fact studying storage or retrieval. In our case, we may not know whether a particular constituent IL concatenation is a result of language transfer or of transfer of training or, perhaps, of both.[26] But this limitation need not deter us, even if we cannot always sort things out absolutely. By applying the constructs suggested in this paper, I believe that relevant data can be found in the very many second language learning situations around us.

The second problem is: how can we systematize the notion fossilization so that from the basis of theoretical constructs, we can predict which items in which interlingual situations will be fossilized? To illustrate the difficulty of attempting to answer this question, note in the following example the nonreversibility of fossilization effects for no apparent reason. According to a contrastive analysis, Spanish speakers should have no difficulty with the *he/she* distinction in English, nor should English speakers have any difficulty with the corresponding distinction in Spanish. The facts are quite different, however: Spanish speakers do, indeed, regularly have trouble with this distinction, while the reverse does not seem to occur with English learners of Spanish.[27] Unlike the Serbo-Croatian example mentioned above, in this case there is no clear-cut explanation why Spanish speakers have trouble and English speakers do not. In cases such as these, it may turn out that one process, e.g., language transfer or transfer of training, overrides other considerations, but the stating of the governing conditions may prove very difficult indeed.

In principle, one feels forced to agree with Stephanie Harries (personal communication) who claims that until a theory of second language learning can answer questions like: "How do I recognize fossilizable structures in advance?" or "Why do some things fossilize and others do not?", all experiments conducted within the framework provided in this paper must be regarded as exploratory in nature. (To put things in more familiar jargon: with regard to fossilization, our results are descriptive and not explanatory in nature.) But this task of prediction may prove to be impossible; certainly as Fred Lukoff points out (personal communication) this task, on the face of it, may be even tougher than trying to predict errors in second language performance—a task notably lacking in success.

The major justification one has for writing about the construct fossilization at this stage of knowledge is that descriptive knowledge about ILs which turns out to suggest predictions verifiable in meaningful performance situations, leads the way to a systematic collection of the relevant data; this task, one which is impossible without this construct, is expected to be relevant to serious theory construction in a psychology of second language learning.

The third problem to be treated here concerns the apparent difficulty of fitting the following type of question into the idealized domain I have been sketching: how does a second language learning novice become able to produce IL utterances whose surface constituents are correct, i.e., correct with respect to the TL whose norm he is attempting to produce? This question finally brings us face to face with the notion of success in absolute terms: productive performance in the TL by the second language learner which is identical to that produced by the native speaker of that TL.[28] We noted this earlier so as to exclude from our idealized domain of inquiry those learners of second languages who reactivate[29] the latent language structure that is realized into a native language. In this article, we are concentrating on attempted learning of a second language, unsuccessful in this absolute sense. Of course, success in second language learning need not be defined so absolutely. The teacher or the learner can be satisfied with the learner's achieving what has been called "communicative competence" (see, for example, Jakobovits 1970, or Hymes 1972). But this is not the issue here. As was pointed out in the introduction, the emphasis upon what the teacher has to do in order to help the learner achieve successful learning belongs to the teaching perspective, which is not the perspective of this paper. Perhaps the rather curious confusion in the literature of learning a second language with teaching a second language (see note 2) can be explained by the failure to see a psychology of second language learning in terms other than those related to success. For example, typical learning theory experiments when done in the domain of second language learning would demand knowledge of where the learner will tend to end up, not where we would like him to end up. Experiments of this type would also demand knowledge of where the second language learner begins. We would claim that prerequisite to both these types of knowledge are detailed descriptions of ILs—descriptions not presently available to us. Thus, such experiments at present are premature, with the results bound to prove confusing.

Specifically concerning the problem raised in the first sentence of this section, it seems to me that this question, though relevant to the psychology of second language learning, is one that should also not be asked for the present since its asking depends upon our understanding clearly the psychological extent of interlingual identifications. For example, before we can discover how surface constituents in an IL get reorganized to identity with the TL, we must have a clear idea of what is in that IL, even if we cannot explain why it is there. In Selinker (1969) I believe I have shown that within a very limited interlingual situation, the basis from which linguistic material must be reorganized in order to be correct has been operationally and unambiguously established. But I have there said nothing about the way in which successful learners do in fact reorganize linguistic material from this particular IL. Here we can speculate that as part of a definition of learning a second language, successful learning of a second language for most learners, involves, to a large extent, the reorganization of linguistic material from an IL to identity with a particular TL.

The fourth problem is: (a) what are the relevant units of this hypothesized latent psychological structure within which interlingual identifications exist and (b) is there any evidence for the existence of these units?
If the relevant data of the psychology of second language learning are in
fact parallel utterances in three linguistic systems (NL, IL, and TL), then
it seems to me reasonable to hypothesize that the only relevant, one
might say, psychologically real, interlingual unit is one which can be
described simultaneously for parallel data in the three systems, and, if
possible, for experimentally induced data in those systems.

Concerning underlying linguistic structure, we should perhaps not
be too surprised if it turns out not to matter whose model we need, if an
eclectic one will do, or even if such notions *as the cycle, tree pruning,* or
even *derivation* prove not to have much relevance. If it is reasonable to
assume that the only linguistically relevant unit of a theory of second
language learning is one which is identified interlingually across three
linguistic systems (NL, TL, and IL) by means of fossilization and the
processes described earlier, then it follows that no unit of linguistic theory, as these units are currently conceived, could fit this criterion. More
generally, we should state that there is no necessary connection between
relevant units of linguistic theory and linguistically relevant units of a
psychology of second language learning.[30] That this assumption is obviously correct is clear to me; that many linguists will not be convinced is
also clear.

For evidence of the relevant unit of surface syntactic structure, applying at one and the same time to these three linguistic systems, I refer
the reader to experimental evidence appearing in my paper on language
transfer (Selinker 1969). In those experiments subjects responded orally
in their native language to questions presented orally in their NL and
attempted to respond in English to parallel questions presented in English. The questions came from an interview designed to elicit manifestations of specific types of surface structures in certain syntactic domains.
The only experimental instruction given was for each subject to speak in a
"complete sentence." Replicated results showed that the interlingual unit
of surface syntactic structure transferred from NL to IL (*not* to TL) was a
unit roughly equivalent to the traditional direct object or to an adverb of
place, an adverb of time, an adverb of degree, and so on. I would claim
that this unit, a surface constituent labeled the *syntactic string*, has a
behavioral unity both in the experimental situation and in meaningful
performance situations,[31] and thus, if the results were replicated in other
interlingual situations (i.e., other combinations of NL, TL, and IL),
would account for a large class of IL events.

With regard to a *realizational unit,* i.e., a syntactic string tied to a specific semantic notion, replicated results from this same series of experiments show that responses concerning a topic such as "subjects studied in school," as opposed to other topics such as "buying and receiving things" and "seeing movies and parades," affected very drastically the surface concatenation of the above-mentioned strings.[32] This semantic effect on surface syntactic order in an interlingual study, if further replicated in other interlingual situations, would provide very powerful evidence for the transfer of the whole realizational unit as well as for its candidacy as the unit of realizational structure in interlingual identifications.

Concerning the notion of relevant units on the phonological level, it seems to me that Brière (1968) has demonstrated that for his data there are several relevant units. The relevant units do not always correspond to known linguistic units, but rather would depend on the sounds involved; sometimes the taxonomic phoneme is the unit, but the unit in other cases seems not to be describable in purely linguistic terms. Brière evolved an experimental technique which imitated to a large extent actual methods of teaching advocated by applied structural linguists: listening to TL sounds, attempted imitation, use of phonemic transcription, physiological explanations, and so on. If I may be allowed to reinterpret Brière's data, it seems to me that he has been working, in another interlingual situation, with exactly the three systems we are discussing here, NL, TL, and IL: first, NL utterances which were hypothesized utterances in American English; second, TL utterances which were actual utterances in the composite language Brière set up, each utterance having been produced by a native speaker of French, Arabic, or Vietnamese; third, IL utterances which were actual utterances produced by native speakers of this NL when attempting to produce this particular TL norm. Regarding the sounds /ž/ and /ŋ/ in his TL corpus, the unit identified interlingually across these three systems is the taxonomic phoneme defined distributionally within the syllable as opposed to within the word (Brière 1968, p. 73). For other sounds the relevant phonological unit of interlingual identifications is not the taxonomic phoneme, but may be based on phonetic parameters some of which, he says, are probably not known (Brière 1968, pp. 73 and 64).

If these units in the domain of interlingual identifications are not necessarily the same units as those in the native-speaker domain, then where do they come from? An interesting bit of speculation about native-speaker performance units is provided by Haggard (1967, p. 335) who states that searching for "the unit" in native-speaker speech perception is a waste of time. Alternative units may be available to native speakers, for example under noise conditions.[33] While other explanations are surely possible for the well-known fact that noise conditions affect performance in a second language, and sometimes drastically, we cannot ignore the possible relevance of Haggard's intriguing suggestion: that alternative language units are available to individuals and that these units are activated under certain conditions. It fits in very well with the perspective outlined in this paper to postulate a new type of psycholinguistic unit, available to an individual whenever he attempts to produce sentences in a second langauge. This interlingual unit stretches, we hypothesize, across three linguistic systems: NL, IL, and TL, and becomes available to the idealized second language learner who will not achieve native-speaker competence in the TL, whenever he attempts to express meanings, which he may already have, in a TL he is learning, i.e., whenever he attempts to produce a TL norm. These units become available to the learner only after he has switched his psychic set or state from the native-speaker domain to the new domain of interlingual identifications. I would like to postulate further that these relevant units of interlingual identifications do not come from anywhere; they are latent in the brain in a latent psychological structure, available to an individual whenever he wishes to attempt to produce the norm of any TL.

The final difficulty with this perspective which we will treat here is the following: how can we experiment with three linguistic systems, creating the same experimental conditions for each, with one unit which is identified interlingually across these systems? I can only refer the reader once again to my own experiments on language transfer (Selinker 1969) where manifestations of desired concatenations of particular surface syntactic structures were obtained in what, I believe, was an efficient and valid manner. An oral interview technique was used; the purpose of the interview was to achieve a similar framework in the three systems which served the interviewer as a guide in his attempt to elicit certain types of sentences from the subjects. Upon request, I am prepared to make available a transcript of this interview as well as some thoughts for its improvement. Future experimental work, to be undertaken within this perspective, will go toward investigating the kind and extent of linguistic structures amenable to this particular technique.

Summary

The following are some assumptions which are necessary for research into the linguistic aspects of the psychology of second language learning and which have been suggested by the above discussion.

1. In a theory of second language learning, those behavioral events which are to be counted as relevant data are not immediately obvious.

2. These data have to be organized with the help of certain theoretical constructs.

3. Some theoretical constructs relevant to the way in which adults actually learn second languages are: interlingual identifications, native language (NL), target language (TL), interlanguage (IL), fossilization, syntactic string, taxonomic phoneme, phonetic feature.

4. The psychologically relevant data of second language learning are utterances in TL by native speakers, and in NL and IL by second language learners.

5. Interlingual identification by second language learners is what unites the three linguistic systems (NL, TL, and IL) psychologically. These learners focus upon one norm of the TL.

6. Theoretical predictions in a relevant psychology of second language learning must be the surface structures of IL sentences.

7. Successful second language learning, for most learners, is the reorganization of linguistic material from an IL to identity with a particular TL.

8. There exist five distinct processes which are central to second language learning: language transfer, transfer of training, strategies of second language learning, strategies of second language communication, and overgeneralization of TL linguistic material.

9. Each prediction in 6 should be made, if possible, relative to one of the five processes in 8.

10. There is no necessary connection between relevant units of linguistic theory and linguistically relevant units of a psychology of second language learning.

11. The only linguistically relevant unit of a psychology of second language learning is one which is identified interlingually across the three linguistic systems: NL, TL, and IL.

12. The syntactic string is the unit of surface structure transfer and part of the unit of realizational transfer.

13. The taxonomic phoneme is, in the case of some sounds, the unit of interlingual phonology, while in other cases no purely linguistic unit seems relevant.

14. There exists a latent psychological structure, i.e., an already formulated arrangement in the brain, which is activated whenever an adult attempts to produce meanings, which he may have, in a second language which he is learning.

15. Interlingual identifications, the units mentioned in 12 und 13, and the processes listed in 8 exist in this latent psychological structure.

16. Fossilization, a mechanism which also exists in this latent psychological structure, underlies surface linguistic material which speakers will tend to keep in their IL productive performance, no matter what the age of the learner or the amount of instruction he receives in the TL.

17. The fossilization mechanism accounts for the phenomenon of the regular reappearance in IL productive performance of linguistic material which was thought to be eradicated.

18. This latent psychological structure, for most learners, is different from and exists in addition to the latent language structure described by Lenneberg (1967, pp. 374–79).

19. These two latent structures differ in the following ways: (a) the latent psychological structure has no genetic timetable; (b) it has no direct counterpart to any grammatical concept; (c) it may not be activated at all; (d) it may never be realized into a natural language; and (e) it may overlap with other intellectual structures.

20. The qualification ("for most learners") in 7 and 18 is necessary, since those adults who seem to achieve native-speaker competence, i.e., those who learn a second language so that their performance is indistinguishable from that of native speakers (perhaps a mere 5 percent of all learners), have not been taught this performance through explanation and instruction but have somehow reactivated this latent language structure.

21. Since it is assumed that the two structures mentioned in 18 are different and since we know very little about the latent language structure and its activation, then the 5 percent mentioned in 20 should be ignored in setting up the idealizations which guide us to the psychologically relevant data of second language learning.

Notes

1. This paper was begun during the 1968–69 academic year while I was a visitor at the Department of Applied Linguistics, University of Edinburgh. Many students and teachers at Edinburgh and at Washington, through their persistent calls for clarity, have helped me to crystallize the ideas presented in this paper to whatever level of clarity is attained herein. I wish to thank them and I especially wish to thank Ruth Clark, Fred Lukoff, Frederick Newmeyer, and Paul Van Buren. An earlier version of this paper was read at the Second International Congress of Applied Linguistics, Cambridge University, September, 1969.

2. It is not unfair to say that almost all of the vast literature attempting to relate psycholinguistics to second language learning, whether produced by linguists or psychologists, is characterized by confusion between "learning" a second language and "teaching" a second language. (See also Mackey in Jakobovits 1970, p. ix.). This confusion applies as well to almost all discussions on the topic one hears. For example, one might hear the term "psychology of second language teaching" and not know whether the speaker is referring to what the teacher should do, what the learner should do, or both. This terminological confusion makes one regularly uncertain as to what is being claimed.

3. The answer to this question is not obvious since it is well known that theoretical considerations help point the way to relevant data. See, for example, Fodor (1968, p. 48): ". . . how we count behaviors and what is available as a description depends in part on what conceptual equipment our theories provide. . . ."

4. *Adult* is defined as being over the age of twelve. This notion is derived from Lenneberg (1967, e.g., pp. 156, 176) who claims that after the onset of puberty, it is difficult to master the pronunciation of a second language since a critical period in brain maturation has been passed, and ". . . language development tends to 'freeze' " (Lenneberg 1967, p. 156).

5. First pointed out by Harold Edwards.

6. See Lawler and Selinker (1979) where the relevance of counterfactuals to a theory of second language learning is taken up.

7. Chomsky (1969, p. 68) expresses a very similar view:

> . . . it must be recognized that one does not learn the grammatical structure of a second language through 'explanation and instruction', beyond the most elementary rudiments, for the simple reason that no one has enough explicit knowledge about this structure to provide explanation and instruction.

Chomsky gives as a detailed example a property which is clearly central to grammar: that of nominalization (Chomsky 1969, pp. 68 and 52–60). I see no point in repeating Chomsky's detailed arguments which clearly show that a successful learner of English as a second language could not have learned to make the judgments Chomsky describes through "explanation and instruction."

8. We have also idealized out of our consideration differences between individual learners, which makes this framework quite incomplete. A theory of second language learning that does not provide a central place for individual differences among learners *cannot* be considered acceptable. See Lawler and Selinker (1979) for a discussion of this tricky question in terms of profiles of idealized learners who differ one from the other with respect to types of linguistic rules and types of meaningful performance in a second language.

9. There has been a great deal of misunderstanding (personal communication) of this point: I am not taking an antimentalist position here. Neither am I ruling out on an a priori basis perceptual studies in a second language. However, the reader should be aware that in addition to the usual problems with determining whether a subject perceives or understands an utterance, the analyst in the interlingual domain cannot rely on intuitive grammatical judgments since he will gain information about another system, the one the learner is struggling with, i.e., the TL. (For a similar methodological problem in another domain, see Labov 1969, p. 715). Another, and perhaps the most important, argument against perceptual interlingual studies is that predictions based upon them are not testable in "meaningful performance situations" (see definition above); a reconstruction of the event upon the part of the learner would have to be made in a perceptual interlingual study. Such difficulties do not exist when predictions are related to the shape of utterances produced as the result of the learner attempting to express in the TL meanings which he may already have.

10. Notions of such separate linguistic systems have been developed independently by Jakobovits (1969) and Nemser (1971).

11. The notion *interlanguage* is introduced in Selinker (1969).

12. Gillian Brown has pointed out (personal communication) that we should work here toward a dynamic model where fossilization would be defined relative to various, perhaps arbitrary, chronological age groups.

13. John Laver has helped me to clarify this point.

14. Several people have pointed out (personal communication) that, in this paragraph, there appears to be a connection solely between fossilization and errors. This connection is not intended since it turns out that "correct" things can also reemerge when thought to be eradicated, especially if they are caused by processes other than language transfer.

15. Keith Brown (personal communication) has argued that the sociolinguistic status of the languages or dialects called Indian English, Filipino English, West African English, West African French, and so on, places them in a different category from that of the IL situation which I have been describing. From the sociolinguistic point of view this argument might be justified, but I am concerned in this paper with a psychological perspective and the relevant idealizations seem to me to be identical in all of these cases.

16. To describe this situation, Jain (1969) speaks of *functional competence.* Corder (1967), using the term *transitional competence,* focuses on the provisional aspect of developing competence in a second language. Both these notions owe their existence in the first place, to Chomsky's (1965) notion of linguistic competence which is to be distinguished from actual linguistic performance.

17. An *interlingual situation* is defined as a specific combination of NL, TL, and IL.

18. This sentence and sentences like it were in fact produced consistently by a middle-aged Israeli who was *very* fluent in English.
19. I am indebted to Wayles Browne (personal communication) for clarification of this point.
20. Reported by George McCready (personal communication).
21. Ian Pearson (personal communication).
22. Elaine Tarone (personal communication).
23. That is, what Corder refers to as the learner's "built-in syllabus" (Corder 1967).
24. Example from Tom Huckin (personal communication).
25. Example from Briana Stateman (personal communication).
26. The *drive a bicycle* example may, in fact, fit this situation (see Jain 1969, p. 24).
27. Example from Sol Saporta (personal communication).
28. As was pointed out in note 7, Chomsky (1969, p. 68) also adds the ability to provide native-speaker-like grammaticality judgments.
29. Note that this reactivation may be the only explanation possible for an individual who learns *any* part of a second language well. In this light, Cheryl Goodenough (personal communication) has objected to the qualitative split between the 5 percent who succeed and the rest of all second language learners. Since in this article we are not concentrating on success in a second language, as one would in the teaching approach, but on the attempt to isolate the latent psychological structure which determines, for any learner, the system underlying attempted production of a TL norm where the total effect of this output is clearly nonidentity with the hypothesized TL norm, then resolution of this issue should not affect the discussion. The importance of isolating this 5 percent is the speculation that these individuals may not go through an IL.

    Reibel (1969) stresses the role of the latent language structure in second language learning by suggesting that it is only when second language learners do the wrong things that they do not "succeed," i.e., "we seek to explain differences between adult learners, not in terms of differences in the innate learning abilities, but rather in terms of the way in which they are applied" (p. 8). Kline (1970) attempts to provide a point of contact between Reibel's views and mine by suggesting that any reorganization of an IL to identity with a TL must use the kinds of capacities and abilities Reibel describes.

    A different opposing view to the perspective of this article has been presented by Sandra Hamlett and Michael Seitz (personal communication) who have argued that, even for the vast majority of second language learners, there is no already formulated arrangment existing in the brain, but that the latent psychological structure alluded to here is developed, partly at least, by strategies which change up to the age of twelve and remain with an individual for the rest of his life. There seems to be at present no critical empirical test for deciding between these two alternatives.

30. It is important to bear in mind that we are here working in the domain of interlingual identifications and thus are in a different counterfactual domain (Lawler and Selinker 1979) than linguists who work in the domain of the ideal speaker-listener (Chomsky 1965). It seems to me that researchers in the psychology of second language learning are in the analogous position of the language teacher who, Chomsky (1966) admonishes, has the burden of deciding what in linguistics and psychology is relevant to his needs.

    Nevertheless, the linguistic status of ILs has still to be determined. One would like to know, for example, whether such things as transformations occur in IL grammars. Watkin (1970) asks whether the rules of IL are of the same general construction or shape as the rules for the same phenomena in the second language, "or are they in a 'recoded' form?". Watkin's data implies the same type of fossilization related to some similarity among rules of different ILs.

31. The surface domain considered was constituent concatenation after the verb. Sample results showed statistically-significant parallel trends for NL (Hebrew) and IL (English) *object* and *time* constituents on the one hand and (direct) *object* and *adverb* (of degree) on the other. That is, whenever an *object* constituent and a *time* constituent occurred after the verb, the statistically-dominant surface order was *object-time*, and not the reverse, both concerning NL responses, e.g., 9, and IL responses, e.g., 10:

    9. raiti [et haseret haze] [lifney švuaim]
        "I saw that movie two weeks ago"
    10. I met [Mrs. Cosman] [today]

    But whenever an *object* constituent and an *adverb* constituent occurred after the verb, the statistically-dominant surface order was *adverb-object*, and not the reverse, both concerning NL responses, e.g., 11 and IL responses, e.g., 12:

    11. ani ohev [meod] [sratim] 'I like movies very much'
    12. I like [very much] [movies]

    Importantly, these and all other experimental results were controlled informally by observing speakers of all ages over twelve, from this interlingual situation, producing IL utterances in meaningful performance situations.

32. That is, when the responses concerned the topic "subjects studied at school," there occurred an almost absolute trend toward the NL (Hebrew) order *place-object$_{noun}$* after the verb, e.g., 13, and toward the same IL (English) order of surface constituents, e.g., 14:

    13. ani roca lilmod [bauniversita] [biologia]
        "I want to study biology at the university"

14. I will study [in the university] [biology]

But when the responses concerned topics such as the other two topics mentioned in the text, there occurred an almost absolute trend toward both the
NL order *object$_{noun}$ place* after the verb, e.g., 15 and toward the same IL
order of surface constituents, e.g., 16:

15. kaniti [et hašaon] [baxanut]
     "I bought the watch in the store"
16. I bought [my watch] [in Tel Aviv]

For further details, see Selinker (1969) sections 3.41 and 3.42.
33. The fact that Haggard is concerned with alternative units which are inclusive
in larger units has no bearing on the issue under discussion in this section.

References

Brière, Eugène J. *A Psycholinguistic Study of Phonological Interference.* The
     Hague: Mouton, 1968.
Chomsky, Noam. *Aspects of the Theory of Syntax.* Cambridge, Mass.: MIT Press,
     1965.
———. "Linguistic Theory." In *Language Teaching: Broader Contexts.* Report of
     the *Northeast Conference on the Teaching of Foreign Languages,* Menasha,
     Wis., 1966. Pp. 43–49.
———. "Linguistics and Philosophy." In *Language and Philosophy,* edited by
     Sidney Hook. New York: New York University Press, 1969. Pp. 51–94.
Corder, S. Pit. "The Significance of Learners' Errors," *IRAL* 5 (1967):161–70.
Coulter, Kenneth. "Linguistic Error-Analysis of the Spoken English of Two Na-
     tive Russians." Master's thesis, University of Washington, 1968.
Crothers, Edward, and Suppes, Patrick. *Experiments in Second-Language Learn-
     ing.* New York: Academic Press, 1967.
Fodor, Jerry A. *Psychological Explanation: An Introduction to the Philosophy of
     Psychology.* New York: Random House, 1968.
Haggard, Mark P. "Models and Data in Speech Perception." In *Models for the
     Perception of Speech and Visual Form,* edited by Weiant Wathen-Dunn, pp.
     331–39. Cambridge, Mass.: MIT Press, 1967.
Hymes, Dell. *On Communicative Competence.* In *Sociolinguistics,* edited by J. B.
     Pride and J. Holmes. Harmondsworth, England: Penguin, 1972.
Jain, Mahavir. "Error Analysis of an Indian English Corpus." Unpublished
     paper, University of Edinburgh, 1969.
Jakobovits, Leon A. "Second Language Learning and Transfer Theory: a Theo-
     retical Assessment." *Language Learning* 19 (June, 1969):55–86.

Jakobovits, Leon A. *Foreign Language Learning: A Psycholinguistic Analysis of the Issues.* Rowley, Mass.: Newbury House, 1970.

Kline, Helen. "Research in the Psychology of Second-Language Learning." Unpublished paper, University of Minnesota, 1970.

Labov, William. "Contraction, Deletion, and Inherent Variability of the English Copula." *Language* 45, no. 4 (1969):715–62.

Lakoff, George. "On Generative Semantics." In *Semantics—An Interdisciplinary Reader in Philosophy, Linguistics, Anthropology and Psychology,* edited by Danny Steinberg and Leon Jakobovits. Cambridge: At the University Press, 1971.

Lawler, John, and Selinker, Larry. "On Paradoxes, Rules, and Research in Second-Language Learning." *Language Learning* 29, no. 2 (1979):363–76.

Lenneberg, Eric H. *Biological Foundations of Language.* New York: John Wiley and Sons, 1967.

Nemser, William. "Approximative Systems of Foreign Language Learners." *IRAL* 9 (1971):115–23.

Reibel, D. A. "Language Learning Strategies for the Adult." Paper read at Second International Congress of Applied Linguistics, Cambridge University, September, 1969.

Richards, Jack C. "A Non-Contrastive Approach to Error Analysis." Paper delivered at TESOL Convention, San Francisco, March, 1970.

Selinker, Larry. "Language Transfer." *General Linguistics* 9 (1969):67–92.

Watkin, K. L. "Fossilization and its Implications Regarding the Interlanguage Hypothesis." Unpublished paper, University of Washington, 1970.

Weinreich, Uriel. *Languages in Contact.* New York: Linguistic Circle of New York, 1953.

A Noncontrastive Approach
to Error Analysis

Jack C. Richards

Introduction

The identification and analysis of interference between languages in contact has traditionally been a central aspect of the study of bilingualism.[1]
The intrusion of features of one language into another in the speech of
bilinguals has been studied at the levels of phonology, morphology, and
syntax. The systems of the contact languages themselves have sometimes
been contrasted, and an important outcome of contrastive studies has
been the notion that they allow for prediction of the difficulties involved
in acquiring a second language. "Those elements that are similar to the
(learner's) native language will be simple for him, and those areas that
are different will be difficult" (Lado 1957, p. 2). In the last two decades
language teaching has derived considerable impetus from the application
of contrastive studies. As recently as 1967, Politzer affirmed: "Perhaps
the least questioned and least questionable application of linguistics is the
contribution of contrastive analysis. Especially in the teaching of languages for which no considerable and systematic teaching experience is
available, contrastive analysis can highlight and predict the difficulties of
the pupils" (Politzer 1967, p. 151).

Studies of second language acquisition, however, have tended to
imply that contrastive analysis may be most predictive at the level of
phonology, and least predictive at the syntactic level. A recent study of
Spanish-English bilingualism, for example, states:

> Many people assume, following logic that is easy to understand, that
> the errors made by bilinguals are caused by their mixing Spanish
> and English. One of the most important conclusions this writer
> draws from the research in this project is that interference from

Reprinted with permission of the publisher and the author from *English Language Teaching Journal* 25 (1971):204–19, published by Oxford University Press
and the British Council.

Spanish is not a major factor in the way bilinguals construct sentences and use the language. [Smith 1969]

This article focuses on several types of errors, observed in the acquisition of English as a second language, which do not derive from transfer from another language. Excluded from discussion are what may be called interlanguage errors; that is, errors caused by the interference of the learner's mother tongue. A different class of errors is represented by sentences such as *did he comed, what you are doing, he coming from Israel, make him to do it, I can to speak French.* Errors of this nature are frequent, regardless of the learner's language background. They may be called intralingual and developmental errors. Rather than reflecting the learner's inability to separate two languages, intralingual and developmental errors reflect the learner's competence at a particular stage, and illustrate some of the general characteristics of language acquisition. Their origins are found within the structure of English itself, and through reference to the strategy by which a second language is acquired and taught (cf. Cook 1969; Stern 1969). A sample of such errors is shown in tables 1–6 (see appendix). These are representative of the sorts of errors we might expect from anyone learning English as a second language. They are typical of systematic errors in English usage which are found in numerous case studies of the English errors of speakers of particular mother tongues. They are the sorts of mistakes which persist from week to week and which recur from one year to the next with any group of learners. They cannot be described as mere failures to memorize a segment of language, or as occasional lapses in performance due to memory limitations, fatigue, and the like (Corder 1967). In some learners they represent final grammatical competence; in others they may be indications of transitional competence.

Sources of the Present Study

Tables 1–6 are taken from studies of English errors produced by speakers of Japanese, Chinese, Burmese, French, Czech, Polish, Tagalog, Maori, Maltese, and the major Indian and West African languages.[2] From these sources I have selected those errors which occurred in a cross section of the samples. By studying intralingual and developmental errors within the framework of a theory of second language learning, and through examining typical cases of the teaching of the forms from which they are derived, it may be possible to see the way toward teaching procedures that take account of the learner's strategy for acquiring a second language.

Types and Causes of Intralingual and Developmental Errors

An examination of the errors in tables 1–6 suggests that intralingual errors are those which reflect the general characteristics of rule learning, such as faulty generalization, incomplete application of rules, and failure to learn conditions under which rules apply. Developmental errors illustrate the learner attempting to build up hypotheses about the English language from his limited experience of it in the classroom or textbook. For convenience of presentation, tables 1–6 will be discussed in terms of: 1) overgeneralization, 2) ignorance of rule restrictions, 3) incomplete application of rules, 4) false concepts hypothesized.

Overgeneralization

Jakobovits defines generalization or transfer as "the use of previously available strategies in new situations. . . . In second-language learning . . . some of these strategies will prove helpful in organizing the facts about the second language, but others, perhaps due to superficial similarities, will be misleading and inapplicable" (Jakobovits 1969a, p. 32; see also Jakobovits 1969b). Overgeneralization covers instances where the learner creates a deviant structure on the basis of his experience of other structures in the target language. For example (see table 1, parts 1, 3, 4, 8), *he can sings, we are hope, it is occurs, he come from.* Overgeneralization generally involves the creation of one deviant structure in place of two regular structures. It may be the result of the learner reducing his linguistic burden. With the omission of the third person *-s,* overgeneralization removes the necessity for concord, thus relieving the learner of considerable effort. Dušková, discussing the omission of third person *-s,* notes:

> Since (in English) all grammatical persons take the same zero verbal ending except the third person singular in the present tense . . . omissions of the *-s* in the third person singular may be accounted for by the heavy pressure of all other endingless forms. The endingless form is generalised for all persons, just as the form *was* is generalised for all persons and both numbers in the past tense. . . . Errors in the opposite direction like *there does not exist any exact rules* may be explained either as being due to hypercorrection . . . or as being due to generalisation of the 3rd person singular ending for the 3rd person plural. [Dušková 1969, p. 20].

Overgeneralization is associated with redundancy reduction. It may occur, for instance, with items which are contrasted in the grammar of the language but which do not carry significant and obvious contrast for the learner. The -ed marker, in narrative or in other past contexts, often appears to carry no meaning, since pastness is usually indicated lexically in stories, and the essential notion of sequence in narrative can be expressed equally well in the present—*Yesterday I go to the university and I meet my new professor.* Thus the learner cuts down the tasks involved in sentence production. Ervin-Tripp suggests that "possibly the morphological and syntactic simplifications of second language learners correspond to some simplification common among children (i.e., mother tongue speakers) learning the same language" (Ervin-Tripp 1969, p. 33).

Certain types of teaching techniques increase the frequency of overgeneralized structures. Many pattern drills and transform exercises are made up of utterances that can interfere with each other to produce a hybrid structure:

Teacher	Instruction	Student
He walks quickly.	Change to continuous form	*He is walks quickly.*

This has been described as overlearning of a structure (Wolfe 1967, p. 180). At other times, *he walks* may be contrasted with *he is walking, he sings* with *he can sing,* and a week later, without any teaching of the forms, the learner produces *he can sings, he is walks.*

Ignorance of Rule Restrictions

Closely related to the generalization of deviant structures is failure to observe the restrictions of existing structures, that is, the application of rules to contexts where they do not apply. *The man who I saw him* (table 3, pt. 2) violates the limitation on subjects in structures with *who. I made him to do it* (table 4) ignores restrictions on the distribution of *make.* These are again a type of generalization or transfer, since the learner is making use of a previously acquired rule in a new situation. Some rule restriction errors may be accounted for in terms of analogy; other instances may result from the rote learning of rules.

Analogy seems to be a major factor in the misuse of prepositions (table 4). The learner, encountering a particular preposition with one type of verb, attempts by analogy to use the same preposition with similar verbs. *He showed me the book* leads to *he explained me the book; he said to me* gives *he asked to me; we talked about it,* therefore *we discussed about it; ask him to do it* produces *make him to do it; go with him* gives *follow with him.* Some pattern exercises appear to encourage incorrect rules being applied through analogy. Here is part of a pattern exercise which practices *enable, allow, make, cause, permit.*

$$
\left.\begin{matrix} \text{Expansion joints} \\ \text{Safety valves} \\ \text{We} \end{matrix}\right\} \begin{matrix} \textit{permit} \\ \textit{allow} \end{matrix} \left\{\begin{matrix} \text{the pipes} \\ \text{the steam} \\ \text{the metal} \end{matrix}\right\} \textit{to} \left\{\begin{matrix} \text{expand or contract.} \\ \text{escape from the boiler.} \\ \text{cool slowly.} \end{matrix}\right.
$$

$$
\left.\begin{matrix} \text{The heat} \\ \text{Weakness in the metal} \end{matrix}\right\} \textit{caused} \left\{\begin{matrix} \text{the metal} \\ \text{it} \end{matrix}\right\} \textit{to} \left\{\begin{matrix} \text{melt.} \\ \text{fracture under tension.} \end{matrix}\right.
$$

$$
\left.\begin{matrix} \text{The heat} \\ \text{Weakness in the metal} \end{matrix}\right\} \textit{made} \left\{\begin{matrix} \text{the metal melt.} \\ \text{it fracture under tension.} \end{matrix}\right.
$$

It is followed by an exercise in which the student is instructed to complete a number of statements using verbs and prepositions from the table: *The rise in temperature—the mercury—rise up the tube. The risk of an explosion—the workers—leave the factory. The speed of the train—it—leave the rails on the curve. . . .*

From a class of twenty-three with mixed language backgrounds, no fewer than thirteen produced sentences like *The rise in temperature made the mercury to rise up the tube.* Practising *make* in the same context as *allow it to, permit it to, enable it to,* precipitates confusion. Other instances of analogous constructions may be less easy to avoid. Table 3, part 2 includes *this is not fit to drink it, the man who I saw him.* By analogy with the learner's previous experience of subject + verb + object constructions, the learner feels that there is something incomplete about *that's the man who I saw,* and so adds the object, after the verb, as he has been taught to do elsewhere.

Failure to observe restrictions in article usage may also derive from analogy, the learner rationalizing a deviant usage from his previous experience of English. This may happen even when the mother tongue is close to the English usage. F. G. French gives the following example of how a common article mistake is produced by rational analogy (French 1949). In English we say *The sparrow is a small bird. Sparrows are small birds.* Since the statements are exactly parallel, a logical substitute for the second language would be *The sparrows are small birds.* In Burmese, the equivalents would be

sa gale thi	*nge thaw*	*nget*	*pyit thi*
The sparrow	small	bird	is

and in the plural

sa gale mya thi	*nge thaw*	*nget mya*	*pyit kya thi*
The sparrows	small	birds	are

Instead of following the form of the mother tongue, however, the learner, having first produced *The sparrows are* from *The sparrow is*, sees a parallel between *sparrows* and *birds,* and produces the common error *The sparrows are the small birds.* A similar example is noted by Aguas, from Tagalog-speaking students (Aguas 1964).

Incomplete Application of Rules

Under this category we may note the occurrence of structures whose deviancy represents the degree of development of the rules required to produce acceptable utterances. For example, across background languages, systematic difficulty in the use of questions can be observed. A statement form may be used as a question, one of the transformations in a series may be omitted, or a question word may simply be added to the statement form. Despite extensive teaching of both the question and the statement forms, a grammatical question form may never become part of competence in the second language. Redundancy may be an explanatory factor. The second language learner, interested perhaps primarily in communication, can achieve quite efficient communication without the need for mastering more than the elementary rules of question usage. Motivation to achieve communication may exceed motivation to produce grammatically correct sentences. A further clue may be provided by classroom use of questions.

The use of questions is a common teaching device. Typically they are used, not to find out something, but as a means of eliciting sentences. Alternatively, the statement form may be used as a means of eliciting questions through a transform exercise. Classroom observation suggests that the use of questions may be unrelated to the skills it is meant to establish. Here are some examples:

Teacher's Question	*Student's Response*
Do you read much?	Yes, I read much.
Do you cook very much?	Yes, I cook very much.

Ask her what the last film she saw was called.	What was called the last film you saw?
What was she saying?	She saying she would ask him.
What does she tell him?	She tell him to hurry.
What's he doing?	He opening the door.
Ask her how long it takes.	How long it takes?
Will they soon be ready?	Yes, they soon be ready.
How much does it cost?	It cost one dollar.
What does he have to do?	He have to do write the address.
What does he ask his mother?	He ask his mother for the address.

As the above sample illustrates, when a question is used to elicit sentences, the answer often has to be corrected by the teacher to counteract the influence of his question. Some course books proceed almost entirely through the use of questions; others avoid excessive use of questions by utilizing signals to indicate the type of sentence required. These may reduce the total number of deviant sentences produced.

False Concepts Hypothesized

In addition to the wide range of intralingual errors which have to do with faulty rule learning at various levels, there is a class of developmental errors which derive from faulty comprehension of distinctions in the target language. These are sometimes due to poor gradation of teaching items. The form *was,* for example, may be interpreted as a marker of the past tense, giving *one day it was happened* (table 1, pt. 2) and *is* may be understood to be the corresponding marker of the present tense: *he is speaks French* (table 1, pt. 1). In table 2, pt. 4 we find the continuous form instead of the simple past in narrative; elsewhere we encounter confusion between *too, so,* and *very,* between *come* and *go,* and so on. In particular instances I have traced errors of this sort to classroom presentation, and to presentation which is based on contrastive analysis of English and another language or on contrasts within English itself.

Here is an example of how the present continuous came to be understood as a narrative tense. The simple present tense in English is the normal tense used for actions seen as a whole, for events which develop according to a plan, or for sequences of events taking place at the present moment (cf. Hirtle 1967, p. 40–41; Close 1959, p. 59). Thus the sports commentator's *Now Anderson takes the ball, passes it to Smith . . .*

and the cooking demonstrator's *I take two eggs, now I add the sugar. . . .* How do we find this use represented in textbooks for teaching English as a second language?

Typically one finds that the continuous form has been used for these functions instead. A recent audiovisual course contains many sequences like the following: *The lift is going down to the ground floor. Ted is getting out of the lift. He is leaving the office building. Ted is standing at the entrance of the office building. He is looking up at the sky. . . .*

This is not a normal use of English. The usual tense for a sequence of events taking place "at the moment" is the present tense, the continuous tense being used only when a single event is extracted from a sequence, the sequence itself being indicated by the present forms. This presentation of the continouus form led a number of students to assume that the continuous form in English is a tense for telling stories and for describing successions of events in either the present or the past.

The reasons for the occurrence of untypical verb uses in many course books appears to be related to a contrastive approach to language teaching. In this example, the course designer has attempted to establish the use of the continuous form in a context in which the present form is appropriate. It is often felt that a considerable amount of time should be devoted to the continuous form, since it does not exist in most learners' mother tongues. Excessive attention to points of difference at the expense of realistic English is a characteristic of much contrastive-based teaching. My experience of such teaching confirms Ritchie's prediction: "A course that concentrates too much on 'the main trouble spots' without due attention to the structure of the foreign language as a whole, will leave the learner with a patchwork of unfruitful, partial generalizations. . ." (Ritchie 1967, p. 129).

Many courses progress on a related assumption, namely, that contrasts within the language are an essential aid to learning. "Presenting items in contrast can lighten the teacher's and the student's work and consequently speed up the learning process" (Hok 1963, p. 129). Here are some examples of actual learning from materials thought out in terms of contrast.

George (1962) notes that a frequent way of introducing the simple and continuous forms is to establish the contrast:

is = present state, *is* + *ing* = present action.

The contrast is in fact quite false to English. When the past is introduced, it is often introduced as a past state. *He was sick.* This lays the groundwork for the learner to complete the picture of present and past in English by analogy:

is = present state, *is* + *ing* = present action,
was = past state ∴ *was* + *ing* =past action.

Thus *was* or *was* + *ing* may be used as past markers. Used together with the verb + *ed* this produces such sentences as *he was climbed the tree.* Interpreted as the form for "past actions" it gives *I was going downtown yesterday* instead of *I went downtown yesterday.*

Table 3 shows examples of the confusion of *too, so,* and *very.* Other substitutions are common, such as the use of *teach* for *learn,* of *do* for *make,* of *come* for *go,* of *bring* for *take.* Learners often feel that the members of such pairs are synonyms, despite every attempt to demonstrate that they have contrastive meanings. Such confusion is sometimes attributable to premature contrastive presentation.

Here are the occurrences of *too* and *very* in a first reader which tells the story of a group of children who light a fire in the snow in front of an old house: *The house is empty because it's old . . . I'm very cold. England is too cold . . . The fire is very big . . . It's very big. It's a very big fire. The firemen are going to put water on the fire because it's too big.*

The course designers intended to establish a contrast between *too* and *very,* but in so doing they completely confuse the meaning of the two forms. From the presentation—and from the viewpoint of a young learner—they have the same meanings. Thus we have the parallelism between:

It's too big and it's dangerous.
The fire is dangerous. It's very big.

How could a child, following such a presentation, avoid saying *This is a too big house? Too* would be more safely taught out of association with *very,* and in contexts where it did not appear to be a substitute for *very,* as, for example, in a structure with *too* + adjective + infinitive—*this box is too heavy to lift.*

Other courses succeed in establishing confusion between *too, so,* and *very* by offering exercises like these:

1. Reword the following sentences, using *too. This coffee is so hot that I can't drink it. I've got so fat that I can't wear this dress now . . . .*

Example: *This soup is very hot. I can't drink it. This soup is too hot (for me) to drink.*
2. Remake these sentences using *too. This hat is very big; he's only a little boy. This grammar is very difficult; a child can't understand it.*

This type of exercise leads to the errors in table 3, pt. 4. The common confusion of *since* and *for* (table 4, pt. 4) is sometimes reinforced by similar exercises, such as those which require choosing the correct preposition in sentences like:

I have been here (for/since) a week.
We have been in Canada (for/since) 1968.

Constant attempts to contrast related areas of English can thus have quite different results from those we intend. As yet, there is no substantial confirmation that a contrastive approach to teaching is likely to be a priori more effective than any other approach. Classroom experience and common sense often suggest that a safer strategy for instruction is to minimize opportunities for confusion by selecting nonsynonymous contexts for related words, by treating them at different times, and by avoiding exercises based on contrast and transformation.

Conclusions

An analysis of the major types of intralingual and developmental errors—overgeneralization, ignorance of rule restrictions, incomplete application of rules, and the building of false systems or concepts—may lead us to examine our teaching materials for evidence of the language learning assumptions that underlie them. Many current teaching practices are based on the notion that the learner will photographically reproduce anything that is given to him, and that if he does not, it is hardly the business of the teacher or textbook writer. It has been remarked that

Very surprisingly there are few published descriptions of how or what children learn. There are plenty of descriptions of what the teacher did and what materials were presented to the children, but little about what mistakes the children made and how these can be explained, or of what generalizations and learning strategies the children seem to be developing. . . . It may be that the child's strategy of learning is totally or partially independent of the methods by which he is being taught. [Dakin 1969, pp. 107–11]

Interference from the mother tongue is clearly a major source of difficulty in second language learning, and contrastive analysis has proved valuable in locating areas of interlanguage interference. Many errors, however, derive from the strategies employed by the learner in language acquisition, and from the mutual interference of items within the target language. These cannot be accounted for by contrastive analysis. Teaching techniques and procedures should take account of the structural and developmental conflicts that can come about in language learning.

Notes

1. This article is based on a paper presented at the TESOL convention held at San Francisco in March, 1970. I am grateful to William F. Mackey, Bernard Spolsky, and John Macnamara for comments on earlier versions of it.
2. Major sources for tables 1–6 are: French 1949; Dušková 1969; Arabski 1968; Estacia 1964 (especially comments by Meyerstein and Ansre); Richards 1968; Bhaskar 1962; Grelier n.d.; Aguas 1964.

References

Aguas, E. F. "English Composition Errors of Tagalog Speakers and Implications for Analytical Theory." D. Ed. dissertation. University of California, Los Angeles, 1964.

Arabski, J. "A Linguistic Analysis of English Composition Errors made by Polish Students." *Studia Anglica Posnaniensia* 1, nos. 1 and 2, pp. 71–89.

Bhaskar, A. W. S. "An Analysis of Common Errors in P.U.C. English." *Bulletin of the Central Institute of English* (Hyderabad, India), no. 2 (1962):47–57.

Close, R. A. "Concerning the Present Tense." *English Language Teaching* 13 (1959).

Cook, Vivian. "The Analogy between First and Second Language Learning." *IRAL* 7 (1969):207–16.

Corder, S. P. "The Significance of Learners' Errors." *IRAL* 5 (1967):161–69.

Dakin, J. "The Teaching of Reading." In *Applied Linguistics and the Teaching of English,* edited by Fraser and O'Donnell, pp. 107–11. London: Longmans, 1969.

Dušková, L. "On Sources of Errors in Language Learning." *IRAL* 7 (1969):11–36.

Ervin-Tripp, Susan M. Comments on "How and When Do Persons Become Bilingual." In *Description and Measurement of Bilingualism,* edited by L. G. Kelly. Toronto: University of Toronto Press, 1969.

Estacia, C. "English Syntax Problems of Filipinos." In *Proceedings of the Ninth*

International Congress of Linguistics, pp. 217–23. The Hague: Mouton, 1964.

French, F. G. *Common Errors in English*. London: Oxford University Press, 1949.

George, H. V. "Teaching Simple Past and Past Perfect." *Bulletin of the Central Institute of English* (Hyderabad, India), no. 2 (1962):18–31.

Grelier, S. "Recherche des principales interférences dans les systèmes verbaux de l'anglais du wolof et du français." Dakar, Senegal: Centre de Linguistique Appliquée de Dakar, no. 31, n.d.

Hirtle, W. H. *The Simple and Progressive Forms*. Quebec: Laval University Press, 1967.

Hok, Ruth. "Contrast: An Effective Teaching Device." *English Language Teaching* 17, no. 3 (1963).

Jakobovits, Leon A. *A Psycholinguistic Analysis of Second-Language Learning and Bilingualism*. Urbana-Champaign, Ill.: Institute of Communications Research, 1969a.

———. "Second-Language Learning and Transfer Theory." *Language Learning* 19 (1969b):55–86.

Lado, Robert. *Linguistics Across Cultures*. Ann Arbor: University of Michigan Press, 1957.

Menyuk, Paula. *Sentences Children Use*. Cambridge, Mass.: MIT Press, 1969.

Politzer, Robert L. "Toward Psycholinguistic Models of Language Instruction." *TESOL Quarterly* 2, no. 3 (1967).

Richards, Jack. "Language Problems of Maori Children." *Comment* (Wellington, N.Z.), no. 36 (1968):28–32.

Ritchie, William C. "Some Implications of Generative Grammar." *Language Learning* 17 (1967).

Smith, Gail McBride. "Some Comments on the English of Eight Bilinguals." In *A Brief Study of Spanish-English Bilingualism*, edited by Donald M. Lance. San Antonio: Texas A&M University, 1969.

Stern, H. "Foreign Language Learning and the New View of First-Language Acquisition." *Child Study* 30, no. 4 (1969):25–36.

Wolfe, David K. "Some Theoretical Aspects of Language Learning and Language Teaching." *Language Learning* 17, nos. 3 and 4 (1967).

Appendix

TABLE 1. Errors in the Production of Verb Groups

1. *be* + *verb stem* for *verb stem*

We are live in this hut   He is speaks French
The sentence is occurs . . .   The telegraph is remain . . .
We are hope . . .   We are walk to school every day.

2. *be* + *verb stem* + *ed* for *verb stem* + *ed*

Farmers are went to their houses   One day it was happened
He was died last year   They are opened the door

3. Wrong form after *do*

He did not found . . .   He did not asks me
He did not agreed . . .   He does not has . . .
The man does not cares for his life

4. Wrong form after modal verb

Can be regard as . . .   She cannot goes
We can took him out   She cannot to go
I can saw it   They would became
It can drawing heavy loads   We must made
They can used it   We can to see
It can use in state processions   We must worked hard

5. *be* omitted before *verb* + *stem* + *ed* (participle)

He born in England   He disgusted
It used in church during processions   He reminded of the story
They satisfied with their lot

6. *ed* omitted after *be* + *participle verb stem*

The sky is cover with clouds   Some trees are uproot
He was punish

7. *be* omitted before *verb* + *ing*

They running very fast   The industry growing fast
The cows also crying   At 10:30 he going to kill the sheep

8. *verb stem* for *stem* + *s*

He alway talk a lot   She speak German as well
He come from India

TABLE 2. Errors in the Distribution of Verb Groups

1. *be* + *verb* + *ing* for *be* + *verb* + *ed*

   I am interesting in that
   The country was discovering by Columbus

2. *be* + *verb* + *ing* for *verb stem*

   She is coming from Canada
   I am having my hair cut on Thursdays

3. *be* + *not* + *verb* + *ing* for *do* + *not* + *verb*

   I am not liking it
   Correct rules are not existing
   In French we are not having a present continuous tense and we are not know-
   ing when to use it

4. *be* + *verb* + *ing* for *verb* + *ed* in narrative

   . . . in the afternoon we were going back. On Saturday we were going
   downtown, and we were seeing a film and after we were meeting my brother

5. *verb stem* for *verb* + *ed* in narrative

   There were two animals who do not like each other. One day they go into a
   wood and there is no water. The monkey says to the elephant . . .

6. *have* + *verb* + *ed* for *verb* + *ed*

   They had arrived just now
   He had come today
   I have written this letter yesterday
   Some weeks ago I have seen an English film
   He has arrived at noon
   I have learned English at school

7. *have* + *be* + *verb* + *ed* for *be* + *verb* + *ed*

   He has been married long ago
   He has been killed in 1956

   verb (+ *ed*) for *have* + *verb* + *ed*

   We correspond with them up to now
   This is the only country which I visited so far

9. *be* + *verb* + *ed* for *verb stem*

   This money is belonged to me
   The machine is comed from France

210

TABLE 3. Miscellaneous Errors

1. Wrong verb form in adverb of time

   I shall meet him before the train will go
   We must wait here until the train will return

2. Object omitted or included unnecessarily

   We saw him play football and we admired
   This is not fit to drink it
   This is the king's horse which he rides it every day
   That is the man who I saw him

3. Errors in tense sequence

   He said that there is a boy in the garden
   When the evening came we go to the pictures
   When I came back I am tired

4. Confusion of *too, so, very*

   I am very lazy to stay at home
   I am too tired that I cannot work
   I am very tired that I cannot go
   When I first saw him he was too young
   Honey is too much sweet
   The man became so exhausted and fell on the floor

TABLE 4. Errors in the Use of Prepositions

1. *with* instead of	Ø	met with her, married with her
	from	suffering with a cold
	against	fight with tyranny
	of	consist with
	at	laughed with my words
2. *in* instead of	Ø	entered in the room, in the next day
	on	in TV
	with	fallen in love in Ophelia
	for	in this purpose
	at	in this time
	to	go in Poland
	by	the time in your watch
3. *at* instead of	Ø	reached at a place, at last year
	by	held him at the left arm
	in	at the evening; interested at it
	to	went at Stratford
	for	at the first time
4. *for* instead of	Ø	serve for God
	in	one bath for seven days
	of	suspected for, the position for Chinese coolies
	from	a distance for one country to another
	since	been here for the sixth of June
5. *on* instead of	Ø	played on the piano for an hour
	in	on many ways, on that place, going on cars
	at	on the end
	with	angry on him
	of	countries on the world
	to	pays attention on it
6. *of* instead of	Ø	aged of 44, drink less of wine
	in	rich of vitamins
	by	book of Hardy
	on	depends of civilisation
	for	a reason of it
7. *to* instead of	Ø	join to them, went to home, reached to the place
	for	an occupation to them
	of	his love to her

212

TABLE 5. Errors in the Use of Articles

1. Omission of *the*

    a) before unique nouns   Sun is very hot
                                            Himalayas are . . .
    b) before nouns of nationality   Spaniards and Arabs . . .
    c) before nouns made particular   At the conclusion of article
         in context   She goes to bazaar every day
                                              She is mother of that boy
    d) before a noun modified by a   Solution given in this article
         participle
    e) before superlatives   Richest person
    f) before a noun modified by an   Institute of Nuclear Physics
         of-phrase

2. *the* used instead of Ø

    a) before proper names   The Shakespeare, the Sunday
    b) before abstract nouns   The friendship, the nature, the
                                             science
    c) before nouns behaving like   After the school, after the
         abstract nouns   breakfast
    d) before plural nouns   The complex structures are still
                                            developing
    e) before *some*   The some knowledge

3. *a* used instead of *the*

    a) before superlatives   a worst, a best boy in the class
    b) before unique nouns   a sun becomes red

4. *a* instead of Ø

    a) before a plural noun qualified   a holy places, a human beings,
         by an adjective   a bad news
    b) before uncountables   a gold, a work
    c) before an adjective   . . . taken as a definite

5. Omission of *a*

    before class nouns defined by   he was good boy
       adjectives   he was brave man

TABLE 6. Errors in the Use of Questions

1. Omission of inversion

   What was called the film?
   How many brothers she has?
   What she is doing?
   When she will be 15?
   Why this man is cold?
   Why streets are as bright as day?

2. *be* omitted before *verb* + *ing*

   When Jane coming?
   What she doing?
   What he saying?

3. Omission of *do*

   Where it happened?
   How it looks like?
   Why you went?
   How you say it in English
   How much it costs?
   How long it takes?
   What he said?

4. Wrong form of auxiliary, or wrong form after auxiliary

   Do he go there?
   Did he went?
   Did he finished?
   Do he comes from your village?
   Which road did you came by?

5. Inversion retained in embedded sentences

   Please write down what is his name.
   I told him I do not know how old was it.
   I don't know how many are there in the box.

On Sources of Errors in Foreign Language Learning

Libuše Dušková

The assumption of structural linguistics that contrastive analysis predicts the areas of linguistic difficulties encountered by learners of a second language has recently been called in question (Corder 1967; Wilkins 1968). It has been noted by teachers that many of the common errors can hardly be ascribed to interference from the mother tongue. S. P. Corder (1967) proposes as a working hypothesis that a learner's errors provide evidence of the target language system he is using at a particular point in the learning process, i.e., that they reflect his transitional competence. He makes, however, a careful distinction between mistakes, which are defined as adventitious, random errors in performance due to memory lapses, physical states, etc., of which the speaker is immediately aware, and systematic errors, which reflect a defect in knowledge (i.e., in linguistic competence).

Other authors (Wilkins 1968) suggest that many errors are due to overgeneralization of a pattern, to interference between forms and functions of the language being learnt, and to psychological causes, such as inadequate learning. Moreover, doubts are sometimes raised about the necessity for a prior comparison of grammars (Wilkins 1968), the suggestion being made that an error-based analysis is equally satisfactory, more fruitful, and less time consuming.

Having had long experience with teaching English as a foreign language, the present author felt that it might prove fruitful to examine these assumptions in the light of actual errors made by a homogeneous sample of Czech adult learners of English. The subjects were fifty postgraduate students who had sufficient knowledge of English to be able to read their scientific literature and to converse on subjects related to their work. They were asked in Czech to express in English a request for correction of an English letter, to give a brief account of their last journey abroad, and to write the conclusion of a scientific article of a given content. Apart from an adequate rendition of the content, no restrictions were imposed

First published in *IRAL* 7, no. 1 (1969):11–36. Reprinted by permission of the publisher and the author.

on the choice of lexical and grammatical means. The average number of words contained in a paper was 170. Since the error analysis was made on written papers, no account could be taken of errors in pronunciation. Similarly, orthographic errors were disregarded, the analysis being confined to errors in grammar and lexis.

As a first step, it was necessary to determine what a grammatical or a lexical error is. In most cases, this was not difficult, since the degree of deviation from the normal form was such as to leave no doubt of the unacceptability of the form in question. This was the case with nearly all morphological errors, e.g., *this workers; several young physicist; Mr. B., who work in . . . ; others cases; I spoked; I written*, etc.; and in most instances of a misuse or a distortion of a word, e.g., *when I remind* (recall) *my last travel* (journey) *abroad; last year I attended* (visited) *Eastern Germany; we happen* (hope), *however, that . . . ; it was my vacant* (vacation) *journey; throgh* (throw) *light*, etc. Between clearly deviant forms of this kind, which were regarded as errors, and the normal forms there was a whole scale of deviant forms varying in the degree of deviation. In the case of forms displaying a low degree of deviation, it was hard to decide whether or not to regard them as errors. Compare the following examples, arranged in order of increasing deviation (starting with the normal form):

A. 1. It was a very interesting journey
   2. we traveled home by a train (by train)
   3. with a great pleasure (with great pleasure)
   4. I went there for a business (on business)
   5. this is also reason why . . . (the reason why)
   6. for a one month (for a month)
   7. a very good conditions (very good conditions)
B. 1. I hope I shall return there
   2. I'll not speak (I shan't *or* won't speak)
   3. items which shall have to be solved (will have)
   4. I will be very grateful to you (*shall* in British usage)
   5. They promised us a journey to Dresden when we shall learn good (if we learned well = achieved good results)
   6. I'll be wait for a long time (I'll wait for it)
C. 1. I should like to be sure
   2. Would you like to correct this letter (would you mind correcting)
   3. if you have liked there (liked it there)

4. I should be very like (glad)
5. the journey liked me (I liked the journey)
D. 1. I accompanied my husband, who visited the University in Brussels
2. I obtained many fruitful remarks (received)
3. May I ask you for a kindness (ask a favor of you)
4. I have made some friendships (some friends)
5. my last going abroad (journey)
6. I write with two workers from this Institute (correspond)
7. I am still entertaining a relatively rich correspondence (maintaining)
8. The solution proposed in this article should not be concerned as final (considered)

In *A* all examples except 1 display a misuse of the article; with *train* and *pleasure,* the indefinite article is used in other collocations (*we took a slow train, it's a great pleasure);* with *business* the indefinite article is impossible in the meaning intended, just as *reason* in that particular syntactic position is impossible without an article, while 6 and 7 are wholly incompatible with English structure.

B furnishes samples of errors in the future tense. 2 is possible if *not* is heavily stressed, which the writer did not intend. 3 and 4 show confusion of *shall* and *will,* whereas 5 and 6 are gross distortions of English structure.

C gives examples of errors in the treatment of the verb *like.* In 2 the writer expressed a request as if it were an offer; 3, 4, and 5 are not English.

D presents samples of lexical errors. While 2 to 5, though more or less queer, are still understandable, 6 to 8 obstruct communication.

With the exception of 1 in each paragraph, all other examples were treated as errors. It is obvious, however, that there is a considerable difference in the grossness of the error between, e.g., *I'll not speak* and *I'll be wait,* i.e., between errors cited at the lower and those at the upper end of the scale. With respect to forms displaying a low degree of deviation, opinions may vary, and other writers might exclude some of the forms regarded here as errors. As examples of forms which have been excluded in the present study we may cite, e.g., *I like more (I like better),* and *part* and *formula* where *aspect* and *rule* respectively would be more appropriate. Fortunately, the number of cases in which it was hard to decide whether or not an error had been made amounted to about 40 items, i.e., did not exceed 4 percent of all the errors examined.

Another point that requires preliminary comment is the quantitative aspect of the present study. The study makes no claim to completeness since it was not intended as a statistical count, but merely as a tentative probe which might suggest some points for further investigation. The papers examined certainly do not cover all errors. As for the quantitative aspect of the errors that have been observed, it should be borne in mind that the subjects were free to choose how to express the given content. As a result, while some grammatical points (such as the articles, the past tense, the plural) were bound to occur in all papers, others (e.g., adverbs, relative pronouns, the future tense) appeared only in some. Thus lower frequency of an error need not necessarily mean that the point in question is less difficult, but simply that the point itself occurred only in some (not in all) papers.

Nevertheless, it is hoped that a sufficiently large number and variety of errors were collected to provide material for a qualitative analysis.

Deviant forms were registered, classified according to their nature and examined in an attempt to find an answer to the following questions:

1. Is the distinction between mistakes (errors in performance) and errors (errors in linguistic competence), made by S. P. Corder, justified?
2. What is the predictive value of contrastive analysis in view of actual errors?
3. Which other interference factors, besides the mother tongue, play a role?
4. Is there any difference between errors made in perception of a foreign language and those made in its production?
5. Can contrastive analysis of the mother tongue and the target language be entirely replaced by an error-based analysis?

In the process of classification it appeared that a considerable number of errors could not be classified at all. For instance, of the 48 errors made in word order, it was possible to divide 31 into four subgroups; the remaining 17, however, defied all attempts at classification, being unique in character, nonrecurrent, and not readily traceable to their sources, e.g., *the complex structures still are developing* (complex structures are still developing), *the solution in this article suggested would not . . .* (the solution suggested in this article). Of the total number of 1,007 errors that were collected, about a quarter (251, i.e., 24.9 percent) was of this kind. In the different groups, however, the proportion of recurrent, systemic errors to nonce mistakes varied. The largest number of nonce mistakes were registered among prepositions (38 out of 57, i.e., 66.6 percent), relatively few were observed in morphology (7.7 percent), modal verbs and the tenses (see table 1).

It is tempting to denote nonce mistakes as mistakes in performance. This, however, cannot be done, if mistakes in performance are defined as those of which the speaker is immediately aware in the same way as a native speaker is immediately conscious of a slip of the tongue. Although there are some nonce mistakes that are true slips (e.g., *I am written a letter, I did not made*), which most learners perceive and which they are able to correct themselves when their attention is drawn to them, this certainly does not apply to all nonce mistakes. On the other hand, many of the recurrent errors of systemic character, which we might be inclined to describe as errors in competence, reflect no real defect in knowledge, since most learners know the pertinent rule and can readily apply it, but the mechanism of application does not yet work automatically (this applies in particular to morphological errors). Still, there is a large group of recurrent, systemic errors that seem to reflect a defect in competence, namely errors in the use of the articles.

For the purposes of teaching, nonce mistakes appear to be of small value since the conclusions that can be drawn from them, if any, apply only to one particular learner and unless some system can be discovered in them, they are of little value even in the case of the learner who commits them.

We are of the opinion that an error analysis should be based primarily on recurrent, systemic errors that are made by a number of learners and that can be readily traced to their sources, no matter whether they reflect defects in knowledge or whether they result from inadequate habit formation.

Recurrent systemic errors, when examined with regard to their possible sources, appear to be of diverse nature.

Interference from the mother tongue (i.e., Czech in the present study) was plainly obvious in errors in word order and sentence construction, i.e., on the syntactic level (though not all syntactic errors are accounted for by this factor), see tables 7 and 8.

The word order errors consisted in (*a*) placing the direct object after an adverbial modifier, e.g., *I met there some Germans,* 14[1] (I met some Germans there); (*b*) placing the object before the finite verb, e.g., *the solution suggested in this paper we cannot take as definitive,* 9 (the solution suggested in this paper cannot be taken as definitive); (*c*) postverbal position of the subject, e.g., *in this case do not exist any definite rules,* 2 (in this case there are no definite rules); (*d*) placing a temporal modifier before a local one, e.g., *I returned last month from P.,* 6 (I returned from P. last month, last month I returned from P.).

All these types of errors are clearly traceable to the Czech word order patterns: *Potkal jsem tam nějaké Němce; řešení navržené v tomto článku nemůžeme považovat za definitivní; v tomto případě neexistují žádná určitá pravidla; vrátil jsem se munulý týden z P.* Here the learners, observing the laws of the functional sentence perspective, arranged the words as in Czech, forgetting the grammatical restrictions to which word order is subjected in English.

It is true that *b* and *c* do on occasion occur in native English as marked forms due to the operation of the emotive word order principle (Firbas 1964). They resemble forms like *I'll not speak.* Since, however, the occasion on which they were used clearly called for the use of the normal, unmarked form, they were regarded as errors. Particularly in the situation of teaching English to Czech learners, acceptance of the marked forms *b* and *c* might prove harmful as word order in Czech is not controlled by grammatical restrictions but by the requirements of the functional sentence perspective (Mathesius 1961, 1942, 1929; Firbas 1956, 1964). Consequently, most Czech learners have a natural tendency to disregard also the grammatical restrictions in English word order, with the result that they produce a large number of sentences with out-of-place marked word order. As the eradication of this tendency is a major problem with most Czech learners, sentences like *b* and *c*—in spite of their occasional occurrence in native English—should always be corrected except with most advanced learners who use them for a purpose.

d is somewhat different. Here the neutral word order in Czech is to place the temporal modifier first, while in English this position is occupied by the adverb(ial phrase) of place. If the position of the two modifiers is reversed, both in English and in Czech the modifier placed late receives particular emphasis. In all specimens of *d*, however, the arrangement of the modifiers was not due to any reason requiring the marked, emphatic word order, but to the underlying neutral Czech word order pattern. Consequently, they were treated as errors.

Interference from Czech is equally evident in errors in sentence construction and government in general. For example, an expression like *be so kind to correct me this English letter,* 13, is due to the learners' construing the verb in the same way as in Czech (*opravte mi tento dopis*). Similarly the construction *using of complex structures,* 15, instead of *the use of complex structures* is consistent with the corresponding Czech construction, where a verbal noun followed by a genitive is used. Other examples of this kind are *there are many other cases to solving (případy k řešení*—cases to be solved*), the journey liked me (cesta se mi líbila*—I liked the journey*), it is therefore because, it is therefore that (je to proto, (proto)že*—it is because*), another my friend (jiný můj přítel*—another friend of mine*),* which are all word for word translations of the corresponding Czech expressions.

Similarly some of the misuses of the prepositions were due to interference of the corresponding Czech prepositional phrases, e.g., *by this manner (tímto způsobem*—in this manner*), I went there on three days only (jel jsem tam jen na tři dny*—for three days*), from the reason (z důvodu*—for the reason*), kind from you (laskavé od vás*—kind of you*),* see table 9.

Contrastive analysis predicts learning problems not only in areas where the source and the target language differ, but also in the case of linguistic features unknown in the source language (Lado 1961). This assumption is fully confirmed by the errors made in the use of the articles. There being no articles in Czech, Czech learners possess no frame of reference which might facilitate comprehension and mastery of their uses. Moreover, the presentation of this grammatical feature in current textbooks is so inadequate that learners are largely obliged to build up their own system by intuition. Considerable linguistic experience is certainly necessary where the uses of the articles are conditioned by extralingual reference. The uses which are signalled by linguistic devices, however, can be taught systematically and this might be the first step towards an improvement of this unsatisfactory state of affairs.

Although the difficulty in mastering the uses of the articles is ultimately due to the absence of this grammatical category in Czech, once the learner starts internalizing their system, interference from the other terms of the article system and their functions begins to operate as an additional factor, which can be shown by the variety of the errors made.

Of the 260 errors made in the use of the articles, 228 were recurrent errors classifiable into groups and 32 were nonce mistakes. The largest number of errors consisted in omission of the article:

- *a)* Omission of the indefinite article in cases like *I should like to learn foreign language; it was very interesting journey,* 40.
- *b)* Omission of the definite article with a singular countable noun, e.g., *We shall use present solution,* 27.
- *c)* Omission of the definite article with nouns modified by an *of*-phrase or a participle (phrase): *I visited Institute of Nuclear*

Energy in Ljublana, 21; *preceding notes, mechanisms involved in . . . ,* 52.

d) Omission of the definite article with names of countries and mountains, e.g., *in Soviet Union, in Alps,* 13.

e) Failure in treatment of nouns used generically: no article with a singular noun, e.g., *the use of complex structure,* 20.

f) Use of the definite article with a plural noun in cases like *As in many other cases the precise rules do not exist,* 33; *we met with the (some) physicists from Poland,* 2.

g) Use of the definite article instead of the indefinite, e.g., *working on the similar problem as I,* 15.

As examples of the 32 nonce mistakes we may cite *around the Slovakia* (round Slovakia*), we were travelling by the bus* (by bus*), we were ten days in mountains* (in the mountains*),* see table 5.

While failure to use any article might be attributed to interference from Czech (except perhaps *d* where analogy with other geographical names may play a role), the use of the definite article instead of the indefinite or the zero article is probably due to interference between the various functions of the articles themselves.

A large number of errors seem to have little, if any, connection with the mother tongue. They are above all morphological errors, the total number of which was 180, including 14 nonce mistakes. The errors were classified into the following groups:

a) Omission of the plural ending in the noun, e.g., *two month; new structure that are developed,* 26.

b) Lack of agreement between the subject noun and its verb, e.g., *there does not exist any exact rules; we was,* 21, including 6 omissions of the third person singular ending *-s,* e.g., *this paper help in . . .*

c) Confusion of the infinitive and the past participle, e.g., *the above rules may be consider as . . . ,* 15; *I am going to attended,* 5.

d) Confusion of the present and the past participle, e.g., *the mentioned rules can be treating as . . . ,* 5; *the complex structures are still developed,* 6.

e) Lack of agreement between adjective and its noun: *this workers,* 12; *another points,* 6.

f) Confusion of adverb and adjective: *learn good, exactly rules,* 6.

g) Errors in the forms of irregular verbs: *I have wrote, I gone, we spended*, 12.

h) Omission of *be: would you so kind*, 6.

i) Active voice instead of the passive: *the solution should not consider as . . .* , 6.

j) Finally, in 4 cases the subjects failed to express the genitive relation, there were 4 errors in relative pronouns, 4 in the possessive case and 13 confusions of the parts of speech.

Examples of nonce mistakes are, e.g., *I did not made* (make*); we cannot take this solution supposes* (suggested*) in this paper as . . .* , see table 2. Let us consider these errors group by group.

The omission of the plural ending in nouns does not seem to have been connected to the noun system in Czech, since Czech nouns (with the exception of a few minor unproductive groups) distinguish between the singular and the plural, e.g., *muž–muži (man–men), žena–ženy (woman–women), zákon–zkony (law–laws), pravidlo–pravidla (rule–rules), pole–pole (field–fields)*. The learners, therefore, are accustomed to making this distinction in their mother tongue, and yet they neglect it in English. French teachers are sometimes apt to attribute this error to the influence of spoken French. This assumption does not hold, however, since the error is made by learners who have never learnt French. This error might be described as a mistake in performance because the learner is aware of it when it is pointed out to him and is able to correct it himself. There can hardly be any doubt about semiadvanced learners' linguistic competence in this grammatical point: they can certainly formulate the rule, as well as apply it without any difficulty. A plausible explanation of this error is hard to find. Some suggestions are made in connection with the substitution of the present tense for the past.

Lack of agreement between the subject and its verb is not so difficult to explain, although it is not a case of interference from the system of Czech. Here again the finite verb agrees with its subject in person and number (and in some forms in gender as well). An explanation of this error may be found in the system of the English verbal personal endings. Since all grammatical persons take the same zero verbal ending except the third person singular in the present tense, which is the only verbal form with a distinctive personal ending (apart from the anomalous *am*) omission of the -*s* in the third person singular may be accounted for by the heavy pressure of all the other endingless forms. The endingless form is generalized for all persons, just as the form *was* is generalized for all persons and both numbers in the past tense. Omission of the third person singular ending *-s* is a very persistent error with most Czech learners and is much more common than would appear from the quantitative data obtained in this study.

Errors in the opposite direction like *there does not exist any exact rules* may be explained either as being due to hypercorrection—learners are so often corrected when they say *he work* that they occasionally overcompensate in an effort to avoid the pitfall—or as being due to generalization of the third person singular ending for the third person plural. Again we have interference from the other term of the two-term system of English personal endings.

These errors are again mistakes in performance. When the learner's attention is drawn to the fact that he has made a mistake, he is usually able to correct it. If, however, he is not specially told, he will not generally realize it himself. From the methodical point of view it would be interesting to have the papers corrected by the learners in order to find out which errors they could detect themselves.

Nearly all the other morphological errors may be accounted for in the same way, i.e., they are interferences between the other terms of the English subsystem in question. Thus confusion of the past participle and the infinitive is probably due to the fact that in some verbal forms the auxiliary is followed by the past participle (in the perfect tenses and in the passive voice), in others by the infinitive (in the future tense and the conditional), which may lead to doubt as to which form to use. The same applies to confusion of the present and the past participle. These errors occur even in cases where the English form is quite analogous to the corresponding Czech form, e.g., *the rules should not be consider*—pravidla by neměla být považována. If the learner translated the Czech verbal form word for word into English (*by neměla*—should not; *být*—be; *považována*—considered) he could not go wrong. Similarly the errors in the forms of irregular verbs are quite obviously caused by interference from the other forms of the verb in question (*have wrote, I gone;* the present writer has witnessed persistent incapacity to distinguish between forms like *began–begun, drank–drunk*) or forms of other verbs (*we spended, I writed*).

The errors in lack of agreement between an adjective and its noun are again evident examples of interference from the English adjectival system. Forms like *this workers* can have nothing to do with Czech since the corresponding word *tento,* like all other adjectives ending in hard stems, makes a distinction between the singular and the plural (besides gender): *tito*. In English, however, all adjectives have the same form both in the singular and the plural, except two: *this* and *that*. Therefore it is not surprising that under the overwhelming pressure of all other adjectives these two words are also treated as unchangeable.

Errors like *another points* may be explained by mutual interference between the forms *other–another*, and also by the fact that most learners are unable to identify *an-* in *another* with the indefinite article.

It might be argued that errors like *others cases*, 11, are due to interference from Czech. But surely the fact that no other adjectives ever appear with a plural ending—Czech learners do not produce forms like *greats difficulties* (compare also *this workers* above)—justifies the conclusion that *others cases* is due rather to interference from the other forms of the system *other–another–others*.

In some of the minor groups of morphological errors the influence of Czech may be traced, though perhaps not quite so conclusively as discussed earlier. Omission of *be* after *would* or *will (would/will you so kind)* may be due to interference from the corresponding Czech form *byl byste/ buďte tak laskav*, where there is no infinitive. It is worth mentioning, however, that it is only the verb *to be* whose infinitive is ever omitted. Perhaps the forms *would, will* are wrongly identified with *byl by, bude*.

Similarly in the 4 cases of failure to express the genitive relation, e.g., *in the field nuclear reactions*, the source of the error is probably the corresponding Czech noun phrase *v oblasti mukleárních reakcí* where the genitive relation is not expressed by a separate word but by the case ending.

Also the use of the relative *which* instead of *who*, which is a much more common error among Czech learners than the figures in this study might suggest, is usually ascribed to the influence of Czech, because most learners internalize *which* as *který* and *who* as *kdo*. *Který* being the universal relative pronoun in Czech (whereas *kdo* is mostly used as an interrogative), it is not surprising that *which* is generalized as the universal relative pronoun for English as well.

Confusion of the passive and the active voice may be due to the fact that in Czech the passive voice is formed in two ways, one corresponding to the English manner *(metoda je užívána*—the method is used*)*, the other by means of the reflexive particle *se (užívá se)*. The expression of the passive voice, however, is only one of the functions of the reflexive particle, the others being reflexivity *(hájit se*—defend oneself*)*, intransitivity *(konat se*—take place*)*, and in a number of verbs it is purely tautological *(smát se, dívat se*—laugh, look*)*. The fact that the Czech *se-* verbs are expressed in English on the one hand by the passive voice (where *se* has the passive function) and on the other hand by the active voice (in all other cases) may give rise to doubt as to which voice to use, and occasionally to confusion. The present writer herself felt uncertainty on this point in the initial stages of learning Latin (at the age of thirteen).

On the whole, the number of morphological errors due to the influence from Czech, as compared with the number caused by interference between related English forms is small (19 of the total of 166 systemic errors).

Some of the syntactic errors may also be traced to interference between English forms rather than from Czech ones, viz. confusion of anticipatory *it* and *there (there was not my first stay abroad,* 2; *they are/it is many other points to be solved,* 8). It might be argued that *it is many other points to be solved* corresponds to the Czech *je mnoho jiných bodů . . .* , but then *there* would not appear in place of *it*. Besides the examples of errors observed in this study, Czech learners make errors like *there is possible.*

Similarly inversion in indirect questions (*notice whom did you meet there*—state whom you met there, 8) and confusion of *some* and *any*, 5, are examples of interference from other English forms, see table 7.

All Czech teachers of English will confirm that most Czech learners have great difficulty with modal verbs. In the present study the number of errors observed was 17. All except one consisted in the learners' intending to say *should* and using something else instead, e.g., *the solution would (could, might) not be considered as definitive.* These errors are clearly due to interference from the forms and meanings of the other English modals, since once the learner has developed a permanent link between each English modal and its Czech equivalent, he no longer confuses them. The only nonce mistake here was the use of the past conditional instead of the present (see table 3).

Another problem for Czech learners is presented by the system of the English tenses. Here the difficulty is predicted by contrastive analysis, as the temporal systems in the two languages greatly differ. The actual source of most errors, however, is again interference from the other terms of the English system, and only rarely from the corresponding Czech form. The influence of Czech is apparent in errors like *I shall do it when (if) I shall have time* (in temporal and conditional clauses with reference to the future Czech uses the future tense), and in *I work (am working) here for two years* instead of *I have worked (have been working)*, where Czech uses the present. The proportion of these errors in the bulk of temporal errors is small: in the present study, of 50 errors 4 were of this kind. All the other errors were due to confusion of two English tenses: perfect instead of preterite in narration or with a past temporal modifier, e.g., *to the end* (towards the end) *of my stay there I have made a trip . . .* , 12; preterite instead of perfect in cases like *this is the only country which I visited,* 3; pluperfect instead of preterite, e.g., *It was a very nice journey because I had been able to see many interesting things,* 7; continuous instead of simple forms and vice versa, e.g., *correct rules are not existing, I send you an English letter,* 4; perfect instead of present, e.g., *we have hoped, however, that . . .* , 3, see table 4.

Among the errors in tenses there is one that is hard to explain. It is the use of the present instead of the past, e.g., *their study is started in 1965; last year I have the opportunity to . . .* , 11. This error cannot be caused by interference from Czech, where the past tense is used and where distinction between the present, the past, and the future is generally made. This error may be described as a mistake in performance, a true slip, similar to omission of the plural ending. Perhaps the present tense, as well as the singular, which a learner internalizes first, are impressed on his mind as basic forms which he resorts to as substitutes for all other forms not yet adequately learned. A further contributing factor may be the fairly common idea of English as a language without grammar.

Errors in lexis presented much less homogeneous material for study than errors in grammar. With regard to their possible sources they were classified into the following groups:

a) Confusion of words on the ground of formal similarity. In 48 cases the subjects confused words like *than–then, think–thing, role–rule, take part–take place, suppose–suggest, respect–aspect, plan–plane, ones–once,* etc.

b) Confusion of words also occurred between related words with similar meaning, 20, and related phrases, 9, e.g., *institution–institute, latter–last, interesting–interested, usage–use, lie–lay, definite–definitive; in the least–at least, at first–for the first time.*

In these two groups the source of the error appears to be interference from another English form.

c) On the other hand, a major group of lexical errors comprises misuses of words due to the fact that a Czech word has several equivalents in English, 54, e.g., *do–make* (dělat), *way–journey* (cesta), *repair–correct* (spravit), *include–involve* (zahrnout), *attend–visit* (navštívit), *next–further–other* (další), etc. Difficulties of this kind are predicted by contrastive analysis.

d) A number of lexical errors consisted in distortions, 25, e.g., *evolute, evolvate* (evolve), *eluciete* (elucidate), *physist* (physicist), *realants* (relations), *desolve* (solve), etc., which were included among lexical nonce mistakes. Of the total number of 233 lexical errors, nonce mistakes accounted for 95 (including 25 distortions). Examples of the other nonce mistakes are, e.g., *it was within* (during) *my studies, the solution assumed* (suggested) *in this paper; we hope, although* (however), *that . . . ; put in* (throw) *light,* see table 10.

To sum up what has been found about the sources of large groups of errors we may say that while interference from the mother tongue plays a role, it is not the only interfering factor. There is also interference between the forms of the language being learned, both in grammar and lexis. In grammar, it is the other terms of the particular English subsystem and/or their functions that operate as interfering factors, while in lexis words and phrases are often confused as a result of formal similarity.

In addition, there are other, minor interfering factors such as interference from another foreign language that was learned before English. Czech learners who have previously learned German tend to use words which have identical or similar forms in German and English with their German meanings, e.g., *also* in the sense of *then, become* in the sense of *get, where* is sometimes treated as *who,* and *will* is very often given the function of *want* under the influence of the German *wollen.* The present writer has also noticed interference from German in word order (inversion of the kind *today have I little time*—heute habe ich wenig Zeit) and in phrase construction (*what for a book is it*—was für ein Buch ist es?). This interference is of course a very minor factor and, in comparison with the other two, is largely negligible. In the present study evidence for it was obtained in 7 cases, *college* instead of *colleague,* 4, *oft (often), gast (guest),* and *chef (chief).*

Occasionally, there is interference from French, exemplified in this study by French spelling in two cases, *remarque* and *-ique.*

It might be profitable to compare the results of the present study with the results of a previous study investigating errors in reading comprehension (Dušková 1965–66). Its material consisted of 50 Czech translations of 16 unconnected English sentences taken from scientific texts. The 16 sentences contained 233 words. They were presented to the subjects printed on a sheet.

There is one basic difference between errors made on the production level and those on the reception level, which can be best demonstrated by translation into and from a foreign language. In both cases the quality of the translation—at least in foreign language teaching—is to be judged by the degree to which the translation conveys the information contained in the original. Whereas translation from a foreign language will contain only errors, if any, relative to the original, the utterance in the mother tongue as such being free of morphological, syntactic, lexical, and other errors, translation into a foreign language may, in addition, display errors in the well-formedness of the utterance, resulting from inadequate mastery of the foreign language. Mutatis mutandis this applies to comprehension of a written passage or a heard utterance, and the expression in a foreign language of an intent, or a response to a stimulus.

In comparing the results of the two studies it should be borne in mind that in each case the subjects were asked to perform different operations: in the study of errors in reading comprehension they produced translations, in the present study the papers were free renditions of a given content. It might be interesting to study errors made in translation into a foreign language as compared with those made in free utterances.

Some of the grammatical and lexical points that proved to be problems on the production level—problems in the sense that the subjects made errors in them—are identical with problems involved in the comprehension of a written text. In the study of reading comprehension errors it was possible to distinguish five major groups of errors:

a) Syntactic errors in constructions that are different in English and Czech, 160.

b) Morphological errors consisting in interpreting the plural as the singular, 32 and vice versa, 39; the present as the past, 29; and some minor groups.

c) 159 errors in modal verbs, due largely to a misunderstanding of the lexical meaning of the modal in question.

d) 34 lexical errors caused by formal similarity of words: the subjects confused words like *case–cause, clearly–cleanly, cautiously–causally, instead–indeed, depth–death, aim–aid, ad-*

vantage–advance–adventure,   incline–decline,   think–thank,
omission–emission, and others.

e)   Lexical errors occurred mostly with polysemic abstracts like
     provide, appear, matter, common.

The highest degree of similarity between reading comprehension and production errors can be observed in groups *c, d,* and *e.* Modal verbs appear to present difficulties both on the production and the reception level. From the number of errors (159 in reception, 17 in production) it would seem that they are far more difficult to comprehend than to produce. Actually, however, the small number of errors on the production level is due to the fact that in free utterances, most learners will spontaneously produce only *can* and *can't.* If the necessity arises for them to produce other shades of modal meanings, the number of errors substantially increases. Similarly, on both levels a frequent source of lexical errors appears to be formal likeness of words (34 in reception, 48 in production).

As to the other sources of lexical errors, one-to-many correspondence between Czech and English lexical units appears to play a role on both levels. On the production level, 54 errors were observed in cases where a Czech word has two or more equivalents in English. Similarly on the reception level, 62 errors were noticed in cases where English words have several Czech equivalents.

The difficulty of abstract words, ascertained on the reception level, is evidenced in the present study by confusion of words like *suppose–suggest, concern–consider, involve–include, assume–suggest.*

In the remaining groups (*a* and *b*), there are both similar and different features. The morphological errors that were observed in the reading comprehension study were also registered on the production level. However, there are also many other morphological errors on the production level that do not occur in reception, in particular in irregular forms. This is quite natural since recognition of a form is much easier than its production. Most learners will recognize e.g., *wrote* as the preterite of *write,* by its position and formal resemblance with *write,* without being necessarily able to produce the form themselves. In general, morphology appears to be much more difficult on the production than on the reception level.

Passing to syntactic errors, we can see that they occur on both levels but that they are of a different nature. On the level of comprehension, the main difficulty seems to be detection of the syntactic relations in the sentence since these are signaled by other devices than in Czech. Moreover, learning problems are presented by constructions that do not exist in Czech (e.g., infinitival, gerundive, and participial). On the production level, the difficulties lie in different government, different constructions and word order. For example, a construction like *the idea most likely to have been used in connection with . . .* , nonexistent in Czech, will not present problems on the production level simply because hardly any learner will spontaneously use it, whereas in reception he cannot choose what he is faced with. On the other hand in different constructions and with different kinds of government, learners may go wrong in speaking and writing where in reading they would not make an error, e.g., *there are many other cases to solving, this journey liked me, would you mind to read, I said my leader*—all of which are readily comprehensible if corrected to: *cases to be solved, I liked the journey, mind reading, I said to my commander.*

Finally there are errors that occur predominantly on the production level. They are errors in word order, in the use of the articles and prepositions. On the reception level, errors in any of these three points are rare. In the study of reading comprehension errors, only one error was observed in each category: misinterpretation of a past participle placed after its noun (a word order pattern nonexistent in Czech), *the assumption made avoids the necessity of . . .* , 9; failure to translate the article with a numeral, *the two* meaning in Czech *ti dva* or *oba* whereas *two dva*, 18; 3 errors in equivalents of the preposition *against*. In the present study errors in the use of the articles rank first, while word order and prepositions account for 48 and 57 errors.

As to the sources of errors made on the reception level, errors in groups *a* and *e* confirm the assumption that contrastive analysis predicts the areas of difficulties: syntactic constructions and phrases that do not occur in Czech appear to be learning problems, just as are lexical items which have several Czech equivalents. Errors in groups *b*, *c*, and *d* are of a different nature. Misinterpretation of grammatical number, which undoubtedly does not involve any failure in competence, but only failure in performance, may be due to the fact that for many Czech speakers one signal of the number in the noun is insufficient, since from Czech they are used to two signals, one in the noun and another in the verb. The errors in tenses and the modal verbs are obviously caused by interference from the other terms of the respective systems. The errors in group *d* provide evidence of the operation of formal similarity as an interfering factor.

Thus we have observed the same two major sources of errors as on the production level: negative transfer, or rather nonexistence of certain features in the mother tongue, and interference from other forms of the target language.

In conclusion, we shall attempt to answer the last question raised in this study as to whether contrastive analysis of the source and the target language can be entirely replaced by an error-based analysis. The present findings do not seem to justify such a procedure. They rather suggest that contrastive analysis might be profitably supplemented by the results of error-based analyses, particularly in the preparation of teaching materials. The value of contrastive analysis in the preparation of teaching materials is generally recognized, both as a means of prevention and of remedying errors (Halliday, McIntosh, and Strevens 1964; Nickel and Wagner 1968). A further improvement of teaching materials based on contrastive analysis might be achieved by inclusion of the most common errors occurring outside the sphere predicted by contrastive analysis alone.

There is another conclusion that may be drawn from the present findings, as far as the productive skills are concerned. Categories that exist in both languages but display differences in their functions and distribution, although giving rise to many errors, do not seem to be the most potent source of errors, i.e., they do not represent the greatest difficulties in the foreign language being learned. What proves to be still more difficult is a category nonexistent in the mother tongue. Here the learner has no frame of reference to which he can relate his expression in the foreign language. The teacher is faced with the problem of developing intuition for the foreign language category independently of the mother tongue. This is ultimately the aim of teaching any foreign language category, but in the case of similar categories it is facilitated in the initial and intermediary stages of study by the possibility of reference to the mother tongue.

An example of a category of this kind is provided by the articles in English when taught to Czech speakers. The great difficulty of this feature is borne out not only by the number of errors observed in this study but also by the fact that the articles remain the last sphere in which Czech (and other Slav) speakers continue to make occasional errors even in the case of a near-native command of English.

Note

1. The figure refers to the number of occurrences.

References

Corder, S. P. "The Significance of Learners' Errors." *IRAL* 5 (1967):161–70.
Dušková, Libuše. "K otázce chyb v cizím jazyce" (On the question of errors in a foreign language). *Cizí jazyky ve škole* 9 (1965–66):440–54.

Firbas, J. "Poznámky k problematice anglického slovního pořádku z hlediska aktuálního členění větňho" (Notes on the problem of English word order from the point of view of functional sentence perspective). *Sbornik praci filosofické fakulty brněnské university*, A, no. 4 (1956):93–107.

———. "From Comparative Word-Order Studies." *Brno Studies in English* (Prague), 4 (1964):111–26.

Halliday, M. A. K.; McIntosh, Angus; and Strevens, Peter. *The Linguistic Sciences and Language Teaching*. Bloomington: Indiana University Press, 1964, pp. 118–19.

Lado, Robert. *Language Testing*. New York: McGraw-Hill, 1961. Pp. 15–16 and 24.

Mathesius, V. "Zur Satzperspektive im modernen Englisch." *Archiv für das Studium der neueren Sprachen* 155, no. 84 (1929):202–10.

———. "Ze srovnávacích studií slovosledných" (From comparative word-order studies). *Časopis pro moderní filologii* 28 (1942):181–90 and 302–7.

———. *Obsahový rozbor současné angličtiny na základě obecně lingvistickém (A functional analysis of present-day English on a general linguistic basis)*. Edited by J. Vachek (Prague 1961).

Nickel, Gerhard, and Wagner, K. Heinz. "Contrastive Linguistics and Language Learning." *IRAL* 6 (1968):233–55.

Wilkins, D. A. Review of A. Valdman, *Trends in Language Teaching*. *IRAL* 6 (1968):99–107.

Appendix

TABLE 1

	Recurrent Systemic Errors		Nonce Mistakes		
	Abs.	Percent	Abs.	Percent	Total
Morphology	166	92.3	14	7.7	180
Modal verbs	16	94.2	1	5.8	17
Tenses	50	100.0	—	—	50
Articles	228	87.7	32	12.3	260
Word order	31	64.5	17	35.5	48
Syntax	54	78.3	15	21.7	69
Construction, government	54	58.1	39	41.9	93
Prepositions	19	33.4	38	66.6	57
Lexis	138	59.2	95	40.8	233
Total	756	75.1	251	24.9	1,007

TABLE 2. Morphological Errors

Omission of the plural ending in the noun *(many other point)*	26
Inappropriate plural ending *(peoples, informations)*	4
Lack of agreement between subject and its verb *(foregoing notes has cleared, we was, few people is engaged)*	15
Omission of third person singular ending *-s (this solution correspond)*	6
Infinitive instead of past participle *(the mention rules, rules can be regard as)*	15
Past participle instead of infinitive *(would not been considered, we must solved)*	5
Present participle instead of past participle *(solution submitting in this paper, mechanisms including in the use of . . .)*	5
Past participle instead of present participle *(complex structures are still developed)*	6
Lack of agreement between adjective and its noun *(this notes)*	12
Errors in treatment of *other: others points*	11
another examples	6
Confusion of adverb and adjective *(we cannot take the solution as a definitively one, complex structures are steady developed)*	6
Irregular verbs *(I writed, I spoked, I written)*	12
Omission of *be (would you so kind)*	6
Active voice instead of passive *(the solution would not regard as definitive)*	6
Possessive case *(abroads' journey)*	4
Omission of genitival *of (some aspect mechanisms)*	4
Relative pronouns *(persons which, a girl which, rules what, with who)*	4
Confusion of parts of speech *(interest–interesting, comparative–compare, Russian–Russia, correspondent–correspond)*	13
	166
Nonce mistakes *(we are hope, my friend bought something for your [his] wife)*	14
Total	180

TABLE 3. Errors in Modal Verbs

Would instead of *should (= ought) (would not be regarded)*	12
Could instead of *should (could not be considered)*	3
Might instead of *should (might not be held)*	1
	16
Nonce mistakes (past conditional instead of present conditional)	1
Total	17

TABLE 4. Errors in Tenses

Present instead of preterite *(we are there only four days, I visit some historical towns)*	11
Present instead of perfect *(we correspond with them up to now)*	3
Perfect instead of present *(in this time I have prepared another journey—* at present I am preparing for another journey)	3
Perfect instead of preterite *(I have written this letter yesterday; I traveled with my family in an old Volkswagen, we have been camping all the time)*	12
Preterite instead of perfect *(this is the only foreign country which I visited)*	3
Pluperfect instead of preterite *(I had met parent* [the parents] *of my wife and had spent a wonderful time* [spent]	7
Confusion of simple and continuous forms *(in the afternoon we were going back)*	4
Errors in the future tense *(we will have to solve)*	7
Total	50

TABLE 5. Errors in the Use of the Articles

Omission of the definite article with a singular countable noun *(my knowledge of German language, the conclusion of article)*	27
Omission of the definite article with a noun modified by an *of*-phrase *(in Institute of Nuclear Physics)*	21
Omission of the definite article with a noun modified by a participle (phrase) *(solution given in this article; however we hope* [that] *foregoing remarks enlighted* [enlightened]*)*	52
Omission of the definite article with the name of a country or a mountain range *(from USA, in High Tatras)*	13
Failure in treatment of a noun used generically *(the use of complex structure)*	20
Omission of the indefinite article *(it is only tentative solution, we worked in brewery)*	40
Inappropriate use of the definite article with a plural noun *(the complex structures are still developing, the observation will give the new materials)*	35
The definite article instead of the indefinite *(my last visit to the foreign country)*	15
The indefinite article with an adjective *(could not be taken as a definite)*	5
	228
Nonce mistakes *(in a many other cases, I spent most of time)*	32
Total	260

TABLE 6. Errors in Word Order

Adverbial modifier placed before an object *(I met there many colleagues)*	14
Object in position before the finite verb *(the mountains there I like more)*	9
Subject after the finite verb *(as in many other cases do not exist any exact rules)*	2
Temporal modifier before a local one *(I was one year ago in Russian [Russia])*	6
	31
Nonce mistakes *(there was there a seminar about theoretical physics)*	17
Total	48

TABLE 7. Syntactic Errors

There is instead of *it is (there was a very cold time* [it was very cold]*)*	2
It is (they are) instead of *there is (there are) (they are no correct rules, it is many further points that would have to be solved)*	8
Inversion in indirect question *(give* [state] *please for what purpose did you go there)*	8
Confusion of *some* and *any (give* [state] *please if you have traveled with somebody, gave some light in any things)*	5
Errors in negation *(there are not precise rules)*	7
Omission of subject or object *(which wrote myself, if you have liked there)*	4
Repetition of subject *(following ones they could)*	3
Addition of an inappropriate indirect object *(be so kind to correct me this English letter)*	14
Preposition treated as a conjunction *(it is due to a complex structure is still developing)*	3
	54
Nonce mistakes *(it is written clear English, there were many people interesting* [interested] *in the same problems as I do* [in clear English, as I am]*)*	15
Total	69

TABLE 8. Errors in Construction and Government

Influence of Czech (*this is in part for it that*—to je zčásti proto, že; *I should be very like*—byl bych velmi rád [this is partly because; I should be very glad])	54
Nonce mistakes (*remarks to have been given* [the preceding remarks])	39
Total	93

TABLE 9. Errors in the Use of Prepositions

In instead of *to* (*I will go in Poland*)	11
Influence of Czech (*kind from you, on a week* [of you, for a week])	8
	19
Nonce mistakes (*in this conference* [at], *journey on abroad* [journey abroad], *at any case* [in]	38
Total	57

TABLE 10. Lexical Errors

Confusion of words on the ground of formal similarity (*flee–fly, same–some, happen–hope, maid–main*)	48
Confusion of related words with similar meaning (*farther–further, latest–last, precedent–preceding*)	20
Confusion of related phrases (*lastly–last time, at first–first*)	9
Misuses of words in the case of one-to-several correspondence between Czech and English (*stránka*—page, aspect; *ještě*—still, yet; *před*—before, ago)	54
Influence of German (*college–colleague, oft–often, gast–guest, chef–chief*)	7
	138
Distortions (*throgh* [throw], *similary* [similarly], *desolve* [solve])	25
Other nonce mistakes (*change letters* [exchange], *be presented like definitive* [as], *I wrote down to my colleague* [I wrote to my colleague])	70
Total	233

Patterned Phonetic Variability in Second Language Speech: A Gradual Diffusion Model

Elizabeth Gatbonton

One striking characteristic of second language speech is its extreme phonetic heterogeneity arising from the fact that second language speakers often have different ways of rendering many sounds in their target language. A second language speaker of English, for example, may pronounce the English word *these* as [di:z], [di:s], [dði:z], [ði:z] or [ði:s], in which case he has three variants for the initial interdental and two for the final /s/. Some of his variants may be similar to what native English speakers say and therefore considered correct; others may be quite different and therefore considered incorrect.

Two questions can be asked concerning this variability. First, is it systematic, that is, is the use of one or the other form predictable for each target sound? Second, what is the source of the systematicity or randomness of the data?

Recent investigations of phonetic variability in second language speech suggest that it might be systematic. L. Dickerson (1975) and W. Dickerson (1976) investigated the English speech of Japanese informants and found their variable pronunciation of the English /z/ in words like *these* and *size* and /l/ in *light* to be constrained by phonetic (the surrounding sounds), stylistic (casualness or formality of speech situation) and other factors (e.g., length of study of English). W. Dickerson (1976), moreover, found that as time went by more words containing the target variable took on progressively more advanced variants in a progressively greater number of environments, suggesting a systematic development on this variable through time. Schmidt (1977) also investigated the English speech of Arabic speakers and found their pronunciation of the English interdental to vary systematically according to speech style in the same way as pronunciation of these same variables in their native speech seems to vary.

Reprinted from the *Canadian Modern Language Review/La Revue canadienne des langues vivantes* 34, no. 3 (February, 1978):335–47. By permission of the editor, Anthony Mollica, and the author.

With regards to the possible source of the systematicity or randomness of variable second language data, there is today only speculation of what it might be. W. Dickerson suggests that the source may be a variable linguistic competence which the learner acquires as he learns his second language: "The learner's phonological system (and undoubtedly his syntactic system as well) is a system of variable rules" (W. Dickerson 1976, p. 229). Variable rules, which indicate the probability that one or the other variation of a certain variable may be favored by a given context, were proposed by Labov (1969) and later developed by Cedergren and Sankoff (1974) to account for systematic variability in first language data. But although it may be possible to provide an adequate description of variable performance in terms of variable rules, not all linguists studying variability accept the rules as the source of variability. Bickerton (1973), for example, suggests that the source of first language variability is not variable rules, but certain changes in the language occurring over time, for example, the replacement of an old rule by a new one where the replacement is complete only after both rules have competed in the same context for a time.

Similarly, an alternative explanation to the variable rule position of Dickerson may be taken for second language data. For example, it is possible that the manner of acquisition of correct variants and replacement of incorrect ones in speech underlie systematic phonetic variability in second language speech. If the manner in which the variants are acquired and/or replaced is systematic, it is possible that the distribution of the variants in speech at any stage of development would also be systematic. Likewise, if this acquisition-replacement process is random, the distribution of the variants in speech would also be random.

In this paper, a study is reported exploring the relationship between observed variability in second language data and the process in which correct variants are acquired and incorrect ones replaced. In particular, three phonological variables in the English speech of French Canadian second language speakers in Montréal, Québec, were investigated to find out whether the occurrence of correct and incorrect variants in their speech at any one stage is predictable and whether the systematicity or randomness of the data is related to the acquisition and replacement of correct and incorrect variants.

These issues are investigated as follows. First, a hypothesis concerning the way correct variants are acquired and incorrect variants are replaced was defined, and a model of acquisition based on this hypothesis was constructed. Second, the speech samples of the second language informants were examined to see whether the patterns of variability in their speech matched to a statistically significant degree the patterns predicted by the acquisition-replacement model. The approach taken is adapted from the dynamic paradigm approach as proposed and employed by Bickerton (1973) in showing that first language variability could be accounted for by a model of linguistic changes occurring in speech through time.

The acquisition-replacement process proposed to underlie second language variability here may be called a *gradual diffusion* process involving first the acquisition of correct variants in all the relevant contexts and then the replacement of all incorrect variants there. It is assumed that at the initial stages the learner unsuccessfully pronounces some of his target sounds and substitutes for them others from his native language or from elsewhere. Both the acquisition and the replacement processes occur gradually, starting with the environmental category most favorable to the new sound and proceeding to the last, one at a time. Thus, as acquisition proceeds the number of environmental categories where both variants occur increases, but as replacement proceeds this number decreases until all the relevant categories show only the correct variants, unless the change process is halted by some outside interference before this point is reached. This view of development may be illustrated by a matrix such as in table 1.

Here, the columns indicate the phonetic contexts (for illustration purposes, only three are presented: the actual number depends upon the data) where the different variants occur. The rows indicate the different stages the learner may go through as he acquires the target sound.

In this matrix only incorrect variants (1) are shown in all the environmental categories (EC1) in stage *a* and only correct variants (2) are shown in all the environmental categories in the last stage (stage *g*) indicating that the learner begins with unsuccessful substitutions in all contexts and ends by acquiring correct variants in these same contexts. In the intervening stages (stages *b* to *f*) the acquisition of the correct variants is shown to occur first in EC1 and last in EC3. Since the incorrect variants are not replaced automatically by correct variants there are contexts which contain both variants together (1, 2), the number of which increases as acquisition proceeds. The replacement of the incorrect sounds also proceeds from EC1 to EC3. As the replacement proceeds the number of ECs containing both variants decreases while the number containing correct variants alone increases.

TABLE 1. A Sample Matrix Representing the Manner in which the Correct Pronunciation (2) of a Target Language Variable Is Acquired and the Manner in which the Incorrect Pronunciation (1) of This Same Variable Is Replaced in Three Environmental Categories in the Speech of a Second Language Learner

Stages	EC1	EC2	EC3
Acquisition Phase			
a	1	1	1
b	1, 2	1	1
c	1, 2	1, 2	1
d	1, 2	1, 2	1, 2
Replacement Phase			
e	2	1, 2	1, 2
f	2	2	1, 2
g	2	2	2

Method

Informants

Twenty-seven French Canadian male university students and junior college teachers aged nineteen through thirty were the informants in this study. All were native to Montréal except for one from Trois Rivières, Québec, and another from New Brunswick.

Phonological Variables Examined

The three phonological variables examined were: the voiced *th* (/ð/) as in *brother, the,* and *soothe;* the voiceless *th* (/θ/) as in *teeth, think,* and *ether* and the voiceless velar glide (/h/) as in *behind* and *he.* These variables were chosen because preliminary testing revealed them to be among the most variable in the informants' English and among the most noticeable elements contributing to the accented quality of their speech, as judged by native English speakers.

The data containing the variables were taken from each informant's taped readings of two English diagnostic paragraphs and twenty-seven sentences containing minimal word pairs (here referred to as the read data), as well as from their recorded spontaneous speech (spontaneous data).

The analysis involved these steps:

1. The variants of each variable were identified and classified as correct or incorrect variants. Classification was made with the aid of native speakers of English who listened to each informant's taped reading of one of the diagnostic paragraphs and indicated on an accompanying typewritten text those sounds which they thought were not pronounced natively. Variants which were so noted were considered incorrect while the rest were considered correct.

2. The linguistic contexts containing variants of each variable were identified, categorized, and ordered. The categorization was as follows. Phonetic environments were grouped together if they shared features distinguishing them from other possible groupings. For example, [p], [t], [k] were combined into a category because they all share the features of voicelessness, nonnasality, noncontinuance, and consonance and can be distinguished from a similar group, ([b], [d], [g]) by voicing. Two or more such categories were combined to form a larger category if the following conditions were met. First, the resulting category itself is distinct from other categories. For example, [p], [t], [k] may be combined with [b], [d], [g] to form a nonnasal noncontinuant category distinct from a group formed by [m], [n], [ŋ] which is nasal. Or, [b], [d], [g] and [m], [n], [ŋ] may be combined to form a voiced noncontinuant consonantal category distinguishable from another formed by [p], [t], [k] by voicing. However, [p], [t], [k], and [m], [n], [ŋ] may not be combined since they share only the features noncontinuance and consonance and cannot be distinguished from a category formed by [b], [d], [g] by these features alone. Secondly, the resulting category does not differ from the original smaller categories being combined in the type of variants used there by most informants. For example, a category formed by [p], [t], [k] may be combined with another formed by [b], [d], [g] only if in each of these categories at least 85 percent of the informants used similar patterns of correct and incorrect variants. The two categories may not be merged if most of the informants used similar patterns in one category but different patterns in the other. The latter combination would result in a category that would differ from one of the original categories.

The final sets of categories were ordered according to the proportion of correct or incorrect variants they contained when the speech of all the informants was combined. Categories containing the largest proportion of correct variants were placed highest in the hierarchy while those containing the smallest proportion were lowest in the hierarchy.

3. Models (such as in table 1) of the linguistic changes believed to underlie second language variability were constructed. In constructing these models the number of environmental categories relevant for each variable and the ranking of the categories were taken into account. It was assumed that the category favoring correct variants would be the first category where the acquisition and the replacement processes described earlier would occur.

4. The speech patterns of each informant for each variable were then analyzed and compared to the speech patterns specified in the model matrices. The degree of correspondence between the two sets of patterns was statistically evaluated. A close fit was interpreted as support for patterned variability which reflects patterning in the underlying developmental sequence.

5. To further test the validity of the models, the assignment of each informant's speech pattern to a stage in the model was compared to the way native English speakers rated his speech on an accent scale.

Results

Because of space considerations, only the results of the analyses of the voiced *th* variable in the read speech are discussed in detail here. Others are summarized.

The Voiced th *Variable; READ Data*

The read speech corpus contained seventy-two words with the voiced *th* /ð/ variable, in both stressed and unstressed, as well as in sentence initial and medial positions. Only the words containing /ð/ in sentence medial and in unstressed positions (e.g., *saw the effect; read the book*) were analyzed since the other samples were too small to base a proper generalization on.

Variants of the variable. Four variants of /ð/ were found: a dental stop, [d] (e.g., [ində] as *in the*), an affricate, [dð], as in [adðər] *other*, a fricative, [ð], as in [braðərz] *brothers,* and a zero, [∅], as when the /ð/ is not pronounced at all (e.g., [for əm] *for them*).

Only the occurrence of the dental stop variant was frequently noted by the native English speakers to be nonnativelike. The dental stop variant was therefore considered the incorrect variant while the rest, the correct variants.

Linguistic environments. Five linguistic environments were found to be relevant for the /ð/ variable. These are presented with the percentage of correct variants that they each yielded in the speech of all the informants combined: EC1: a preceding + vocalic, − consonantal segment as in [i] in *either* or [u] as in *to the electricians* (43 percent correct variants); EC2: a preceding + voice, + continuant, + consonantal segment as in [r] in *are they* or [l] as in *will they* (38 percent correct variants); EC3: a preceding + voice, − continuant, + consonantal segment as in [d] in *would they* (27 percent correct variants); EC4: a preceding − voice, + continuant, + consonantal segment as in [s] in *produce this sunset effect* (25 percent correct variants); EC5: a preceding − voice, − continuant, + consonantal segment as in [k] or [t] in *ask the author* or *not their only job,* respectively (14 percent correct variants).

Model matrix. Table 2 represents a model matrix representing the changes believed to occur in the speech of French Canadians learning /ð/.

In this matrix, 1 again stands for the incorrect variant and 2 for the correct variant. Because there are five environmental categories, the model requires eleven stages. Stages *a–f* correspond to the acquisition phase where correct pronunciations are acquired without automatically displacing the incorrect variants. Stages *g–k* represent stages in the replacement phase where incorrect pronunciations are slowly displaced by the correct ones. Table 2 indicates that both the acquisition and the replacement phases begin in the vocalic environment, proceed to the voiced continuant, the voiced noncontinuant, and the voiceless continuant consonantal categories, in that order, and end in the voiceless noncontinuant consonantal category.

Comparison of the observed patterns and model patterns. Twenty-one observed speech patterns were found to correspond perfectly to patterns in the model, as indicated in the right hand column of table 2. Six patterns deviated from the model. The binomial test performed on this twenty-one to six split indicates highly significant support for the model (p<.001). This suggests that the distribution of correct and incorrect variants in the informant's speech is not random but is patterned in the way depicted in the model.

This observation is further supported by the fact that all but three patterns in the model matrix are realized by one or more informants. Since the model was constructed to contain all the theoretically possible speech patterns in the group it was not expected that all patterns would be realized in the sample of informants examined. The fact that most of these are so realized is encouraging empirical support for the hypothesized stages in the model.

An example of the binomial test calculation might be helpful. Consider the simple model analysis of the read /ð/ data. Examination of the

TABLE 2. A Model Matrix Appropriate for the /ð/ in Read Situation Showing the Acquisition Phase (stages *a–f*) and the Replacement Phase (stages *g–k*) of the Acquisition Process It Depicts

Stage	EC1 $\begin{bmatrix} +\text{voc} \\ -\text{cns} \end{bmatrix}$ (##) – ## –	EC2 $\begin{bmatrix} +\text{cns} \\ +\text{vce} \\ +\text{cnt} \end{bmatrix}$ ## –	EC3 $\begin{bmatrix} +\text{cns} \\ +\text{vce} \\ -\text{cnt} \end{bmatrix}$ ## –	EC4 $\begin{bmatrix} +\text{cns} \\ -\text{vce} \\ +\text{cnt} \end{bmatrix}$ ## –	EC5 $\begin{bmatrix} +\text{cns} \\ -\text{vce} \\ -\text{cnt} \end{bmatrix}$ ## –	Informants Matching Model Patterns*
Acquisition Phase						
a	1	1	1	1	1	2; 11; 17
b	1, 2	1	1	1	1	1; 10; 12; 13; 15; 16; 19
c	1, 2	1, 2	1	1	1	3; 6; 29
d	1, 2	1, 2	1, 2	1	1	
e	1, 2	1, 2	1, 2	1, 2	1	4; 28
f	1, 2	1, 2	1, 2	1, 2	1, 2	24; 25
Replacement Phase						
g	2	1, 2	1, 2	1, 2	1, 2	14; 22; 27
h	2	2	1, 2	1, 2	1, 2	21
i	2	2	2	1, 2	1, 2	26
j	2	2	2	2	1, 2	
k	2	2	2	2	2	

Note: voc = vocalic, cns = consonantal, cnt = continuant, vce = voiced

*The numbers on the right are those of the informants whose speech patterns perfectly match patterns at the different stages.

speech of the 27 informants reveals that .67 of them (18) displayed only incorrect elements in EC5. Similarly, in EC4 and EC3 the proportions of informants with only incorrect elements were .59 and .52 respectively. In EC2 and EC1 the proportions of informants showing both correct and incorrect elements were .44 and .67 respectively. These figures provide the basis for estimating the probability of a speaker displaying a pattern that follows the one corresponding to stage c in the model:

	EC1	EC2	EC3	EC4	EC5
Stage c	1, 2	1, 2	1	1	1

This is the product of the five probabilities of displaying each of the patterns in each of the environmental categories (here, .061). Note that if the equal probability assumption is kept for the events represented by 1; 1, 2; and 2 in the model then the probability for obtaining a stage c pattern under the null hypothesis is $1/3^5$ or .004.

The probabilities for each of the eleven stages in the model are thus calculated and summed, yielding the total probability of obtaining a pattern matching one represented in the model. In the present example that probability is .24, considerably higher than .045 calculated under the assumption of equal probability. This indicates that if the population at large has tendencies to distribute correct and incorrect elements in the five environments as do these 27 informants but that otherwise the distribution of the elements in these categories is random, then .24 of any set of informants may be expected to show patterns matching the eleven patterns in the model by chance alone.

The finding that 21 out of 27 informants had patterns matching the model can be evaluated with the binomial test. That is, the event of a match with any one pattern in the model has a chance probability of .24 while the probability of a mismatch is .76. By the binomial test the likelihood of obtaining 21 matches out of 27 is less than .001 and so the null hypothesis that no systematic patterning underlies the distribution can be rejected.

Native speakers' rating. A comparison of the informants' ranking on a 1 to 9 accent rating scale (heavy accent indicating low rank) as given by native speaking judges and their ranking on the model matrix (stage a indicating low rank, k, a high rank) showed a high correlation (Spearman $r = .79$, $p < .01$) between native speakers' perception of accent and the analysis offered by the model.

Voiceless th: *READ Data*

There were 16 words containing the voiceless *th* /θ/ with 3 phonetic variants ([ð], [tᵒ], [t]) occurring in 4 environmental categories (e.g., before and after an [r] segment as in *never thought* and *throw*, respectively, after a vowel as in *in the theatre*, and after other consonants as in *much thought*). Of the 27 observed speech patterns, 22 matched the appropriate model speech patterns while 5 did not. The binomial test indicated this 22 to 5 split to be significantly in favor of the model ($p < .001$). The distribution of the speech patterns to stages in the model matrix correlated positively with the native speakers' ratings of accents ($rs = .85$, $p < .01$).

Voiceless Velar Glide: READ Data

There were 54 words containing the voiceless velar glide /h/ with 3 phonetic variants ([h], [ʔ], [∅]) occurring in 5 environmental categories (after a vowel as in *rehearsal*, a voiceless stop as in *at home*, a voiced stop as in *the big houses*, a voiced continuant as in *for himself* and a voiceless continuant as in *lift him up* where *lift* is pronounced as [lif]).

Of the 27 observed speech patterns, 24 matched the appropriate model speech patterns and 3 did not. This 24 to 3 split was found to be significantly in support of the model ($p < .001$, binomial test). The distribution of the speech patterns to stages in the model correlated positively with the native speakers' ratings of accents (Spearman $r = .86$, $p < .01$).

Voiced th *in Spontaneous Data*

There were 1,363 tokens of /ð/ in the spontaneous speech situation for all the informants combined. The same 4 variants of /ð/ found in the read situation were also found occurring in 5 environmental categories (same as in table 2) in the spontaneous speech situation. Of the 27 observed speech patterns, 23 matched patterns in the appropriate model and 4 did not. This 23 to 4 split was found to be a statistically significant support for the model ($p < .001$).

Compared to the distribution of the speech patterns in the read situation where most were spread across the matrix, most of the spontaneous speech patterns were clustered in the early section of the model. Moreover, for many of the informants fewer correct variants were used in the spontaneous than in the read speech situation and these also occurred in a smaller number of categories.

The distribution of the spontaneous speech patterns to stages in the model matrix correlated positively with the native judges' ratings of the informants' accents (rs = .81, p<.01).

Discussion

The results may be summarized as follows. The patterning of the variants of /ð/, /θ/, and /h/ in the read speech and also of /ð/ in the spontaneous speech samples matched to a statistically significant degree the patterning predicted by a gradual diffusion model of second language phonetic variability. Also, in each case the ranking of the observed speech patterns according to stages specified in the model correlated highly with their ranking on an accent scale by native speakers of English. These findings support the view that phonetic variability in second language speech is patterned, not random, and that the source of this variability and systematicity is the process by which the learner masters new elements of the target language.

Although most of the speech patterns examined here supported the model, there were nevertheless a few which deviated from them. Examination of these patterns, however, shows that often only one category is involved. An example is a speech pattern such as:

EC1	EC2	EC3	EC4	EC5
1	1	1	1	1, 2

which deviates from a model matrix such as the one presented in table 2 only in having two entries in EC5 where only one is expected. A new element (2) is not expected to occur in this environmental category since it has not yet appeared in the earlier categories. Examination of all the patterns produced indicates no consistent pattern with regards to the types of categories involved and so on.

Thus, it is not easy to decide why the deviations occurred. They may possibly reflect errors not related to underlying linguistic processes; for example, errors due to distractions, nervousness, and so on. Or they may simply reflect the possibility that not all second language speakers categorize and order their environments in the same way. The present study assumed that a group of speakers with the same mother tongue background, learning the same target language, in the same general context would be fairly similar in the way they acquired their second language. The present data largely bear out this assumption. Nevertheless, the model of acquisition proposed here does not have to assume consensus in the group regarding the ordering of categories in order to be valid. All the model really specifies is that for each individual some environmental categories are ordered, so that mastery of target sounds is characterized first by the gradual acquisition of correct variants across these categories and then by the gradual elimination of incorrect ones in exactly the same orderly manner. Individuals could, in principle, differ in the precise ordering of the categories. Only a longitudinal study, of course, could examine this possibility.

It is appropriate at this point to draw attention to some characteristics of the acquisition process that appear to underlie phonetic variability here. One is that it proceeds in two phases: the acquisition of correct elements and the replacement of incorrect ones, with each phase having different stages. The question that arises is whether the learners go through all the stages proposed. It seems possible that they do but this proposal has yet to be fully assessed in a further study, for example, in a longitudinal observation of second language learners. The other important characteristic is that the acquisition-replacement process implies a hierarchically ordered set of categories for it to proceed as it does. It is not clear in this study why the categories are ordered or what determines their ordering although some speculations are possible. For example, it is possible that target variables are learned best when they occur in a phonetic context that contrasts highly with them, for example, a vocalic environment for a consonantal target variable and vice versa. Examination of the /ð/ variable (table 2) reveals that the environmental category where its correct variant is acquired earliest is the vocalic (EC1) instead of the consonantal (EC2–EC5) categories indicating some support for a choice of this type. It is also, of course, possible that when the target and the phonetic contexts are of the same class (for example, both are consonants or vowels) the phonetic similarity between them may be important. If one examines the consonantal contexts of the /ð/ variable (EC2–EC5) one finds that those sharing most features with the target variable (EC4) seem to be more favorable to it than others sharing fewer features (e.g., EC5 in table 2).

Another possibility is that certain lexical items containing certain environmental categories are more salient and therefore learned earlier than other items containing other environmental categories. For example, words like *father* and *brother* may be heard more often or heard more in socially salient contexts than words like *further* and *although,* and therefore are learned earlier. Because of this the intervocalic context for the /ð/ variable in the first pair of words may become the locus for the acquisition of the correct variants earlier than the context in the second pair. Once acquired in this context the correct variant is then generalized to other words containing similar phonetic contexts. The spread of newly acquired elements in the language through the lexicon (lexical diffusion) has been proposed by some researchers (cf. Chen and Wang 1975; Ferguson and Farwell 1975) to account for changes occurring in the speech of first language learners and for changes occurring in language in general.

The discovery of a hierarchy of phonetic contexts raises the issue of whether the learners employ systematic strategies in learning the language. While it is not always exactly clear in what sense theorists use the term *strategy* it is usually implied that the learner actively assesses the target language structures being learned (makes an hypothesis about them) and then adjusts his speech accordingly. Dulay and Burt, for example, state that second language learners "gradually reconstruct rules for the speech they hear, guided by universal innate mechanisms which cause them to use certain strategies to organize that linguistic input, until the mismatch between the language system they are exposed to and what they produce is resolved" (Dulay and Burt 1974, p. 73).

The usual evidence offered for learner strategies is the existence of any patterned behavior not directly attributable to the target or mother tongue system. In the field of error analysis these are patterned errors not due to mother tongue interference (cf. Corder 1971). In other studies it is the existence of a hierarchy of difficulty in the items learned (cf. Burt and Dulay 1976; Dulay and Burt 1975).

Sampson (1971) also claims second language learners to be using a strategy when they make phonetic substitution for target language segments not found in their native speech. The strategy consists of assessing the features of the target segment and then matching it against sets of features in the native language. If the language lacks a segment with the same features as the target segment they will use the segment containing features closest to the target features (cf. Michaels 1974; Ritchie 1968).

In the present study the existence of a hierarchy of environmental categories may be taken as evidence for a learner strategy. For example, one could, following the approach of Sampson, argue that the learner assesses the environmental categories by ordering them and then selectively focuses upon them one at a time as the locus for acquiring correct variants of target sounds. Stating the situation this way, however, attributes too much conscious processing to the learner. It is more likely that some perceptual constraints which cannot yet be specified restrict the rate of learning so that acquisition can only proceed context by context.

Implications

The approach taken in this study involves examining the distribution of correct and incorrect elements in the second language data and relating it to the manner in which new elements may be acquired and old ones eliminated as learning proceeds. This approach differs from most others in the language learning literature in that it focuses upon both errors and nonerrors *together*, instead of upon each in isolation; error analysis, for example, focuses only on errors and learner systems analysis focuses only on elements already correctly mastered (cf. Richards 1974; Burt and Dulay 1976; Sampson and Richards 1973). By looking at errors and nonerrors together one is forced to deal with the variability of the data and to seek means for its analysis. Unfortunately, the variability of second language data has, in some respects, often been viewed as an impediment to the full investigation of autonomous second language learner systems and it has made difficult the study of the rules of grammar that may govern the functioning of such systems (cf. Corder 1971; Nemser 1971; Selinker 1972).

Most investigations of autonomous learner systems have looked for regularities (patterns in the errors, common orders of morpheme acquisition, etc.) buried in the highly variable speech performance; the variability itself being regarded more as an inconvenience to the researcher than anything else. That variability in the data seems amenable to linguistic analysis indicates that a grammatical description of the second language system may no longer be a remote possibility.

In the present paper second language speech was examined in the context of a gradual diffusion model of language acquisition. The use of this model, which is based on one developed for first language variability, raises the interesting question regarding the possible parallel between change in language history and change in second language acquisition. In what respects, for example, is there a similarity or difference between the two change processes? W. Dickerson (1976) also raises the issue in connection with his proposal for variable rules for second language speech. Another question concerns the linguistic competence acquired by second language speakers. Dickerson suggests that variable rules are acquired and what are changed as the individual progresses are the probability coefficients of the rules. In the gradual diffusion model, progress in learning consists in the acquisition of new rules and replacement of old ones at each stage of development; that is, the person possesses two competing rules applying alternately. The question then is whether indeed one needs variable rules to account for the variable behavior of the second language learner. If variable rules are not appropriate, what then does the linguistic competence of the learner consist of?

Finally, perhaps some speculation may be permitted about possible implications for second language teaching. Since the model specifies what environmental categories are involved in the acquisition-replacement process and how these are ordered, the model may be useful in determining how materials should be sequenced to meet the needs of students. For example, knowing at which level a student is located can permit the teachers to program the materials to be taught so that the sets containing categories where correct variants are likely to enter in early are presented first and drilled upon most. This way, perhaps teachers can help hasten the learner's progress towards acquiring this variable.

Note

This study, based on work submitted by the author in partial fulfillment of requirements for a Ph.D. at McGill University, was supported by a Canada Council Grant to Professor W. E. Lambert and Professor G. R. Tucker. The author would like to thank Dr. Rosemary Weber and Dr. Norman Segalowitz for their valuable comments on earlier versions of this paper

References

Bickerton, D. "Quantitative Versus Dynamic Paradigms: The Case of Montreal, 'Que'." In *New Ways of Analyzing Variations in English,* edited by C. J. Bailey and R. W. Shuy, pp. 23–43. Washington, D.C.: Georgetown University Press, 1973.

Burt, M., and Dulay, H. C. "Creative Construction in Second Language Learning and Teaching." In *Papers in Second Language Acquisition,* edited by H. Douglas Brown, pp. 65–80. Ann Arbor: Research Club in Language Learning, 1976.

Cedergren, H., and Sankoff, D. "Variable Rules: Performance as a Statistical Reflection of Competence." *Language* 50 (1974):333–55.

Chen, M., and Wang, W. S-Y. "Sound Change: Actuation and Implementation." *Language* 51 (1975):255–81.

Corder, S. Pit. "Idiosyncratic Dialects and Error Analysis." *IRAL* 9 (1971):146–60.

Dickerson, L. "The Learner's Interlanguage as a System of Variable Rules." *TESOL Quarterly* 9 (1975):401–7.

Dickerson, W. "The Psycholinguistic Unity of Language Learning and Language Change." *Language Learning* 26 (1976):215–31.

Dulay, H. C., and Burt, M. K. "A New Perspective on the Creative Construction Process in Child Language Acquisition." *Working Papers on Bilingualism* 4 (1974):71–98.

Dulay, H. C., and Burt, M. K., eds. *New Directions in Second Language Learning, Teaching and Bilingual Education.* Washington, D.C.: TESOL, 1975.

Ferguson, C. A., and Farwell, C. B. "Words and Sounds in Early Language Acquisition." *Language* 51 (1975):419–39.

Labov, W. "Contraction, Deletion and Inherent Variability of the English Copula." *Language* 45 (1969):715–62.

Michaels, D. "Sound Replacements and Phonological Systems." *Linguistics* 126 (1974):69–81.

Nemser, W. "Approximative Systems of Foreign Language Learners." *IRAL* 9 (1971):115–23.

Richards, J. C. *Error Analysis: Perspective on Second Language Acquisition.* London: Longmans, 1974.

Ritchie, W. C. "On the Explanation of Phonic Interference." *Language Learning* 18 (1968):183–97.

Sampson, G. P. "The Strategies of Cantonese Speakers Learning English." In *Linguistic Diversity in Canadian Setting,* edited by Regna Darnell, pp. 175–280. Edmonton: Linguistic Research, Inc., 1971.

Sampson, G. P., and Richards, J. C. "Language Learner Systems." *Language Sciences* 19 (1973):19–25.

Schmidt, R. W. "Sociolinguistic Variation and Language Transfer in Phonology." *Working Papers in Bilingualism* 12 (1977):79–95.

Selinker, L. "Interlanguage." *IRAL* 10 (1972):209–31.

Induced Errors

Nancy Stenson

Introduction

In this article, I would like to describe some types of student errors in a language classroom that result more from the classroom situation than from either the students' incomplete competence in English grammar or first language interference. Students are easily led into making errors in the course of classroom participation by the structure of the situation. These are errors which it is doubtful they would produce in spontaneous speech. Such induced errors tell us little about the level of the students' language competence but are worthy of study in that they are easy to overlook, may easily cause inaccurate assessment of students' ability, and, if ignored, may reinforce misunderstanding and form the basis for later problems. Any analysis of student errors must also take such mistakes into account as phenomena separate from errors of spontaneous speech.

The data from which my examples are drawn were gathered in Tunis, Tunisia, during the summer of 1971 from observation of adult English classes at the Institut Bourguiba des Langues Vivantes, and from high school students during practice teaching sessions of the 1971 Peace Corps TEFL training program in Mahdia, Tunisia. Most of the students were in intermediate or advanced classes.

Vocabulary

A teacher may inadvertently mislead students by the way he defines a lexical item, or by the order in which he presents material. For example, given *worship* as a general word for *pray*, the students immediately attached to the new word the same preposition that they knew to be required with the familiar one, and began speaking of "worshipping to God." Habits which may develop from such analogies between two re-

Reprinted from *New Frontiers in Second Language Learning,* edited by John H. Schumann and Nancy Stenson, pp. 54–70 (Rowley, Mass.: Newbury House, 1974), by permission of the author.

lated items seem especially difficult to break; several students made this mistake in succession, even after the teacher had corrected the first of them.

The problems of both word definition and order of presentation were brought into focus when students were confronted for the first time with a single lexical item consisting of a verb + particle. They were given the definition of *point out* through example sentences with appropriate gestures, and then asked to use it in sentences. Those students who did not merely paraphrase the teacher's examples were all clearly treating the construction as two separate lexical items, *point,* which they already knew, and the preposition *out.* Thus, the new lexical item came out sounding to them like just another way to say *point to* or *point at.* One student with a little more imagination offered "When I see a ship in the sea, I point out," which the teacher corrected to ". . . I point it out to my friends." This is probably not what the student meant at all. The chances are at least equally good that he was using *out* as a directional: "I point out (to sea, to the ship, etc.) . . ." That he intended *out* in his sentence to indicate direction is plausible, since all students were having a great deal of trouble with *point out,* and since omission of a direct object pronoun where one is required was rare, if not unheard of, at least among these students. If this were the case, the teacher's insertion of the pronoun *it* is no help at all to the student. It doesn't help him learn the real meaning of *point out,* which both the teacher and he assume he knows, and if he is a very attentive student, given to quick generalizations, he might even be led, by a correction like this, to start inserting *it* incorrectly with other directionals. Treating verb + particle forms as a unit at some point would at least give a tool for correcting individual lexical items.

Immediately after *point out,* and without fully understanding it, the students were given *notice* and asked to use it in sentences. This led to the sentence "The barometer noticed that it wouldn't be fine." This student appears to have confused the two new vocabulary items and, since one word bears a causative relation to the other, this serves to reinforce the confusion. The student might not make a mistake like this in a normal conversation—he would be more inclined to use a word he is sure of, like *show,* if he ever needed to talk about barometer readings—but once he has misused a word or (worse) a pair of words, even under drill conditions, he will probably, if not set straight, remain confused and make additional errors. This is not to suggest that a teacher should necessarily avoid teaching related words together. Indeed, such a device can be a very useful teaching technique, and whether to use it or not must depend on the situation and the class. However, a teacher who is attuned to such relationships between words (not always evident on the surface of things) can do much to avoid difficulties or clear them up once they present themselves.

A final type of induced vocabulary error came from students being forced to demonstrate a distinction that they were vaguely aware of, but unable to explain adequately. For example, asked to demonstrate the difference between *should* and *must,* a student said: "We should have worked in order to buy clothes, but we must have worked in order to eat." This class knew that *must* was in some way stronger than *should,* but were apparently not entirely clear on just how—in general, they steered clear of *should* and used *must* everywhere. The student who had to demonstrate the difference did indeed make a distinction of degree, but in so doing, he transferred the force of necessity from the end to the means.

A similar error arose when a student attempted to characterize the difference between *at* and *into:* "We look at the moon, but Armstrong looked into the moon." The distinction had been demonstrated solely by examples and pantomime ("Now I'm looking at the bag; now I'm looking *into* the bag" [moving closer to the bag to indicate peering into it]) and this student probably got the idea that the distinction was one of thoroughness or closeness rather than of surface versus interior. Just saying "no" to a student with such a misconception teaches him nothing, yet a teacher unaware of what is going on can do little else.

Situations like these can tell us a lot we would not otherwise learn about what a student knows and does not know. It is impossible to measure his competence with structures and vocabulary he never uses. Since errors are our only way of determining what aspects of language the student has not yet acquired, one could easily be led to assume (without the help of induced errors) that nonappearance of a certain structure rather than deviant appearance indicates acquisition of that structure. In many cases nothing could be farther from the truth. The difference between systematic errors which reflect possible rule differences, interference, etc., and those errors arising from gaps in student grammar should be obvious. The latter constructions are extremely difficult to get at, since they are rarely (and never systematically) reflected in the student's speech. Thus a tremendous number of differences between a student's competence and that of a native speaker may go unobserved or unexplained because there is no data to work from. Here, then, is an area where the importance of induced errors as distinguished from spontaneous errors is apparent. The former provide otherwise unobtainable information about student competence. Two points follow from this: first, that vocabulary misuse may reflect nonacquisition of certain structural elements in the language rather than misunderstanding of a lexical definition; second, errors that might be *describable* in terms of differences in rule formulation between student and native grammar will not necessarily be *explained* in this way. The following section further illustrates this.

Syntax

Grammatical errors that would not ordinarily occur may also be induced through misunderstanding of meaning or usage, or, occasionally, through faulty explanation. Students in one advanced class were asked if they knew the meaning of *any,* and, when all said yes, to give some examples, with the following result: "In this class there are any students who speak German (= not any, no students)," "In a private garden anyone can enter (= no one)" and "Anybody has to work." Apparently these students were once told something to the effect that *any* is used in negatives, or has negative connotations, and they interpreted that to mean that it was itself a negative word, like *never* or *nothing.* Thus, in the first two sentences above, the students left the negative marker off the verb as redundant, producing, in the first case, a deviant sentence, and in the second a polarity switch. The third sentence seems to involve a confusion between *any* and *every* (cf. " $\left\{ \begin{array}{l} \text{Everybody} \\ \text{Anybody} \end{array} \right\}$ may leave now").

That these are situation-induced errors is suggested by the fact that students, even at advanced levels, tend not to use *any* and other words involving feature shifts at all, though they would probably understand them if encountered in someone else's speech. In fact, "I don't have some NP" is a common type of student error; on the other hand, I found no other cases of misuse of negative polarity words, probably because such words are among the last things learned, and hence almost never used, even at advanced levels.

One teacher defined *as if* as more or less synonymous with *like* and then asked students to transform sentences with *like* into sentences with *as if* (e.g., "He climbs like a monkey" into "He climbs as if he were a monkey"). But one student, given the sentence "She cries like a baby" responded with "She cries as if the baby cries" which would be fine if *like* were really just a synonym for *as if.* In fact, however, there is a structural change involved in this exercise as well. The sentence the student was asked to transform is ambiguous; it could be paraphrased in either of the following ways:

Her crying is like that of a baby. (She cries like a baby cries.)
In that she cries, she is just like a baby. (She cries like she is a
 baby.)

It is only in the second of these two readings that *as if* can be used. The
student has inserted *as if* in the first sentence with incorrect results. The
average native speaker of English would not normally be conscious of the
above ambiguity until an incorrect sentence appeared such as the one this
student produced. It is crucial, however, that the teacher be aware of
such potential ambiguities and avoid inadequate explanations like the one
given in this case. A thorough understanding of the syntax of sentences
with *like* in them is the only way to make clear to the student when *as if*
can be substituted for *like* and when it cannot.

A final danger lies in overreliance on grammatical terminology without sufficient attention to function in the sentence. Thus, after several
examples involving *absolutely impossible,* students asked to use the adjective form of *absolutely* produced: "It's absolute impossible to do." These
students had fairly thorough familiarity with grammatical terminology and
usage, so it may have been sheer laziness that produced this sentence. In
any case, such an error is simple enough to correct, especially where the
students are acquainted with the terms. But it is not the sort of mistake
they usually made spontaneously and can thus be attibuted to careless
reliance on terminology at the expense of the usage it represents, rather
than to real confusion over form and function. As such, it is probably not
worth spending much time on, and should be recognized for what it is.

Drills

It is easy to fall into the pattern of a structural drill and forget that the
sentences being produced have semantic content; in reducing textbook
exercises to rote mechanical repetition, students produce some bizarre
semantic violations that would be unlikely to appear in real speech. An
intermediate level drill gave students the choice of several phrases as
possible reponses to a yes-no quesiton:

No, but I
{
hope to
ought to
must
expect to
have to
etc.
}

Thus, "Do you want to study?" "No, but I have to." Some of the students responded with no apparent regard for any semantic relationship between the question and their choice of response: "Are you going to the movies?" "No, but I hope to"; "Do you want to study tonight?" "No, but I hope to"; "Does she understand French?" "No, but she must."[1] It may have been mere lack of attention that caused such errors (only the students can know), but even those students who were listening in seemed to notice nothing peculiar in them. From the reponses students were making, it appeared that they didn't really understand the exercise or the meaning of the tag they were being asked to put on their answers. Again, this sort of thing would not occur in normal speech, but probably only because they have not in fact learned the construction and hence wouldn't use it spontaneously. Such exercises need to be carefully monitored to prevent students from making a mistake set up for them by a possible wrong choice, and above all to avoid reinforcing misconceptions. Where this is not done, students are likely either to not understand or to mislearn. The first would render the drill meaningless; the second would make it detrimental.

Another sort of exercise has the opposite effect of rigidly dictating the students' responses where there are other valid possibilities. Thus, a *not*-insertion drill was preceded by the following instructions:

> If the negative can be contracted with an auxiliary do so. Otherwise, put *not* before the infinitive.

as in: "John can write" → "John can't write"; "John prefers to write" → "John prefers not to write." In the first example above, it is the modal *can* which is being negated, not the verb *write*, whereas in the second case negation is associated with *write* rather than the preceding *prefer*. As if it weren't enough that students had two different structures to work with in the same drill, the majority of sentences of the second type involved matrix verbs of the *expect* type, where there are two possibilities for negative placement, with a corresponding difference in scope and meaning. Moreover, the "correct" response was often the less common of the two possibilities. Students were expected to say:

$$\text{John} \left\{ \begin{array}{l} \text{expects} \\ \text{wants} \\ \text{etc.} \end{array} \right\} \text{not to go.}$$

with the predictable result that they were torn between what they were instructed to say and what they had so often heard and tried to imitate:

"John doesn't expect to go." In addition, they had to cope with input sentences like "He will continue to answer" where both contraction-after-modal or *not*-before-infinitive are possible, and "He needs to study" with its variety of possibilities for negation:

$$
\text{He} \left\{ \begin{array}{l} \text{doesn't need to} \\ \text{needs not to} \\ \text{need not (needn't)} \end{array} \right\} \text{study}
$$

the latter in its uncontracted form being the one taught, for no discernible reason and with no explanation.[2]

A third potential source of trouble in exercises can be found in those drills which involve the joining of two simple sentences in which grammatical transformations have applied which would not apply in the complex sentence. Thus, for example, students were asked to embed one of two sentences in the other by using one of the conjunctions *unless, because, if, although, whenever, whether or not*, as in the following:

The air conditioner isn't working. The students enjoy the class. →

$$
\text{The students enjoy the class} \left\{ \begin{array}{l} \text{unless} \\ \text{although} \\ \text{etc.} \end{array} \right\} \text{the air conditioner isn't working.}
$$

Taking an imperative sentence as part of his input, one student produced the following: "I can't buy any new shoes unless lend me some money." (From "Lend me some money. I can't buy any new shoes.") That is, he joined the surface strings, as they were given to him, and of course imperatives can't occur in the resulting environment.

What is interesting is not so much this mistake (which is not surprising and is easy to correct) as the fact that in other cases where students were thus given an opportunity to make a mistake from the input to their drill, they did not. One pair of sentences given in the same exercise as that just discussed was this: "Paul is too busy. He takes a nap every afternoon." Joining these with *unless*, one would expect "*He takes a nap every afternoon unless Paul is too busy" which is a violation of the rules of pronoun reference. In fact, however, this did not occur. Students changed the sentence to avoid this deviance: "He takes a nap every afternoon unless he is too busy" or "Paul takes a nap every afternoon unless he is too busy," and in other cases, students were able to form various complex sentences involving pronominalization, always keeping the pronoun-antecedent relations straight.

Clues to the question of which possible errors students avoid despite inducements to make them may lie in the notion of linguistic universals. The notion of command relationships and the constraints on pronominalization associated with them have been proposed as universal to all languages. See Langacker (1969) for a discussion of the notion of command. Bever (1970) has formulated this as a perceptual constraint to the effect that one element cannot stand for another unless a connection has already been established or it is apparent (as through a marker of subordination) that such a connection is about to be established. In either case, it would not be surprising for a student to avoid violating a universal constraint. Imperative formation, on the other hand, differs from language to language (although some form of imperative is universal). Thus, Arabic does not distinguish imperative sentences from declaratives by subject deletion as does English. It would be interesting to examine whether students whose native language does form imperatives by subject deletion would make the same mistake. This is an area where theoretical linguistics and teaching can perhaps be mutually useful, the research on universals (syntactic or cognitive) providing a possible explanation for the occurrence and nonoccurrence of certain errors, and the classroom providing a place to test hypotheses about universals.

Unexpected Errors

Common Errors

There were other types of errors that students insisted on making, despite strong inducements to avoid them, for example, students at all levels often substituted *his* for *her* and *her* for *their*, both in free speech and in reading, when the correct form was right in front of them. They had particular trouble with the final *s* of the plural (noun) and third person singular (verb) and often left it out, even when reading, as in "How's the work these day, Jack?" (from a reading exercise). An example of just how difficult the -*s* ending is can be seen in the following: in a simple substitution drill where students were to change the subject of a sentence as indicated by the teacher and change the form of the verb where necessary, the following exchange took place:

Student 1: He is often here.
Teacher: The students
Student 2: The student is often here.
Teacher: Studentsssss

Student 2:   They are often here.
Teacher: Say studentsssss.
Student 2:   The student are often here.

This student clearly knew, at least by the end of the exchange, that a plural was involved, and knew how to form the plural for the verb, but try as he would the teacher could not get her to pronounce the plural morpheme -*s* on the noun.

Tense was another frequent problem, and particularly certain sequence of tense rules. Thus, there were mistakes such as "[In the old days, parents arranged weddings and] the boy didn't know the girl he is going to marry" or "After a long travel, I returned to my house and see a lot of dust." The following sentence "He acts as if he knows Habib Bourguiba" was given in response to the exercise changing *like* to *as if* (contrary to fact). The students had been told repeatedly that *as if* requires a past verb for a counterfactual meaning, and in this case the input sentence given by the teacher already had the correct verb form in it ("He acts as if he knew H. B."), so that there was no change or choice that the student needed to make to produce the expected "He acts as if he knew Habib Bourguiba." Yet he changed the tense, and thus the meaning of the sentence. In cases like this, apparently the student's difficulty with the form overcame all the positive clues he was given.

In general, students had far less trouble with the past tense in simple sentences, although errors such as "I forget to say to you that . . . " and "Do they have lunch yesterday?" did occur on a random basis, even among advanced students.

Atypical Errors

Not all errors made in these circumstances are typical in other contexts, however. A common instance of a situation where all the right information is available is the pattern drill, where students have just one transformation to perform, leaving the rest of the sentence intact. One of the purposes of this sort of drill is precisely to militate against extraneous, irrelevant errors, and as has been discussed earlier, students tend to take this sort of instruction quite literally, and where an exercise is not carefully written, may in fact produce a deviant sentence by choosing the wrong lexical item to insert or by failing to make some secondary change which goes along with the transformation being drilled. But where there is truly only one change to be made, one expects the student to leave the rest of the sentence alone (and herein lies the ease in ignoring its meaning altogether). It is therefore surprising to find a student reordering other elements in a sentence in the course of a drill, even where word order may be troublesome elsewhere in his speech. In a passive formation drill, a student given "We always keep our knives in this drawer" produced the following: "Our knives are kept in this drawer always." While some students have difficulty with the order of constituents in English, adverb placement, at least with simple tenses, is not generally a troublemaker. The fact that the simple present is changed to an auxiliary + participle construction may be the source of trouble, but what one would expect, on the basis of similar spontaneously made errors, would be something like "Our knives are kept always in this drawer." I know of no precedent or explanation for reordering the adverb with respect to the prepositional phrase in the course of the drill.

In a dialogue that was being learned by repetition and memorization, the following sentences were produced: "Ours is much newer model" and "His must be a one of the newest models." In a similar case, students were forming sentences on the pattern "Verb + ing is fun," "X-ing is hard work"; one student said "Walking is a good exercise." The first of these sentences represents one of the most common mistakes made by Tunisian students—omission of the article. In the next two cases, however, an article has been inserted, something far rarer in free conversation. These may be cases of overcorrection; a grammatical explanation could no doubt also be found. It is peculiar, however, that this occurs here, where the model for the correct sentence without the article is available to the student and is the more natural one for him in any case.

The above error types represent an entirely different situation from those described in earlier sections. The sentences discussed as common errors are examples of patterns that also occur frequently in spontaneous speech, and which are so strongly a part of the student's grammar that they are preferred even where the correct form is obvious. The examples in this section, on the other hand, represent a peculiar subset of induced errors. Like induced errors, the cases described above do not occur in normal speech, but here the situation in the classroom is set up not for them *to be made,* but for them *NOT to be made.* Yet they occur despite everything and are, apparently, thoroughly internalized into the student's grammar. Thus they should perhaps not be considered errors in the same sense as those discussed in the bulk of this article, but rather as Corder (1971) suggests, manifestations of rule differences between the student's idiosyncratic dialect and the native dialect he is learning.

The Problem of Meaning

It is often unclear what a student means to say when he produces an ungrammatical sentence, particularly when it has no context, as in answer to a teacher's request to "give me a sentence using X." One student, when asked to give a sentence using *as if* (which had just been defined as a synonym of *like* with the second clause in the past for negative implication), said "I am glad as if I had slept." It is not at all clear what is wrong with this sentence because the meaning that the student had in mind is obscure (does he mean: glad because I slept, glad that I slept, would be glad if I'd slept, would like to have slept, didn't sleep but feel as if I had?). Since the teacher didn't ask the student to explain, he could not do more than just say "you can't say that in English," and we can do no more than mention it as an unclear example.

In a lesson on gerunds, students were questioned in such a way that they produced sentences with gerundive subjects:

Teacher:	What do you do on the weekend?
Student 1:	I go swimming.
Teacher:	Is it fun?
Student 1:	Yes.
Teacher:	What's fun?
Student 2:	Swimming is fun.

One such sequence went as follows:

Teacher:	What does your father do?
Student 1:	He's director of a bank.
Teacher:	Is it hard work?
Student 1:	Yes.
Teacher:	What's hard work?
Student 2:	Hard work is the director of a bank.

This is an example of the error type discussed earlier as atypical errors, where the student ignores a drill situation which sets him up for the correct response, and produces a deviant sentence as a result. The clue to what might be happening in these cases must be sought in the student's intended meaning. One could hypothesize several different possibilities for this sentence, taken in isolation. Notice, for example, that the above response is identical in form to a different type of *WH*-question-answer pair:

Q: What is an apple?
A: An apple is a fruit.

where the questioned noun phrase subject is defined by qualification in the predicate. That is, in one case, the predicate provides the new information, and in the other, the subject does. The question here is whether the student really has confused the two: did he misunderstand the question or simply not know how to form the answer? It seems unlikely in a case where several correct sentences on the same pattern had already been elicited that he would suddenly do a semantic reverse like this. In fact, we have already seen that evidence seems to indicate that the opposite is more often the case. That is, if in the middle of a series of sentence pairs of the pattern "What is fun?" "Swimming is fun," the teacher said "What is an apple?", a student with poor command of *wh*-questions might respond, in the same pattern, with "Fruit is an apple." The pattern is not broken, even when it should be. It is more likely in this instance that the student understood the question and had the correct answer in mind. It was only coincidental that, in garbling the grammar of his answer, he stumbled upon *another* English syntactic pattern. The question then remains, why did he make a mistake, and what should the teacher do about it? Is it enough simply to give the right answer, with no explanation of why the sentence was wrong? Or should the teacher take the time to find out exactly what the student meant, and show him why he didn't succeed in expressing it? If his problem is something as simple as not knowing what to do with the object of the gerund, merely hearing the correct sentence might be enough. But the teacher must know his student well to be sure the problem isn't deeper, especially where the student's sentence falls so close to another correct English pattern *and* where the drill situation would lead one to expect the right answer. Even if he didn't have the definition-type sentence in mind, he might still notice the resemblance later and get confused. Alternatively, the student may, as has been suggested by Corder (1967), simply be testing a hypothesis about the new language by the sentence he has produced and will accept the correction. The only way to tell in such cases is by studying the persistence of errors over time. The teacher, who sees his students regularly over a period of time, has access to the evidence necessary for an accurate determination, and can thus provide a valuable service to the researcher doing error analysis.

It may not even be clear in every case whether a sentence a student produces is deviant or not. For example, in a class asked to make up sentences using *should,* one student said, "They should need another book." If *should* is taken to mean expectation on the part of the speaker, this sentence is fine ("They should need another book by next week, because they're on the last chapter of this one already"). But it is unlikely that this is what the student meant, since this class was just learning modals for the first time, and *should,* even in its more common sense of *ought to* was not an active part of their vocabulary. On the other hand, co-occurrence restrictions such as these are seldom violated in spontaneous speech, and it is unlikely that a sentence such as this would have been produced if the student had not been put on the spot. An analysis which does not take this into account overlooks an important principle which every teacher knows: the importance of context as an aid in deciphering student speech.

Of course, the time spent in trying to figure out what a student meant may not always be justifiable in the classroom. But it is important for the teacher to be aware of all the possibilities in order to make this decision. Correcting the wrong thing, or the right thing for the wrong reason, or not correcting enough, can easily make matters worse.

Summary and Conclusions

In the weak version of contrastive analysis, as in all forms of error analysis, the source of the error is an important issue (unlike the strong version of contrastive analysis, where the source is assumed). A great deal of evidence has come to light indicating that contrastive analysis is inadequate to explain the source of certain types of error. My research in Tunisia has reaffirmed this. But error analysis, as it is usually defined, also begs the question. Too many variables are involved to say that the idiosyncrasies of learner language are explainable solely in terms of either interference or target-language internal rules, or even a combination of the two. In this article, I have concentrated on errors which are related to the classroom situation itself. These fall into several categories. The first, and most obvious, are the errors which students wouldn't make in free speech, but which are elicited by the teacher's questions or by drills. These may be due to incomplete acquisition of the lexical item or grammatical structure involved, to analogy suggested by the order of presentation, or to a number of other possible causes, as yet unexplored.

I also touched briefly on some errors which one might expect to find within this framework, but which students manage to avoid. The relationship of potential errors which do not actually occur to putative linguistic universals such as coreference restrictions, semantic restrictions, meaning conflicts, etc., is worth exploring. To this end, a thorough study of what errors are *not* made will be necessary. In addition, there are errors that recur despite a teaching situation designed to avoid them. These errors may provide evidence for the hypothesis-strategy approach to language leaning suggested by Corder. If such is the case, it may turn out not to be worthwhile to force extensive drill of these issues when the learner isn't ready to absorb them.

The discussions above are intended to be highly tentative, as evidenced by the fact that no attempt is made to provide any solutions. It is first necessary to point out the *possible* sources of error, in order to increase awareness of the problems. Doubtless induced errors should be treated differently in the classroom (as well as in research) from those which actually reflect the students' developing competence, but it is not clear just how this is to be done.

Several issues are involved here. In preparing materials and writing drills, it is important to keep in mind that surface relationships could lead to misunderstanding on a deeper level, and that any inexplicit explanation may be open to misinterpretation by the student. The teacher must be on guard to monitor drills and explanations to be certain that they do not lead to false generalizations. In this way, many induced errors could be avoided or caught before they cause any real trouble. There is also the question of what to do about those errors which will crop up and persist despite all attempts to control them. It is here that the issue of ascertaining the student's meaning plays an important role. The clearer a teacher's understanding of the sources of student errors, the better he will be able to judge which ones are most worth concentrating on. Finally, an understanding of the effect on the student of miscorrection through misinterpretation of his intent is vital to adequate language teaching. No teacher would disagree that correcting the wrong thing could be disastrous; however, it is not always obvious, especially to the inexperienced teacher, what is the right and what is the wrong thing. Only after this is determined, and only over an extended period of time, can the nature and extent of damage that such cases might cause be measured.

For the linguist studying second language acquisition, the distinction between classroom-induced errors and spontaneous student errors is also valuable. It is crucial to bear this distinction in mind when attempting to account for student language, for to ignore it is to risk faulty analysis. It could cloud the issues to attribute to a developing grammar an error that the student wouldn't ordinarily make. It is of course quite possible to *describe* many, and perhaps all, of the errors discussed above solely in terms of rule deviance. For example, one could describe the confusion between *point out* and *notice* described in the vocabulary section as simply a patient-agent confusion in the student's grammar, or the inability to distinguish between *should* and *must* by formally giving them a slightly different meaning from that of standard English. But such statements would be misleading if the description of student language is to have any reality in terms of the student's acquisition of the language, for these errors do not in fact represent any internalized part of his grammar, and do not therefore occur systematically in the same way that certain errors of tense usage or word order might occur. "Whenever a student of a second language creates an utterance in the second language, he reveals something about his competence (or his lack of competence)" (Wardhaugh 1967, p. 25). The errors discussed above suggest something about what the student does *not* know rather than about what he does know. We must not make the mistake of attributing them to a system where none exists. An approach to student language *description* which does not distinguish between spontaneous, systematic errors and those forced by the situation will do nothing to *explain* where the student is in the second language acquisition process, how he got there, or what the process is.

Notes

This work was supported in part by Contract OEC-0-70-4986 from the U.S. Office of Education to the Language Research Foundation. I am endebted to many people who helped me in my research both here and in Tunisia. I would like especially to express my thanks to Mohammed Maamouri of the Institut Bourguiba des Langues Vivantes, Tunis, who arranged for me to attend English classes there, to DeWayne Coambs, Leslie and Lewis Tremaine, Mike Vale, and other Peace Corps staff members for access to their classrooms, and for helpful discussions of their own experiences at the beginning stages of my research, and to Bruce Fraser, Walt Olson, Patty Regan, and John Schumann for their valuable comments on earlier versions of this paper.

1. This latter example is not necessarily an example of a semantic violation; in fact it may reflect a common spontaneous error type among students at this level: the substitution of *must* for *should*. Note that a response "No, but she should" would have been perfectly acceptable. This may well be what the student was saying. The same may be true of other examples I have used. This points up once again the extreme tentativeness of any claim about what the student actually meant to say.
2. This is a classic example of the deep/surface structure conflict: two sentences which have the same structure on the surface are quite different at a deeper, more abstract level. An awareness of current research in transformational linguistics can help the teacher find and avoid many such areas of difficulty.

References

Banathy, Bela H., and Madarasz, Paul H. "Contrastive Analysis and Error Analysis." *Journal of English as a Second Language* 4, no. 2 (1969):77–92.

Bever, Thomas G. "The Cognitive Basis for Linguistic Structures." In *Cognition and the Development of Language,* edited by John R. Hayes. New York and London: John Wiley and Sons, 1970.

Bowen, J. Donald. "Contrastive Analysis and the Language Classroom." In *On Teaching English to Speakers of Other Languages, Series III,* edited by Betty Wallace Robinett. Papers read at the TESOL Conference, New York, March 17–19, 1966. Washington, D.C.: TESOL, 1967.

Burt, M. K., and Kiparsky, Carol. *The Gooficon.* Rowley, Mass.: Newbury House Publishers, 1972.

Buteau, Magdelhayne F. "Students' Errors and the Learning of French as a Second Language: A Pilot Study." *IRAL* 8, no. 3 (1970):133–45.

Chomsky, Noam. *Aspects of the Theory of Syntax.* Cambridge, Mass.: MIT Press, 1965.

———. "Linguistic Theory." In *Language Teaching: Broader Contexts.* Report of the Northeast Conference on the Teaching of Foreign Languages, 1966, pp. 43–49.

Corder, S. P. "The Significance of Learners' Errors." *IRAL* 5, no. 4 (1967):161–69.

———. "Idiosyncratic Dialects and Error Analysis." *IRAL* 9, no. 2 (1971):147–59.

Dušková, Libuše. "On Sources of Errors in Foreign Language Learning." *IRAL* 7, no. 1 (1969):11–36.

Jacobs, Roderick. "Linguistic Universals and Their Relevance to TESOL." *TESOL Quarterly* 3, no. 2 (1969):117–22.

James, Carl. "Deeper Contrastive Study." *IRAL* 7, no. 2 (1969):83–95.

Langacker, Ronald W. "Pronominalization and the Chain of Command." In *Modern Studies in English,* edited by D. Reibel and S. Schane. Englewood Cliffs, N.J.: Prentice Hall, 1969.

Richards, Jack C. "A Non-Contrastive Approach to Error Analysis." *English Language Teaching Journal* 25 (1971):204–19.

———. "Error Analysis and Second Language Strategies." *Language Sciences,* no. 17 (1971):12–22.

Rutherford, William E. "Deep Structure, Surface Structure, and Language Drill." *TESOL Quarterly* 2, no. 2 (1968):71–79.

Strevens, Peter. "Two Ways of Looking at Error Analysis." ERIC, ED 037 714, 1969.

Wardhaugh, Ronald. "Some Current Problems in Second Language Teaching." *Language Learning* 27, nos. 1 and 2 (1967):21–26.

———. "The Contrastive Analysis Hypothesis." *TESOL Quarterly* 4, no. 2 (1970):123–29.

Some Reservations Concerning Error Analysis

Jacquelyn Schachter and Marianne Celce-Murcia

Introduction

For several years now a debate has taken place as to whether contrastive analysis (hereafter CA), or error analysis (hereafter EA), or perhaps both of them should play a role in the construction of language teaching materials and the explanation of the second language acquisition process.

CA advocates (e.g., Fries 1945; Lado 1957; Di Pietro 1971) have claimed that a systematic comparison of the source language and the target language at all levels of structure will generate predictions about the areas of learning difficulty in the target language for speakers of the source language. Furthermore, they have maintained that the best teaching materials will emphasize those features of the target language that differ markedly from corresponding features of the source language.

EA proponents, on the other hand, have challenged the usefulness of CA both on theoretical and practical grounds. Their counterclaim is that a careful study of a large corpus of errors committed by speakers of the source language attempting to express themselves in the target language provides factual empirical data—rather than theoretical speculation—for developing a syllabus or a model of second language acquisition. Furthermore, they point out that the analysis of production errors shows quite clearly that not all systematic errors produced by the learner can be attributed to interference from the source language. In fact, they claim that such errors provide evidence for a much more complex view of the learning process, one in which the learner is seen as an active participant in the formation of and revision of hypotheses regarding the rules of the target language.

Reprinted from *TESOL Quarterly* 11 (1971):441–51, copyright 1977 by Teachers of English to Speakers of Other Languages, by permission of the publisher and the authors.

The authors are most appreciative of the perceptive comments and suggestions given them by Diane Larsen-Freeman on an earlier version of this article.

272

In view of such criticism of both the pedagogical value and the theoretical justification of CA, it is not surprising that proponents of the CA hypothesis are dwindling rapidly and that the theory behind it has lost its prestige and popularity. Nor is it surprising that a new and different approach should be so well received. In this case, the newly elaborated methodological tool, EA, follows closely the psycholinguistic search for an alternative to the behaviorist's habit-formation theory of language acquisition—one that attempts to explain the essentially creative nature of the language acquisition process as described by Chomsky (1965). This alternative involves viewing the learner as one who interacts actively with the new language, developing new hypotheses about the structure of the language he is learning as well as modifying and discarding earlier formed ones. The claim is that the systematic errors produced by the learner provide evidence for this view. EA has thus become a rallying point for those who would affirm their rejection of a behavioristic view of the language learner.

A cursory glance at the titles and abstracts in recent issues of journals (such as *TESOL Quarterly, Language Learning* and *IRAL*) would indicate that the advocates of EA have prevailed and that EA currently appears to be the "darling" of the seventies. The concern of the authors is that the pendulum has swung too far in reaction against the CA hypothesis and its now clearly identified problems. We feel that although proponents of EA have provided convincing arguments regarding the weaknesses of CA, they have to a large extent failed to focus their attention on the possibility that there are corresponding weaknesses in EA which would make error-based theories and materials as inadequate and one-sided as contrastively based theories and materials are. It is this point that we wish to address here. Before doing so, however, it would be well to review the development of EA, and some of the claims that have been made about it.

An Overview of Error Analysis

Trained and sophisticated language teachers have undoubtedly applied EA to one degree or another for decades. They have studied their students' recurring mistakes, classified them into categories, and used them as the basis for preparing lessons and materials designed to remediate such errors. Lee (1957) provides one of the early comprehensive statements of this practice and further develops the procedure—which is simple in concept but laborious and complex in practice. For language learners with the same mother tongue, Lee proposes that errors be collected at all learning stages (i.e., beginning, intermediate, and advanced) so that persistent errors—errors still being made by advanced students—can be distinguished from the earlier self-correcting errors typical of beginners.[1]

Richards (1971*b*) characterizes the field as follows: "The field of error analysis may be defined as dealing with *the differences* [italics ours] between the way people learning a language speak, and the way adult native speakers of the language use the language" (Oller and Richards 1973, p. 114).

Richards (1971*a*) proposes a three-way classification of errors:

1. interference errors
2. intralingual errors
3. developmental errors

The interference errors are those caused by the influence of the learner's mother tongue on production of the target language in presumably those areas where the languages clearly differ.

The intralingual errors are those originating within the structure of English itself. Complex rule-learning behavior is typically characterized by overgeneralization, incomplete application of rules, and failure to learn conditions for rule application. When the complexity of English structure encourages such learning problems, all learners, regardless of background language, tend to commit similar errors.

The developmental errors reflect the strategies by which the learner acquires the language. These errors show that the learner—oftentimes completely independent of the native language—is making false hypotheses about the target language based on limited exposure to it. A major justification for labeling an error as developmental comes from noting similarities to errors produced by children who are acquiring the target language as their mother tongue.

Richards provides the reader with a number of charts exemplifying certain intralingual and developmental errors which he claims cannot be explained on the basis of CA. While Richards does not totally reject CA, when compared with the positions taken by previous researchers he clearly minimizes its role:

> Interference from the mother tongue is clearly a major source of difficulty in second language learning, and contrastive analysis has proved valuable in locating areas of interlanguage interference. Many errors, however, derive from the strategies employed by the

learner in language acquisition and the mutual interference of items within the target language. These cannot be accounted for by contrastive analysis. Teaching-techniques and procedures should take account of the structural and developmental conflicts that can come about in language learning. [Richards 1971*a*, p. 214]

In several important articles Corder has done more than anyone else to develop the highly sophisticated view of error analysis that many researchers adhere to today. He has also had great impact on those who are directly concerned with the teaching process and it is useful to reiterate his contributions. In "The Significance of Learners' Errors" (1967), for example, he argues that first and second language learning share basically the same processes and that whatever differences exist are explainable in terms of motivation. He cautions that random errors of the types that even native speakers may make (i.e., *mistakes*) must be carefully distinguished from errors which are systematic in nature and reflect a learner's transitional competence (i.e., *errors*). By paying attention to the learner's errors, Corder feels we will come to better understand his/her needs and stop assuming we know what to learn and when to learn it. He claims that errors can be significant in three ways: (1) they tell the teacher how far the learner has come and what s/he still must learn; (2) they give the researcher evidence of how language is learned (i.e., strategies and procedures used); (3) they are a device the learner uses to test out hypotheses concerning the language s/he is learning.

In a later article, "Describing the Language Learner's Language" (1972), Corder explicitly distinguishes remedial EA from developmental EA—the former type of EA facilitating teacher evaluation and correction, the latter being used to describe the successive transitional dialects of a language learner.

Weaknesses in Error Analysis Research

The distinction between remedial, classroom-oriented EA and developmental EA is a useful one; and if one's particular project is in the realm of developmental EA, the distinction may be clear-cut. However, if the goals of a particular project are pedagogically oriented, the line between developmental and remedial EA becomes very difficult to draw. This is because one's view on how the learner processes the second language data s/he is exposed to should influence one's views on the pedagogical implications of a particular study. In practice many, if not most, studies are concerned with both developmental and pedagogical implications.

Thus in the following discussion of the current weaknesses in the state of the art, we address ourselves to both classroom teachers and researchers in the field.

Although no two EA projects are alike, it is possible to discuss a group of weaknesses exhibited by many of them.[2] In doing this we are not claiming that any actual EA study exhibits all of the potential weaknesses described below. Nor do we assert that our own previous work (or student research we have supervised) is free of such weaknesses.

The Analysis of Errors in Isolation

The first step in an error analysis is the extraction of errors from the corpus. In many cases the corpus is then excluded from further consideration as the investigator focuses on the task of organizing the errors. This seemingly innocuous move (abandoning the corpus) provides what some consider to be the most devastating criticism of the whole EA enterprise. To consider only what the learner produces in error and to exclude from consideration the learner's nonerrors is tantamount to describing a code of manners on the basis of the observed breaches of the code. Several of those who have commented on EA have argued similarly (Svartvik 1973; Corder 1973; Hammarberg 1974). A striking example of the inadequacy of this approach is provided by Andersen (1977). His study of errors in article usage by Spanish learners of English[3] indicated that these learners produced many errors in using the article *a/an* and few errors in using the article *the,* which in isolation are not very interesting facts. Deeper analysis of the data, including close inspection of the cases in which the articles were used correctly, led Andersen to a considerably more interesting conclusion, i.e., that many of the subjects were using the strategy of providing the English equivalent of the article that was required in Spanish in that context. This resulted in few *the* errors and many *a/an* errors. This strategy could not have been discovered without careful consideration of both errors and nonerrors.

The Proper Classification of Identified Errors

Errors are typically described with regard to the target language system. The question is asked: "Is this a deviation from the target language?" As all investigators know it is not always easy to decide. But even when this decision is possible the next question is really the critical one: "What structure is this an error in?" Numerous questionable decisions are made at this point, which is the critical stage of an EA project. It is also the problem that is least discussed in the literature. Some examples may prove useful. (The examples cited all result from the personal experience of the authors and their associates.)

Suppose one is concerned with characterizing syntactic errors in English produced by Chinese learners and comes across several sentences of the following type:

a) There are so many Taiwan people * live around the lake.
b) There were lots of events * happen in my country.
c) . . . and there is a mountain * separate two lakes.
d) . . . and there are so many tourist * visit there.

The reaction of several analysts to these sentences was that they exhibit errors in English subject relative clause production; and the analysts were led to the conclusion that Chinese learners typically fail to insert the relative subject markers *that, who,* and *which.* This conclusion is probably wrong. That is, if looked at from the point of view of what the learner is trying to produce, these errors can also be viewed as attempts to establish a topic and follow it with a comment, a process that is syntactically and pragmatically acceptable in Chinese.[4]

An even more difficult case is exhibited by the following sentence, produced by a Japanese learner:

Americans are *easy* to get guns.

It is possible to analyze this as an instance of a wrongly applied rule that raises the subject, in this case, out of an extraposed clause, on analogy with "Americans are easy to please."[5] However, it may also be the case that the learner has categorized *easy* as an adjective which allows infinitival complements, like *able* in the sentence "Americans are *able* to get guns," where the subject of *able* is also the subject of the infinitive. Under this interpretation the raising rule is irrelevant. That the second interpretation is more likely (though not proven) is given added weight by the fact that children acquiring English as a native language also interpret the subject of *easy* as the subject of the infinitive (C. Chomsky 1969).

Statements of Error Frequency

Some EA-based projects make very informal statements of error frequency, merely pointing out that certain systematic errors are especially frequent in the speech or writing of nonnative speakers of English, e.g.,

Burt and Kiparsky (1972). Other studies have examined more rigorously a specific corpus and have provided extensive numerical totals so that the reader can see how frequently one kind of error occurs vis-à-vis another (see, for example, Neuman 1977). The informal type of EA study inevitably suffers from serious omissions although the discussion of the structures treated may provide good pedagogical suggestions. The studies supplying numerical error totals allow us to arrive at sounder pedagogical conclusions (e.g., that errors in the usage of articles and prepositions are among the most frequent of all ESL error types); however, they are less useful than studies that treat error frequency with greater sophistication—i.e., studies which consider the number of times it would have been possible for the learner(s) to make a given error as well as the number of times the error occurred (i.e., articles and prepositions are frequent errors because the need to use them arises so often).

In more sophisticated EA studies the emphasis is on *relative* as opposed to *absolute* frequency of error types (see, for example, Agnello 1977). In such a study relative frequency refers to a fraction obtained by using as numerator the number of times an error was committed and as denominator the number of times the error type could have occurred. It also considers the extent of the corpus—i.e., the number of words or sentences. This allows us to arrive at a percentage of accuracy and also to learn how often the nonnative speaker uses this structure both correctly and incorrectly in a given corpus.

Certainly such relative statements of frequency are more informative than earlier absolute statements from both a pedagogical and a developmental point of view; however, even here only obligatory—and not optional—contexts can be studied and quantified with accuracy for any given error type. This is because only the obligatory contexts supply the researcher with the total number of required occurrences of any element or structure in a given corpus; this total is then used as a basis for comparison with the numbers of instances where the element of structure actually occurs. No such total can be computed for optional contexts.

The Identification of Points of Difficulty
in the Target Language

The determination of what is most difficult, which is of primary importance for the classroom, derives from the previous classification of errors and the statement of their frequency, plus one assumption that is seldom made clear. That assumption is that points of difficulty in the target language are nondistinguishable from points at which errors are frequent.

We would argue that although there may be a great deal of overlap between the difficulty of a given element or structure and its error frequency, there may also be areas of difficulty that are not revealed by a high frequency of production errors. We refer here to the possibility that learners avoid producing constructions which they find difficult both in terms of the actual formation of such structures *and* the conditions for their use. Both kinds of avoidance have been reported on recently. Schachter (1974) presented evidence indicating that Chinese and Japanese learners avoid producing relative clauses in English; and Kleinmann (1977) presents even more convincing evidence that Arabic-speaking learners avoid the English passive construction. It is noteworthy that in neither of these cases would an analysis of errors alone have identified these apparent areas of difficulty for Japanese, Chinese, and Arabic learners of English. For classroom purposes particularly, it is as important to know what the learner *won't* do, and why, as it is to know what he will do, and why. The most comprehensive EA will only provide evidence on the latter, not the former.

The Ascription of Causes to Systematic Errors

This is an area of particular concern since to find the cause of an error is to find the source for a view of the language learner which will undoubtedly have an impact on classroom methods and materials in the future. It would be wise, then, for investigators to suggest causes of error only very cautiously. What we see happening, however, is just the reverse.

There are, for example, large numbers of learner errors that are ambiguous as to whether they are interlingual or developmental. Consider the case of the obligatory copula in English. For native speakers of Chinese, Arabic, and certain other languages nonoccurrence of this form can in part be explained as interference (i.e., interlingual errors) because of structural differences between the target and the source languages. However, this very same error could also be described as essentially developmental since monolingual English learners (i.e., children) and native speakers of languages like Spanish, which exhibits no structural differences with English in this area, also produce this "error" when learning English. There has been a tug-of-war going on—that has not been resolved to date—concerning which theory such an error supports.[6]

There is also a related problem concerning the interlingual/intralangual distinction mentioned earlier. Several studies (see, for example, Kleinmann 1973 and Suwatthigul 1973) have assumed that an error made by a mixed group of non-English speakers representing various language backgrounds was, of necessity, due to intralingual rather than interlingual factors—i.e., due to the inherent complexity of English rather than interference from the native language. However, such reasoning could easily lead one to arrive at linguistically inaccurate conclusions. Suppose a researcher was looking at errors in the contrastive use of reflexive and reciprocal pronouns in English (e.g., They were talking to themselves/each other.) Suppose further that this researcher had noticed that all of his subjects (who happened to be speakers of Romance languages, Bantu languages, etc.) overgeneralized the plural reflexive pronoun and used it inaccurately to signal both meanings in English. The researcher then could conclude that this error was intralingual (i.e., due to the inherent complexity of English) since many subjects speaking several related and unrelated languages were systematically producing the same error. However, this researcher would have overlooked the fact that speakers of certain other languages such as German—who happened to be absent in his particular group of subjects—would *not* overgeneralize the plural reflexive pronoun and furthermore that they would have a contrast parallel to the one occurring in English (i.e., *sich/ein ander*). Only a detailed typological survey makes explicit the fact that German and English share this lexical reflexive/reciprocal contrast—a contrast lacking in many other languages. For speakers of these other languages such errors may in fact be due to interlingual interference.

Thus one must be extremely cautious when claiming to have identified the cause of any given error type.[7]

The Biased Nature of Sampling Procedures

Researchers using EA data tend to overlook the fact that they may be working with a very limited and biased sampling in any one of the following areas:

1. background languages (assuming a heterogeneous group is being studied)
2. subjects
3. data samples (from any given subject)

Furthermore, the sampling in any of these ares is rarely (if ever) random in the statistical sense of the word since researchers work with available subjects, do research with existing classes of students, etc. Therefore, trying to draw statistically significant findings from such samples may be a priori a questionable practice. The above example concerning the interpretation of errors made in the use of English reflexive and reciprocal pronouns illustrates the kind of problem that can occur if background languages have not been properly sampled (from a linguistic point of view).

The problem of gathering authentic samples of data from an individual subject has also been underrated. An experience of one of the authors will serve to illustrate this. In gathering English and French lexical data for a longitudinal study on a bilingual child, it was noticed that the child did not produce the French word for rabbit (i.e., *lapin*) during a scheduled taping session even though the child had a pet rabbit and was well acquainted with both the English and French words and during the taping produced the English one. Had the investigator not had considerable previous exposure to the child, she might have concluded that the child did not actively use the French form. This would have been a false conclusion, and it underscores the dilemma researchers face when working exclusively with performance data. That is to say, the researcher is at the mercy of the subject's lapses, whims, and perhaps occasional noncooperation. Such performance errors can easily be analyzed as competence errors in those cases where the investigator has a purely casual acquaintance with the subject. Therefore, those doing any kind of EA should always be aware of this problem, which applies to groups of subjects as well as individuals. There is the ever present danger of treating performance data as if they were the only and ultimate truth.[8]

Conclusion

We hope that the six potential weaknesses listed above will help teachers and students better judge the merits and limitations of the many EA projects that they read about and hear about. In addition, we would hope that researchers carrying out EA projects would attend to these potential pitfalls so that the overall quality of EA research might improve.

In retrospect, if anything was learned from the so-called rise and fall of CA, it should be that one single view of the language learning process, attractive though it may be, will not account for the diverse phenomena that exist. If we are to make substantial progress in our study of language learning and language pedagogy, we must guard against the notion that EA, even though it is associated with a rich and complex psycholinguistic view of the learner, should supplant CA as the exclusive basis for developing teaching materials or for discovering language acquisition strategies. Sophisticated use of EA is in its infancy as is the field of second language acquisition, in which EA should be just one of many tools.

Certainly ESL/EFL teachers should be aware of what is going on in the field of EA, for from many studies we can gain new insights that will help us to view our students in a new light. Nevertheless, we owe it to ourselves and our students to maintain our perspective and to refuse to be swayed by overinflated claims made by proponents of any theory.

We can in the future expect to gain a great deal from research done using EA, but only if we do not expect too much now.

Notes

1. Lee encourages the use of CA to explain errors whenever possible and cites some examples of errors which could not be interpreted without the use of CA. Similarly, Wardhaugh (1970) later takes the position that CA's role be limited to that of a tool used in the interpretation of systematic production errors (i.e., the weak CA hypothesis).
2. For purposes of this discussion, it makes no difference whether the backgrounds of the learners are single or multiple, so long as each group is focusing on a single target language.
3. The articles a/an and the were two of several morphemes Andersen studied for this project.
4. This interpretation was suggested by Fred Tsao (personal communication), a native speaker of Mandarin and a linguist.
5. For this interpretation, the sentence would be derived from a grammatical intermediate structure such as "It is easy for Americans to get guns," on analogy with "It is easy (for anyone) to please John."
6. To our knowledge, no one has investigated the possibility that such an "ambiguous" error would be more persistent and difficult to overcome if the nonnative speaker's systematic error could be *simultaneously explained* as either developmental or interlingual (i.e., interference based).
7. For further arguments along these lines and an enlightening discussion of the difficulties involved in discovering the causes of errors produced by speakers of English learning French, see Swain (1975).
8. Closely related to the sampling issues discussed in this section is the related problem of specifying the language data to be collected, i.e., the task the learner must perform. Previous research (Olsson 1972; Larsen-Freeman 1975) has shown that the language activity in which the element or structure occurs (e.g., spontaneous speech, elicited speech, dictation, translation, composition, multiple choice exercises, etc.) will influence the types and the frequencies of errors that occur.

References

Agnello, Francesca. "Exploring the Pidginization Hypothesis." Master's thesis in TESL, University of California, Los Angeles, 1977.

Andersen, Roger. "The Improved State of Cross-Sectional Morpheme Acquisition/Accuracy Methodology." Paper presented at the Los Angeles Second Language Research Forum, University of California, Los Angeles, February, 1977.

Burt, Marina K., and Kiparsky, Carol. *The Gooficon: A Repair Manual For English.* Rowley, Mass.: Newbury House, 1972.

Chomsky, Carol. *The Acquisition of Syntax in Children from 5 to 10.* Cambridge, Mass.: MIT Press, 1969.

Chomsky, Noam. *Aspects of the Theory of Syntax.* Cambridge, Mass.: MIT Press, 1965.

Corder, S. Pit. "The Significance of Learners' Errors." *IRAL* 5, no. 4 (1967):161–70.

———. "Describing the Language Learner's Language." In *CILT Reports and Papers* (Center for Information on Language Teaching), no. 6 (1972):57–64.

———. "The Elicitation of Interlanguage." In *Errata,* edited by Jan Svartvik. Lund, Sweden: C. W. K. Gleerup, 1973.

Di Pietro, Robert J. *Language Structures in Contrast.* Rowley, Mass.: Newbury House, 1971.

Fries, C. C. *Teaching and Learning English as a Foreign Language.* Ann Arbor: Univeristy of Michigan Press, 1945.

Hammarberg, Bjorn. "The Insufficiency of Error Analysis." *IRAL* 12, no. 3 (1974).

Kleinmann, Howard. "Transformational Grammar and the Processing of Certain English Sentence Types." Master's thesis in TESL, University of California, Los Angeles, 1973.

———. "Avoidance Behavior in Adult Second Language Acquisition." *Language Learning* 27, no. 1 (1977):93–107.

Lado, Robert. *Linguistics Across Cultures.* Ann Arbor: University of Michigan Press, 1957.

Larsen-Freeman, Diane. "The Acquisition of Grammatical Morphemes by Adult Learners of English as a Second Language." Ph.D. Dissertation, University of Michigan, 1975.

Lee, W. R. "The Linguistic Context of Language Teaching." *English Language Teaching* 11, April–June, 1957.

Neuman, Regina. "An Attempt to Define Through Error Analysis the Intermediate Level at UCLA." Master's thesis in TESL, University of California, Los Angeles, 1977.

Oller, John, and Richards, Jack C. eds. *Focus on the Learner.* Rowley, Mass.: Newbury House, 1973.

Olsson, Margareta. "Intelligibility: A Study of Errors and their Importance."
    Research Bulletin no. 12, Department of Educational Research Gothen-
    burg School of Gothenburg, Sweden (ERIC), 1972.
Richards, Jack G. "A Non-Contrastive Approach to Error Analysis." *English
    Language Teaching* 25, no. 3 (1971a).
———. "Error Analysis and Second Language Strategies." *Language Science* 17
    (1971b). Reprinted in revised form in Oller and Richards, 1973.
Schachter, Jacquelyn. "An Error in Error Analysis." *Language Learning* 24, no.
    2 (1974):205–14.
Suwatthigul, Pimpaporn. "Thai Students' Performance in the Usage of Modal
    Auxiliaries in English. Master's thesis in TESL, University of California,
    Los Angeles, 1973.
Svartvik, Jan. Introduction to *Errata*. Lund, Sweden: C. W. K. Gleerup, 1973.
Swain, Merrill. "Changes in Errors: Random or Systematic." Paper presented at
    the Fourth International Congress of Applied Linguists, Stuttgart, August,
    1975.
Wardhaugh, Ronald. "The Contrastive Analysis Hypothesis." *TESOL Quarterly*
    4, no. 2 (1970):123–30.

Questions

1. Look at group 7 in table 1 and group 1 in table 2 of the Richards data. Do you think these can both be intralingual error types? Support your answer.

2. If you have access to a body of written data that contains errors in categories mentioned in Dušková (tense, article, word order, preposition), list the number of errors in each category. Rank order both the errors from your data and the errors in the same categories in Dušková. How would you explain the similarities and differences in the rank orders? If you are unable to obtain your own data, compare the rank ordering in Dušková with that from the data in the Time I study in the article by M. S. Scott and G. R. Tucker, "Error Analysis and English Language Strategies of Arab Students," *Language Learning* 24, no. 1 (1974):69–97.

3. George, Corder, and Selinker all differ somewhat on the sources of learners' errors. State the position of each and the arguments of each for his own claims. Which position do you favor and why?

Problems

A. Hungarian Morphology*

1. een laatok ed' fiuut	I see a boy.
2. te laats ed' fiuut	You see a boy.
3. øø laat ed' fiuut	He sees a boy.
4. een laatom a fiuut	I see the boy.
5. te laatod a haazat	You see the house.
6. øø laatja a fiuut	He sees the boy.
7. ed' fiuu laat engem	A boy sees me.
8. ed' fiuu laat teeged	A boy sees you.
9. ed' fiuu laatja øøt	A boy sees him.
10. a fiuu laat engem	The boy sees me.
11. a fiuu laat teeged	The boy sees you.
12. a fiuu laatja øøt	The boy sees him.
13. ed' fiuu laatja a fiuut	A boy sees the boy.
14. a fiuu laat ed' fiuut	The boy sees a boy.
15. een laatom øøt	I see him.
16. te laats engem	You see me.
17. te laatod øøt	You see him.
18. øø laat teeged	He sees you.
19. øø laat engem	He sees me.

But not:

*a fiuu laat teegedat	*a fiuu laat engemat
*a fiuu laatja teeged	*a fiuu laatja a fiuu
*een laatok	*a fiuu laatja ed' fiuut
*a fiuu laatja engem	

As a preliminary to the questions below state the differences between Hungarian and English verb conjugations and subject/object case forms.

*This problem is adapted from a problem in *Workbook in Syntax* by Andreas Koutsoudas (New York: McGraw-Hill, 1969, now out of print) by permission of the author.

Attested errors of English speakers learning Hungarian

**een laatok a fiuut	very persistent
**te laats a haazat	very persistent
**laat a fiuut	very persistent
**een laatok ed' fiuu	less common
**te laatod a fiuu	less common
**ed' fiuu laatja engem	not common
**ed fiuu laatja teeged	not common
**te laatod engem	not common

1. What is the relationship between the first three errors?
2. What about the next two?
3. And the last three?
4. Are any of these errors accounted for easily by interference?

B. English Syntax

1. This revolution called White Revolution because nobody killed.
2. The Chinese government refused to sign the agreement which made by the meeting of Washington.
3. I was immigrated to the U.S. with my family.
4. It called Kamikochi, very beautiful nature views.
5. The two might have been coexisted.
6. No revolution can be succeeded by the force of power.
7. In this battle heroes born.
8. I arrived two months ago and I was attended to the English course.
9. Another event was the fight between Iran and the Arabs. It caused by Islam.
10. He was grown up and lived the deep far of upper Egypt.

1. These sentences were produced by a group of intermediate learners of English from different language backgrounds. They exhibit two *systematic* error types. What are they? Which sentences exhibit the first error type and which the second?
2. What is the underlying difference between these two error types? Does the Richards article help? (cf. pp. 197–214) Which error type do you think will be harder to eliminate? Why?
3. What remedial work would you propose to deal with these errors?

C. English Phonology

1. bátən mísıŋ	button missing
2. hítənrə́n	hit and run
3. mítən lɔ́st	mitten lost
4. šʊ́dənt gów	shouldn't go
5. mænhǽtən stríyts	Manhattan streets
6. kúdənt síy	couldn't see
7. láytən ðiy lówd	lighten the load
8. bǽtəndmít	bat and mitt
9. rítən fɔ́rm	written form
10. núwtənzlɔ́	Newton's law
11. gétənɛgzǽmpəl	get an example
12. wúwdəntláyk tuw	wouldn't like to

1. What is the *major* phonological problem of the learners who produced the data above?
2. Isolate the environments in which that problem occurs.
3. Rank order those environments in terms of possible difficulty. Give arguments for your order.

Related Aspects

Introduction

Whereas the previous sections each contained a relatively coherent perspective on the learner, this section appears to do just the opposite. It represents attempts of researchers to break away from the constraints imposed by contrastive and error analysis, and to explore other factors that contribute to the second language learning process.

The contrastive analysis approach focused on the native and target languages of the learner and the error analysis approach on the learner's systematic errors. This section contains articles dealing with yet other phenomena: some deal with the shared characteristics of learners other than the errors they make; others deal with the shared characteristics of languages insofar as they can be viewed as representative of larger language groupings; yet others deal with the shared characteristics of native speakers and teachers as they provide language input to the learner. Each of the factors dealt with herein is important and cannot be ignored if we are eventually to understand how it is that we learn second languages.

Celce-Murcia argues that language universals and the typological characteristics of native languages as compared with target languages should have an effect on the ease or difficulty with which the learner can incorporate some new feature of the target language. Schachter and Rutherford present a set of data which they use to claim that such typological factors are in fact at work. In addition to providing an example of the Celce-Murcia argument, the Schachter and Rutherford article is notable for two other claims. The first is that analyses of learner production must not focus simply on the form of the utterance produced by the learner but rather must focus on the relation between form and function. They point out that certain forms in a learner's interlanguage are serving a function determined by certain characteristics of the learner's native language, characteristics that the language shares with others. The second is that in learner interlanguages one finds what they label "overproduction" of certain structures by learners of certain backgrounds and not others, a phenomenon which must be accounted for. The Schachter (1974) article can also be viewed as providing evidence for typological factors at work in language learning, although it was not presented as such. The avoidance phenomenon is, she claims, the result of a typological parameter regarding which English and certain other languages differ.

Just as one can consider the notion that there are characteristics basic to all languages that can affect the learning process, one can also pursue the idea that there are characteristics inherent in all language learners which also affect the process. Bailey, Madden, and Krashen make just this claim. They find an accuracy order of certain morphemes by adults that correlates highly with the order found for child second language learners, both of which differ from the order found for child first language learners. Bailey, Madden, and Krashen claim that the results show common strategies for second language learning and suggest that the results show a common order of acquisition as well. Larsen-Freeman searches for a cause for this phenomenon and finds that the accuracy/acquisition order correlates well with the frequency order of the morphemes of certain ESL teachers, thus suggesting an external cause rather than an internal one. Hatch and Wagner-Gough consider other proposed "natural" sequences and discuss various suggestions made to account both for the sequences and for attested variations from them.

Yet another phenomenon to be considered is that proposed by Schachter, avoidance. She argues that in certain cases learners avoid producing structures they find difficult to incorporate into their interlanguage. They produce fewer instances of the structure than learners of other language backgrounds and, along with this, fewer error percentages. Schachter did not test for the possibility that the learners who appeared to exhibit avoidance behavior might in fact not have comprehended the structure in question as well as speakers from other language backgrounds. Kleinmann controlled for this possibility in a well-designed experiment, which again showed avoidance behavior by speakers of certain language groups and other constructions than the ones Schachter observed. This phenomenon is particularly disturbing for teachers since it is much more difficult to detect and deal with something that does not occur in the learner's speech than with something that does.

Ferguson, Henzl, and Freed provide evidence that yet another phenomenon must be taken into account: that native speakers in talking to learners alter their speech in certain systematic ways, now known as Foreigner Talk. In his article, Ferguson attempts to verify his hypothesis that there is a conventional foreigner talk for English and takes certain steps toward characterizing it. His pioneer work spawned many studies, among which are the two included here. Freed's study is of casual conversations between natives and nonnatives while Henzl's is of classroom talk by teachers. The consequences of our developing knowledge in this area may be great, but at this stage one must exercise caution in coming to decisions on what this implies for the classroom.

The final phenomenon dealt with in this section involves the description and consequences of correcting moves by teachers when students have produced oral errors in the target language. Chaudron has made a careful study of such moves by teachers in a French immersion program in Canada, categorizing them and noting the effectiveness of the various types. Long, after reviewing various studies and pointing out problems in the interpretation of certain correcting moves, concludes by questioning the value of error correction as an essential part of classroom procedure.

Second language learning is a complex and challenging task, more difficult by far than the learning of chess or calculus. And while many succeed at this task, many others fail. We have made important gains in recent years in isolating and explicating factors that influence this task—characteristics of the language, the learner, and also of the input. The work will continue. And perhaps you, our readers, will contribute to it.

The Universalist Hypothesis: Some Implications for Contrastive Syntax and Language Teaching

Marianne Celce-Murcia

Background

Theories of second language teaching, implicitly or explicitly, are based on some linguistic model. The model on which most previous work is based assumes that "languages can differ from each other unpredictably and without limit" (Joos 1954, p. 96n). The proponents of this approach believe that each language is a unique social and cultural product, sharing nonrandom similarities only with genetically related languages (i.e., languages having a common ancestry, as for example, French, Spanish, Italian, and Portuguese, all of which derive from Latin.)

As opposed to this view, there are linguists who believe that all languages share universal properties, that, in fact, the differences existing among languages are to a great extent superficial (Chomsky 1965). These linguists are concerned with both the investigation of individual grammars of particular languages, and in the development of a theory of linguistic universals. Thus, from a study of particular grammars, the linguist will make predictions about language universals (Chomsky 1968). Like all scientific hypotheses, such "universals" can be "disproved" should any particular language provide contrary evidence. Empirical explorations of the "universalist hypothesis" have been carried out (Greenberg 1962, 1966), and the available evidence strongly suggests that the hypothesis is well motivated and merits further serious study.

These two different perspectives toward language and the study of languages lead to different assumptions with respect to what theoretical linguistic information should be used in the preparation of optimally effective language teaching materials. Linguists of the nonuniversalist bent have been active in promoting contrastive analysis studies of a certain

Reprinted by permission of the publisher and the author from *Workpapers in TESL, UCLA* 6 (June, 1972):11–16.

kind. Such studies are typically concerned only with the superficial structures of two languages: the native language of the student and the language he is trying to learn, i.e., the target language. This, for example, is the approach used by Kufner (1962) in his study of the grammatical structures of English and German.[1] In fact, in this study Kufner asserts that the " . . . search for a universal grammar has proved futile. . ." (p. 64).

Given this attitude, it is not surprising that the universalist hypothesis has been neither adequately considered nor applied to language teaching pedagogy thus far.[2] All too frequently it has been cavalierly dismissed as is shown in the quote from Kufner cited above. The more superficial contrastive analysis approach, however, has undergone much subsidized research and has been applied constantly over the past twenty years. We are all aware, however, that there remain many problems in the teaching of foreign or second languages.

The remainder of this article suggests an alternative approach to contrastive syntax that takes into account facts about language typology and language universals; it is argued that such an approach is necessary if meaningful work is to be done in the area of contrastive syntax (i.e., work that will yield truly useful information to the language teacher and to persons engaged in the preparation of materials).

Proposal

The universalist hypothesis suggests the possibility of establishing universal matrices, revealing the finite set of grammatical elements, as well as the finite set of combinatory and hierarchical principles, available to any human language. Two given languages could then be compared with reference to these "universals" to determine precisely what differences of substance and form they entail and whether these differences are superficial or deep. A further hypothesis is that differences that exist at the superficial level will constitute a minor (or nonexistent) learning task whereas those differences existing in deep structure (i.e., underlying structure) will pose a more serious learning problem.

Since all languages of the world appear to have some way of expressing comparison, constructions of comparison have been selected as the specific problem for discussion in this article. Although such constructions are singled out for illustrative purposes, it is hoped that the implications for contrastive studies in syntax and for language teaching will be general and far reaching.

Typological Considerations

Following the universalist hypothesis, I assume that there is a finite number of ways in which any given language may express comparison, and
further, that there are certain constraints with respect to these constructions that all languages must obey. One possible way of taking language
universals into account is to construct a typology for comparative constructions, based on an investigation of this construction in English and
several other carefully selected languages that will provide broad representation of comparative constructions found in the languages of the
world. Using the results of this typology, a number of predictions should
emerge concerning the ease or difficulty with which the speakers of these
languages could learn English sentences expressing comparison. The typology should be based not on an analysis of surface constructions in
these languages but on a comparison of underlying syntactic and semantic
processes. For languages of the same type, it is, of course, also necessary
to establish a matrix of surface structures, showing the transformations
(i.e., permutations, deletions, etc.) that apply. In this way it also becomes
clear to what extent languages of the same type include the same set of
transformational rules.

A preliminary investigation (reported in more detail in Celce-Murcia
1972) indicates that there are three different types of comparative constructions found in the languages of the world. I shall refer to the first type
as the *degree comparative*. This type is exemplified by English and other
Indo-European languages (1).

  1. John is taller than Mary.

These languages are described as having a degree comparative since they
make use of morphemes of degree such as *more/-er* and *less*.

A second syntactic type of comparison is referred to as the *limited
universe comparative* and is exemplified by languages such as Mandarin
(2) and Japanese (3), which do not make use of morphemes such as *more*
and *less* to express comparison. Instead, they make use of uninflected
relative adjectives equivalent to *tall, short, pretty,* etc., and limit the
reference of the adjective through the use of two individuals (i.e., arguments) rather than one.

  2. John compared to Mary is tall. (English paraphrase of the Man-
     darin sentence "John bi Mary gao")
  3. Next to Mary Helen is pretty. (English paraphrase of the Japa-
     nese sentence "Mary yori Helen no hoo ga kirei-da")

While the English paraphrases provided above are possible sentences, a more usual translation of (2) would be (1) whereas (3) would normally be translated as (4).

    4. Helen is prettier than Mary.

The third type of syntactic comparison is the *surpass comparative* found in languages such as Igbo (5), a Niger-Congo language of West Africa, as well as in most Bantu languages of East and South Africa.

    5. John ka Mary ogologo. "John surpasses Mary (in) height."

There is an interesting psycholinguistic aspect to languages having surpass comparatives; this will be discussed shortly.

Psycholinguistic Considerations

Since measurable properties of objects such as age, height, size, weight, number, etc., are at the heart of most expressions of comparison, it is useful to point out the special properties of such concepts.

    For example, sentences such as those in (6) can be paraphrased by sentences such as those in (7):

    6. *a)* John is heavier than Bill.
       b) Bill is shorter than John.
    7. *a)* John's weight is greater than Bill's (weight).
       b) Bill's height is less than John's (height).

In English and many other languages, such measurable properties in predicates of comparison tend to be expressed in terms of adjectives that form pairs of oppositions as in (8)—i.e., the construction used in (6) is more common than the construction used in (7).

8. *Measurable Property*

	Predicating Opposition	
	Unmarked Form	Marked Form
age	old	young
height	tall	short
size	{ big	little
	{ large	small
weight	heavy	light

Measurable Property	*Predicating Opposition*	
	Unmarked Form	Marked Form
length	long	short
width	wide	narrow
depth	deep	shallow
amount	many/much	few/little
temperature	{ hot	cold
	warm	cool
strength	strong	weak
etc.		

As I have suggested in (8) by the use of the headings *unmarked form* and *marked form,* the predicating oppositions listed above have psychological implications as well as logical import. These psychological implications can be described by the notion of markedness (see Chomsky and Halle 1968 and others). Thus far the concept of markedness has been applied largely to phonological problems; in pairs of phonological oppositions, one member of the pair is typically unmarked (i.e., more natural, more frequently found in languages, more frequent in occurrence in any one language, first learned by children, etc.) and the other member typically marked (i.e., less natural, more complex, etc.). It has been found, for example, that where such oppositions are neutralized, (i.e., where only one member occurs to the exclusion of the other), it is the unmarked member which occurs.

It would be appropriate at this point to offer some preliminary evidence with regard to the hypothesized unmarked and marked forms given in (8). For example, with respect to *age,* it would appear that *old* is the unmarked member of the pair, since one normally says (9) and not (10).

9. John is twenty years old.
10. John is twenty years young.

Also one typically asks question (11) rather than (12). Where (12) is used, it is accompanied by special stress and intonation, i.e., *marked* prosodic features.

11. How old is John?
12. How young is John?

Example (12) could be acceptable in response to a statement that John would be good for a certain job but that he is rather young. By extension, the unmarked version of a sentence expressing comparison would be (13) rather than (14):

13. John is older than Mary.
14. Mary is younger than John.

That is, (13) would tend to be used in both neutral informational contexts, and contexts focussing on the question of who the older one of the two is. On the other hand, (14) would tend to occur only in the contexts that focus on who the younger one is.

Only a few studies have been concerned with syntactic or semantic markedness. This concept can, however, play an important role in second language teaching. Its theoretical implications regarding psychological conceptualizations are extremely important. With regard to unmarked and marked comparatives, however, an experiment has been conducted (see Celce-Murcia 1972) to establish empirically markedness values for English with regard to oppositions such as those listed in (8). It was found that 40 subjects responded to 36 stimuli designed to elicit comparisons[3] by using the hypothesized unmarked form significantly more frequently than the marked counterpart (i.e., about 87 percent of all the responses were unmarked).

Implications for Language Teaching

If it is found that for the oppositions discussed above there are universally marked and unmarked forms, this will have a great effect on the teaching of comparative constructions. It is interesting to note that in Igbo and in the Bantu languages only the unmarked form corresponding to (15) is possible. Both (13) and (14) must be expressed in Igbo and other languages having surpass comparatives as something approximating (15).

15. John surpasses Mary in age.

In other words, there is a neutralization of the *old/young* opposition in Igbo and Bantu, with only the unmarked form occurring. Given this knowledge, one can easily see implications for language teaching. For speakers of Igbo and Bantu learning English, a systematic presentation and drilling of such marked and unmarked comparative constructions would be required, utilizing explanations and drills which would have to differ from those used with speakers of langauges where oppositions such as *old/young* are not neutralized.

The use of adjective oppositions that relate to measurable properties is an aspect of comparison in English that is ignored in most
standard texts used for teaching English to foreigners. For example, in
Praninskas (1957), the relatedness or complementarity of the adjective
oppositions such as *long/short* with respect to comparative constructions
goes unmentioned. Yet the exercises direct the learner to perform tasks
such as "Compare two pencils with respect to length" (p. 204). There is,
of course, no mention of the preference in English for the use of the
unmarked *longer* versus the marked *shorter* when comparing two objects
with respect to length, or the use of *faster* versus *slower,* when comparing
two objects with respect to speed.[4] Praninskas is not an isolated case. The
exercises and examples in Rutherford (1968, pp. 194–207) and Hornby
(1961, pp. 135–44) give even less indication that comparison in English
involves internalization of such information. In fact, I have found no
materials in any reference books or texts written and used for the teaching of English as a second/foreign language that systematically treat the
problems mentioned above.

Conclusion

My suggestion is that serious omissions in teaching materials of the sort I
have discussed above with reference to the comparative construction may
be avoidable in the future if an effort is made to apply the universalist
hypothesis—as expressed in transformational theory—to contrastive
studies in syntax. In other words, for each major sentence type being
contrasted (e.g., indirect object constructions, embedded noun clauses,
alternative questions, contrary-to-fact sentences, etc.)[5] it would be extremely desirable to know something about the ways in which different
languages of the world express the given construction before proceeding
with either a specific contrastive analysis of the construction in two particular languages or the preparation of language teaching materials designed to teach the construction to classes either with a homogeneous or
heterogeneous language background.

Obviously, a great deal of typological syntactic research must be
undertaken before such materials will be available to those who wish to
carry out contrastive studies in syntax or prepare language teaching materials. However, given the current state of the art in contrastive syntax, it
appears that application of the universalist hypothesis will result in more
insightful studies and thus better teaching materials than most previous
contrastive syntax studies have produced.

Notes

I would like to express my deep indebtedness to Professor Victoria A. Fromkin who is the primary source of my interest in language universals and who, on various occasions, has discussed with me most of the ideas expressed in this article. The article has benefited greatly from these discussions; however, all errors and infelicities that appear are solely my responsibility.

1. See Hammer (1965) for a comprehensive list of the contrastive studies that had been carried out at that time. Almost all of these studies were carried out in the structuralist, nonuniversalist tradition.
2. A notable exception to this generalization is the pioneering work presented in Schachter (1967), Wilson (1967), and McIntosh (1967). In this series of papers, Schachter presents an analysis of relative clauses that takes language universals into consideration; Wilson, following the same frame of reference, then takes note of specific differences existing between relative clauses in English and Tagalog; McIntosh subsequently presents some language lessons for teaching English relative clauses to native speakers of Tagalog that were designed based on the differences discussed in Schachter and Wilson.
3. To give an example of the stimuli used in this experiment, there were two pencils identical in all features except length (i.e., one was slightly longer than the other). The subject was shown these two pencils and asked to make a comparison. Interestingly enough, subjects typically responded with "this pencil is longer" rather than "this pencil is shorter."
4. If we should find, however, that all languages view the same members of the pairs as unmarked, this kind of explanation will be unnecessary.
5. Relevant materials of the type being proposed, are, of course, presently available with regard to relative clauses—see Schachter (1967) and comparative constructions—see Celce-Murcia (1972). However, this material is only a sketchy beginning, something suggestive of the enormous task which still needs to be done.

References

Celce-Murcia, M. "A Syntactic and Psycholinguistic Study of Comparison in English." Ph.D. Dissertation in Linguistics, University of California, Los Angeles, Department of Linguistics. Ann Arbor, Mich.: University Microfilms, 1972.

Chomsky, Noam. *Aspects of the Theory of Syntax.* Cambridge, Mass.: MIT Press, 1965.

———. *Language and Mind.* New York: Harcourt, Brace and World, 1968.

Chomsky, Noam, and Halle, Morris. *The Sound Pattern of English.* New York: Harper and Row, 1968.

Greenberg, Joseph H. *Universals of Language.* Cambridge, Mass.: MIT Press, 1962.

————. *Language Universals.* The Hague: Mouton, 1966.

Hammer, John. *A Bibliography of Contrastive Linguistics.* Washington, D.C.: Center for Applied Linguistics, 1965.

Hornby, A. S. *The Teaching of Structural Words and Structural Patterns: Stage II.* London: Oxford University Press, 1961.

Joos, Martin. *Readings in Linguistics.* 2d ed. New York: American Council of Learned Societies, 1958.

Kufner, Herber L. *The Grammatical Structures of English and German.* Contrastive Structure Series. Chicago: University of Chicago Press, 1962.

McIntosh, Lois. "Language Lessons Based on Transformational Analysis." In *Workpapers in English as a Second Language,* vol. 1. University of California, Los Angeles, Department of English, 1967.

Praninskas, Jean. *A Rapid Review of English Grammar.* Englewood Cliffs, N.J.: Prentice-Hall, 1957.

Rutherford, William E. *Modern English: A Textbook for Foreign Students,* (New York: Harcourt, Brace and World, 1968.

Schachter, Paul. "Transformational Grammar and Contrastive Analysis." In *Workpapers in English as a Second Language,* vol. 1. University of California, Los Angeles, Department of English, 1967. Reprinted in *Teaching English as a Second Language: A Book of Readings,* edited by H. B. Allen and R. N. Campbell. 2d ed. New York: McGraw-Hill, 1972.

Wilson, Robert D. "A Contrastive Analysis of Segments of Transformational Grammars." In *Workpapers in English as a Second Language,* vol. 1. University of California, Los Angeles, Department of English, 1967.

Discourse Function and Language Transfer

Jacquelyn Schachter and William Rutherford

It is well known that at any stage in the learning of a language by adults there are observable features of learner production that can be attributed to influence by the learner's native language. Such influences, when manifested as identifiable errors, are what one usually refers to as "negative transfer" or "interference" errors. It is also the case that past studies of L_1 influence upon L_2 learning have drawn their data from just those language subareas that comprised what until recently was properly held to be the field of mainstream linguistics, those areas being phonology, morphology, syntax, and to some extent semantics. We wish to ask, however, whether this conventional phonology-to-semantics framework is really adequate for the study of L_1-L_2 influence, and whether there are possibly other perhaps less obvious ways in which L_2 production is affected by L_1. We are aware, for example, that many of the rules of English syntax, apart from their proposed formal analyses, seem to have their own reason or purpose for being and that a number of recent studies have been investigating this.[1] Therefore, if L_1 can influence L_2 with respect to the observable features of surface syntax, is it not also possible that influence can be manifested as well by whatever purpose such L_1 features are designed to serve? More specifically, we wish to ask the following:

1. Does any part of written English that is identifiable as nonnative reflect attempts by the learner to match features of English syntax to certain discourse functions, especially in cases where such functions are marked differently in the learner's native language than they are in English?
2. Are learner attempts to encode in English the notions topic/comment, theme/rheme, etc., different from those of a native speaker of English? If so, what syntactic devices do different learners resort to for such purposes?

Reprinted by permission of the publisher and the authors from *Working Papers on Bilingualism* 19 (November, 1979):3–12.

Our answer to such questions is an affirmative one, and in the remainder of this article we will first provide evidence for our conclusions and then propose some new perspectives for the consideration of the notions of overproduction and transfer error. Finally, we will suggest some promising directions that future research in these areas might take.

We begin by calling your attention to some facts gleaned from inspection by us of samples of written English produced by foreign students taking English at the American Language Institute at the University of Southern California.

A. The English surface form that results from application of the rule called *extraposition*[2] is one that is produced with surprising frequency by learners whose native language is Japanese—more often, in fact, than by those who speak Spanish, Arabic, Persian, and Mandarin. A count of the instances of extraposition sentences in 525 compositions, for example, shows that the Japanese learners produced an average of 3 extraposition sentences in every 4 compositions whereas learners with these other native language backgrounds produced only an average of 2 extraposition sentences in every 5 compositions. It would appear that the Japanese learners are overproducing these constructions. Examples:

1. It is believed that sweet flag leaves contain the power to expel sickness and evil (J17).
2. It is very unfortunate . . . that prosperity of our country only results from a sacrifice of workers (J7).

Also produced by the Japanese learners is an extraposition error type that we do not find in the writing of the other groups: Examples:

3. ?The computer is called the "brain" because it is the very important thing that the computer can remember (J1).
4. ?It is a tendency that such friendly restaurants become less in the big city (J12).

B. Existential constructions with dummy subject *there* are also produced with surprising regularity by learners whose native language is Chinese—again more often than by the Spanish, Arab, Persian, and Japanese learners, although the difference in frequency is not as great as the one mentioned above. In a count of existential constructions in 100 compositions, the Chinese learners produced an average of 4 existentials in every 5 compositions, whereas the learners of other native languages produced an average of 3 in every 4 compositions. Examples:

5. There is a small restaurant near my house in my country. Many things of the restaurant are like those of Marty's luncheonette (C22).
6. There are many different races that you can find in a small island such as Singapore. The Malays are what you call the natives (C24).

Also produced by the Chinese learners is an error type in existential sentences that we do not find in the writing of other groups. Examples:

7. ?There is a tire hanging from the roof served as their playground (C40).
8. ?There were many new patriots in my country gathered together and established a new country (C6).

Now obviously it should occasion no surprise that learners with particular native languages, in this case Japanese and Chinese, will produce specific error types in their use of the target language construction in question. In fact, the term *interference error* has been coined for reference to just those cases where a feature of L_1 has been erroneously carried over into production of L_2. And instances of error types unique to learners of a particular native language background are customarily assumed to be interference errors. What is interesting about the examples cited above, however, is that although they are produced with noticeable regularity, there are no constructions in the surface structure of either Japanese or Chinese that correspond to English extrapositions and existentials. Japanese and Chinese share characteristics that, among other things, often make it unnecessary for subject position to be filled at all, much less filled with dummy elements corresponding to English *it* or *there*. One might reasonably expect, therefore, that speakers of these languages would produce fewer such constructions in English. What then leads them to resort more often to the use of such constructions? We do not claim to have the answer to this question, but we do have what we consider to be a first order hypothesis that we will offer for your consideration. We wish to lead into this, however, by way of a brief discussion of some aspects of the cross-language coding of certain discourse functions.

It is commonly recognized that many of the syntactic structures of a language serve definable functions within discourse. It is also true that a given structure may serve a variety of discourse functions and that a given function may be implemented by more than one structure. There is, in other words, no necessary one-to-one correspondence. For example, the double form-function requirement in English—(a) that subject position always be filled, and (b) that in the neutrally marked topic-comment pattern new information occurs in the highest verb phrase constituent— has spawned a number of sentence constructions that are generated through movement transformations (i.e., raising, lowering, fronting, and backing). The choice of which construction to use—or in which syntactic "package" (Chafe 1976) to wrap the semantic content—would be controlled by the discourse considerations of information arrangement. Thus, a choice between, for example, the sentential subject and extraposition versions of the second sentence in the following pairs would be determined by what has preceded:

A. 1. Dr. Weiss is carefully considering tomorrow's experiment.
    2. *It is his opinion at the moment that it might not work.*
B. 1. Several scientists are of the opinion that tomorrow's experiment might not be successful.
    2. *That it might not work is also Dr. Weiss's opinion.*

In other words, some part of the semantic content of the contextual sentences (A1 and B1) constitutes the topic of the italicized sentences (A2 and B2), thereby constraining the available syntactic choices.

Although it is not nearly so well known how other, especially radically different, languages encode discourse functions, progress is beginning to be made in this area, as revealed by a number of current studies. A recent seminal article by Li and Thompson (1976), "Subject and Topic: A New Typology of Language," provides a useful framework for observing aspects of discourse-function encoding across languages. Li and Thompson hold that it is more meaningful to divide languages typologically not in terms of the traditional SVO/SOV/etc., word order distinction but rather on the basis of whether languages manifest as basic grammatical relations subject-predicate on the one hand or topic-comment on the other. Given such a typological framework, the distinction between the notions of subject and topic becomes crucial. For a detailed discussion on the criteria underlying the distinction we refer you to the article just mentioned; we quote here only a portion of their summation:

> We may single out 3 basic factors underlying these criteria . . . for distinguishing between T[opic] and S[ubject]: discourse strategy, noun-verb relations, and grammatical processes. The subject has a minimal discourse function in contrast with the topic. . . . the topic, but not necessarily the subject, is discourse-dependent, serves as the center of attention in the sentence, and must be definite. As for N-V relations and grammatical processes, it is the subject rather than the topic that figures prominently. Thus subject is normally determined by the verb and selectionally related to the verb; and the subject often obligatorily controls verb agreement. These properties of the subject are *not* shared by the topic. In conclusion the topic is a discourse notion whereas the subject is to a greater extent a sentence-internal notion. . . . [P. 466]

Li and Thompson show that unlike English, whose sentences can be talked about most meaningfully with reference to the grammatical relation subject-predicate, in topic-prominent languages the most basic constructions display rather the discourse relation, topic-comment. (That is, in such languages, in contrast to English, the topic-comment construction cannot be viewed as being derived from any sentence type.) The tendencies for languages to give prominence, or not, to one or the other of these two systems provide Li and Thompson with a four-way typological distinction:

1. Subject-prominent languages (e.g., English)
2. Topic-prominent languages (e.g., Mandarin)
3. Both subject-prominent and topic-prominent (e.g., Japanese)
4. Neither subject-prominent nor topic-prominent (e.g., Tagalog)

We wish to make it clear, however, that although topic-comment constructions are not basic to subject-prominent languages, these languages do have topicalization devices that can reflect this sentence type. For example, the subject-predicate relation in English is typified by a sentence like "John prefers Picasso" but we also have topic-comment constructions such as the sentence "As for modern art, John prefers Picasso." Conversely, although topic-comment constructions are basic to topic-prominent languages, some also have sentences which exhibit subject-predicate form. The English translation of a typical Mandarin topic-comment sentence might be "Airplanes, the 747 is big." Also grammatical in Mandarin is the subject-predicate sentence whose English translation would be "The 747 is big." It should be understood, then, that many topic-prominent languages can still have subjects and many subject-prominent languages can still have topics; the typological distinctions we speak of are rather reflections of a given language's *basic* sentential relationships.

Topic-prominent languages have other characteristics which set them apart from subject-prominent languages like English. Some of these characteristics are as follows:

1. In surface coding: Topic (although not necessarily subject) is always coded in topic-prominent languages. In Chinese, for example, topic always occurs in sentence-initial position; in Japanese topic normally occurs sentence initially and is always marked with the particle *wa*.
2. In expression of voice: The passive construction, as it is seen in English, either is rare, doesn't occur at all, or occurs but carries some special meaning. For example, in Chinese the passive is extremely rare in both speech and writing and in both Chinese and Japanese it can carry a connotation of adversity.
3. With regard to grammatical place holders: Sentences with dummy subjects like *it* in extraposition sentences and *there* in existential sentences of English don't occur in topic-prominent languages. In such languages, sentences in which no subject is called for semantically can simply do without one.
4. With regard to language typology: Topic-prominent languages tend to be those whose canonical sentence form puts the verb in final position. In Japanese this rule is a fairly rigid one.
5. With regard to basic sentence form: Sentences of the topic-comment form are to be considered as basic in topic-prominent languages and not automatically derivable from some other sentence type.

Topic-prominent languages also set themselves apart from English in another way. They tend to use word order for the expression of discourse function, whereas English, a subject-prominent language, uses word order almost exclusively to signal grammatical relations. Related to this is the fact that deletion in Chinese and Japanese is determined by discourse factors and is not subject to the kind of syntactic constraints that control deletion in English. One clear indication of this is revealed in a kind of error that Chinese and Japanese learners of English make as they are, apparently, trying to sort out the radically different and complex characteristics of grammatical word order and subject prominence. They make errors like these (italics indicate the relevant portions of the sentences):

9. ?*Most of food* which is served in such restaurant *have cooked already* (J).
10. ?Irrational emotions are bad but *rational emotions must use for judging* (J).
11. ?*Chiang's food must make in the kitchen of the restaurant* but *Marty's food could make in his house* (C).
12. ?If I have finished these four jobs, I am confident that *my company can list* in the biggest 100 companies in the world (C).

Now what is interesting is that a random sample of our language teachers at the American Language Institute unanimously diagnosed the above errors as having to do with a confusion between active and passive. They would argue for instance that (9) should have been "Most of the food which is served at such a restaurant *has been* cooked already." In arguing thus, they conform to the constraints, typical in subject-prominent languages, which require that there be a surface subject ("most of the food" in this case) and also require that the surface subject control verb agreement, thus "has been cooked." But in fact these sentences are a direct reflection of the surface syntax of Chinese and Japanese and topic-comment form. Bilingual English-Chinese and English-Japanese speakers inform us that it is far more plausible to interpret the initial noun phrases in each example as a topic, unrelated grammatically to the following verb, whose actual subject and often object are simply not required by the native language discourse conventions. By this reasoning, fuller readings of 9–12, for example, would be:

9a. Most of the food which is served in such restaurants [they] have cooked [it] already.
10a. Irrational emotions are bad, but rational emotions, [one] must use [them] for judging.
11a. Chiang's food [he] must make [it] in the kitchen of the restaurant, but Marty's food [he] could make [it] in his house.
12a. If I have finished these four jobs, I am confident that my company [they] can list [it] in the biggest 100 companies in the world.

These sentences are therefore very probably not examples of malformed passives but rather examples of the carry-over into the target language of native language function-form characteristics.

In topic-prominent languages like Chinese and Japanese (which is also of course subject-prominent), canonical sentence form puts topic first and comment second. Topic is always "given," has already been raised to consciousness, so to speak, while comment represents "new" information, or what is said about the topic. It follows then that before something becomes a topic it has to be introduced, or raised to consciousness. An introduced referent that is to become a topic is therefore itself "new" and, by the conventions of discourse in topic-prominent languages, will appear in the comment.

Let us now return to a consideration of the learner production cited earlier. Recall that we are dealing with efforts in written English of adult learners whose native languages are topic-prominent and whose expectations about (or experiences with) discourse functions are presumably at wide variance with those of native English speakers. We feel it is reasonable to assume that they would bring to the task of learning English the following (probably subconscious) expectations:

1. That word order is indicative, among other things, of discourse function.
2. That the position of leftmost, preverbal noun phrases is often reserved for topics.
3. That new information, destined to become a topic, will not occur in sentence-initial position.

Now since we find the Chinese and Japanese speakers producing the English extraposition and existential dummy subject sentences at a great rate, we need to ask what discourse functions the learners are using them for. If we look more closely at the samples of learner production in examples 1–4 we find that English extraposition constructions are being used almost exclusively by Japanese learners to make generic statements concerning general facts and beliefs, which serve as settings for future topics. In examples 1a–4a the bracketed constituents are the generic statements.

1a. It is believed [that sweet flag leaves contain the power to expel sickness and evil] (J17).
2a. It is very unfortunate . . . [that prosperity of our country only results from a sacrifice of workers] (J7).

3a. ?The computer is called the 'brain' because it is the very important thing [that the computer can remember] (J1).

4a. ?It is a tendency [that such friendly restaurants become less in
the big city] (J12).

We do not find extraposition sentences, for example, such as "It will be
difficult to finish the composition" where the main verb is predicated of a
nongeneric noun phrase.

We also find that English existential constructions are being used
almost exclusively by Chinese learners to introduce new referents which
serve as subsequent topics. In examples 5a–8a the underlined constructions serve to introduce new topics.

5a. *There is a small restaurant* near my house in my country. Many
things of this restaurant are like those of Marty's luncheonette
(C22).

6a. *There are many different races* that you can find in a small island
such as Singapore. The Malays are what you call the natives
(C24).

7a. ?*There is a tire* hanging from the roof served as their playground
(C40).

8a. ?*There were many new patriots* in my country gathered together
and established a new country (C6).

We do not find existential sentences, for example, such as the second of
the following pair (intended as a partial conversation) where the existential construction includes a noun phrase which has previously been introduced as a topic:

9a. Good restaurants are hard to find.

9b. *There's a good restaurant down the street.*

There is other evidence available to support the contention that L_1
discourse patterns can influence L_2 syntax. A study by Thomas Huebner
(1979) reveals, among other things, that the familiar morpheme acquisition order method of research fails to provide an explanation for certain
aspects of the acquisition of the English determiner system by a speaker
of Hmong, a topic-prominent language of the Sino-Tibetan group in
Southeast Asia. This speaker's interlanguage consistently omitted the English definite article for subject position noun phrases though not for
noun phrases in object position. Huebner's conclusion is that the topic-

prominent typological characteristics of Hmong have contributed to an interlanguage hypothesis of the learner in which he identifies as a topic in English any sentence-initial noun phrase carrying the feature of definiteness. But since topics in topic-prominent languages are typically definite (in that they represent information already introduced into the discourse) and since they therefore are often not marked as topics (other than by position), then the learner also sees no need to mark (redundantly) what he perceives as a topic in English. Hence the occurrence in the interlanguage of this learner, of subject noun phrases with missing definite articles, and a striking example of the influence of a feature of L_1 discourse upon the acquisition of L_2 syntax.

With these observations in mind, we hypothesize that learners of English whose native language is topic-prominent might be employing a strategy of the following kind:

1. They learn the form of a construction in the target language.
2. They hypothesize (partially correctly) that the form is used to express a particular discourse function; this hypothesis is consistent with the constraints within their own native language upon the interplay between syntactic form and discourse function in topic-prominent languages.
3. When the need arises within a target language context to express that particular discourse function, they use the form they have hypothesized is associated with that function.
4. The result is twofold: (*a*) a kind of "overproduction" of the construction in question (since that one construction is being made to serve a discourse function that in target language use is served by other constructions as well), and (*b*) the production of a unique error type (since the grammatical restrictions on the syntactic environment in which the form can occur have to be broken occasionally in order that the form may bear the heavy discourse function load being demanded of it).

If we have interpreted the data accurately, then the results have some important implications for the future study of L_2 learner production. We believe that the notions *overproduction* and *transfer* need to be reconsidered along the following lines. Whatever at first inspection looks like overproduction of a particular form by learners with a homogeneous native-language background should be closely scrutinized to see if the form is being made to support a discourse function that is too heavy. If so, then that overproduction is an instance of a new and different variety of language transfer, namely from L_1 function to L_2 form. If within the overproduction there occur systematic error types produced exclusively by those same learners, then those error types should be considered cases of a new and different variety of transfer errors, namely one that represents a carry-over not of surface syntax from L_1 to L_2 but rather of L_1 function-form constraints to L_2. Thus we are suggesting that the cases of overproduction and error types discussed here be considered as special cases of language transfer and that therefore the notion of language transfer itself should be widened accordingly.

Behind the issues that we have touched upon in this paper there is an implicit assumption which we wish now to make explicit. This assumption is that for any research that purports to shed light on the dynamic processes of language acquisition, it is necessary that the researcher focus attention on that particular property that makes of language itself a dynamic phenomenon: namely, discourse. This is not to say (as some appear to be doing) that a search for insights into language function and discourse is incompatible with the segmentation and classification procedures of traditional linguistic analysis. On the contrary, it is the very discreteness of linguistic elements that renders identifiable the various ways in which linguistic form is encoded for the realization of language function. We feel, however, that it is potentially counterproductive for language acquisition research to attempt to base conclusions exclusively upon the distributional patterns of observable language isolates in surface syntax.

There is a growing body of important literature in theoretical linguistics (e.g., the papers in Grossman et al. 1975) which has been reexamining from the perspective of function, discourse, and human processing techniques, the nature of syntactic phenomena that until recently were considered totally accounted for. There is also a growing body of literature in second language research which has been investigating the acquisition by children of discourse function (e.g., Hatch 1978; Keller-Cohen and Gracey 1976; Wagner-Gough and Hatch 1975). In this same spirit, we believe that research in language transfer should, whenever possible, transcend study of the patterning of the formal exponents of language and focus as well upon the inevitable systematic attempts by the learner to make the formal exponents serve functional ends.

Notes

The initial research on this paper was supported by the Center for the Humanities, University of Southern California. We wish to extend our most sincere thanks to Masakazu Watabe for many ideas and observations. Other helpful suggestions have come from Thomas Huebner and Amy Sheldon.

1. Different functional accounts of English extraposition, for example, appear in Ziv (1975), Jacobs (1975), Tannenhaus and Carroll (1975), Langacker (1974), and Thompson (1978).
2. Although *extraposition* usually refers to a process, we will henceforth use that term to designate as well the construction resulting from implementation of the process. We will thus have recourse to phrases like "learner production of extraposition," etc.

References

Chafe, Wallace. "Givenness, Contrastiveness, Definiteness, Subjects, Topics, and Point of View." In *Subject and Topic*, edited by Charles Li. New York: Academic Press, 1976.

Grossman, Robin E. L.; San, James; and Vance, Timothy J., eds. *Papers from the Parasession on Functionalism*. Chicago: Chicago Linguistic Society, 1975.

Hatch, Evelyn. "Discourse Analysis and Second Language Acquisition." In *Second Language Acquisition*, edited by E. Hatch. Rowley, Mass.: Newbury House, 1978.

Huebner, Thomas G. "Order-of-Acquisition vs. Dynamic Paradigm: A Comparison of Method in Interlanguage Research." *TESOL Quarterly* 13, no. 1 (1979):21–28.

Jacobs, Roderick A. "Promotion and thematization processes in English, or how to get a head." In *Papers from the Parasession on Functionalism*, edited by Robin E. L. Grossman et al. Chicago: Chicago Linguistic Society, 1975.

Keller-Cohen, Deborah, and Gracey, Cheryl. "Repetition and Turn-Allocation in the Non-Native Acquisition of Discourse." *Papers and Reports on Child Language Development* 12. Stanford: Stanford University Department of Linguistics, 1976.

Langacker, Ronald. "Movement Rules in Functional Perspective." *Language* 50, no. 4 (1974).

Li, Charles, ed. *Subject and Topic*. New York: Academic Press, 1976.

Li, Charles, and Thompson, Sandra. "Subject and Topic: A New Typology of Language." In *Subject and Topic*, edited by Charles Li. New York: Academic Press, 1976.

Tannenhaus, Michael K., and Carroll, John M. "The Clausal Processing Hierarchy . . . And Nouniness." In *Papers from the Parasession on Functionalism*, edited by Robin E. L. Grossman et al. Chicago: Chicago Linguistic Society, 1975.

Thompson, Sandra. "Modern English from a Typological Point of View: Some Implications of the Function of Word Order." *Linguistiche Berichte* 54 (1978).

Wagner-Gough, Judy, and Hatch, E. "The Importance of Input Data in Second Language Acquisition." *Language Learning* 25, no. 2 (1975):297–308.

Ziv, Yael. "On the Relevance of Content to the Form-Function Correlation." In *Papers from the Parasession on Functionalism,* edited by Robin E. L. Grossman et al. Chicago: Chicago Linguistic Society, 1975.

Is There a "Natural Sequence" in Adult Second Language Learning?

Nathalie Bailey, Carolyn Madden, and Stephen D. Krashen

On the basis of intensive analysis of the speech of three children as well as the study of available literature on child language acquisition, R. Brown (1973) concluded that the order of acquisition of certain functors (or grammatical morphemes) in English is invariant; despite differing rates of first language acquisition, there seems to be a surprisingly uniform developmental course that all children take in learning English. Brown analyzed the speech of three children longitudinally, and noted the presence or absence of each functor in each "obligatory context," that is, in each locus where adult syntax would require the presence of the functor. A functor was considered acquired when it was supplied in 90 percent of obligatory contexts for three successive recording sessions. A slightly different method was used by de Villiers and de Villiers (1973) in a cross-sectional study; they simply ranked functors according to relative accuracy in obligatory contexts. This alternative method correlated significantly with Brown's results.

Dulay and Burt (1973), studying a subset of the 14 functors Brown dealt with, presented evidence that 5-to-8-year-old children learning English as a second language also show a high degree of agreement with each other with respect to degree of accuracy of functors. Dulay and Burt concluded that "there does seem to be a common order of acquisition for certain structures in L₂ acquisition" (p. 256); however, the actual difficulty ordering found by Dulay and Burt was not the same as that found in first language acquisition studies (see table 1).

To explain this difference, Dulay and Burt note that the order of acquisition posited for older learners is not affected by the cognitive and conceptual development the first language learning child undergoes while learning his first language.

Dulay and Burt's findings are consistent with another observation reported in the same paper (Dulay and Burt 1973); the overwhelming majority of errors made by children in learning English as a second language are "developmental" rather than "interference," that is, they are

Reprinted by permission of the publisher and the authors from *Language Learning* 24, no. 2 (1974):235–43. 1973, for their help.

TABLE 1. Difficulty Order of Functors[1]

First Language Learners (de Villiers and de Villers 1973)	*Second Language Learners* (Dulay and Burt 1973)[2]
1. plural (-*s*)	1. plural (-*s*)
2. progressive (-*ing*)	2. progressive (-*ing*)
3. past irregular	3. contractible copula
4. articles (*a, the*)	4. contractible auxiliary
5. contractible copula	5. articles (*a, the*)
6. possessive (*'s*)	6. past irregular
7. third person singular (-*s*)	7. third person singular (-*s*)
8. contractible auxiliary	8. possessive (*'s*)

1. De Villiers and de Villiers (1973) studied 14 functors in all; included here are the 8 functors covered in both studies. Difficulty orders from the 2 studies do not correlate significantly (rho = .59, n.s.).
2. Taken from Dulay and Burt's largest subgroup (Sacramento).

similar in kind to errors made by children learning English as a first language and not the result of interference from the learners' first language habits. Dulay and Burt conclude from these results that first and second language learning in children involves similar kinds of processing of linguistic data. Specifically, the process of learning English as a second language must involve the "creative construction" and testing of hypotheses about the target language.

Recent studies have emphasized that errors made by adults in second language learning are to a large extent (1) common to learners with different mother tongues, and (2) analyzable as incorrect hypotheses about the target language (Richards 1971*a* and 1971*b*, Buteau 1970, Dušková 1969, Bailey and Madden 1973). Such results encourage the hypothesis that adult second language learning may also involve a natural sequence of acquisition. One would not expect the adult sequence to match that of the child's learning of his first language. Rather, since adults are more similar to 5-to-8-year olds with respect to cognitive maturity, the adult order should be closer to that of the older child learning English as a second language. In this study, the following two hypotheses will be tested:

1. Adults learning English as a second language will show agreement with each other in the relative difficulty of functors in English.
2. The adult rankings will be similar to that of the child learning English as a second language, rather than to that of children learning English as a first language.

Procedure

Seventy-three adult subjects (ages 17 to 55) were tested. The subjects were members of eight classes in ESL (the first four levels of each of two programs) at Queens College, New York. One program, the English Language Institute program, is an intensive, all day program for foreign students preparing to study in American colleges, and the other, the Continuing Education program, is a 4-hour-per-week adult education course. Generally, the adult education subjects had more exposure to English outside the classroom. The subjects were also classified as Spanish or non-Spanish speaking. The Spanish speaking group consisted of 33 students and the non-Spanish group consisted of 40 students representing 11 different mother tongues (Greek, Persian, Italian, Turkish, Japanese, Chinese, Thai, Afghan, Hebrew, Arabic, and Vietnamese).

As in Dulay and Burt's (1973) study, language data was elicited with the Bilingual Syntax Measure (BSM) (Burt, Dulay, and Hernandez 1973). Despite the fact that the Bilingual Syntax Measure was originally designed for children, it was successfully used with adults here. The BSM consists of 7 colored cartoons accompanied by preliminary questions and testing questions. The preliminary questions are designed to insure the subjects' knowledge of lexical items. The testing questions are designed to elicit the use of the eight selected English functors listed in table 1.

Each subject was tested individually by a team of 2 undergraduate students from the Queens College Linguistics Department. One E (examiner) showed a picture to the S (subject), asked the pertinent preliminary questions, then proceeded to the test questions. The second E recorded the S's answers to the test questions on the BSM answer sheet.

As in previous studies, accuracy of usage was determined by the ratio of the correctly formed and used functors to the obligatory occasions for them. Following Dulay and Burt (1973) a correctly used functor was scored as one point, a misformed functor as .5 and a missing functor as zero, e.g.,

They   birds   (missing functor = 0)
They is   birds   (misformed functor = .5)
They are birds   (correct functor = 1)

Results

Pearson product-moment correlations were performed on the relative accuracy of use of the 8 grammatical morphemes between Spanish and non-Spanish speakers and among the 8 instruction levels.

There was a significant correlation between relative accuracies of function words for Spanish and non-Spanish speakers (r = .926, p < .005, one-tailed test). The scores are portrayed in figure 1. Correlations among the eight instruction groups are given in table 2. There was a high degree of agreement as to the relative difficulty of the functors among all groups, with the exception of level 3 in the English Language Institute program, which may be due to a ceiling effect caused by a high level of English language proficiency in this group. Percentages of accuracy are given in table 3.

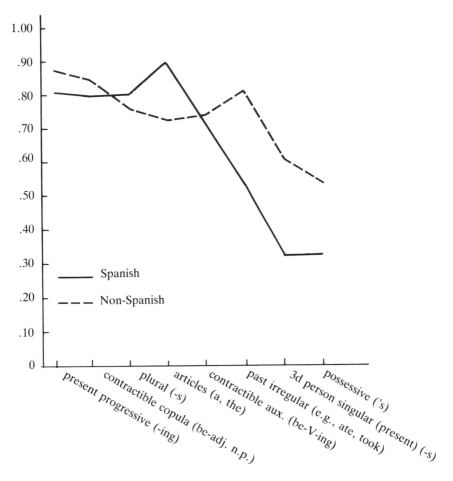

Fig. 1. Comparison of Spanish and non-Spanish adults; relative accuracies for 8 functors

TABLE 2. Correlations between Groups of ESL Students for Function Word Accuracy

	ELI 1[1]	ELI 2	ELI 3	ELI 4	CON ED 1[2]	CON ED 2A	CON ED 2B
ELI 2	.85[b]						
ELI 3	.53	.79[b]					
ELI 4	.93[b]	.82[b]	.51				
CON ED 1	.78[a]	.83[b]	.43	.69[a]			
CON ED 2A	.93[b]	.86[b]	.49	.88[b]	.90[b]		
CON ED 2B	.84[b]	.68[a]	.16	.78[a]	.84[b]	.93[b]	
CON ED 3	.71[a]	.80[b]	.52	.69[a]	.84[b]	.63[a]	.94[b]

1. English Language Institute
2. Continuing Education Program

a. p < .05 (one-tailed)
b. p < .01 (one-tailed)

TABLE 3. Percentage of Accuracy for Adult ESL Learners in Eight Functors

	-ing	cont. cop.	plural	art.	cont. aux.	past irr.	third per.	poss.
ELI 1	.84	.85	.72	.80	.77	.61	.34	.31
ELI 2	.87	.77	.71	.59	.55	.48	.38	.38
ELI 3	.90	.90	.88	.70	.66	.82	.65	.72
ELI 4	.90	.88	.81	.82	.81	.77	.54	.47
CON ED 1	.82	.80	.69	.81	.50	.25	.47	.21
CON ED 2A	.63	.64	.66	.83	.76	.13	.21	.13
CON ED 2B	.90	.88	.94	.93	.75	.40	.28	.19
CON ED 3	.89	.82	.88	.79	.33	.45	.32	.36

To test hypothesis 2, adult relative accuracies were compared to Dulay and Burt's (1973) data for 5-to-8-year-old children learning English as a second language. Relative accuracies for their Sacramento group (consisting of 96 children with a relatively large amount of exposure to English) correlated significantly for both parametric and nonparametric measures ($r = .893$, $p < .005$, one tailed test, rho $= .91$, $p < .01$). Also, correlation between our subjects and Dulay and Burt's San Ysidro group (26 Mexican children exposed to English only in school) was significant ($r = .97$, $p < .005$, one tail, rho $= .94$, $p < .01$). The correlation between the adults and Dulay and Burt's East Harlem group (30 Puerto Rican children in a balanced bilingual program) did not quite reach statistical significance with the Pearson r but did with the Spearman rho ($r = .60$, $p < .10$, rho $= .88$, $p < .01$). Figure 2 exhibits the relative accuracies of the 4 groups. The lower correlation with the East Harlem group may reflect the fact that Black English is often the target language for these children since their main divergence from the order of the other two groups is due to lower accuracy in the use of the copula and contractible auxiliary, commonly deleted in Black English.

As predicted, the adult order did not correlate significantly with relative accuracies for functors reported by de Villiers and de Villiers (1973) for children (rho $= .57$, n.s.).

Discussion

Despite the differences in adult learners in amount of instruction, exposure to English, and mother tongue, there is a high degree of agreement as to the relative difficulty of the set of grammatical morphemes examined here, supporting hypothesis 1. This result in conjunction with error analysis research indicates that adults use common strategies for second language learning. In addition, if relative difficulty corresponds to order of acquisition as implied by de Villiers and de Villiers's (1973) results with children, this result also suggests a common order of acquisition for functors in adults.

Comparison with Dulay and Burt's data reveals that relative accuracy in adults is quite similar to the relative accuracies shown by children learning English as a second language for the same functors, supporting hypothesis 2. Thus, while adults may in general not achieve the level of performance achieved by first language learners or children learning English as a second language, and may need the isolation of linguistic structures and feedback provided by the classroom, these results indicate that they process linguistic data in ways similar to younger learners.

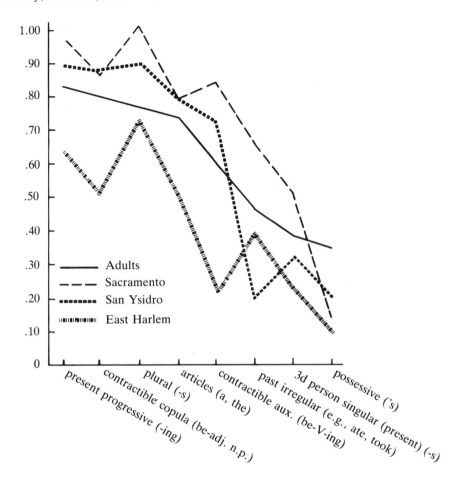

Fig. 2. Comparison of child and adult relative accuracies for 8 functors

Since subjects with different first languages performed similarly, the results are also consistent with findings that errors in second language learning are not all the result of interference from the first language. Along with studies of errors in second language learning cited above, this argues against any strong version of the contrastive analysis hypothesis. While casual observation affirms that errors due to mother tongue interference do occur in second language learning in adults, our data imply that a major source of errors is intra- rather than interlingual, and are due to the use of universal language processing strategies.

Further evidence may be found for the use of universal language processing strategies in the study of aphasia, a noninterference situation.

A very recent cross-sectional study of nonfluent aphasia (de Villiers 1974) reports a relative order of difficulty in functors nearly identical to that found here for adults learning English as a second language (for those 6 functors covered in both studies, rho = .94, p < .05). There thus seem to be 2 invariant orderings for functors: one for children learning English as a first language, and the other shared by children learning English as a second language, adults learning English as a second language, and adult nonfluent aphasics. It remains to be determined what combinations of factors account for this apparent uniformity in adult processing and why the adult order differs from the child's.

Finally, we need to consider the role of the classroom. Dulay and Burt (1973) conclude that their findings of an invariant order of acquisition in children learning English as a second language and its implications for a developmental theory imply that "we should leave the learning to the children" (p. 257); teaching syntax is not necessary. It may be the case that second language learning in children can effectively take place in the absence of a formal linguistic environment. The conclusion, however, while possibly correct, does not follow from their results on relative accuracy of function words. Adults, as demonstrated here, show nearly the same rankings and a similar degree of invariance, and as empirical studies (Krashen and Seliger 1976; Krashen, Seliger, and Hartnett 1974; Krashen, Jones, Zelinski, and Usprich 1978) and years of experience in language learning and teaching show, instruction is directly related to English language proficiency in adults, while exposure to English in informal environments is not.

We are thus faced with an interesting conclusion: adults seem to profit from instruction, an instruction that often presents the grammatical morphemes in an order different from that implied here. An interesting and testable hypothesis is that the most effective instruction is that which follows the observed order of difficulty, one with a "natural syllabus." We will be prepared for such an experiment when we confirm the implied sequence longitudinally, and discover which aspects of language follow a universal sequence, and understand what factors determine such a sequence.

Note

We thank Helen Cairns, Miriam Eisenstein, and the students from Linguistics 19, Queens College, Spring, 1973, for their help.

References

Bailey, N., and Madden, C. "Is Second Language Learning Like First Language Learning?" Presentation given at C.U.N.Y. Conference, Commodore Hotel, New York, 1973.

Brown, R. *A First Language; the Early Stages.* Cambridge, Mass.: Harvard University Press, 1973.

Burt, M. K.; Dulay, H. C.; and Hernandez-Chavez, E. *Bilingual Syntax Measure.* Restricted ed. New York: Harcourt Brace Jovanovich, 1973.

Buteau, M. "Students' Errors and the Learning of French as a Second Language: A Pilot Study." *International Review of Applied Linguistics* 8 (1970):133–45.

Cook, V. "The Analogy Between First and Second Language Learning." *International Review of Applied Linguistics* 7 (1969):207–16.

Corder, S. P. "The Significance of Learners' Errors." *International Review of Applied Linguistics* 4 (1967):161–69.

de Villiers, J. G. "Quantitative Aspects of Agrammatism in Aphasia." *Cortex* 10 (1974):36–54.

de Villiers, J. G., and de Villiers, P. A. "A Cross-sectional Study of the Acquisition of Grammatical Morphemes in Child Speech." *Journal of Psycholinguistics Research* 2 (1973):267–78.

Dulay, H. C., and Burt, M. K. "Should We Teach Children Syntax?" *Language Learning* 23 (1973):245–58.

Dušková, L. "On Sources of Errors in Foreign Language Learning." *International Review of Applied Linguistics* 7 (1970):11–36.

Krashen, S.; Jones, C.; Zelinski, S.; and Usprich, C. "How Important Is Instruction?" *English Language Teaching Journal* 32, no. 4 (1978):257–60.

Krashen, S., and Seliger, H. "The Role of Formal and Informal Environments in Second Language Learning: A Pilot Study." *International Journal of Psycholinguistics* 3 (1976):15–21.

Krashen, S.; Seliger, H.; and Hartnett, D. "Two Studies in Adult Second Language Learning." *Kritikon Litterarum* 2/3 (1974):220–28.

Richards J. "Error Analysis and Second Language Strategies." *Language Sciences* 17 (1971a):12–22.

———. "A Noncontrastive Approach to Error Analysis." *English Language Teachings* 25 (1971b):204–19.

Implications of the Morpheme Studies for Second Language Acquisition

Diane Larsen-Freeman

In 1973 second language acquisition researchers Dulay and Burt reported that they had discovered an "order of acquisition" for eight English morphemes among Spanish-speaking children learning English as a second language (ESL). Their claim that certain morphemes were acquired earlier than others was based on the relative number of times their subjects correctly supplied these morphemes in obligatory contexts.

Subsequent to Dulay and Burt's report, further morpheme studies were undertaken. The results of these studies showed that the morpheme order originally reported for Spanish-speaking children was also characteristic of Chinese-speaking children learning ESL (Dulay and Burt 1974) and of adult ESL learners representing various native language backgrounds (Bailey, Madden, and Krashen 1974; Larsen-Freeman 1975b). Although the morpheme orders for these different groups of learners were not invariant, there was still a strikingly similar pattern among the orders from the various subject populations. Furthermore, although tasks involving different modalities did elicit different morpheme orders, certain morphemes in oral production tasks (speaking and elicited imitation) were consistently used more accurately than others by all learners (Larsen-Freeman 1975b).

Prompted to search for the reason why learners regularly produce certain morphemes more accurately than others, Larsen-Freeman (1976a) examined the common oral production morpheme sequence in light of possible determinant(s). Morpheme complexity, learner variables, instructional procedures, operating strategies, perceptual saliency and the frequency of occurrence of the morphemes in spoken English were all considered. Significant positive correlations were only obtained when the morpheme acquisition order[1] was compared with the frequency of occurrence of these same morphemes in native-speaker speech.[2]

Since the morpheme frequencies used in this comparison were based on speech samples of English-speaking parents conversing with their chil-

Reprinted by permission of the publisher and the author from *ITL* (*Review of Applied Linguistics*) 39–40 (1978):93–102.

dren, it was felt that it was premature to claim that frequency of occurrence was the principal determinant of the ESL acquisition order. For us to feel more secure with such a claim, it would be necessary to examine morpheme frequencies in the type of language input an ESL learner would be likely to encounter. In order to accomplish this, it was decided to record the speech of ESL teachers during classroom instruction.

Volunteers were solicited from among the staff of ESL instructors at the University of California, Los Angeles (UCLA). Two teachers of different low-level classes agreed to participate. Their classes were each tape recorded for one hour a week over a ten-week period. Although the classes were at comparable levels of proficiency, each instructor devised her own course syllabus. From a total of twenty hours of recorded instruction, three hours were randomly selected from the tapes of each class. For the one class, the tapes selected were from weeks one, three, and seven. For the other class, the tapes were from weeks two, six, and nine. The six hours were transcribed and morpheme frequency counts were made from the teachers' speech for the nine morphemes most often studied by second language acquisition researchers. (For a detailed description see Larsen-Freeman 1975a).

Table 1 reveals the frequency ranks of the nine morphemes in descending order for both classes for the six hours of transcribed tapes.

The similarity across classes is readily apparent. A Kendall's coefficient of concordance was performed and was significant at the .001 level.

Next, Spearman Rank correlation coefficients were calculated be-

TABLE 1. Frequency Ranks for Nine Morphemes

Morphemes	Class A Tapes			Class B Tapes		
	1	3	7	2	6	9
Article	1	1	1	1	1	1
Copula	2	2	2	3	2	3
Plural	3	3	3	2	3	2
Progressive -ing	4	4	4	4	5.5	6
Third person sing.	5	5	5	6	7	7
Regular past tense	6	7	6	5	5.5	4
Progressive auxiliary	7	8	8	8	8	8
Possessive	8	9	9	9	9	9
Irregular past tense	9	6	7	7	4*	5

*The grammar component of this class dealt with irregular past tense which would account for its higher rank.

tween each of the teacher speech frequency orders and Brown's (1973) reported frequency order determined by a count of the morphemes in the speech of English-speaking parents to their children. Table 2 gives these correlations. Thus, in four of six possible cases the morpheme frequency ranks were correlated significantly at the .05 level.

TABLE 2. Spearman Rank Order Correlation Coefficients between Morpheme Frequency Counts from ESL Teacher Speech and Brown (1973)

	Class A Tapes			Class B Tapes		
	1	3	7	2	6	9
Brown* (1973)	.633	.666	.616	.533	.585	.416
	$p < .034$	$p < .025$	$p < .038$	$p < .070$	$p < .049$	$p < .132$

*Brown's order
1. copula
2. article
3. progressive -ing
4. progressive auxiliary
5. plural
6. irregular past tense
7. possessive
8. third person singular
9. regular past tense

The morpheme frequencies in the teachers' speech were next compared to an oral production morpheme acquisition order from Larsen-Freeman (1975b). Table 3 gives the Spearman Rank correlation coefficients. Again we see in four of the six comparisons, the morpheme ranks from two sources were correlated significantly at the .05 level.

TABLE 3. Spearman Rank Correlation Coefficients between Morpheme Frequency Counts from ESL Teacher Speech and Larsen-Freeman (1975b)

	Class A Tapes			Class B Tapes		
	1	3	7	2	6	9
Larsen-Freeman* (1975b)	.733	.650	.683	.650	.493	.433
	$p < .012$	$p < .029$	$p < .021$	$p < .029$	$p < .088$	$p < .122$

*Larsen-Freeman's order Phase I (Speaking Task-data elicited using the Bilingual Syntax Measure)[3]
1. progressive -ing
2. copula
3. article
4. progressive auxiliary
5. plural
6. regular past
7. third person singular
8. irregular past tense
9. possessive

Finally, the frequencies of the morphemes in the ESL teachers' speech were compared to Dulay and Burt's morpheme acquisition order (1974). Table 4 gives the resulting Spearman Rank correlation coefficients.

As table 4 shows, all six correlations are significant, including four at the .01 level. The increase in significance obtained in correlating the Dulay and Burt morpheme order with the ESL teacher speech frequency order is probably due to the fact that the subject population studied by Dulay and Burt, 115, was much larger than the 24 subjects studied by Larsen-Freeman.

TABLE 4. Spearman Rank Correlation Coefficients between Morpheme Frequency Counts from ESL Teacher Speech and Dulay and Burt (1974)

	Class A Tapes			Class B Tapes		
	1	3	7	2	6	9
Dulay and Burt*	.783	.750	.766	.783	.744	.700
(1974)	p < .006	p < .010	p < .008	p < .006	p < .011	p < .018

*Dulay and Burt's order

1. article	4. plural	7. irregular past tense
2. copula	5. progressive auxiliary	8. possessive
3. progressive -ing	6. regular past tense	9. third person singular

The final statistical measure employed was the Kendall coefficient of concordance among twelve morpheme orders: six from the ESL teacher speech, four from Larsen-Freeman's 1975 study (orders from a speaking task and an elicited imitation task each administered twice), Brown's 1973 frequency order, and Dulay and Burt's 1974 acquisition order. The coefficient of concordance was found to be signicant at the .001 level. The evidence cited here was felt to be supportive of the hypothesis that the frequency of occurrence of the nine morphemes in English native-speaker speech is the principal determinant of the oral production ESL morpheme acquisition order. While the identifying of a variable correlating significantly with the morpheme acquisition order was satisfying, what this reveals about language acquisition is far from clear. The implications of this finding would depend very much on one's view of the language acquisition process. For instance, a behaviorist might feel that the fact that the morpheme acquisition sequence mirrors the frequency of occurrence supports a stimulus-response view of language acquisition. The more frequently a stimulus is encountered, the more the opportunities for reinforcement occur and the more quickly a rule becomes inculcated.

On the other hand, from the same finding one could argue just as convincingly that a cognitive model of language acquisition is justified. The cognitivist would say the learner is engaged in working out the rules from the speech to which he is exposed. Structures with high frequencies would supply the learner with more data on which to base and refine his hypotheses about those rules. Indeed, in keeping with Slobin's notion of operating principles, a cognitivist could postulate a preprogrammed principle existing in learners' minds that advises learners to pay attention to the frequency of structures in the input and to concentrate their efforts on figuring out the rules initially for those structures occurring most often.

In both the aforementioned views of language acquisition, the learner's speech product is treated analytically. The learner is seen to be struggling to master the rules governing the usage of particular morphemes. In a first language acquisition study by Peters (1976)[4] one gains an entirely different perspective of what the learner might be attempting to do. Peters found that the subject she investigated tried to match the "gestalt" of a *sentence* in his speech rather than limiting his production to one- or two-word *phrases*.

> The result was utterances in which, although the segmental fidelity was not very great, the combination of number of syllables, stress, intonation, and such segments as could be distinguished combined to give a very good impression of sentencehood. I will call this type of speech Gestalt since like Tunes[5] which it includes, it seems to be aiming at whole phrases or sentences rather than at single words. [Pp. 4–5]

Given the appropriate context, it was often possible for Peters to attribute some meaning to these utterances despite the fact that no single constituent clearly was identical with the adult native-speaker form. A potentially important implication for our study is suggested by Peter's observation that:

> Some of Minh's early Tunes incorporated both fairly well analyzed parts and "filler syllables" which seemed to be used as place holders to fill out not yet analyzed parts of a phrase. [P. 5]

Extrapolating from this finding, it is possible that nonnative speakers learn to insert the appropriate morphemes in their speech in an attempt to match the gestalt of the native-speaker input to which they are exposed. Rather than treating the morphemes analytically and grappling with the rules that govern each, the learner might be attempting to have his speech product conform to the contour of the input—and morphemes are the "filler syllables" which aid him to sound more nativelike.

From this same unanalytic perspective, researchers Brown (1973), Hatch and Gough (1974), Hakuta (1974) and Fillmore (1976) have all talked about a common acquisition strategy among language learners whereby the learner incorporates a memorized "routine," "formula," or "prefabricated pattern" into his repertoire without first analyzing its constituent parts. Learners store such patterns as "It's time to + VERB" (Butterworth 1972) as they would an individual lexical item and learn to use the pattern appropriately long before they have analyzed the underlying rules governing the individual segments. It is possible that learners supply morphemes correctly in obligatory contexts, not because the learners control the rules for correct morpheme suppliance, but because these morphemes are present in unanalyzed memorized patterns which the learners have incorporated into their repertoires. Indeed, it seems the morphemes which are clustered at the top of the acquisition order are the ones most likely to enter into memorized patterns. Brown notes that patterns such as "It's here" or "I'm here" which his subjects tended to treat monomorphemically have "very high frequency in parental speech" (1973, p. 396). On the other hand, morphemes at the bottom of the order, such as possessive and third person singular, probably occur so infrequently that they are unlikely to be present in chunks of speech which become memorized wholes.

Although we have perhaps not exhausted all possible explanations for our finding, we have not wanted for variety: we have considered the analytic perspective on language acquisition of the behaviorists and the cognitivists; we have considered the unanalytic perspective on language acquisition that the learner supplies certain morphemes correctly because he is attempting to match the gestalt of the speech he hears or that these certain morphemes occur in speech patterns that he has memorized.

It is difficult at this point to imagine how these varying points of view could ever be resolved empirically. It may very well be, however, that no one explanation would ever work for all learners and that different learners might rely on differing strategies depending upon the nature of the input they receive, their own cognitive style and their level of proficiency in the target language.

Notes

1. The term *acquisition order* was first used by Dulay and Burt and is the one most often seen in print. Bailey, Madden, and Krashen, however, chose to use *difficulty order*. It seems to me the term *accuracy order* may be the most

precise since the order is established by calculating the percentage of times a subject *accurately* supplies a morpheme in obligatory contexts.

2. As there was no general morpheme frequency count available, the morpheme frequencies Brown (1973) determined for the three sets of native English-speaking parents of the subjects in his first language acquisition study were used. Brown's frequency counts were made from transcripts of recordings taped during the periodic visits by researchers to the subjects' homes. Since Brown states that there are significantly high correlations for the morpheme frequency orders among the three sets of parents, the frequencies are probably representative of their actual occurrence in native-speaker speech.

3. There were three other oral production tasks in the Larsen-Freeman (1975) study. None of them correlated as highly with the morpheme frequency counts as did the order for the task reported in table 3. However, there still was an obvious similarity among all the orders. This is supported statistically by the high Kendall's coefficient of concordance obtained. As I have pointed out earlier (Perkins and Larsen-Freeman 1975), the rank ordering of morphemes to obtain an acquisition order seems a questionable practice since differences between ranks appear to be slight when comparing two orders and yet result in insignificant correlations.

4. I am grateful to Steve Krashen for calling this working paper to my attention.

5. By "tunes" Peters refers to a learner's uttering a phrase with a "melody," i.e., intonation contour, unique enough to allow it to be recognized even if the segments of the phrase are mumbled. Peters gives several examples: uh oh! [¯ ˍ] look at that [ˍˌ].

References

Bailey, N.; Madden, C.; and Krashen, S. "Is there a 'Natural Sequence' in Adult Second Language Learning?" *Language Learning* 24 (1974):235–43.

Brown, R. *A First Language.* Cambridge, Mass.: Harvard University Press, 1973.

Butterworth, G. "A Spanish-speaking Adolescent's Acquisition of English Syntax." Master's thesis, University of California, Los Angeles, 1972.

Dulay, H., and Burt, M. "Should We Teach Children Syntax?" *Language Learning* 23 (1973):245–58.

———. "Natural Sequences in Child Second Language Acquisition." *Language Learning* 24 (1974):37–44.

Fillmore, L. W. "The Second Time Around: Cognitive and Social Structures in Second Language Acquisition." Ph.D. dissertation, University of California, Berkeley, 1976.

Hakuta, K. "Prefabricated Patterns and the Emergence of Structure in Second Language Acquisition." *Language Learning* 24 (1974):287–97.

Hatch, E., and Gough, J. W. "Second Language Acquisition," *An Introduction to the Teaching of English as a Second Language,* edited by M. Celce-Murcia. Prepublication version, 1974.

Larsen-Freeman, D. "The Acquisition of Grammatical Morphemes by Adult Learners of English as a Second Language." Ph.D. dissertation, University of Michigan, 1975*a*.

———. "The Acquisition of Grammatical Morphemes by Adult ESL Students." *TESOL Quarterly* 9 (1975*b*):409–20.

———. "An Explanation for the Morpheme Acquisition Order of Second Language Learners." *Language Learning* 26 (1976*a*):125–34.

———. "ESL Teacher Speech as Input to the ESL Learner." *UCLA Workpapers in Teaching English as a Second Language* 10, (1976*b*):45–50.

Perkins, K., and Larsen-Freeman, D. "The Effect of Formal Language Instruction on the Order of Morpheme Acquisition." *Language Learning* 25 (1975):237–43.

Peters, A. "Language Learning Strategies: Does the Whole Equal the Sum of the Parts." *Working Papers in Linguistics* (University of Hawaii) 8 (1976).

Explaining Sequence and Variation in Second Language Acquisition

Evelyn Hatch and Judy Wagner-Gough

All of us who work with second language learners soon become aware that there is a pattern to the errors that our students make. If we look at second language data long enough and over enough studies, a recognizable pattern emerges, a pattern that changes over time as the learner becomes more and more proficient in the second language. This pattern of language acquisition has been called *interlanguage*, an *approximative system*, or an *interim set of grammars*. Since we believe that there are shared characteristics in second language learning, we also believe that second language learning, just like first language learning, can be studied and described.

This does not mean that we all agree on what must appear in that pattern, nor does it mean that the order of acquisition of various parts of the system is an invariant order. It does mean that if you and others look at data taken during a longitudinal study of a child's second language learning, you can get a general consensus for a sequence in language acquisition. It may not be exactly the same as that for our subjects and it may not be the same as that identified by Dulay and Burt. But you can discover a general tendency that the learner will acquire A before B and both before C. For example, we can say that the order of question development for English second language learners is something like that shown in table 1. Rising intonation is either learned or transferred from the first language, *wh*-fronting occurs and *what* and *where* questions appear first, *can* is the first inversion form for the modals. Finally *be* appears in questions and much later *do*-support is acquired in question forms. Throughout this sequence, inversions are avoided as much as possible; the learner uses rising intonation instead. This general sequence is similar to that found in first language studies and, as such, these shared characteristics of learners have been called universals by many, including myself. You may object, and many have, that a universal is not a universal if you can find one example to disprove it; "what good is a universal if it isn't a univer-

Reprinted by permission of the publisher and the authors from *Language Learning*, special issue no. 4 (1976):39–57.

sal?" In that case, there is nothing in second language learning, or in first language learning, that is universal. You will find children who acquire C before B and B before A. You may find children who acquire all three simultaneously, and you will find children who do not acquire (using the criterion of 70 percent, 80 percent, or 90 percent correct in obligatory contexts over a two-week period) the forms at all but use them in seeming free variation with other forms for many functions. Homer, the Iranian child, for example, used *-ing* forms for imperatives, continuous aspect, past, and future in variation with unmarked verbs. You will find children who will acquire a form (meet the above criterion for acquisition) and then revert to an old pattern or invent a new one. Enrique, a Spanish-speaking child, for example, finally acquired the definite article in English and then invented the article *le* which seemed to be a combination of Spanish articles and *the*.

TABLE 1. Sequence of Question Development

1. Rising Intonation
   This tree? (Paul)
   You go? (Zoila)
   This name? (Homer)
2. Tag Questions
   You Joe, okay? (Paul)
   You want tea, no? (Zoila)
   George come school, no? (Ken)
3. *wh*-fronting
   ∅ Copula
   Where my ball? (Rune)
   What you knitting? (Rune)
   ∅ do-support
   Why you speak French? (Chamot)
   When you up? (Zoila)
   Why we not live in Scotland? (Rune)

4. Modal inversion
   How can I finish? (Chamot)
   Can I play? (Paul)
   Can Ken have juice? (Paul)
5. *be*-inversion
   Is it Misty? (Homer)
   Are you play? (Homer)
   Is this yours house? (Paul)
   Variation data
   Like you ice cream? (Rune)
   Drive you car yesterday? (Adams)
   What draw a boy? (Adams)
6. "Embedded" (?) questions
   I no know what is it. (Chamot)
   I don't know where is mines. (Adams)

Since we do find a great deal of variation in the data from some children, you may feel, and many do, that we should not look for explanatory universals for the data until we really know what the descriptive facts are. If we are not precisely sure what the universal-invariant order of structure acquisition in a second language might be, and if we are certain to find exceptions to the "invariant" order, then how can we start looking for explanations for such a sequence. Obviously that has never stopped anyone interested in language acquisition before. We expect linguists to start analyzing their field data and search for alternative explanations for the data from the first day of data gathering. We could spend a lifetime arguing about how best to write the description of the sequence of rules acquired by second language learners. That is important work, of course, but more interesting to almost everyone, we think, is why the data looks the way it does, what it tells us about the acquisition *process.*

Many suggestions have been made to explain our "universal" order of acquisition and some have been made that might explain the variations from the sequence as well. Perhaps immodestly, some of these suggestions have been called universals too. The purpose of this article is to review the explanations that have been given.

Table 1 illustrates at least one thing which is quite different from the data for first language learners. Rune, a Norwegian child, tried to invert the whole verb to form a question. How do we explain this variation? The immediate answer is contrastive analysis. In Norwegian one can invert subject and verb to form a question.

Contrastive Analysis

Contrastive Analysis (CA) is perhaps the best known of all hypotheses; it's been with us the longest. Certainly it can account for much of the variation we find in order of acquisition and for the forms used in variation data. If L_1 and L_2 have similar processes or different processes, similar or dissimilar division of structural function, one should be able to predict or at least explain some variation in data as interference or transfer. Examples of this abound in the literature.

If contrastive analysis were the complete answer to variation in our data, we should then like to be able to apply it universally. And, in fact, we can't. Table 2 shows that Paul, a Chinese child, did not use the copula. If we try to use contrastive analysis to explain this, we find that Paul does not follow the predictions we would have to make. Ravem, in his report on Rune, also shows that Rune did not (except for the few examples given in table 1) consistently follow first language patterns to form questions.

While we may wish to discard a strong version of the CA hypothesis it can explain a great deal of the variation. No one, for example, would guess that the following utterance was from anyone but a Spanish speaker:

I no speak very well English. Maybe in one year and two year more I a little more better. All my English is only də listen də people. I

TABLE 2. Contrastive Analysis Prediction Examples

	Taiwanese		Predictions	Actual Utterances
NP1 = demonstrative pronoun				
	cheh shi dzu cheh dzu	This is book This book	This kite.	This kite.
	heh shi dzu he dzu	That is book That book	That car.	That car.
	cheh m shi dzu *cheh m dzu.	This not is book.	This not is freeway.	This not freeway.
	heh m shi dzu. *heh m dzu	That not is book.	That not is Brent.	That not Brent.
NP2 = personal pronoun				
	ni shi sien-sen *ni sien-sen	You are teacher	You are Edmond.	You Edmond.
NP1 = proper noun				
	Bun-dao shi ngin-nan. *Bun-dao ngin-nan	Bundao is boy.	Bozo is clown.	Bozo clown.
	Bundao m shi ngin-nam. *Bun-dao m ngin-nan.	Bundao not is boy.	Brent not is baby.	Brent not baby.

listen you voice and when I listen the . . . cosa? . . . in the tape is different completely. Də last week I see the book de Adams. "I no believing in the men" is the name de my book. I liking much. A story de girl. Same all the story, is the man is love for the girl and the girl is love for the man. Tell me que is very nice. Is no one story in one book, is continue. Is good. When you want (ε) stay relax in you bed. The husband de Vicky is crazy, es too liking many girls. Is before, now is again. [Zoila]

Further, one should realize that the CA model is not just a screen which lets the learner squeeze through wherever the languages are similar and blocks him where they are different. The Stockwell, Bowen, and Martin (1965) hierarchy of difficulty is a much more sophisticated use of CA to identify ease and difficulty of learning. It looks at structural similarity not just as present or absent but in a number of other ways (see fig. 1). In its simplest form it looks for correspondence (where form and function are the same); for splitting up of one category from the first language into several in the second language; for collapses where several categories in the first language now become one in the second; for new and absent categories in the new language; and for interacting splits and collapses between forms or functions in the two languages. The notion that the number of forms for a particular structure contributes to ease or difficulty

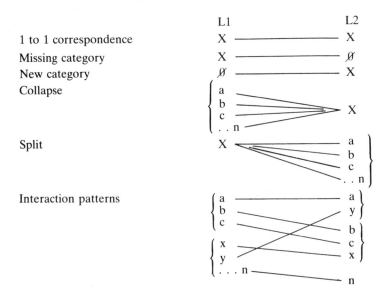

Fig. 1. Correspondences in contrastive analysis

of learning may seem obvious to us now, but this is the first discussion of it in CA literature.

The hierarchy of difficulty, however, is still more complex than the notation mentioned above. Categories are also marked for optional or obligatory rules. Semantic function is treated in much more depth in later literature, but it is important to remember that Stockwell, Bowen, and Martin (1965) included it as part of the CA hypothesis. Their hierarchy of difficulty included information on correlation of semantic function as well as structure equivalence. This gives a very complex prediction of ease and difficulty in learning a second language (see table 3).

TABLE 3. Hierarchy of Difficulty

Level of Difficulty	L_1 English Type of Choice	Structural Correspondence	Func./Seman. Correspondence	L_2 Spanish Type of Choice
1	Ø	≠		Ob
2	Ø	≠		Op
3	Op	≠	≡	Op
4	Ob	≠	≡	Ob
5	Op	≠	≡	Ob
6	Ob	≠	≡	Op
7	Ob	≠		Ø
8	Op	≠		Ø
9	Op	=	≢	Op
10	Ob	=	≢	Ob
11	Op	=	≢	Ob
12	Ob	=	≢	Op
13	Op	=	≡	Ob
14	Ob	=	≡	Op
15	Op	=	≡	Op
16	Ob	=	≡	Ob

Source: From Stockwell, Bowen, and Martin 1965, pp. 283–84.

Ø no choice
= structural correspondence
≠ lacks structural correspondence
≡ functional/semantic correspondence
≢ lacks functional/semantic correspondence
Ob obligatory choice
Op optional choice

Language Universals

Many researchers became discouraged when they found that CA did not
work in all the ways they wished it to. Many of these people turned to a
second approach. If differences between first and second language cannot explain all the data, perhaps similarities between many languages
would. That is, if we know something about language universals, perhaps we can explain why some facets of English are easy or difficult to
learn. Language universals are being identified by Greenberg (1966),
Keenan (1974), and others. Some of their statements about the substructures which all languages share are simple universals, such as "all languages have conditional clauses," "all languages differentiate nouns
from verbs," "all languages have a nominalizing process which changes
sentences, VPs or verbs into nouns," or "not all languages have reflexive pronouns," "not all languages have passives," "not all languages
have prepositions." The universals may be conditional, such as "if a
verb agrees with objects it also agrees with subjects." Or they may be
biconditional, such as "the more explicit verb agreement is with NPs,
the greater the amount of NP and Pro deletion." (Note that a greater
amount of subject and pronoun deletion is allowed in Spanish with its
explicit verb agreement than is allowed in English with its nonexplicit
verb agreement.) Using a word order typology, Keenan has also given
us information on what one might expect of languages which are SVO,
SOV, or verb initial—for example, that most SVO languages are prepositional while SOV languages are postpositional. While Keenan would
not use this information as a predictor of ease or difficulty in language
learning nor even suggest that it might explain some of the data, this has
not stopped some of us from trying to see whether such information
might be helpful in examining second language learning data. (Certainly
it is useful for the teacher who deals with students from many different
language groups. Knowing something about the universality of various
substructures and general characteristics of languages of various word
order typology groups can be helpful.)

Ross (1974) has recently proposed a centralness-peripheral dichot-
omy based on language universals some of which he has enumerated (see
fig. 2). Ross notes that no laws apply *only* to the periphery, but some
apply *only* to the center (e.g., "no processes apply only in embedded
clauses, but some apply only in independent clauses" or "no processes
require the predicates that undergo them to be stative, but some require
actives"). Ross states that the implications of a systematic center-periphery distinction for psychology and education are obvious. It is suggested

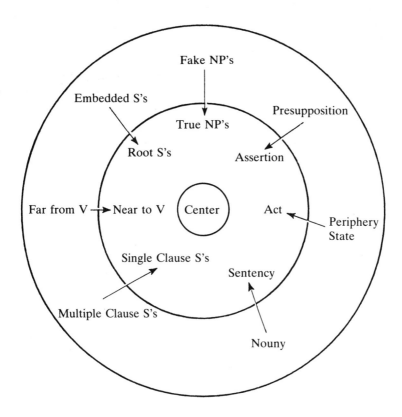

Fig. 2. Ross's center-periphery diagram. (Adapted from Ross 1974.)

that one could apply Ross's center hypothesis (The Law of the Center: the center first) to second language data. The hypotheses include:

> 1. In linguistics, there is a center/periphery distinction. 2. In child language acquisition, kids learn the center first. 3. In L_2 acquisition, people learn center of L_2 first. 4. In aphasia, the periphery is lost first. 5. In language death, the periphery is lost first. 6. In pidgins and creoles, the center remains. 7. Variation is greater at the periphery than at the center. [Hakuta 1975]

Knowledge of work in language universals and of the center hypothesis based on language universal processes is important, but direct application of either of these two approaches can lead us into error. We do not want to say that articles are learned late because they are not language universal. If we did, we would also have to say that adjectives are learned late since they are not universal (when in fact they are learned early). We would have to say that pronouns are acquired early when they aren't. All languages have nominalizing processes but certainly that does not mean that learners will quickly recognize and begin to use such processes immediately in the second language. Instead, we might want to consider this information valuable in the light of whether or not the learner has already acquired the cognitive function of these forms in the first language. If he has and if he still follows the same order of acquisition of the forms as a child learning English as a first language, we may need to rethink many of the explanations given for order of acquisition of structures by first language learners.

It is difficult to know just how applicable the center hypothesis may be to second language learning. Cohen (1975) has some data that show that language forgetting (Ross calls it language death) does not strictly follow the center hypothesis; the last thing learned (the periphery?) is not always the first thing forgotten. The problem at the moment is not knowing precisely what the center consists of aside from true NPs, acts, single clause sentences, etc., those parts of the language on which the most processes can work. If it includes the most concrete of nouns, the most wide-ranging action/want verbs (*do, want, got, go, eat,* etc.), pronoun forms *me, you,* modifiers like *more, big, nice, pretty, bad,* demonstratives *this, that,* a negative marker, rising-falling intonation and SVO stringing, you could match beginning utterances of most first and second language learners of English, the language of many retarded children, the language of certain aphasic patients, and many English-based pidgins. The center, however, appears to contain much more. Perhaps a diagram that is circles within circles will evolve.

Relexification

As Schumann has pointed out, pidgins do share a number of data characteristics with those of individual case studies of second language acquisition. Suggestions have been made that there may be some sort of pan-pidgin which with relexification could match (if not account for) universals in beginning stages of second language acquisition. In fact, one could claim that it is this simplified structure that must be universal to all language acquisition.

The relexification notion has been viewed in another way as well, the notion that we simply keep the "core" of the first language and relexify it. That is, we change the vocabulary to that of the new language. There are many amusing examples of relexification in the literature (and even in comic strips). Clyne (1975) has many interesting examples of Australian and German factory language, some of which could be interpreted in this way. Perhaps a clearer example of this process is the systematic change made in Ameslan (American Sign Language, a language with its own syntax quite different from English) by English speakers who use Ameslan signs in English word order and have even added new signed endings for English morphology to Ameslan signs.

The pidginization hypothesis is often called a simplification process. Perhaps we might want to consider whether the learner is starting with what he hears and applying some sort of simplification rules to that input in order to create his own output or whether he's starting with some sort of central core (the center). This leads us to a fourth hypothesis, one concerned with the input data a second language learner has to deal with.

Input

Hatch (1974) has shown there is a correlation between the frequency of various *wh*-question forms in input data directed at children and the order in which they acquire question forms. Obviously there is an overlap between frequency, structural complexity, and cognitive difficulty, but certainly frequency cannot be ruled out. Table 4 shows this interaction clearly. Adults speaking to this child must subconsciously have been aware of structural and cognitive difficulty of questions asked since they so carefully programmed the sequence of questions directed toward the child. Why should a child who has equivalent questions in his first language and the cognitive prerequisites to, for example, answer a *why* question, acquire *wh*-questions in the same general order as a first-language learner? Part of the explanation must be input. Paul simply was not asked *why* questions.

Gough (1975) has pointed out that the language input to children learning second languages and adults learning second languages is quite different. The input to adults is not as carefully programmed. Adults are expected to understand *why* questions almost immediately. Not only is the structural sequence quite different in the speech of persons talking to adult learners but the variety of topics is almost unlimited. They are not asked, as the child is, to identify objects around them. Instead, they are asked about a wide variety of abstract and sophisticated topics. Some variation in data over the age range of learners can be explained in these terms.

But even when input is quite controlled, different learners attend to it differently. This brings us to many factors which we often lump together as idiosyncratic.

TABLE 4. Input Frequency and Question Production

Input in Order of Frequency	Paul's Question Production

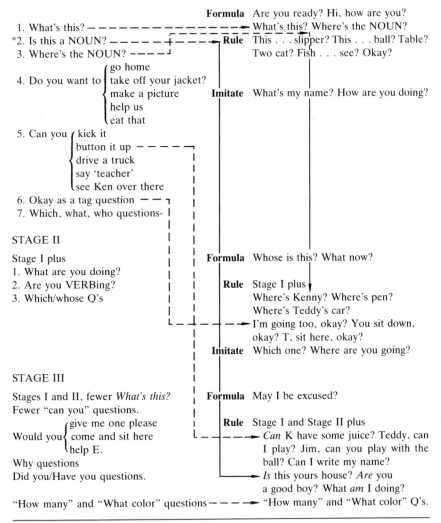

STAGE I

Formula Are you ready? Hi, how are you?

1. What's this? — — — — — — — — — — — — → What's this? Where's the NOUN?

*2. Is this a NOUN? — — — — — — + — — — → **Rule** This . . . slipper? This . . . ball? Table?

3. Where's the NOUN? — — — — ⅃ Two cat? Fish . . . see? Okay?

4. Do you want to ⎰ go home
⎪ take off your jacket?
⎨ make a picture   **Imitate** What's my name? How are you doing?
⎪ help us
⎱ eat that

5. Can you ⎧ kick it
⎪ button it up — — — — ⌐
⎨ drive a truck
⎪ say 'teacher'
⎩ see Ken over there

6. Okay as a tag question — — ⌐

7. Which, what, who questions- │

STAGE II

Stage I plus

1. What are you doing?   **Formula** Whose is this? What now?

2. Are you VERBing?   **Rule** Stage I plus

3. Which/whose Q's Where's Kenny? Where's pen?
Where's Teddy's car?

L — ⅃ — + — — → I'm going too, okay? You sit down,
okay? T, sit here, okay?

Imitate Which one? Where are you going?

STAGE III

Stages I and II, fewer *What's this?*   **Formula** May I be excused?

Fewer "can you" questions.

Would you ⎰ give me one please   **Rule** Stage I and Stage II plus
⎨ come and sit here L — ⅃ — — — → *Can* K have some juice? Teddy, can
⎱ help E. I play? Jim, can you play with the

Why questions ball? Can I write my name?

Did you/Have you questions. └——→ *Is* this yours house? *Are* you
a good boy? What *am* I doing?

"How many" and "What color" questions — — — → "How many" and "What color" Q's.

Idiosyncratic Explanations

Another way of explaining our data is to say they are just idiosyncratic. For example, some learners avoid listening to the second language whenever possible. The more studies of young children one reads, the less convincing the statement that children learn second language easily and quickly. Many run out of the room, pretend to go deaf, hide under the table, or cry; they are as skilled as adults in avoiding second language encounters. Some children attend carefully but do not produce language unless they must; they prefer an extended listening period before language production. This does not always mean instant bloomers in all cases, not everyone who shows an extended listening period is really listening. Other children begin babbling English immediately on being exposed to a speaker of the new language. Olmstead-Gary (1974) has also shown that children respond quite differently to extended listening versus immediate practice as teaching strategies. This area of seeming idiosyncratic response has not been considered in depth in trying to account for variation in data.

Work done on learning styles by education researchers and on hemispheric preference has also been ignored as a possible source of explanation of variation in our data. Bogen (1969) has outlined the general characteristics of left and right hemisphere function. Krashen, Seliger, and Hartnett (1974) have shown that students with right or left hemisphere preference do enroll in classes which match their learning style (inductive versus deductive methodologies) when given a choice. Hartnett (1975) has shown that they not only enroll in the appropriate class but make greater gains in proficiency (measured by cloze and dictation) if they are in a course which matches their hemispheric preference.

Our data from children shows a great deal of variation in obviousness of whether or not the child is using analytical processes in learning the language. The distinction between "data gatherers" and "rule formers" is a very general one (any and all such two-way dichotomies are always wrong) but helpful in describing what seem to be learner characteristics. Some of the analytically oriented children even give overt information on the rules that they have formed. In contrast to the famous Brown and Bellugi anecdote where in response to the question "Adam, which is right, 'two shoe' or 'two shoes'?", Adam replied "Pop goes the weasel!", we can find children who not only would say which is right but also give you the rules. Ronjat's child Louie, for example, explained how to make various sounds: "Pour *a*, on ouvre tout; pour *m*, tout est fermé, et pour *p*, d'abord fermé, puis ouvert."

The areas of attitude, motivation, and personality (openness, inhibition, etc.) research may yet give us ways of identifying differences not only in speed and global proficiency terms but also for variations in acquisition that now seem idiosyncratic. No direct application of the information that we have in these areas has been made to explain case data.

The idiosyncratic claim should not include these areas since they apply to groups of learners; the idiosyncratic claim should be resorted to only as a last-ditch explanation. We need to look at research in all of the above areas to help us explain variation. It may be that some of the strategies that individual children use can be explained by such studies.

Strategies or Operating Principles

Slobin (1971), Brown (1973), and others have identified a number of "universal" strategies that children use in learning a first language. Many of these are helpful in explaining second language data as well. Those which seem most useful are (1) perceptual saliency—that which is easily perceived is easier to learn. For example, articles, which in English do not receive stress, are not as easily perceived as nouns, verbs, etc., which do receive sentence stress. (2) Number of forms—the learner will begin with one form, then add others first in correct ways, then use the forms in variation, then gradually sort out the correct use of each of the forms. For example, children may acquire the /s/ plural first, then add the /z/ plural, add a few /iz/ plurals correctly, then mix them all up, then gradually sort out the forms according to the environment in which it appears. (3) Number of functions—if a form has only one function, it should be easy to learn; if it has many, and if the forms overlap in some of the functions, it will be more difficult. For example, Homer began using the -ing form very early, a common phenomenon for both first and second language learners. We can say this is due to its perceptual saliency, its high frequency in the input data, and its phonological stability (one form). However, the function of the progressive is more complex. Depending on included adverbial markers of a mutually understood context, it shows (a) activity of temporary duration; (b) activity which is just about to happen; (c) various future events. Homer was unable to discover the boundaries between the -ing form and other tense and aspect markers (if he was searching for them at all). (4) Communication importance—if a form is not crucial for communication, it will not appear in initial acquisition data. The late development of the morphological system of English by most learners (learning what Leopold has called "the icing on the cake") is a case in point. Articles, the copula, and most of the auxiliary system are not necessary for communication and they usually are developed rather slowly. (5) Word order—learners do pay attention to word order. Most of our data shows that this applies to second language learning as well as first. There are some interesting exceptions, however, which are not explainable in terms of contrastive analysis, such as:

Two hours in car me.
Maybe finish 11:30 Spanish.
He in face one cloth. (The wrestler was wearing a mask.)
Me in play one hour possible.
He for long hair ties it. (He wears his hair in a ponytail.)

Nevertheless, second language learners do pay attention to word order. One does not, for example, find Japanese speakers trying to put relative clauses in front of nouns in English as they do in Japanese. Exceptions to English word order do occur in our data but they also occur in the data of first language learners (cf. Stern and Stern 1907).

While it is true that not all children use these strategies all of the time, Slobin's (1971) principles are very helpful in explaining why the sequence in second language acquisition is so similar to that of first language learners. The problem is that if our analysis of data does not allow us to look beyond the appearance or nonappearance of a form, we may not really notice whether or not the child uses a form for functions which are not "obligatory contexts," we may miss seeing the strategies that the learner is using to acquire form and function.

If we do look at all the data, some very interesting facts emerge. Being given a framework, a way of analyzing data, has encouraged many of us to throw out data that doesn't fit the framework. Trying to figure out data that doesn't fit our ways of analyzing data is the most interesting (and the most frustrating) task of all. Sometimes it is impossible for us to understand what the child is doing but sometimes interesting guesses can be made.

Brown (1973), in his discussion of the acquisition of *wh*-questions by first language learners, argued that one need not use transformational rules to account for early stages of question formation, though of course that might be the easiest way to make the data conform to descriptive rules proposed at that time by transformational grammarians. Clark (1974), Gough (1975), and Hakuta (1975) have recently shown that we are so prone to thinking about linguistic description that we are blind to the psycholinguistic processes; we pay little attention to what the learner really does. For example, how should we describe the "embedded questions" in table 1? Are they really examples of embedded questions or are they really just examples of learners juxtaposing an "I don't know" and a question? Hakuta has discussed similar examples in depth. Clark and Gough have looked at another phenomenon, incorporation, to explain data that, at first glance, seems very strange. Homer had many examples of sentences which began with *what: What this is airplane. What is this is car. What is this is.* It soon became apparent that he formed his *wh-*pattern by using both the question he had just heard along with his response. For example, *What is this?* and *This is truck* became *What is this this is truck.* Then he added a deletion rule to get "What is this truck" and "What this is truck." Once the process was discovered, one could account for other data such as "Where is Mark is school." "Where are you going is house." "Yeah, can you do that." Such samples do not correspond to our usual notions that learners (as well as linguists) derive *wh-*questions from declarative sentences, not vice versa. Homer was using both questions and statements together in order to work out the form for discourse.

Another process which we frequently ignore in looking at data is how the learner discovers the boundaries of a particular structure via rule testing. We can't discover that unless we look at the acquisition of various substructures in detail. The relationship of form and function in the emerging grammars of children is important in second language learning as well as in first language learning.

Perhaps a combination of processes such as those mentioned above with the strategies Slobin has delineated will be the most productive in explaining the sequence and variations in our data. With adult learners of second languages, it might even be possible to find out whether or not rule testing is a conscious process or not.

Introspection

A final explanation of much language variation can come from the learner himself. Variations in control have been reported both by John-ston and Boyd (personal communication). Johnston notes that after stu-dying French for a year, she went to France and there tried to keep close watch on the effect of such language immersion. She soon found this an impossible task, but she was aware of a progression in her interlanguage: (1) she made errors and was entirely unaware that she made them; (2) she made the same errors and realized "on hearing herself" that she made them; (3) she "heard" an error about to surface, but could not stop herself from making it; (4) she "heard" an error about to surface, and stopped herself in time; (5) she no longer was aware of any problem with the structure. This kind of information has something to say about the kind of variation we find in data—sometimes the speaker "knows better" but cannot prevent the error; other times he can. Perhaps some of the data offered as proof that there is no such thing as interlanguage is really evidence for Johnston's hypothesis on steps one goes through in control of forms instead.

As you can see in figure 3, this leaves us with lots of different explanations, lots of "universals" of second language acquisition to choose from in explaining the sequence of acquisition of various substructures of English and the variations in data. Perhaps there is some way of deciding that some universals are more universal than others. Can they be

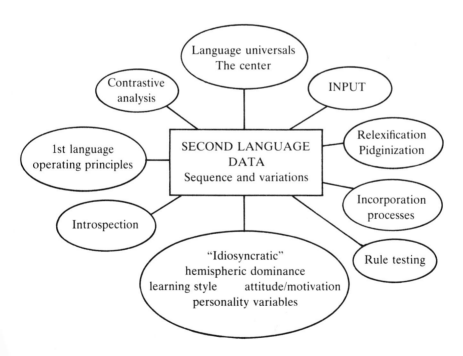

Fig. 3. Possible factors underlying second language sequences and variations

arranged into some sort of order of importance as Stockwell, Bowen, and Martin (1965) tried to do with their hierarchy of difficulty? Can a flow chart be designed? We are sure that each of us could on the basis of our own favorite explanations. Everyone of us has our biases and could assign priority to our favorites. For example, we happen to think that low semantic value, number of forms, number of functions, and perceptual salience account for late acquisition of the English definite article much more clearly than language universals or contrastive analysis. Most people who have taught students from Japan, Korea, and China would disagree. Lumping everything into either a developmental or interference problem doesn't appeal to us very much either, but it shows that in each case the investigator has chosen one solution over others (at least temporarily). So it is obvious that researchers do have some way of choosing among all the proposals. Since they do, it ought to be possible to find some preference order for explanations for sets of data.

Perhaps an interesting experiment might be set up where we ask everyone who is working on second language learning (and that is an amazingly long list of people) to look at sets of data and give explanations for each. Finally, they could rank or weight their explanations as they like. That makes the search for universals a popularity contest but I think we could learn much from it. We might even come up with some more illuminating universals to consider.

We should not take the search for descriptions or explanations lightly. Nor should we be dismayed at the number of factors that seem to be operating. We all would like universals that really work. At the Denver TESOL conference, we said again and again, "No, that's wrong and here is the data to prove it." We wanted universals to be truly universal and we wanted operating principles to operate all the time for all data. And they never will. How universal must a universal be? Perhaps the terminology is wrong and we should more modestly speak of major patterns and possible explanations but to do so may lead people to believe that we have no way of answering such questions as "What is the usual sequence of acquisition of various second language structures?" and "What kinds of variation from that sequence are common, and how can we explain the sequence and the variations from it?"

We have a good start on all of these questions. We have a wealth of data to look at. Each of the hypotheses that have been presented deserves to be tested against the data that we have. And combinations of weighted hypotheses should also be tested. New methods of eliciting data for this can also be worked out. We are working in language acquisition at a very exciting time. In 1969, there was no one around to even talk to about it. Now there are new studies appearing every day. With all the interest and all the ideas that have been presented to us, we can make a real contribution to one of the most important questions ever asked: how is it that people learn languages?

Note

The authors wish to acknowledge the contributions of innumerable graduate students whose ideas and data are presented here. We especially thank Kenji Hakuta and Ed Keenan and accept responsibility for any inaccuracies in reporting on their research.

References

Adams, M. S. "The Acquisition of Academic Skills and a Second Language Through a Program of Total Immersion." Master's thesis. Los Angeles: University of California, 1974.

Bogen, J. "The Other Side of the Brain II: An Appositional Mind." *Bulletin of the Los Angeles Neurological Society* 34 (1969):135–62.

Boyd, P. "Second Language Learning: The Development of Anglo Children Learning Through Spanish." Master's thesis. Los Angeles: University of California, 1974.

Brown, R. *A First Language.* Cambridge, Mass.: Harvard University Press, 1973.

Butterworth, G. "A Spanish Speaking Adolescent's Acquisition of English Syntax." Master's thesis. Los Angeles: University of California, 1972.

Chamot, A. U. "Grammatical Problems in Learning English as a Third Language." Ph.D. dissertation. Austin: University of Texas.

Clark, R. "Performing Without Competence." *Journal of Child Language* 1 (1974):1–10.

Clyne, M. G. "German and English Working Pidgins." Paper presented at the International Congress on Pidgins and Creoles, Honolulu, Hawaii, January, 1975.

Cohen, A. D. "Forgetting a Second Language." Paper presented at the Second Language Acquisition Workshop, TESOL Conference, Los Angeles, March, 1975.

Dulay, H., and Burt, M. "A New Perspective on the Creative Construction Process in Child Second Language Acquisition." *Working Papers on Bilingualism* 4 (1974):71–97.

Gough, J. D. "Comparative Studies in Second Language Learning." Master's thesis. Los Angeles: University of California, 1975.

Greenberg, J. H. "Some Universals of Grammar. In *Universals of Language*, edited by J. H. Greenberg. Cambridge, Mass.: MIT Press, 1966.

Hakuta, K. "Prefabricated Patterns and the Emergence of Structure in Second Language Learning." *Language Learning* 24 (1974):287–97.

———. "The Role of Imitation in Second Language Acquisition." *Report in the Inter-University Seminar on Second Language Acquisition* pp. 24–31. Cambridge, Mass.: Harvard University Press, 1975.

Hartnett, D. D. "The Relation of Cognitive Style and Hemisphere Preference to Deductive and Inductive Second Language Learning." Master's thesis. Los Angeles: University of California, 1975.

Hatch, E. "Second Language Universals?" Paper presented at TESOL Conference, Denver, March, 1974.

Hatch, E. and Wagner-Gough, J. "Second Language Acquisition." In *An Introduction to the Teaching of English as a Second Language,* edited by M. Celce-Murcia and L. McIntosh. Prepublication manuscript. Los Angeles: University of California, 1974.

Huang, J. "A Chinese Child's Acquisition of English Syntax." Master's thesis. Los Angeles: University of California, 1970.

Johnston, M. W. "Observations on Learning French by Immersion." Unpublished. University of California, Los Angeles, 1972.

Keenan, E. L. "Design for a Language." Unpublished. University of California, Los Angeles, Department of Linguistics, 1974.

Krashen, S.; Seliger, H.; and Hartnett, D. "Two Studies in Adult Second Language Learning." *Kritikon Litterarum* 3 (1974):218–28.

Leopold, W. F. *Speech Development of a Bilingual Child: A Linguist's Record, I–IV*. Evanston, Ill.: Northwestern University Press, 1949.

Olmstead-Gary, J. G. "The Effects on Children of Delayed Oral Practice in Initial Stages of Second Language Learning." Ph.D. dissertation. Los Angeles: University of California, 1974.

Ravem, R. "Language Acquisition in a Second Language Environment." *International Review of Applied Linguistics* 7 (1968):175–85.

Ronjat, J. *Le Développement du Langage Observé chez un Enfant Bilingue*. Paris: Champion, 1913.

Ross, J. "The Center." Paper presented at New Ways of Analyzing Variation in English Conference, Georgetown University, October 8, 1974.

Shapira, R. "An Adult Spanish Speaker Learns English." Master's thesis. Los Angeles: University of California, 1976.

Slobin, D. I. "Developmental Psycholinguistics." In *A Survey of Linguistic Science,* edited by W. O. Dingwall. College Park: University of Maryland Press, 1971.

Stern, C., and Stern, W. *Die Kindersprache*. Leipzig: Barth, 1907.

Stockwell, R. P.; Bowen, J. D.; and Martin, J. W. *The Grammatical Structures of English and Spanish.* Chicago: University of Chicago Press, 1965.

Young, D. I. "The Acquisition of English Syntax by Three Spanish-speaking Children." Master's thesis. Los Angeles: University of California, 1974.

An Error in Error Analysis

Jacquelyn Schachter

In the course of the intense debate on the value of the contrastive analysis (CA) hypothesis in the last ten years, two clearly differentiated versions have emerged: CA a priori, which is also called the predictive or strong version, and CA a posteriori, which is sometimes called the explanatory or weak version. The terminological distinction "a priori versus a posteriori" proposed by H. Gradman (1971a) appears to be more purely descriptive and less evaluative than the distinctions "strong versus weak" or "predictive versus explanatory." CA a priori is said to be a point by point analysis of the phonological, morphological, syntactic, or other subsystem of two languages. Given two theoretically compatible linguistic descriptions of one of these subsystems of language A and language B, investigators can analyze them and discover the similarities and differences between them. They do this so that they can make predictions about what will be the points of difficulty for a speaker of language A, for example, who is attempting to learn language B, on the assumption that similarities will be easier to learn and differences harder. CA a priori advocates generally concede that the prediction of areas of difficulty will not account for all of the learning problems that occur in the classroom. There will also be problems caused by such variables as previous teaching and motivation.

The proponents of CA a posteriori take a different methodological approach. Assuming that speakers of language A are found by the process of error analysis to make recurring errors in a particular construction in their attempts to learn language B, the investigator makes an analysis of the construction in language B, and the comparable construction in language A, in order to discover why the errors occur. CA a posteriori is said to be a subcomponent of the more encompassing field of error analysis. Those who propose an error analysis approach to the study of second language acquisition point out that both linguists and teachers have paid too much attention to predicting what the learner will do, and have not paid enough attention to the study of what the learner actually does. They stress the claim that many language learning errors do not result

Reprinted by permission of the publisher and the author from *Language Learning* 24, no. 2 (1974):205–14.

from native language interference but rather from the strategies employed by the learner in the acquisition of the target language and also from the mutual interference of items within the target language. There is sufficient evidence at this point to indicate that these claims are correct, and that error analysis is a useful tool in the study of second language acquisition.

However, there are a number of people who are currently taking a more extreme view. (Lee 1957; Whitman and Jackson 1972; Gradman 1971*a,* 1971*b;* Ritchie 1967.) They argue that the only version of CA that has any validity, either for the classroom or for the investigation of second language acquisition, is CA a posteriori. In the numerous articles which present arguments against the a priori version, there are two objections that occur repeatedly. The first is that CA a priori sometimes predicts difficulties that do not occur, especially in the syntactic subcomponent of a language, resulting in a waste of time in the classroom. And it is argued that if wrong predictions are made using the a priori hypothesis, then the hypothesis itself must be wrong. The second recurring claim is that CA a posteriori provides a shortcut to the long and arduous job of doing CA at all. It allows the investigator to focus one's energy and attention on just those areas that are proven, by error analysis, to be the difficult ones.

It is necessary at this point to make the assumptions underlying the a posteriori approach explicit, especially since its advocates have so far failed to do so. The main assumption is that error analysis will reveal to the investigator just what difficulties the learners in fact have, that difficulties in the target language will show up as errors in production. The second assumption is that the frequency of occurrence of specific errors will give evidence of their relative difficulty.

While the a posteriori approach appears, on the surface, to have certain merits, it is my contention that the weaknesses of this approach are more serious than the weaknesses of the a priori approach. In both the a priori and a posteriori approach, there are weaknesses in the CA of phonological systems (the area in which most CA work has been done), for reasons which I will attempt to explain later. But the a posteriori weaknesses, which are due to the previously mentioned assumptions, become glaringly obvious in the area of syntax.

In order to support this claim I would like to present certain facts that I have discovered about the difficulties that different groups of foreign students have with the acquisition of English relative clauses. As background for this research I compared the major restrictive relative clause formation (RCF) strategies of four unrelated languages, Persian,

Arabic, Chinese, Japanese, with the major restrictive RCF strategies of English. From this comparison I was able to make predictions of probable areas of difficulty for the speakers of each group in producing relative clauses in English. I made no attempt to set up a hierarchy of difficulty since I feel that at this point hierarchies of difficulty are premature. I then analyzed "free" (no controls for structure) compositions of some Persian, Arab, Chinese, and Japanese students studying English at the American Language Institute, in the University of Southern California. There were fifty compositions from each language group, twenty-five compositions from intermediate level classes, and twenty-five from the advanced level. I extracted all of the relative clauses from these compositions, and analyzed them with respect to certain criteria which I will mention shortly. I reasoned that if the a posteriori advocates were correct, the information that I had gained from the a priori comparison would provide less in the way of explanation of errors than the information some other investigator would have gained from error analysis and CA a posteriori alone. Furthermore, again if the a posteriori advocates were correct, I would have predicted some difficulties which did not in fact occur.

The information on RCF strategies in the particular language was derived for the most part from the work of Keenan and Comrie (1972) who have investigated RCF in some forty languages. Their material is rich and complex and cannot be completely summarized here. What I shall do is mention three main dimensions with regard to which, as they point out, languages can differ in their RCF strategies, describing for each dimension only the five languages of concern to this paper. Information on Japanese was provided by Matt Shibatani and Masakazu Watabe; information on Chinese was provided by Charles Li. (Another dimension considered in this study was what noun phrases can be relativized, but I found that I had insufficient evidence to make conclusions with regard to it.)

Dimension 1: Position of relative clause with respect to the head noun. Relative clauses can occur either to the left of the head NP (Chinese and Japanese) or to the right of it (English, Persian, Arabic) or both (no languages in this study). With respect to this dimension, the prediction is that the Japanese and Chinese would have difficulty, but the Persians and Arabs would not.

Dimension 2: How relative clauses are marked. Relative clauses are marked as subordinate in a number of ways. The only ones relevant to this study are: (1) the introduction of an arbitrary subordination marker between the head NP and the relative clause (English *that*, Persian *ke*, Arabic *illi*, Chinese *də*); (2) the insertion of a pronominal particle between the head NP and the relative clause (English *who, whom, which, whose*); (3) no subordination marker or pronoun, but subordinate affixes in the restrictive clause (Japanese). The prediction in this case is that the Japanese learners would have difficulty with both the subordination marker *that,* and with the relative pronouns *who, whom, which, whose,* whereas the others would have difficulty only with the latter.

Dimension 3: The occurrence of a pronominal reflex. English does not have these pronouns, but the other four languages do, although not in all NP positions. Table 1 summarizes the possibilities in the five languages of concern here (where + is obligatory, − is obligatorily absent, (+) is ambiguous between sometimes obligatory and optional).

TABLE 1. Pronominal Reflexes in Five Languages

	Subj.	Dir. Obj.	Ind. Obj.	Obj. Prep.	PossNP	Obj. Comp. Part
Persian	(+)	+	+	+	+	+
Arabic	(+)	(+)	+	+	+	+
Chinese	−	−	+	+	+	+
Japanese	−	−	−	(+)		
English	−	−	−	−	−	−

If English did have these pronouns, the following would be examples:

Subj: the boy that *he* came
Dir. obj: the boy that John hit *him*
Ind. obj: the boy that I sent a letter to *him*
Obj. prep: the boy that I sat near *him*
Poss NP: the boy that *his* father died
Obj. comp. part: the boy that John is taller than *him*

The prediction of difficulty here varies for each language, with Japanese learners predicted to have least and Persian learners most difficulties.

After the a priori predictions were identified, I then undertook an error analysis. I wanted to ascertain how many errors were made by each group relative to the total number of RCs produced, and then, what kinds of errors each group made.

All restrictive relative clauses—both correct and incorrect—were identified for each language group. (I counted as a restrictive relative clause any clause contiguous to a NP which had the semantic effect of modifying the NP. Any clause which might be interpretable as either a restrictive or a nonrestrictive clause was counted as the former). Both the correct and the error groups were further divided on the basis of the NP in the relative clause that was relativized, i.e., Subj., Dir. Obj., Ind. Obj., etc.

The overall totals for each group, including an American control group consisting of a freshman composition class, are listed in table 2.

TABLE 2. Relative Clause Production in Five Language Groups

	Correct	Error	Total	Percentage of Errors
Persian	131	43	174	25
Arab	123	31	154	20
Chinese	67	9	76	12
Japanese	58	5	63	8
American	173	0	173	—

The differences in the total number of relative clauses for each group are surprising. But for the moment let us focus solely on the errors. From an inspection of the number of errors of the four groups one would be led to suspect that the Persian and Arab learners have far more difficulty producing relative clauses than do the Chinese and Japanese learners. It might be argued, however, that since the Persians and Arabs produced more relative clauses they would be expected to produce more errors also. The significant figures would be the percentage of relative clause errors compared to the number of relative clauses produced.

According to these figures and the CA a posteriori hypothesis, the Japanese and Chinese students have considerably less difficulty in the acquisition of relative clauses than do the Persian and Arab students; although they produce fewer relative clauses, the percentage of errors is significantly less ($p < .025$). Notice that if one were to do an error analysis of the Chinese or Japanese students alone, he would discover extremely few relative clause errors in the data and would thus be led to conclude, given the a posteriori assumptions, that RCF is a quite minor problem for speakers of these languages learning English.

However, what I find striking is the difference in the total number of relative clauses produced between the Persian (174) and Arab (154) students on the one hand, and the Chinese (76) and Japanese (63) students on the other. Why should the former group spontaneously produce so many more relative clauses than the latter group?

A partial answer to this question lies, I think, in the difference between the two groups with regard to dimension 1, the position of the relative clause with regard to the head NP. Persian and Arabic students already have postnominal relative clauses in their native languages. Chinese and Japanese students have prenominal relative clauses in their native languages and must learn to switch relative clauses to a postnominal position in the process of learning English. (The switching from pre- to postnominal position is not the only problem for the Japanese and Chinese students; in most cases they must also change the internal order of the main constituents within the relative clause.) This difficulty, which was predicted by the a priori approach, surfaces not in the number of errors they make, but rather in the number of relative clauses they make. It is plausible and I think correct to suppose that they produce fewer relative clauses in English because they are trying to avoid them, and that they only produce them in English when they are relatively sure that they are correct, which would also account for the extremely small number of errors they make. What we encounter is a phenomenon of avoidance due to a difficulty which was predicted by the a priori approach, but which the a posteriori approach can not handle at all.

I claim that Persian and Arab learners, on the other hand, find RCF in English to be so similar to RCF in their native languages that they assume they can directly transfer their native language forms to English. This not only accounts for the larger number of relative clauses that they make in English, but also for the larger number of errors, and for the type of errors most commonly made. The number of relative clauses produced by the Persian and Arab learners in this study is quite close to the number produced by typical American freshman college students (as seen in table 2). Given that the Persian and Arab learners transfer their native language forms to English, one would expect numerous errors in pronominalization (dimension 3) and this is precisely what the data show. This pronominalization occurs in most NP positions in both languages, and it is reflected in English in the following sentences (where the parenthesized number is the actual number of occurrence of errors of the type).

Arab
S: activities which *they* are hard   (2)
O: the time I spent *it* in practice   (6)
OP: education which they don't work for *it*   (4)
Persian
S: the people that *they* are interested in space
       research   (14)
O: oil which we sell *it* to other countries   (12)

> OP: a little pool which the water for *it* comes
>   from the mountains   (9)

The evidence with regard to dimension 2, the marking of relative clauses as subordinate, does not provide arguments for either approach. The a priori prediction is that all groups will have difficulty in producing the English relative pronouns, *who, which, whom, whose,* and there is some evidence that this is the case.

> Persian: persons *which* I have to spend most of my life with them
> Arab: the college *who* asked my some questions
> Chinese: to help the student *whom* is going to join in this contest

(There were no Japanese errors of this type in the study, but this is hardly surprising, since there were only five total errors. I have some examples of errors of this type, but they are not part of the study.)

Let me summarize the evidence that has been presented with regard to the two dimensions in which the two approaches differ. In the a priori approach, the prediction was that the Chinese and Japanese learners would have difficulty with the placement of the RC, and that the Persian and Arab, and to some extent the Chinese learners would have difficulty with pronominalization. The evidence shows that this was the case. In the a posteriori approach, with its dependence on error counts, only the pronominalization problems of the Persian and Arab learners surfaced. Given the number of errors made by the Chinese and Japanese learners, a total of fourteen, the investigator would be led to assume the Chinese and Japanese students did not have any difficulty producing RC structures in English, a conclusion that I think is completely erroneous.

The total weight of the evidence from this study strongly supports the a priori approach. The learner apparently constructs hypotheses about the target language based on knowledge he already has about his own language. If the constructions are similar in the learner's mind, he will transfer his native language strategy to the target language. If they are radically different, he will either reject the new construction or use it only with extreme caution. On the other hand, error analysis without a priori predictions simply fails to account for the avoidance phenomenon. If the student does not produce the constructions he finds difficult, no amount of error analysis is going to explain why. But this statement needs to be tempered somewhat. It is quite possible that the avoidance phenomenon does not occur in the acquisition of the phonological subcomponent of the target language, and that there is a qualitative difference in the acquisition of the phonological as opposed to the syntactic subcomponents. In the syntactic subcomponent, the possibility of paraphrase exists, and the student can take advantage of paraphrase relations to avoid constructions he finds difficult, while still getting his idea across. Examples from the compositions of Japanese and Chinese students bear this out.

Chinese: We put them in boxes we call them rice boxes.

Japanese: Japan Islands are located right on the Pacific volcanic zone; that is why we have such kind of disaster.

As far as you are a human being, that is a normal thing. Every teacher has to get through.

However, there is no such thing as phonological paraphrase, and therefore the avoidance phenomenon is difficult, if not impossible. Imagine a student who has trouble making the *th* sounds in English trying to avoid using words that contain them by substituting other words with the same meaning but without the *th* sounds. What happens in fact is that the student is forced to use the words and therefore to make errors in the production of the sounds.

It is instructive to look at this controversy from another point of view. It has often been claimed that CA a priori has predicted difficulties that do not turn out to be difficulties in the classroom. This could be due to poor analysis or poor predictions about what is difficult and what is not. But it could be due to another factor. CA a priori is neutral between comprehension and production. CA a posteriori is based on production. If a student finds a particular construction in the target language difficult to comprehend it is very likely that he will try to avoid producing it. Since the difficulty lies in the comprehension, an a priori prediction that the construction will be difficult will not be contradicted by the lack of production of that construction in the target language. We may very well be deluding ourselves into thinking that we have done such a good job teaching a particular construction that the students are not having any trouble with it at all, whereas in fact the students have so much trouble with it they refuse to produce it.

I regard the CA a posteriori hypothesis as untenable and think it should be abandoned. In the analysis of the difficulties of English RCF for the speakers of the four languages in this study, the a posteriori approach alone would not have accounted for the phenomena that occurred. However, the technique of error analysis proved extremely useful, and I would not like to see that technique abandoned. It was the error analysis that showed how the learners react to new phenomena. I think it likely that more work in error analysis will provide us with data from which useful insights about the second language acquisition process can be derived. There is no reason to assume, however, as many people do, that one and only one approach will provide us with all the answers to our questions about second language acquisition. It seems much more reasonable to suppose that only by a combination of approaches, say CA a priori predictions, error analysis, and comprehension testing, will we begin to amass some reasonably unassailable information on what the second language learning process is all about.

Note

This is a revised version of a paper presented at the summer meeting of the Linguistic Society of America, Amherst, Massachusetts, July, 1974.

References

Corder, S. P. "The Significance of Learners' Errors." *International Review of Applied Linguistics* 5 (1967):161–70.

Gradman, Harry. "The Limitations of Contrastive Analysis Predictions." *PCCLLU Papers* 3/4, 1971a

———. "What Methodologists Ignore in 'Contrastive Teaching.' " *PCCLLU Papers* 3/4, 1971b.

Keenan, Edward, and Comrie, Bernard. "NP Accessibility and Universal Grammar." *Linguistic Inquiry* 8 (1977):63–99.

Lee, W. R. "The Linguistic Context of Language Teaching." *English Language Teaching* 11 (1957):77–85.

Richards, J. C. "A Non-Contrastive Approach to Error Analysis." *English Language Teaching* 25 (1971):204–19.

Ritchie, William C. "Some Implications of Generative Grammar for the Construction of Courses in English as a Foreign Language." *Language Learning* 17 (1967):111–31.

Selinker, Larry. "A Brief Reappraisal of Contrastive Linguistics." *PCCLLU Papers* 3/4, 1971.

Wardhaugh, Ronald. "The Contrastive Analysis Hypothesis." *TESOL Quarterly* 4 (1970):123–30.

Whitman, R., and Jackson, K. "The Unpredictability of Contrastive Analysis." *Language Learning* 22 (1972):29–41.

Avoidance Behavior in Adult
Second Language Acquisition

Howard H. Kleinmann

In the last thirty years there have been at least two significant approaches in the analysis of learner difficulty in acquiring a second language. The first approach, contrastive analysis (CA), attempted to predict the areas of difficulty and nondifficulty learners would encounter by comparing the linguistic system of the learners' native language (NL) with that of the target language (TL). Proponents of this approach claimed that those features of the TL which were similar to the learners' NL would be relatively easy to acquire, and that those elements of the TL which differed from the learners' NL would be relatively difficult to acquire (Lado 1957).

The second approach, error analysis (EA), has examined empirically the actual errors in the TL produced by second language learners and has sought to explain their cause. Proponents of this approach make no a priori predictions of learner difficulty based on CA. Instead, the errors in the TL are analyzed, and where appropriate, are attributed to differences between the NL and TL, overgeneralization, strategies of learning and communication, and a variety of other sources (Richards 1971; Selinker 1972).

Recent research has revealed that CA is an inadequate predictor of learner difficulty with TL material. Richards (1971) and Selinker (1972) cited numerous examples of errors which were not attributable to interference from the NL, but which were intralingual and developmental in nature. Whitman and Jackson (1972) confirmed the inadequacy of CA as a predictor of performance for Japanese subjects tested on English syntax, and Dulay and Burt (1973, 1974a, 1974b) demonstrated the developmental nature of second language acquisition in children for certain morphemes, as did Bailey, Madden, and Krashen (1974) for adults. These studies strongly question the CA approach on empirical grounds, and together with Wardhaugh's (1970) observation of the uncertain state of linguistic theory and the lack of a comprehensive contrastive theory,

Reprinted by permission of the publisher and the author from *Language Learning* 27, no. 1 (1977): 93–107.

cast considerable doubt on the ability of CA to predict areas of difficulty and nondifficulty.

Although the evidence from recent EA studies points to the fact that CA is a weak predictor of areas of difficulty and nondifficulty for second language learners, a drawback has been pointed out concerning the EA approach, which takes observed errors and seeks to explain their cause. Dušková (1969) pointed out that the "lower frequency of an error need not necessarily mean that the point in question is less difficult" (p. 15). Although Dušková's statement did not explicitly refer to avoidance, the implication was there. Schachter (1974) went one step further by arguing that the EA approach is deficient because it it incapable of explaining the phenomenon of avoidance. In her study native Chinese and Japanese students committed significantly fewer errors on English relative clauses than did native Persian and Arab students, leading one to believe that English relative clauses were less difficult for the Chinese and Japanese students. But she also observed that the number of relative clauses produced was much lower for the Chinese and Japanese students compared with the Persian and Arab students. This difference was attributed to the fact that the placement of relative clauses in Chinese and Japanese differs so much from their placement in English that the students avoided their use and consequently produced fewer errors.

Several other studies have dealt with the notion of avoidance in the context of second language learning. Swain (1975) reported her subjects, children learning French as a second language in an immersion program in Ottawa, omitted relatively many indirect object pronouns when faced with a repetition task. The high percentage of omission, Swain (1975) suggested, perhaps reflected an avoidance strategy.

Perkins and Larsen-Freeman (1975), in an attempt to elicit certain morphemes, asked subjects to summarize a nondialog film. The researchers stated, "We noticed that our subjects were very adept at avoiding using the morphemes we were interested in" (p. 239).

Tarone, Frauenfelder, and Selinker (1975), also working with children learning French as a second language, presented subjects with several pictures comprising a story which they were supposed to communicate in French. The authors found some subjects avoided talking about concepts represented in the pictures for which their vocabulary was lacking and concluded that a semantic avoidance strategy was operating. Ickenroth (1975) and Varadi (in Cohen 1975) reported a similar compensation for a lack of vocabulary knowledge and cited various "escape routes" (Ickenroth 1975, p. 10) which learners resort to, for example, choosing a synonym or superordinate term, paraphrasing, and others.

Another type of avoidance which has been reported on in the literature on second language learning has been labeled "topic avoidance" and refers to learners' totally avoiding talking about topics for which they lack the vocabulary. Varadi (in Cohen 1975) has labeled this phenomenon "message abandonment."

Several of these last studies are summarized in Tarone, Cohen, and Dumas (1976), who attempt to define and operationalize the general notion of communication strategy of which various types of avoidance are a part. The problem inherent in all these studies is that they do not characterize and describe genuine cases of avoidance. Instead, they discuss situations which deal with a learner's ignorance of some linguistic item and his concomitant nonuse thereof, which in turn is interpreted as avoidance. Such a student can be said to be at the presystematic stage of learning (Corder 1973), which Ringbom (1976) has pointed out is short of the stage of being able to choose "between well-defined and understandably organized alternatives" (p. 9). Clearly at this stage an individual cannot be said to be avoiding a given syntactic structure, morpheme, or lexical item, which he does not have in his linguistic repertoire, any more than he can be said to be avoiding doing anything which he is unable to do. To be able to avoid some linguistic feature presupposes being able to choose not to avoid it, i.e., to use it. It is this notion of avoidance, which presupposes choice, that is the focus of the following study.

Method

Subjects

The subjects in this study consisted of 39 foreign students enrolled in the intermediate English as a second language course offered by the English Language Institute of the University of Pittsburgh during the 1976 winter term. The 39 subjects were divided into 2 groups.

Group I consisted of 24 native speakers of Arabic. Seventeen of the subjects in this group were from Saudi Arabia, 5 were from the United Arab Emirates, and 1 each were from Libya and the Sudan. Their ages ranged from 17 to 29 years old, with 19 of the subjects falling in the 19-to-22 age range.

Group II consisted of 15 subjects, 13 native speakers of Spanish and 2 native speakers of Portuguese. Eleven of the Spanish subjects were from Venezuela, 1 was from Panama, and 1 was from Puerto Rico. The two Portuguese subjects were from Brazil. The subjects in this group ranged from 17-to-42 years of age, with 10 of them falling in the 17-to-29 age range.

Groups I and II comprised the experimental groups. A third group of subjects, consisting of 15 native speakers of English enrolled in an introductory linguistics course, was used as a control group for the picture test component of the indirect preference assessment task described below.

Design

The use of 4 English structures was investigated: passive voice (e.g., *The car was hit by the bus*), infinitive complements (e.g., *I told Mary to leave*), direct object pronouns in sentences containing infinitive complements (e.g., *I told her to leave*), and present progressive (e.g., *The man is running*). A CA between English and Arabic, English and Spanish, and English and Portuguese was performed for these structures, based on which predictions were made as to the relative difficulty subjects in Groups I and II would have with them. The predictions, summarized in table 1, were that Spanish and Portuguese subjects, relative to Arabic subjects, would experience difficulty with infinitive complements and direct object pronouns, and that Arabic subjects, relative to Spanish subjects, would experience difficulty with passive and present progressive structures. It was hypothesized that when presented with an indirect preference assessment task, the difficulty these subjects would have with the above structures would manifest itself in avoidance behavior.

TABLE 1. Difficulty Predictions Based on Contrastive Analysis

English Structure	Group I Arabic	Group II Spanish and Portuguese
Passive	Difficulty	No difficulty
Present progressive	Difficulty	No difficulty
Infinitive complement	No difficulty	Difficulty
Direct object pronoun	No difficulty	Difficulty

Materials and Procedures

Comprehension Testing

Groups I and II were administered a multiple-choice comprehension test on passive, infinitive complement, and present progressive structures.

This was done to ensure that the subjects in fact comprehended the structures so that their nonuse could not be attributed to a lack of knowledge, but instead, to avoidance. No test was given on direct object pronouns since it was assumed that intermediate ESL students knew their meaning.

The subjects also rated their confidence in each of their answers on a 5-point scale ranging from "completely unsure" (0) to "completely sure" (4). Thus, 3 different scores were obtained from this test for each subject: (1) a straightforward measure of the number of items correct for each structure without any consideration of confidence ratings, (2) a weighted comprehension score taking into account confidence ratings, and (3) a straightforward confidence score. These 3 scores were correlated with the frequency of production of the structure elicited on the indirect preference assessment task.

Indirect Preference Assessment Task

Groups I and II were presented with 7 pictures, 4 of which were designed to elicit a passive sentence given the following verbal cue: "What happened to the _____?" The blank represents the word *woman, car, ball,* or *man,* depending on the particular picture. The other 3 pictures were designed to elicit a present progressive sentence given the following cue: "Describe the picture in a sentence." All 7 pictures were presented to the control group, Group III (native speakers of English), to confirm their appropriateness for eliciting the structures just mentioned.

In order to elicit infinitive complements and direct object pronouns, the following situation was devised. Each subject was seated in front of the experimenter and next to another person whom the subject knew or had been introduced to. The experimenter was talking casually with the subject and at some point turned to the third person, called his or her name, and then said either "Leave!", "Stop!", or "Go!" The experimenter then asked the subject,

> (tell)
> "What did I just (order) _____?"
> (ask)

(the blank represents the third person's name) to which the subject was expected to respond. Each subject participated in 3 such vignettes, designed to elicit sentences like "You told him to leave," and met with the experimenter in 2 sessions lasting approximately 5 minutes each.

Anxiety

An adapted version of the Achievement Anxiety Test (Alpert and Haber 1960), designed to measure the facilitating and debilitating effects of anxiety on performance, was administered to Groups I and II. The test statements were adapted to take into account the contexts that the second language learner finds himself expected to perform in and the kinds of performance for which he knows he will be evaluated. Example statements are:

> Nervousness while using English helps me do better.
> Nervousness while using English in class prevents me from doing well.

Each statement was followed by five choices, ranging from "always" to "never," and the subjects were instructed to circle the choice which best described the degree to which the statement applied to them. The subjects were administered translated versions of the test, which were designed to offset any confounding influence the English version might have exerted. The results on this test were correlated with the frequency of production of the various structures on the indirect preference assessment task.

Success-Achievement and Failure-Avoidance Orientation

A translated version of the Success-Failure Inventory (McReynolds and Guevara 1967) was administered to the 2 experimental groups. The test, designed to measure the strength on one's motives to attain success and avoid failure, consisted of 22 statements, each of which was to be answered as either "true" or "false." Example statements are:

> I have a strong desire to be a success in the world.
> I like to follow routines and avoid risks.

The results on this test were also correlated with the frequency of use of the various structures elicited.

Results and Dicussion

Significant differences (see table 2) were found between the Arabic and Spanish-Portuguese groups in the frequency with which they used passive, infinitive complement, and direct object pronoun structures when faced with an indirect preference assessment task. (The *t* value for direct object pronoun narrowly missed the .05 significance level.) The significant differences are attributable neither to a lack of comprehension on the part of the avoiding group nor to a difference in the comprehension of the particular avoided structure by the two groups (table 3), which suggests that a genuine avoidance phenomenon, operating in accordance with CA difficulty predictions, is at play. Furthermore, it does not appear that the nonavoiding group possessed any high degree of productive mastery over the target structures. If that had been the case, one could argue that the group's frequent use of a target structure was a result of its members finding it easy to produce, that is in a mechanical sense, compared to the avoiding group, whose members found it more difficult to produce. What the results in fact show is that both groups generally did not differ meaningfully with respect to productive mastery, as evidenced by the similar rate with which they gave correct and incorrect responses (table 4).

TABLE 2. Significance of Difference between Mean Responses on Indirect Preference Assessment Task: Arabic versus Spanish and Portuguese

Structure	Group	N	$\overline{X}$	SD	t	df
Passive	Arabic	24	1.58	1.35	3.98**	37
	Span. and Port.	15	3.20	1.01		
Pres. prog.	Arabic	24	2.54	0.59	1.34	37
	Span. and Port.	15	2.20	1.01		
Inf. comp.	Arabic	24	2.88	0.34	5.24**	37
	Span. and Port.	15	1.53	1.19		
D.O. pron.	Arabic	24	1.88	1.33	1.68*	37
	Span. and Port.	15	1.13	1.36		

*$p < .06$ (one-tail)
**$p < .01$ (one-tail)

TABLE 3. Differences between Comprehension Scores on Three Structures

Structure	Group	N	$\overline{X}$	SD	% Correct	t	df
Passive	Arabic	24	4.50	0.78	90.00	.61(NS)	37
	Span. and Port.	15	4.33	0.90	86.60		
Pres. prog.	Arabic	24	5.83	1.09	83.29	.30(NS)	37
	Span. and Port.	15	5.93	0.88	84.71		
Inf. comp.	Arabic	24	4.12	1.68	68.75	.23(NS)	37
	Span. and Port.	15	4.00	1.60	66.67		

TABLE 4. Response on Target Structures Elicited

Structure	Response	Arabic	Spanish and Portuguese
Passive	Correct	9 = 24%	15 = 31%
	Incorrect	29 = 76	33 = 69
Pres. prog.	Correct	48 = 79	26 = 79
	Incorrect	13 = 21	7 = 21
Inf. comp.	Correct	48 = 70	8 = 35
	Incorrect	21 = 30	15 = 65
D. O. pron.	Correct	45 = 100	14 = 82
	Incorrect	0 = 0	3 = 18

The notion of productive mastery of the target structure on the part of the nonavoiding group becomes especially dubious when the results on passive are examined (table 4). This structure was actually elicited 48 times out of a possible 60 for the Spanish-Portuguese group, or in other words on 80 percent of the trials. But 69 percent of the time that this structure was produced by this group, it was done so incorrectly. Admittedly, the Arabic group produced the passive incorrectly 76 percent of the time, but even so, one would hardly want to say that the Spanish-Portuguese group's performance was indicative of its members having mastered the passive.

The nonsignificant differences between the groups' use of the present progressive (table 2) is not counterevidence to the proposal that CA is an accurate predictor of avoidance. This result may be attributable to a canceling effect of difficulty due to form as opposed to function. In Arabic there is no present progressive structure as such, but rather, an imperfective form which is also used to express continuous action. In Spanish there is a present progressive form similar to that of English (that is, it contains an inflected form of the auxiliary verb *estar* 'be' followed by a present participle form which consists of a verb and -*ndo* suffix), but its function is different. The Spanish form is not obligatory when the action the verb expresses is observable and one wishes to express ongoingness. In other words currency modification in the verb is not obligatory with observable verbs when there is external currency modification (Stockwell, Bowen, and Martin 1965). Since the subjects in the study were responding to picture cues, where the action was observable, it is understandable why many of them responded with a sentence in the simple present tense, and that as a group they did not perform significantly differently from the Arabic group.

Perhaps a more plausible explanation is one which takes into account pedagogical factors. The present progressive is a structure which has a high frequency in English and is therefore emphasized in ESL classes for both comprehension and production, unlike a structure such as the passive, which is frequently taught primarily for comprehension. It is also a structure which is sequenced relatively early in an ESL syllabus, which gives it maximal review opportunity. This is certainly true of the program at the University of Pittsburgh, in which the subjects in this study were enrolled. Consequently, it is not unlikely that the subjects in this study, regardless of native language background, learned the present progressive to such a degree that they felt comfortable using it, which would account for the nonsignificant differences between the groups' use of this structure. This view is consistent with Berko's finding that in first language acquisition the verb form children learn best is the present progressive (Berko 1958).

Other evidence exists which indicates that avoidance is at least a partially viable explanation for the relative nonuse of certain structures. In particular, within the Arabic group, whose members produced significantly fewer passives than the Spanish-Portuguese group, confidence in the comprehension of passive correlated significantly with use of the structure (table 5). It seems reasonable to think that confidence is a variable that would affect an individual's choice to avoid or not to avoid.

TABLE 5. Correlations between Predictor Variables and Frequency of Use of Structures within Arabic Group

Predictor Variables	N	Passive	Inf. Comp.	Pres. Prog.	D.O. Pron.
Comprehension	24	0.00	0.18	0.49**	
Confidence	24	0.47**	0.11	−0.02	
Weighted comprehension	24	0.12	0.12	0.45*	
Facilitating anxiety	21	0.47*	−0.39	−0.01	−0.06
Debilitating anxiety	21	−0.13	−0.19	0.27	−0.16
Success-achievement	21	0.10	0.35	0.28	0.06
Failure-avoidance	21	−0.01	−0.14	−0.28	0.13

*p < .05 (one-tail)
**p < .01 (one-tail)

Confidence does not necessarily reflect the learner's knowledge of some structure. Rather, it reflects the learner's perception of his knowledge, which may or may not be accurate. It is this perception, at least within the Arabic group, which appears to have partially influenced their choice to use or not to use the passive.

On the other hand, confidence was not significantly related to use of the passive for the Spanish-Portuguese group (table 6). A reasonable conclusion, therefore, is that CA accurately predicts avoidance, but that use of the target structure on the part of the predicted avoiding group is a function of other variables, one of which is confidence. The same line of argument is applicable to the finding that within the Arabic group, facilitating anxiety correlated significantly with the use of the passive (table 5), and in general, for all the significant correlations within the Spanish-Portuguese group (table 6).

TABLE 6. Correlations between Predictor Variables and Frequency of Use of Structures within Spanish-Portuguese Group

Predictor Variables	N	Passive	Inf. Comp.	Pres. Prog.	D.O. Pron.
Comprehension	15	0.08	−0.15	0.41	
Confidence	15	0.38	−0.06	−0.08	
Weighted comprehension	15	0.21	−0.15	0.43	
Facilitating anxiety	14	0.07	0.64**	0.17	0.66**
Debilitating anxiety	14	−0.14	−0.33	−0.44	−0.58*
Success-achievement	14	−0.41	0.47*	−0.67**	0.01
Failure-avoidance	14	0.27	−0.48*	0.47*	−0.17

*$p < .05$ (one-tail)
**$p < .01$ (one-tail)

Although linguistic avoidance is generally not a directly observable phenomenon, there was at least one instance of a response which seemed to be an indication of deliberate avoidance. Presented with a picture intended to elicit a passive sentence and given the cue "What happened to the woman?", one of the Arabic students responded by topicalizing the deep object, as one would do in uttering a passive sentence. After pausing reflectively, he then responded with an active sentence. ("The woman

[PAUSE]. The car hit the woman.") Abuhamdia (personal communication, July 30, 1976) has suggested that this example does not constitute a case of overt avoidance, but rather, that it reflects an object topicalization common in Arabic before uttering an active sentence. This alternate interpretation, however, does not explain why such topicalizations did not occur more frequently in the data or why, in the case cited, the subject paused as if to try to think of the construction. On the other hand, the fact that such examples did not occur more frequently is not counterevidence to the avoidance interpretation. A learner resorting to a strategy of avoidance is not likely to want others to know about it, especially if they are in a position of authority, as a teacher is. More plausible is the notion that a learner will try to cover up his avoidance strategy, for example, by paraphrasing. This view is consistent with Ickenroth's (1975) notion of "escape routes," which implicitly characterizes the learner's objective as a compensation for discomfort with a given linguistic feature.

It will be recalled that no difficulty was predicted for Spanish-Portuguese subjects, relative to Arabic subjects, on the present progressive, and that, therefore, they would produce significantly more of them compared to the Arabic group. This hypothesis, however, was not confirmed. In fact, if we look at the mean scores for the two groups on the present progressive, reported in table 2, the Spanish-Portuguese score is lower than that of the Arabic group. This implies that perhaps the present progressive is not as easy as had been thought for the Spanish-Portuguese group. Evelyn Hatch (personal communication) has suggested that perhaps the Spanish and Portuguese subjects avoided using the present progressive. If they did, we could understand the large negative correlation between success-achievement and use of the present progressive (table 6) in the following way: the subjects realize the actual difficulty of the present progressive because of its *superficial* similarity to their native language, but avoid its use because they realize there is more than meets the eye. Thus, the greater the orientation of the subject to achieve success the less likely he is to produce the English present progressive because he senses the probability of his making an error due to the confusing nature of the present progressive, which, as has already been pointed out, is formally similar but functionally dissimilar to the form in his native language. This interpretation is supported by traditional CA proponents who point out that the linguistic features (of two languages) which "are similar in form but different in meaning constitute a special group very high on a scale of difficulty" (Lado 1955, p. 34). It seems reasonable that such features would be prime candidates for avoidance.

The fact that the Arabic group used the present progressive so frequently (over two-thirds of the time), in apparent contradiction to the CA prediction, might be explainable on the basis that this structure, which is nonexistent in Arabic, differs so much from anything existing in Arabic that it was consequently easier to learn. In other words, what may have been at play was a kind of novelty effect, exerted by the present progressive structure, which allowed the Arabic group to learn this structure so thoroughly that there was no need to avoid it.

The within-group correlations (tables 5 and 6) between the predictor variables and use of the structures revealed a consistent pattern. The use of those structures which were avoided by a particular group was significantly related to various affective variables. Thus, within the Arabic group, who avoided the passive, facilitating anxiety correlated significantly with use of this structure, and within the Spanish-Portuguese group, who avoided infinitive complement and direct objective pronoun structures, facilitating anxiety also correlated significantly with use. The findings suggest avoidance operating as a group phenomenon, but within the particular avoiding group, use of the generally avoided structure is a function of the facilitating anxiety levels of the group's members. This finding is not inconsistent with a study conducted by Chastain (1975), who found a significant negative correlation between test anxiety and final course grade in a university audio-lingual French-as-a-foreign-language class. Obviously, the anxiety there had a delibitating influence. But Chastain also implied a facilitating influence of anxiety based on his findings that anxiety was a significant predictor of success in learning Spanish as a foreign language. The evidence, therefore, seems to support the notion that certain affective measures influence learner behavior in a foreign language.

The significant findings with respect to facilitating anxiety and its predicting the use of various structures deemed difficult by contrastive analysis may also be a reflection of the ability of learners "to overcome the empathetic barriers set up by egoboundariness" (Taylor 1974, p. 34), which Taylor (1974) claims is partly necessary for an adult to become proficient in a second language. Taylor et al. (1969) and Guiora et al. (1972) had originally supported this hypothesis with their finding of a positive relationship between empathy and successful pronunciation of a second language. The present study, therefore, due to the significant positive relationship found between facilitating anxiety levels and use of generally avoided structures, is seen as supporting, in an indirect way, the view of empathy as a correlate of second language learner performance on the syntactic level.

An examination of all of the significant correlations within each group found that they generally fell into the following pattern: for those structures which the particular group avoided on the indirect preference assessment task, various affective variables correlated with use of the structures; for those structures which the particular group did not avoid, the affective variables did not correlate with use. In addition, significant differences between correlation coefficients relating the various affective variables with use of the structures were generally found on those structures which the group avoided. It is this pattern which suggests that the significant correlations are significant in the nonstatistical sense, too. Moreover, this pattern sheds light on the important question of how we can predict when a given structure will be avoided as opposed to when it will be produced with the likelihood of error. The results of this study suggest strongly that CA is a fairly good predictor of avoidance. However, structures which otherwise would be avoided are likely to be produced depending on the affective state of the learner with respect to such variables as confidence, anxiety, and motivational orientation. This conclusion reflects the intersection of linguistic and psychological factors in determining learner behavior in a second language, the linguistic and psychological factors identified in this study being, respectively, contrastive analysis and the affective variables cited above.

The original study on avoidance in second language acquisition by Schachter (1974) concluded that CA should not be abandoned as a diagnostic tool for learner difficulty in the TL because of its unique potential for being able to account for the phenomenon of avoidance. The study reported on here supports that conclusion with its finding that second language learners resort to an avoidance strategy that cannot be attributed to a lack of knowledge of the avoided structure. Furthermore, it has suggested that CA is a fairly good predictor of potential cases of avoidance, although admittedly, it cannot predict when a given structure will be avoided as opposed to when it will be produced with the likelihood of error. Such predictions can only be made with supplemental information concerning various affective characteristics such as confidence, levels of anxiety, and motivational orientation. The need for further research in this area goes without saying. Especially useful would be replication and expansion of the present study to include other affective variables such as risk-taking, about which relatively little is known concerning second language learners. A better profile of potential avoiders and nonavoiders is needed to gain an understanding of the processes which govern a learner's behavior in a second language.

Note

This article is a summary of the author's doctoral dissertation research conducted at the University of Pittsburgh, Department of General Linguistics. The author wishes to thank Christina Bratt Paulston, Charles Perfetti, Thomas Scovel, Charles Stegman, and Sarah Thomason for their invaluable assistance.

References

Alpert, R., and Haber, R. N. "Anxiety in Academic Achievement Situations." *Journal of Abnormal and Social Psychology* 61 (1960):207–15.

Bailey, N.; Madden, C.; and Krashen, S. D. "Is There a 'Natural Sequence' in Adult Second Language Learning?" *Language Learning* 24 (1974):235–43.

Berko, J. "The Child's Learning of English Morphology." *Word* 14 (1958):150–77.

Chastain, K. "Affective and Ability Factors in Second-Language Acquisition." *Language Learning* 25 (1975):153–61.

Cohen, A. D. "Error Correction and the Training of Language Teachers." *Modern Language Journal* 59 (1975):414–22.

Corder, S. P. *Introducing Applied Linguistics.* Harmondsworth: Penguin Books, 1973.

Dulay, H. C., and Burt, M. K. "Should We Teach Children Syntax?" *Language Learning* 23 (1973):245–58.

———. "Errors and Strategies in Child Second Language Acquisition." *TESOL Quarterly* 8 (1974a):129–36.

———. "Natural Sequences in Child Second Language Acquisition." *Language Learning* 24 (1974b):37–53.

Dušková, L. "On Sources of Errors in Foreign Language Learning." *International Review of Applied Linguistics* 7 (1969):11–36.

Guiora, A. Z.; Beit Hallahmi, B.; Brannon, R. C. L.; Dull, C. Y.; and Scovel, T. "The Effects of Experimentally Induced Changes in Ego States on Pronunciation Ability in a Second Language: An Exploratory Study." *Comprehensive Psychiatry* 13 (1972):421–28.

Ickenroth, J. "On the Elusiveness of Interlanguage." Progress report, Utrecht, December, 1975.

Lado, R. "Patterns of Difficulty in Vocabulary." *Language Learning* 6 (1955):23–41.

———. *Linguistics Across Cultures.* Ann Arbor: University of Michigan Press, 1957.

McReynolds, P., and Guevara, C. "Attitudes of Schizophrenics and Normals Toward Success and Failure." *Journal of Abnormal and Social Psychology* 72 (1967):203–10.

Mandler, G., and Sarason, S. B. "A Study of Anxiety and Learning." *Journal of Abnormal and Social Psychology* 47 (1952):166–72.

Perkins, K., and Larsen-Freeman, D. "The Effect of Formal Language Instruction on the Order of Morpheme Acquisition." *Language Learning* 25 (1975):237–43.

Richards, J. C. "A Non-Contrastive Approach to Error Analysis." *English Language Teaching* 25 (1971):204–19.

Ringbom, H. "What Differences are there Between Finns and Swedish-speaking Finns Learning English?" In *Errors Made by Finns and Swedish-speaking Finns in the Learning of English*, vol. 5, edited by H. Ringbom and R. Palmberg. Åbo: AFTIL, 1976

Schachter, J. "An Error in Error Analysis." *Language Learning* 24 (1974):205–14.

Selinker, L. "Interlanguage." *International Review of Applied Linguistics* 10 (1972):209–31.

Stockwell, R. P.; Bowen, J. D.; and Martin J. W. *The Grammatical Structures of English and Spanish*. Chicago: University of Chicago Press, 1965.

Swain, M. "Changes in Errors: Random or Systematic?" Paper presented at the Fourth International Congress of Applied Linguistics, Stuttgart, August, 1975.

Tarone, E.; Cohen, A. D.; and Dumas, G. *A Closer Look at Some Interlanguage Terminology: A Framework for Communication Strategies. Working Papers on Bilingualism* no. 9. Toronto: Ontario Institute for Studies in Education, 1976.

Tarone, E.; Frauenfelder, U.; and Selinker, L. "Systematicity/Variability and Stability/Instability in Interlanguage systems." *Language Learning*, Special Issue no. 4 (January, 1976).

Taylor, B. P. "Toward a Theory of Language Acquisition." *Language Learning* 24 (1974):23–35.

Taylor, J. A. "Personality Scale of Manifest Anxiety." *Journal of Abnormal and Social Psychology* 48 (1953):285–90.

Taylor, L. L.; Guiora, A. Z.; Catford, J. C.; and Lane, H. L. "The Role of Personality Variables in Second Language Behavior." *Comprehensive Psychiatry* 10 (1969):463–74.

Wardhaugh, R. "The Contrastive Analysis Hypothesis." *TESOL Quarterly* 4 (1970):123–30.

Whitman, R. L., and Jackson, K. L. "The Unpredictability of Contrastive Analysis." *Language Learning* 22 (1972):29–41.

Toward a Characterization of English Foreigner Talk

Charles A. Ferguson

The hypothesis has been made (Ferguson 1971) that speech communities tend to have conventional varieties of "simplified" speech which are regarded by the speakers as appropriate for use when the hearers do not have full understanding of the language. These special varieties of simplified speech include baby talk, ways of talking to deaf people, and foreigner talk; these varieties share certain features in common but differ in other features and hence merit separate investigation. A major theoretical justification for the study of varieties of simplified speech is the insight they might give into such notions as basic, simple, or deep, which figure in general theories of language. In addition, the study of baby talk may be of value for understanding the processes of child language development (Ferguson 1964, pp. 109–11; Slobin 1967, pp. 42–45) and the study of foreigner talk seems of value in analyzing the process of pidginization (Schuchardt 1909; Ferguson 1971).

Foreigner talk is commonly regarded in a given speech community as an imitation of the way foreigners speak the language under certain conditions, and it is usually elicited more readily by asking for this kind of imitation than by asking the informant how he would speak to a foreigner. This is reminiscent of the fact that adult users of baby talk will sometimes assert that they are imitating the way young children talk. In both cases, however, the relation between the observable language behavior of young children or foreigners and the simplified varieties of speech conventional in the community is not simple or direct. The historical origins of the conventional baby talk and foreigner talk of a speech community doubtless are complex and may reach back over long periods of time. Also, in actual speech events the influence and imitation may work both ways. From a purely linguistic point of view, the primary locus of the simplified variety is presumably in the competence of the speech community itself rather than in that of the babies or foreigners, since it seems to be optimally characterized by an additional set of rules added to

Reprinted by permission of the publisher and the author from *Anthropological Linguistics* 17, no. 1 (1975):1–14.

the grammar of the language being simplified. From a social psychological point of view, however, it may be important to note the attribution of foreigner talk to the foreigners themselves, since members of the speech community may tend to hear or report actual speech of foreigners in terms of foreigner talk even if the speech is in reality quite different.

As in the case of baby talk, foreigner talk also has extended uses. For example, it may be employed in reporting the speech of foreigners or indicating that a segment of reported speech was spoken by foreigners. Thus, a novelist may use foreigner talk in representing the speech of persons whom he wants to characterize as foreign, even though in the situation portrayed such a person would not in fact speak in that way. The reporting or identifying use of foreigner talk is analogous to the use of baby talk to report or identify children's speech.[1]

A further extension is the use of foreigner talk to represent some-one using a foreign language. In this case there is apparently no intention of suggesting that the structure of the foreign language is reflected by the foreigner talk, but only of marking the speech being reported as being another language while at the same time retaining intelligibility for the reader. An even further extension is the use of foreigner talk to represent an English speaker speaking a foreign language badly. An example of this, from a C. S. Lewis novel, will be used as source material in the present study. The six readily identifiable uses of foreigner talk are summarized in table 1. Parentheses enclose the *x* for foreign language speaker trying to use English, since the actual behavior in this situation may be quite far removed from the coventional foreigner talk of the English-speaking community.

TABLE 1. Uses of English Foreigner Talk (FL = foreign language)

	Primary Use	*Secondary Use (e.g., report)*
English speaker using English to FL speaker	x	x
FL speaker using English to English speaker	(x)	x
FL speaker using FL	—	x
English speaker using FL badly	—	x

The present study attempts to verify the hypothesis that there is a conventional foreigner talk for English and takes preliminary steps toward characterizing it. The method used for verification was to elicit specimens of foreigner talk from university students and the procedure for characterization was to examine a corpus consisting of the specimens elicited from the students together with a body of material taken from a published secondary use of foreigner talk and note common salient characteristics.

The sentence "Me Tarzan, you Jane" will serve as an example of the kind of foreigner talk which is to be specified. It is assumed here that speakers of English have as part of their linguistic competence the ability to produce and respond to such sentences under appropriate conditions. Even if a given speaker may disapprove of such sentences or choose not to use them under appropriate conditions, it is possible to elicit them from him or have them acknowledged as well-formed in the simplified speech which he attributes to others.

In the spring quarter of 1969 at one session of a course of Sociolinguistics, without any previous warning, I asked members of the class to tell me how they thought speakers of English trying to communicate with apparently uneducated non-Europeans would say certain sentences. I made the setting hypothetical and third person since I assumed that at least some members of the class would either disapprove of the use of foreigner talk or would be reluctant to admit their own possible use of it. I specified uneducated non-Europeans in order to avoid other kinds of language behavior such as emphasis on international words, use of French expressions, and the like, which would not be the kind of simplified foreigner talk I was interested in. In addition, I specified that the English speaker they were to describe was acting as a spokesman for a group and speaking to a group—this simply to make the use of plurals or personal pronouns a little more realistic.

Ten sentences or sentence pairs were given to the students and they wrote down what they thought the equivalents might be in the situation. After this, they were asked several questions about their attitudes toward the use of this kind of English, and their papers were collected. Seventeen students turned in papers. The following year the same procedure was followed in the same course, and nineteen papers received. The appendix gives the exact procedure as followed in 1970; the ten elicitation sentences were identical on the two occasions, but there may have been slight differences in the wording of the instructions and the questions.

The whole procedure was quite informal and was originally intended only to provide a basis for class discussion, so that background information about the students is not available. It may be of interest to note that one or two students each year did not turn in papers, about half the students each year were from linguistics with the others coming from a variety of departments, males and females were about equal in number, and apparently the 1970 class had not heard about the 1969 episode and its subsequent classroom discussion.

C. S. Lewis's novel, *Out of the Silent Planet,* tells of two Englishmen who landed on Mars independently and interacted with Martian beings in different ways. One of them learned to speak one variety of Martian language very fluently and accurately and developed considerable respect for the various kinds of Martians and their ways of thought. The other acquired only a smattering of the language and regarded the sentient beings of Mars as savages or animals. When the author is reporting the use of Martian language by the one who spoke it well, he uses ordinary standard English except for several paraphrases, metaphors, and Martian words which are all explained and clearly serve to give a feeling of authenticity to the discourse. When he reports the Martian language use of the other man, however, Lewis invariably employs English foreigner talk, thus indicating the man's imperfect command of the language and possibly also his attitude of superiority toward the Martians.

Sixty-one sentences or sentence sets of the second man talking to Martians appear in the book and these were all excerpted. Apart from four of these, "See! See!" (twice) and "Pretty, pretty!" (twice), all the sentences showed features of foreigner talk which differentiated them from normal English sentences. In each case it was possible from the context to compose a normal sentence which seemed to underlie the sentence of foreigner talk. For example, "We not afraid" was assumed to be the foreigner talk version of "We're not afraid;" "No go to kill him" stood for "We weren't going to kill him;" "You no roar at me" was for "Don't roar at me."

By the nature of the corpus it is difficult to infer any phonological characteristics, but several features may be noted (cf. Kazazis 1969).

1. The only instances in the corpus of addition of a vowel to final consonant are:[2] *talkee-talkee* (CSL 2), *talkie* (E1 II 1); *workee* (E1 II 1), *worka* (E1 II 1); *slippa outa* (E1 I 1); *nexta* (E1 II 1); *giva* (E1 I 1); *datah* (E1 I 1).

2. Reduplicated forms appear for 'talk' and 'gun'; *talkee-talkee* (CSL 2), *talk-talk* (E1 II 1); *bang-bang* (E1 I1, E1 II 1), *boom-boom* (E1 II 1). In addition, CSL has *puff-bang* for 'gun' once and three times has *poof! bang!* to represent shooting (perhaps equivalent to 'bang' in normal English). Besides these apparent lexical reduplications there are instances of repeated words in CSL (*See! See!* 2, *Pretty, pretty!* 2, *run, run* 1).

3. In replying to question C, 15 out of the 17 students in 1969 made some comment about slow, loud, distinct, or exaggerated pronunciation,

including the use of additional pauses and more emphatic stress and intonation. Surprisingly only 3 of the 19 students in 1970 made an unambiguous reference to this kind of special enunciation, and I can only speculate that the difference in reaction may be related to the content of previous class lectures and discussions. This characteristic of special enunciation is comparable to the registral feature of clarification discussed in Weeks 1971.

The special grammatical features found in the corpus include *omissions* (features 4–8) of material ordinarily present in normal language, *expansions* (9–10) by adding material not normally present, and *replacements* or *rearrangements* (11–14) of material such that similar semantic value is conveyed by different forms or constructions. Features will be listed under these three headings, and numbered consecutively, continuing the numbering of the phonological features.

Omissions in the corpus are:

4. One of the most consistent omissions in the corpus is that of the definite article *the*. There are two occurrences of *the* in the elicitation sentences; of the 72 possible occurrences in the elicited foreigner talk sentences, 64 are omitted, 8 are present and 4 are changed to *that*. There are 15 presumed occurrences of *the* in the CSL sentences; none of these appear in the foreigner talk sentences. The evidence for the indefinite article *a, an* is less conclusive, since there are no occurrences in the elicitation sentences, and only four in the presumed model sentences of CSL. All four presumed occurrences, however, show omissions in the foreigner talk sentences of the text.

5. All forms of the English verb *to be* (e.g., is, are, was) in all uses (e.g., equational sentence with noun complement, progressive be . . . -ing) are generally omitted in the corpus. In the elicitation sentences there are 8 occurrences of forms of *to be;* of the 288 possible occurrences in the elicited foreigner talk sentences, 256 are omissions, 4 replace *is* or *are* with *be,* and the remaining 28 maintain the original form. Even allowing for the fact that some of these omissions follow from the omission of the entire predication, omission of *to be* is a striking characteristic of the corpus. There is no clear-cut trend of preference for retention of *to be* or replacement of *be,* but it may be worth noting that none of the replacements are with the auxiliary use (*be* . . . *-ing*) and that 9 out of the 27 retentions are in the sentence "Where's the money. . . ."In the published source there are 19 occurrences of *to be* in the presumed model sentences, and none in the actual text.

6. All inflectional suffixes or internal stem changes signaling the grammatical categories of case, person, tense and number in nouns and

verbs tend to be omitted in the corpus. Specifically, the following morphemes may be omitted: the plural and possessive markers of nouns; third singular present suffix, past tense markers, progressive -*ing*, future *will*, and perfect *have* . . . -*en* of verbs. As an illustration of the strength of this tendency we may note that 30 of the 36 students omitted *have* . . . -*en* and all indications of past time from *haven't seen*, the commonest rendition being *no see* (25). Three of the respondents mentioned the dropping of verb inflections in their replies to the questions; one of them had an interesting rationalization of the dropping of -*s*. The comments are worth quoting in full. (The question answered is in parentheses.)

(Question C) "Drop the progressive and past tense."

(A) "I would simplify some verb forms—such as "She will be going tomorrow" could be "She goes tomorrow." "Do you understand?" I would simplify to 'You understand?' "

(C) "When I look to see what I've done I find tense very hard to express when one deals with yesterday or tomorrow. I dropped the third person singular *s* from *works*, hoping that the verb *work* might be familiar to some of my hearers."

7. All conjunctions, both coordinating and subordinating, tend to be omitted in the corpus. This tendency is very strong. In sentence 5 the conjunction *and* is omitted by 23 of the 36 respondents; 4 of the remainder simplified the sentence by deleting the first clause and hence the *and* also. In the "Come and see me" sentence, half the respondents omitted either the *come* or the *see* and hence also *and*, but of those who kept both verbs 14 omitted *and*, 1 wrote *and* in parentheses, and only 3 retained *and*. In the published source there are at least 17 sentences without conjunctions in which one or more conjunctions could be present for the model sentence, and in all the 61 sentences there are only 2 instances of *and* and 1 of *before* used as a conjunction.

8. In a number of instances in the corpus a verb appears without the required subject pronoun, but it is not clear whether these should all be regarded as omissions of the pronoun, since in most cases they could be interpreted as the omission of a conjunction or even the addition of a verb. For example, "We little people, we only want. . . ." may be a foreigner talk equivalent of "We are little people and (we) only want. . . ." In spite of the uncertainty of analysis in particular cases there is a distinct tendency to omit pronouns when they are redundant from previous mention in the same sentence or a preceding sentence. There are at least 18 instances of the absence of subject pronouns under these conditions in the CSL sentences.

The feature of reduplication which was listed under phonology could equally well be regarded as grammatical or lexical expansion. Also, the occasional use of multiple negation, mentioned below under replacements, could be viewed as adding material. Often sporadic instances of expansion occur, such as "He's working with me. He with me. He work with me." In addition to these occasional examples, two patterns of expansion are worth noting.

9. One of the most frequent expansions in the corpus is the addition of subject *you* to imperatives. Elicitation sentence 4 has three imperatives "Come and see me tomorrow. Don't forget." Eleven of the 32 responses add *you* to the word *come* (4 of the remaining omit the *come* altogether). There are no instances of adding *you* to the second verb, *see*, which is omitted completely by 12 respondents, but there are 4 additions of *you* to *forget*. In consonance with the pattern of pronoun omission mentioned above in 8, it seems likely that the important feature about *come* which is responsible for the pronoun insertion is its position as first in a series of verbs rather than some other factor, such as the difference between affirmative and negative. In the published source there are 6 clear-cut instances of imperatives, of which 4 have *you* added. These are neatly divided into 3 affirmatives and 3 negatives, and 2 of each add *you*.

10. In 8 instances sentences of the corpus have an added tag such as *yes? ok? see? no?* which was absent in the model or presumed model sentence. Although this is a small number of cases it suggests both that such tags are more used in foreigner talk and that the simple "is it right?" kind of tag is preferred to the complex question tags of normal English with their shift of affirmative-negative and use of auxiliaries.

Replacements in the corpus are:

11. The tendency to replace all negative constructions by a *no* preceding the item negated is very strong. In the elicitation sentences there are 2 occurrences of *n't* (*haven't seen, don't forget*); out of 72 possible occurrences in the foreigner talk 46 are *no* and only 7 are *not;* the remainder included 3 instances of retaining *don't* and 13 nonnegative equivalents of "don't forget," such as *remember, ok?*, and the like. There is also an elicitation sentence containing a stressed *not* (*he's not my father*), and this received 18 *no's*, 17 *not's*, and 1 double *not-no*. In the published source there are 18 instances of *no* as a clause negation and 5 cases of *not*. Of the 5 cases of *not*, 3 have a stressed *not* in the presumed model sentence. This tendency to retain *not* when it is uncontracted is reminiscent of the rules for contraction and deletion of the copula discussed in Labov (1969).

12. The normal English possessive construction exemplified by the expression "my brother" is replaced by somewhat different constructions

a significant number of times in the corpus. More commonly the construction is retained or the possessive pronoun is simply omitted, but of greater interest are the instances of replacement. In the elicitation sentences there are 2 occurrences of *my* and 1 of *your* (*my brother, my father, your brother*), thus 108 possible occurrences of the construction in the corpus. Of these 43 retain the possessive, 43 omit it, 3 replace *your* by *you*, and 15 replace the construction by a pronominal form after the noun (e.g., *brother me* [*you*], *brother to me* [*you*], *brother to I, brother to me* [*you*]). This is the clearest example in our limited corpus of the tendency to *analytic paraphase* which is characteristic of pidgins (cf. Agheysi 1971).

13. The Standard English use of the case forms of the pronouns (*I* or *me, he* or *him,* etc.) is complex and fluctuating, but the use of the "nominative" forms *I, he,* etc. as simple subject pronouns immediately preceding a finite verb is completely normal and exceptionless in ordinary Standard English. The use of *me, him,* etc. in this function seems to be regarded as baby talk or foreigner talk. Of the 108 possible occurrences of *I* as subject in the responses, 58 retained *I,* 28 used *me,* and the remainder omitted the pronoun. The sentences with *he* offer some complications; 2 of them have *he* as subject of the copula and 2 have a *he* in a second clause where the pronoun is likely to be omitted. However, if all possible occurrences are lumped together the figures are: *he* 94, *him* 46, omissions 59, 9 occurrences of (*that*) *man,* and 8 miscellaneous. There was only one straightforward instance of subject *she* in the sentences (in 10; the one in 3 was paraphrased in many ways). Of the 36 possible occurrences 27 had *she,* 6 had *her,* and 3 had (*that*) *woman* or *girl.* If we exclude omissions and paraphrases, *me* and *him* occurred 33 percent of the time in place of the nominative, and *her* 18 percent. This is clearly a feature of English foreigner talk.

The tendency to the use the accusative form of the pronoun seems limited to the first person singular in the CSL text. There are 12 instances of *me* as subject compared to 2 of *I,* contrasting with 12 instances of *he* and 20 of *we,* with no examples of *him* or *us.*

Some of the respondents, in their replies to the questions, give evidence of concern about the use of pronouns. In addition to comments about the need for pointing along with pronouns or the desirability of eliminating them completely, several replies mention the use of case forms. The general attitude seems to be that the pronouns constitute a problem, and the accusative is somehow to be expected in this kind of English. Along with this is the notion that the use of accusative is really unfortunate, and several wrote that they themselves would not use it, even though they had put it in their written sentences. The only rationale expressed for the use of the accusative is to reduce the number of forms, but there is no explanation of why the accusative would accomplish this any better than the nominative. The following examples are of interest; the question is indicated in parentheses before the quotation, the respondent's own pronoun score after it.

(C) "I've used accusatives for the pronoun forms by way of simplification, i.e., fewer forms necessary in the total situation. This also because I would have to point to the people I was talking about." (*me* 2, one omission; *him* 4, *he* 0, two omissions; *her* 1.)

(A) "I have a definite feeling that some of these are standard clichés, esp. passive pronouns, e.g., *him* (do something). I might use some of simplified forms, but would def. use active pronouns. (*me* 2, *I* 1; *him* 4, *he* 2; *her* 1).

(A) "I would use pronoun case more accurately." (*me* 2, one omission; *him* 1, *he* 2, three omissions; *she* 1).

(A) "I would not be quite so inclined to use the accusative form of the pronoun as subject . . . I'd rather gesture." (*me* 2, *I* 1; *him* 6; *her* 1) .

(C) "I'm not satisfied with the English pronouns, even though I've limited the case. Perhaps a blend of French, English and the native lang. could be affected." (*I* 2, 1 paraphrase; *him* 3, *he* 2, one omission; *her* 1).

(A) "I think it's more a matter of gestures than whether you use *me* or *I* though." (*me* 3; *him* 5, 1 omission; *her* 1).

14. There are two yes-no questions among the elicitation sentences, both having inversion Did you understand. . .", "is he. . ." For the former all but one respondent omitted the *did* and had no other syntactic sign of interrogation. Presumably intonation alone would signal the question, and four of the students gave explicit indications of interrogative intonation. The sentence with *is* was not decisive on this point since all but four omitted the copula; one of the latter, however, had noninverted order *he be*. It is probably safe to assume that there is a tendency to replace inversion with intonation as question marker.

Although the principal characteristics of foreigner talk seem to be the grammatical omissions, expansion, and rearrangements already discussed, there are also instances of lexical substitution in which a lexical item of the normal language is replaced by a synonym, a paraphrase, or a special expression used only or primarily in foreigner talk. Of the 38 student respondents 24 had at least one instance of lexical substitution, and there are a number of cases in the published source which seem to be lexical substitutions. Because of the lack of overlap in vocabulary there are no examples of identical substitutions in the elicited material and the published source, but similar trends are evident, as will be noted below.

TABLE 2. Lexical Substitutions

Normal Word	Favorite Substitute in Foreign Talk	Number of Students Making Favorite Substitution	Total Number of Students Making a Substitution for This Word (N = 36)
understand	savvy	5	12
tomorrow	next day	5	10
always	all (the) time	5	7
father	papa	4	8
gun	bang-bang	3	5

Five words of normal English were replaced by students of both years by identical expressions, as shown in table 2. The word *yesterday* should probably be added to this list of common substitutions even though no student of one year happened to use exactly the same equivalent as a student of the other year. Altogether seven students made a substitution for it, each slightly different but all, except for one use of a foreign word, containing a word for 'day' and a word for 'past' (e.g., *one day gone, day before this, today last day*). The Lewis material had no instances of *tomorrow, always,* or *yesterday,* but it is interesting to note that in one sentence the expression *all the time* is apparently the substitute for normal English *forever,* showing the same kind of analytic paraphrase of a temporal adverb. Also, in the Lewis material the word *gun* was replaced by *puff-bang,* which is similar to the *bang-bang* and *boom-boom* of the students. The complete list of words for which substitution was made by students follows: *always, brother, carry, come, father, forget, go, gun, man, money, say, tell, talk, tomorrow, understand, where, work, yesterday.* The list of substitutions in the published source is more problematical, but is probably as follows: *bad, because of, die, forever, God, happen, leader, like, look, mean* (= 'intend'), *much/many, over* (= 'finished').

The lexical characteristics of English foreigner talk suggested by the substitutions in the corpus include those listed below as 15–18; examination of more material would undoubtedly suggest others.

15. A few lexical items are regularly used primarily in foreigner talk and are only marginal in normal English. The best known example is *savvy* 'understand' which appears in English-based pidgins and creoles throughout the world. A less certain example is the use of *papa* 'father,' which is probably more frequent in baby talk than foreigner talk. The only other example in the corpus is *moolah/wampum* 'money.' The term

wampum tends to be limited to speech addressed to or attributed to American Indians, while the term *moolah* has more general applicability, being used also in various slangy and humorous contexts in normal English.

Somewhat different from the use of foreigner talk equivalents for English words is the use of certain words in foreigner talk which do not correspond to any particular lexeme of normal English but have a range of meaning and use which is characteristically foreigner talk. The best example in the corpus is the multipurpose intensive *plenty* which recurs three times in the Lewis material. One occurrence has the normal colloquial meaning of *'many, lots of'*; another, *Me know all that plenty* "I know all that very well', is further removed from the normal use of *plenty*. The other occurrence . . . *you plenty keep him* . . . 'you'd better keep him', is quite unlike any use of plenty or its synonyms in normal English. The range of use illustrated here for *plenty* might well be matched in various pidgins either with *plenty* or with other words such as *heap*.

16. There is a tendency to use non-English words even if it is clear that the person addressed is not familiar with the language from which the words are borrowed. The student respondents used fifteen foreign words; all of them were of Latin-Romance origin, generally Spanish or French, but one instance of Latin (*frater* 'brother') and one Italian (*capisce* 'understand'). The word *savvy* mentioned in 15 is itself of Romance origin.

17. In a number of instances a basic (unmarked?) synonym of simpler semantic content and greater frequency of use is preferred to a more precise, less frequent term. For example, three students substituted *take* or *have* for *carry*, and *come* was used in the meaning 'happen' in the Lewis material. Perhaps this represents no more than a shuffling of synonyms as in the exchange among *say, speak, talk, tell* in student responses (*say* and *tell* for *talk*, *speak* and *talk* for *say*). A more interesting example is the use of *dead* as a verb in the Lewis material, suggesting that *dead* was felt somehow to be more basic than *die*.

18. The decomposition of a word into a phrase in which semantic features of the word are separated out in an analytic paraphrase is very common and characteristic of foreigner talk. In addition to the examples of *always, forever, tomorrow,* and *yesterday,* discussed earlier, the following may be cited:

where	which place
like	same as
leader	big head
forget	slippa outa tete

    understand   catch words
    gun   firestick

In principle this lexical characteristic is the same as the kind of analytic paraphrases discussed under grammatical characteristics.

The purposes of this very limited study were to establish the existence of at least one variety of foreigner talk as part of the total communicative competence of speakers of American English and to give a preliminary characterization of it. All but 2 of the 36 students supplied sentences with expected foreigner talk features.[3] There was substantial agreement on basic features of the foreigner talk even though the responses differ in detail and in extent of use of the features. Accordingly, on the basis of the data presented, the 2 purposes have been fulfilled, although possibly more questions have been raised than answered. This brief final section contains comments on the attitudes of the respondents toward foreigner talk, speculation about how the competence is acquired, and a discussion of the limitations of the study.

    Negative attitudes of the American speech community toward the use of baby talk have been recognized (Ferguson 1964) and the present study gives evidence of negative attitudes toward the use of foreigner talk. Although nearly all the respondents supplied sentences which exemplified foreigner talk, many of them expressed some disapproval of its use. Question A asked whether the respondent would use this kind of language himself. If we score the replies to question A on a scale of 4 (definite yes, qualified yes, qualified no, definite no), only 4 students give a definite yes (1 of whom reported he had actually used it in the real-life situation). Twenty out of the 36 students gave a qualified yes indicating either that they would use some of the features exemplified in their sentences or would use that kind of speech under limited conditions (e.g., after trying something else). There were 8 outright expressions of unwillingness—3 qualified and 5 definite nos, and 4 responses were unclear or lacking. The general attitude seemed to be that foreigner talk was not a good thing—it sounds too condescending or would hinder learning good English—but could be used if necessary. Some respondents added a comment about another form of communication which they would either prefer or would use in conjunction with the foreigner talk register. There were 7 mentions of gestures or sign language, 3 of simple but correct English, and 2 of trying a foreign language such as French or Spanish.

    If we accept the notion that in general speakers of American English can modify their speech toward a conventionalized foreigner talk register, the question arises how they learn to do this. For those features which seem to constitute either a simplification (e.g., elimination of inflection) or an addition of redundancy (e.g., reduplication) the argument could conceivably be made that these processes are in some sense universal or a part of general language competence which does not require special learning. Even for these simplifying and clarifying features the arbitrary, conventional nature sometimes seems clear (e.g., why omission of the copula), but other features which seem to serve mostly as registral markers (e.g., *me* for *I, savvy* for *understand*) must certainly be acquired just as much as the arbitrary lexicon and inventory of morphophonemic relations of any language must be acquired.

In discussion with some of the students after the sentences had been administered, the only suggestions made about possible sources were the mass media: a number of students recalled hearing examples of foreigner talk in films or on television. While this may be secondary source contributing in an occasional way to the acquisition of foreigner talk competence, it can hardly be the primary source. My own speculation would be that many features of foreigner talk are acquired, along with practice in using it, during childhood playing in peer groups where children who know transmit to children who know less well or not at all. The widespread familiarity with the American Indian variety of foreigner talk comes only in part from cowboy novels or Western films—children in play learn to use the greeting "How!", the intensifier *heap* 'much, very', *wampum* for 'money', and other linguistic and nonverbal features of the way Indians are supposed to talk. Just as 4- or 5-year-olds can already use a baby talk register with younger children or under other appropriate conditions (Weeks 1971; Gleason 1973), 8-to-12-year-olds can use a number of special registers for playing different roles, and foreigner talk is one of them.

The ultimate source is another issue. When and how did the basic features of English foreigner talk become established? I suspect that features of foreigner talk, like baby talk, may persist for centuries.[4] Further, the whole foreigner talk register may be seen as a relatively little used resource of the speech community which is available for rapid development into a pidgin when a particular situation of language contact calls for it. See Bender et al. (1972) for discussion of the emergence of the Simplified Italian of Ethiopia as an example of this process.

The data of this study are very limited, and caution must be used in generalizing from them. Ten sentences elicited under highly artificial conditions, in reference to one kind of speech situation, from a total of 36 university students are a far cry from the actual use of foreigner talk in any of the functions attributed to it in 1.[5] What is called for is a series of investigations of English foreigner talk by different populations in different contexts as well as comparative study of foreigner talk in other speech communities altogether.[6] Only after such systematic research could the full implications be explored for the role of "simplified" registers in the repertoires of speech communities, the process of simplification in language, and the formation of pidgins.

Appendix: Foreigner Talk Elicitation Instructions

Administrator reads:
I am asking you to tell me how you think an English-speaking person might act in trying to communicate with some non-English speakers. The person whose speech I want you to describe is acting as the spokesman for a group of three and he is addressing a group of non-English speakers who are obviously non-European and illiterate. They may have heard some English before but they are not really able to understand it or speak it. I will read you a sentence in normal English, and I want you to write down the way you think the English speaker might say it. I'll repeat each sentence as many times as you like before going on to the next one.

Sentences:

1. I haven't seen the man you're talking about.
2. He's my brother, he's not my father.
3. Did you understand what she said?
4. Come and see me tomorrow. Don't forget!
5. Yesterday I saw him and gave him some money.
6. He's working with me. He'll work with you too.
7. Who is that man? Is he your brother?
8. He always carries two guns.
9. Where's the money I gave you yesterday?
10. She's going tomorrow.

Administrator asks:
   A. Would you use this kind of language yourself in this situation? Some features of it more likely than others?
   B. Would you make any special use of gestures in connection with this kind of language?
   C. Are there any other features of this communication situation you would like to comment on?

Notes

An earlier version of this paper was included in a presentation on simplified registers made at the Linguistic Institute, State University of New York, Buffalo, Summer 1971. It was presented in abbreviated form at a seminar of Pidgins and Creoles, University of California, Berkeley, May 1972, and at the International Congress of Applied Linguistics, Copenhagen, August, 1972.

1. Cf. Ferguson 1964, p. 111, where examples and references are given.
2. The source identifications in parentheses refer to the first and second class elicitation (EI I, EI II) and the Lewis novel (CSL); the arabic numerals give the number of instances.
3. One of the two whose attempts at simplification were unlike English foreigner talk is not a native speaker of English and came to the United States a few years ago; the other was not identified.
4. As an example, the persistence of the use of the infinitive is discussed in Schuchardt 1909 and Bender et al 1972. The use of the infinitive in the foreigner talk of European languages antedates the original Lingua Franca, however. Giraldus Cambrensis (twelfth century) quotes his conversation with an uneducated pious anchorite, who has picked up enough Latin for his purposes and uses it "per infinitivum nec casus servabat" (Brewer 1861, p. 90). I am indebted to Jean Ure for this reference.
5. After this study was completed two additional administrations of the sentences to Stanford students were carried out, one by Charles B. Kitsman, the other by M. Lionel Bender. The latter had responses from 49 students; the former from 18, but included several additional sentences and was paired with a study eliciting standard English sentences as presumed models for foreigner talk stimulus sentences. The results, which will appear elsewhere, generally confirm the findings of this study.
6. For a study of German foreigner talk as reflected in the German conversation of foreign labor immigrants, cf. Clyne 1965. The author shows "simplifying" tendencies of the kind described here and in addition more surprising (i.e., arbitrary, nonsimplifying) features such as the universal use of *du* and the strong tendency toward use of the infinitive in final position for normal German finite verb forms.

References

Agheyisi, Rebecca. "West African Pidgin English: Simplification and Simplicity." Ph.D. dissertation, Stanford University, 1971.

Bender, M. L.; Cooper, R. L.; and Ferguson, C. A.. "Language in Ethiopia: Implication of a Survey for Sociolinguistic Theory and Method." *Language in Society* 1 (1972):215–33.

Brewer, J. S. *Giraldi Cambrensis Opera,* vol. I, edited by J. S. Brewer. London: Longman, Green, Longman and Roberts, 1861.

Clyne, Michael. "Zum Pidgin-Deutsch der Gastarbeiter." *Z. für Mundartforschung* 34 (1968):130–39.

Ferguson, Charles A. "Baby Talk in Six Languages." In *Ethnography of Communication,* edited by Dell Hymes and John J. Gumperz. *American Anthropologist,* 66, special issue (1964): pt. 2, pp. 103–14.

———. "Absence of Copula and the Notion of Simplicity: A Study of Normal Speech, Baby Talk, Foreigner Talk, and Pidgins." In *Pidginization and Creolization in Language,* edited by Dell Hymes. Cambridge: At the University Press, 1971.

Gleason, Jean Berko. "Code Switching in Children's Language." In *Cognitive Development and the Acquisition of Language,* edited by T. E. Moore. New York: Academic Press, 1973.

Kazazis, Kostas. "Distorted Modern Greek Phonology for Foreigners." *Glossa* 3, no. 2 (1969):198–209.

Labov, William. "Contraction, Deletion and Inherent Variability of the English Copula." *Language* 45 (1969):715–62.

Lewis, C. S. *Out of the Silent Planet.* New York: MacMillan and Co., 1960.

Schuchardt, Hugo. "Die Lingua franca." *Zeitschrift für Romanische Philologie* 33 (1909):441–61.

Slobin, Dan I. *A Field Manual for Cross-cultural Study of the Acquisition of Communicative Competence.* Berkeley: University of California, 1967.

Weeks, Thelma. "Speech Registers in Young Children." *Child Development* 42 (1971):1119–31.

Linguistic Register of Foreign Language Instruction

Vera M. Henzl

Whenever participants in a verbal communication do not have equal facility of the language in use, adjustments in choices of linguistic means may take place. The speaker of a language seems to know intuitively how to talk, for example, to a little child or to a foreigner; he modifies his speech to what he thinks will be simpler and easier for the listener to comprehend. The choices he makes tend to be consistent for speakers of whole speech communities, and, in fact, they may show a systematic patterning that allows us to view the modified speech variety as a subsystem or "register" of the language.

Common characteristics found in language used by foreign language teachers in talking to their students would justify the recognition of a special register. The present study attempts to establish whether such systematic characteristics do exist. The experiment was carried out with a group of educated native speakers of Czech, investigating the language they use in addressing American students of Czech.

Background

It was hypothesized that if such a conventional Foreign Language Classroom Register (FLCR) were isolated, it would bear features reflecting the inequality of the linguistic competence between speaker and hearers, as well as typical features of communication in the classroom setting.

Thus, one set of assumptions relied heavily on the definition of the Foreigner Talk Register (FTR) described by Ferguson (1975); working with a highly inflectional language like Czech, it was predicted that the variety used in talking to foreign students would demonstrate characteristics of grammatical simplification, especially in the level of morphology and syntax. In the lexicon a tendency toward generality was expected, that is toward choices from a semantically basic vocabulary. In speech characteristics, emphatic stress, loud pitch, and slow speech rate were presumed.

Reprinted by permission of the publisher and the author from *Language Learning* 23, no. 2 (1973):207–22.

The predictions related to the second part of the hypothesis were based on characteristics of the variety of Czech which is used as the means of school instruction, i.e., Standard Literary Czech (SLC).[1] This variety, codified by the Czechoslovak Academy of Sciences, constitutes the ideal norm of the language drawn from the classics of the national literature; it contains numerous archaisms in phonology and morphology. By definition it is the norm for the written language, while its application in speech is reserved for special social contexts of strictly formal communication such as official speeches, lectures, theatrical performances, mass media, and also education.[2] In this analysis the conversational form of Czech, which will be conveniently referred to as Colloquial Czech (CC),[3] is a coexisting supradialectal variety of the same language that, contrary to SLC, has incorporated changes brought about in the natural development of the language. It differs from SLC on all levels of the system, though predominantly in phonology and morphology. It was expected that speakers, by virtue of their own experience in a classroom situation, would automatically switch in the direction of SLC in their FLCR. For the same reason, it was assumed they would refrain from dialectal and slang variants.

The present study not only tests the two hypotheses but also views the nature of the interplay between the two hypothetical processes.

Material and Method

Recordings of spoken Czech were obtained from eight subjects, all of whom were born in Czechoslovakia and lived there until recently. They came from different academic backgrounds, but all were exposed during their education to foreign language instruction. The material for recording was selected to regulate stylistic choices of the speakers. The first sample was a contemporary political anecdote which invited an extensive use of dialogue. The second sample represented a short, mostly descriptive sketch by a modern Czech writer, Karel Čapek, and offered a possibility for stylistic elaboration. In individual sessions each subject was asked to tell his own version of each story twice—once to a group of American students who had studied Czech at Stanford University for two years, and once to native speakers of Czech (the order of the tasks was distributed equally among the speakers). In this fashion, four samples were elicited from each subject, and in the analysis are marked in the following order: 1A = anecdote in CC, 1B = anecdote in FLCR, 2A = sketch in CC, and 2B = sketch in FLCR; a double letter, e.g., 1Aa, indicates that an additional recording 1A was made by the same speaker.

In order to minimize the influence of self-consciousness on subjects' performance, both speakers and listeners were kept ignorant about the purpose of the experiment; to the contrary, speakers were led to believe that the students' retention of the stories was being tested.

Analysis of Data

The 36 speech samples were transcribed in the conventional orthography of Standard Czech which has a close phonological correspondence. This allowed for a fairly accurate examination of not only syntax and lexicon, but of most of phonology as well. Phenomena concerning prosodic and expressive features, such as stress, intonation, rhythm, quality and intensity of voice, etc., were not incorporated in the analysis, except for the heuristic purpose of determining sentence boundaries.

Differential quantitative measurements were made of the speech rate in the two language varieties, while pauses and hesitations, except for their distribution in the utterances, were not analyzed nor instrumentally measured.

In the following paragraphs, the most typical distinctions contrasting FLCR and CC speech which were consistently found in the samples, will be listed.

Lexicon

One of the main characteristics of the FLCR samples seems to be the great use of basic vocabulary, while native discourse, as a rule, exhibits an extremely rich diversity in the choices of words. A striking example of this lexical discrimination is the degree to which subjects refrained from elaborating the key word of the anecdote story when addressing a group of nonnatives; with the exception of subjects no. 6 and no. 7, all speakers employed exclusively the basic verb *plakat* 'to weep' in their FLCR speech, whereas in talking to a Czech audience, they felt no inhibitions in incorporating synonyms of various extended meanings. We found, for example, in no. 1-1A: *pláče*, no. 2-1A: *brečí* no. 3-1A: *pláče* ~ *křičí* ~ *řvala*, no. 4-1A: *plakala* ~ *řvala* ~ *bečela* ~ *brečí*, no. 5-1A: *brečí*, and no. 8-1A: *brečela* ~ *bečela* ~ *pláče*. A similar case was observed with the verb *vidět* 'to see'; here, in the speech samples of the same subject, we encountered in FLCR no. 3-2B: *vidí* versus no. 3-2A: *vidí* ~ *kouká* in CC.[4] Differential counts of verb frequencies point to a direct correlation between the occurrence of lexical items and the index of the richness of vocabulary. Generally, in FLCR, speakers tended to utilize maximally each lexical item once it was introduced, while in CC the frequency of individual entries was lower.

In both stories subjects displayed a noticeable effort to talk to the foreigners in concrete terms. Although indefinite pronouns and indefinite adjectives (such as *někdo* 'someone' or *nějaký* 'some') were readily used in CC samples, a significant degree of replacement occurred in FLCR samples by the use of personal pronouns *ty* or *vy* 'you', or by a concrete noun or a fictitious name, such as *pán* 'gentleman' or *pan Novák* 'Mr. Smith.

The reasons for the lexical reduction of a remarkably high proportion of the data need to be sought in other sources than those which can be provided by semantic simplification. The variety of speech in most FLCR samples lacked many words and phrases found frequently in CC, and that, for various reasons, stayed at the periphery of the SLC lexicon. Types of expressions which occurred in this category included typical colloquial expressions, such as no. 3-1A, no. 6-1A: *furt* 'constantly' or no. 2-2A: *ted'kou*, no. 7-1A: *ted'ka* 'now'; defamatory expressions, e.g., no. 6-1A: *Prdlenka*, an invented name; borrowings, such as no. 3-1A: *trafika* 'traffic'; words with transferred meaning, e.g., no. 3-2A: *zdravit hluboce* 'to greet deeply' or *škleb* 'grimace'; compound words, e.g., no. 1-1A: *kolemjdoucí* 'by-passer', especially those made at the spur of the moment, such as no. 2-1A: *s poloúsměvem* 'with a half-smile' or no. 2-2A: *známou-neznámou figuru* 'known-unknown figure (accusative)'; and also idiomatic expressions which form a special corpus of the lexicon, e.g., no. 3-2A: *komu jsem to zase nalít* 'who tricked me again.'

In talking to the foreign students, subjects either omitted the above mentioned expressions completely, or they replaced them by lexical items that are better accommodated within the grammar of SLC. Thus, a colloquialism no. 7-1A: *policajt* 'cop' was changed to its Standard equivalent in the FLCR speech sample, i.e., no. 7-1B: *strážník* 'policeman'; similarly, an idiomatic phrase no. 4-2A: *smeknout klobouk* 'to greet by taking off one's hat' was replaced by a descriptive verb which was used in the sense of 'to take off' generally in any context, i.e., no. 4-2B: *sundat klobouk* 'to take off the hat'.

The use of interjections and onomatopoeia, typical of Baby Talk simplified register, was favored by some subjects in their FLCR speech, but was found in many CC samples as well. For instance, the verb *plakat* 'to weep' was often substituted or at least reinforced by expressions, such as *uá, bé, bébé, bů, bulí*, or *bulila*. On the other hand, words like *jó, no, tak, a, hele, že, žejó, jako, víš*, etc., which do not carry a semantic content in themselves but rather mark a hesitation process in the course of the speech event, were found almost exclusively in the CC talk, though they seemed to be also an inherent characteristic of certain individual speakers.

Syntax

The results of the data only confirm the observations of many recent developmental psycholinguistic studies (Phillips 1970, 1972; Broen 1972; Snow 1972) regarding the sentence structure of simplified linguistic registers. The findings indicate that all speakers without exception tended to speak to the foreign students in short and well-formed sentences. In general, sentences had a smaller number of words in FLCR speech than in CC samples (see table 1). A lesser occurrence of subordinate clauses and the exclusion of unfinished sentences from FLCR speech also reflected the tendency for subjects to speak in concise, well-formed sentences (see table 2).

In the initial hypothesis syntactic simplification was presumed to take place in FLCR. Though the mechanism of grammatical adjustments was different from the kind reported in Foreigner Talk studies (Clyne 1968; Ferguson 1972), the data demonstrate that there was a tendency to lower the inflectional complexity of nominal and verbal categories in the FLCR speech. Nevertheless, I am hesitant to conceive of this decrease as a direct consequence of any conscious effort on the part of the speaker. It can be more feasibly interpreted as a result of the speaker's preference for short and basic sentence structures, where the basic syntactic categories by virtue of their function eliminate inflectional elaboration. This refers primarily to the high percentage of the base cases (nominative and accusative) in FLCR as compared to the higher declensional diversity (e.g., instrumental) in CC.

An increased use of unmarked verbal forms was demonstrated in speech directed to foreigners by the tendency to simplify forms in the ratio of tenses, moods, and voices. Use of the past tense was intentionally avoided by most speakers in FLCR samples (see table 3). Future tense, which in Czech is possible only with imperfective verbs, was not found in the data, as neither one of the stories offered much opportunity to use it. Perfective verbs, whose present tense has a future meaning, appeared in both CC and FLCR samples, but it is not clear whether perfectivization should be ascribed to the speaker's intention to express a temporal relation rather than to his choice of a different lexical meaning.

Indicative mood was used almost exclusively in all samples. Only six speakers employed the conditional at all, in the range of one to three

TABLE 1. Number of Words per Sentence

Story	Speaker 1		Speaker 2		Speaker 3		Speaker 4		Speaker 5		Speaker 6		Speaker 7		Speaker 8	
	1	2	1	2	1	2	1	2	1	2	1	2	1	2	1	2
CC	5.2(5.7)	12.2(11.8)	11.3	38.8	15.8	19.6	4.2	21.3	4.6	14.1	11.2	28.5	10.8	69.0	12.4	17.2(51.5)
FLCR	3.8	10.0	6.9	17.3	5.3	12.5	6.2	8.8	4.3	8.6	11.9	20.7	9.7	12.2	6.3	7.2(7.0)

Note: CC = Colloquial Czech; FLCR = Foreign Language Classroom Register; ( ) = additional recording of the story

TABLE 2. Number of Sentences in CC and FLCR

	Speaker															
	1		2		3		4		5		6		7		8	
Story	1	2	1	2	1	2	1	2	1	2	1	2	1	2	1	2
CC: Total no. of sentences	8(8)	6(6)	20	4	8	7	15	4	10	8	12	11	13	1	11	6(2)
No. of unfinished sentences	–(–)	–(–)	–	1	3	2	–	–	1	–	4	7	1	–	–	–(–)
No. of subordinate clauses	1(2)	2(4)	1	4	5	4	1	9	3	4	2	17	1	6	4	7(7)
FLCR: Total no. of sentences	11	4	23	6	9	4	12	5	10	5	10	3	11	4	12	6(7)
No. of unfinished sentences	–	–	–	–	–	–	–	–	–	–	–	–	–	–	–	–(–)
No. of subordinate clauses	–	2	–	2	–	3	1	1	–	2	2	4	–	4	1	1(2)

Note: CC = Colloquial Czech; FLCR = Foreign Language Classroom Register; ( ) = additional recording of the story

TABLE 3. Number of Occurrences of Verbs in Past Tense: Total Number of Verbs

| | Speaker | | | | | | | | | | | | | | | |
| | 1 | | 2 | | 3 | | 4 | | 5 | | 6 | | 7 | | 8 | |
Story	1	2	1	2	1	2	1	2	1	2	1	2	1	2	1	2
CC: No. of past tense verbs	1 (5)	2 (1)	32	5	15	8	15	12	–	10	21	38	–	1	17	2 (1)
Total no. of verbs	12(13)	12(13)	46	28	30	23	24	28	17	22	36	58	28	10	33	19(16)
FLCR: No. of past tense verbs	–	–	–	–	11	4	20	–	–	6	17	–	–	1	–	–(–)
Total no. of verbs	11	11	41	24	17	13	26	12	15	10	23	16	25	10	25	12(13)

Note: CC = Colloquial Czech; FLCR = Foreign Language Classroom Register; ( ) = additional recording of the story

instances per sample; most of these conditional forms were used in speaking to Czechs, although speaker no. 6 had a ratio of conditional in CC and FLCR of 1:3 in the descriptive sketch.

Social constraints associated with the classroom instruction were responsible for the great part of morphological differences between the speech to foreign students and to natives. Inflectional variants of CC were found in some A-samples, while morphological structures of inflectional forms applied in FLCR samples belong to the SLC system.[5] For example, the common CC infinitive suffix *-t* was used in no. 8-2Aa: *říct* 'to tell'; it resulted from an overgeneralization of the infinitive morphological rule *-ti#* → *-t#* (as in *dělati* → *dělat* 'to make') to an exceptional case (*říci* → *říct* 'to tell' in the example). A similar tendency of CC was illustrated in regularizing the second person singular indicative suffix of the verb "to be," as in no. 2-1A: *seš a jseš* 'you are' (by analogy to the regular form of all other verbs: *děláš* 'you make', *budeš* 'you will be', *víš* 'you know' . . .), while in FLCR, the same speaker switched to the SLC suffix, i.e., no. 2-1B: *jsi* 'you are'. Features of CC were found also in nominal suffixation, for example in 2A subject no. 6 used an instrumental construction *s kloboukama* (plural masculine) 'with the hats' which takes the old dual suffix *-ma* that spread to all genders in CC, whereas SLC differentiates gender (and applies suffix *-y*, i.e., *s klobouky*). In the data, the instrumental case of the plural, for reasons discussed earlier, did not occur in FLCR speech.

Phonology

A comparison of the FLCR and CC samples indicates that speech directed to a group of foreign students is marked by a phonemically more accurate SLC pronunciation than speech addressed to native Czechs. Simplification of consonantal clusters and reduction of vocalic quantity were two characteristic aspects of CC that stood in contrast to the FLCR samples in the analysis. Both of them were closely related to the speech rate.

Consonantal Clusters

The different rate of speech and subsequent different patterning of accentuation was responsible for the reduction of segments in consonantal sequences of the CC samples. In the slow FLCR speech all segments of the same clusters were pronounced:

no. 5-2B: *zvedl* 'he lifted'   no. 5-2A: *natáh ~napřáhl* 'he
                                                       stretched'

       —   no. 3-2A: *nalít* 'he got caught'
no. 6-2B: *sáhl* 'he touched'   vs.   no. 6-2A: *sáh* 'he touched'
           jsem 'I am'   *sem* 'I am'
no. 7-1B: *přijde* 'he'll come'   no. 7-1A: *přite* 'he'll come'

Vocalic Length

A noticeable reduction of the phonemic length of vowels was apparent in
the CC samples, especially in those of the fast speakers. Since instrumental quantitative measurements were not employed, observations were restricted to the most obvious occurrences. Such a case was seen in the
typical shortening of suffixal vowels, as in no. 3-1A: *maji* 'they have', no.
3-2A: *pobavim* 'I'll entertain', or no. 7-1A: *tak se ji ptaji* 'so they ask her',
where all the *i*'s were long in the Standard pronunciation.[6]

Furthermore, the contrastive analysis of materials illustrated that
FLCR speech entirely lacked phonological variations and morphopho-
nemic changes which are typical markers of the substandard CC speech.
Some of the main differences are listed below.

FLCR: *é* vs. CC: *ý* (*í*)

For the SLC vowel *é,* which occurred in the FLCR samples, free CC
speech commonly substitutes a variant *ý* or *í.* In the data the CC variant
was found in some root morphemes, e.g., no. 3-2A: *nalít'* 'he got caught',
or no. 8-2A: *zahlídl* 'he glimpsed', but predominantly in adjectival suffixes of CC speech, where FLCR samples illustrated a consistent choice
of the SLC *é* variant:

no. 1-1B: *nějaké jmeno* 'a name'   no. 1-1Aa: *nějaký jméno* ~
                                                    nějaké jméno
                           vs.
no. 1-2B: *svého známého* 'one's   no. 1-2Aa: *lhostejný zašklebení*
           acquaintance (accusative)'   'apathetic grimace'
no. 2-1B: *nějaké jméno* 'a name'   no. 2-1A: *nějaký lidi* 'some
                                                    people, (accusative)'
       —   no. 2-2A: *takový krásný počasí*
                                                    'such a nice weather'
       —   vs. no. 3-1A: *jaký číslo* 'what
                                                    number'

	všecko možný 'all possible'
	nějaký jméno 'a name'
no. 5-1B: *nějaké jméno* 'a name'	no. 5-1A: *ňaky meno* 'a name'
no. 5-2B: *známého* 'an acquaintance (accusative)'	no. 5-2A: *z takovýho očekávanýho úsměvu* 'from such an expected smile'

FLCR: *ý* versus CC: *ej*

The variant *ej* is one of the most widespread phenomena of CC, recorded already in medieval linguistic literature. The switch to this variant was found in the CC sample with only one subject, which was surprising. Most probably because subjects were particularly aware of the substandard nature of this variant, they refrained from using it when confronted with the tape recorder. Furthermore, in the data *ej* occurred only in final position, though its application in medial position is equally common in CC:

no. 5-2B: *druhý pán* 'the other gentleman'		no. 5-2A: *druhej pán* 'the other gentleman'
—		*udivenej obličej* 'surprised face'
—	vs.	*neurčitej škleb* 'uncertain grimace'
—		*takovej rozpačitej, rozpačitej pohled* 'a hesitant face'

FLCR: *i (í)* versus CC: *y (ý)*

The *y (ý)* variant which occurs in CC inflectional suffixes of adjectives and demonstrative pronouns, was observed in the CC speech of one subject. Very often, as happened in this experiment, the choice of the substandard variant causes a failure to provide environment for palatalization of the root morpheme final consonants, e.g., $k \rightarrow c$ and $t \rightarrow t'$ in our data:

no. 2-1A: *nějaký lidi* 'some people' (SLC: *nějací lidi)*
            ty se ptali 'those asked' (SLC: *ti se ptali,* pronounced [ťi])

FLCR: *o* versus CC: *vo*

Insertion of *v* before the root morpheme initial *o* is a typical aspect of CC speech. Subjects tried to "correct" their pronunciation to the Standard norm in their FLCR samples:

no. 5-2B: *omyl* 'mistake' vs.	no. 5-2A:	*vosel* ~ *obličej* 'ass ~ face'
	no. 2-1A:	*vona* ~ *ona* 'she'
	no. 2-2A:	*vodkašle* 'he clears his throat by coughing'
	no. 1-1Aa:	*vodvedeme* 'we'll lead away'
	no. 1-1A:	(*dovedeme* 'we'll lead into', here prefix *do-* instead of *o-*)

Speech Characteristics

As expected, without exception, all speakers talked louder and slower when addressing the group of foreign students. Though the voice intensity was not measured, speed of talk was recorded, and it was found that the relation between the CC and FLCR samples ranged from 161:73 words per minute (speaker no. 3) to 99:95 words per minute (speaker no. 7). A complete distribution is shown on table 4.

Pauses in speech (/) were definitely more numerous in FLCR than in the speech to the natives, and occurred consistently in positions of constituent boundaries. In CC, where the flow of words was generally fast, some speakers made only breath pauses such as no. 3-2A:

> *Šel pán po ulici a / z dálky už vidí přicházet pana Nováka. Říká si: ,,Ó, jé, Novák, to se s nim dobře pobavim."* ['There was a gentleman walking in the street and / from far already he sees approaching Mr. Novák. He says to himself, "Oh, gee, Novák, sure I'll have a nice chat with him." ']

Hesitation pauses and slips of the tongue were found in an abundant number in the CC speech, while they were almost null in the FLCR samples. This area, however, was not subject of the analysis at this point.

Discussion

In the beginning of this study, I made the assertion that speech directed to foreign language students constitutes an additional linguistic register in

TABLE 4. Rate of Speech, Number of Words per Minute

Story	Speaker															
	1		2		3		4		5		6		7		8	
	1	2	1	2	1	2	1	2	1	2	1	2	1	2	1	2
CC	98(93)	126(85)	140	150	161	131	113	100	118	144	133	144	139	99	123	114(155)
FLCR	71	73	78	111	73	60	61	85	80	81	100	76	111	95	84	63 (67)

Note: CC = Colloquial Czech; FLCR = Foreign Language Classroom Register; ( ) = additional recording of the story

the total repertoire of the communicative competence of a native speaker. I further asserted that, due to similarity in the speech situation caused by the unequal command of the language by the participants of the speech event, speech addressed to the foreigners in the classroom would show the same general characteristics as those observed in registers defined as Baby Talk (Ferguson 1964; Gleason 1971) and Foreigner Talk (Ferguson 1971, 1975; Clyne 1968). The results of the experiment confirmed the validity of this hypothesis to the following extent.

The organization of speech shows that, in a foreign language class-room situation, speakers make the linguistic choices in accordance to their judgement of what is easy, simple, and clear for the listener to hear, perceive, and comprehend. In doing so, they systematically pattern their speech to match the level of limited competence of the hearer. Phenomena belonging to this rubric include the application of emphatic stress and loud pitch in combination with the low rate of speech and high frequency of pauses. An attempt at clarity motivates the tendency for a pedantic differentiation of phonologically relevant features, such as correct pronunciation of phonological segments in consonantal clusters, or preservation of phonemic quantity in vowels.

Observations in syntax reveal that speakers manipulate linguistic variables which are at their disposal, with considerable delicacy, in response to their intuitive knowledge of grammatical simplicity. Since linguistic theory fails to provide us with an operational definition of what the notion of simplicity in language entails, the analytic work suffers from subjective assumptions. Data of the experiment give some cues that allow interpretation of simplification as a systematic phenomenon. The high ratio of short basic and coordinate sentences, found in the FLCR samples, necessarily bears on the high occurrence of simpler, i.e., less marked, and therefore more universal, constructions, such as base case nominal phrases and active present indicative verb phrases. The limited reduction in morphological complexity may be viewed as a by-product of the preference for a simple sentence structure rather than as a result of an inflectional modification as such.

Comparison of lexical choices in speech oriented to foreign students with those found in speech to natives, provides strong evidence that, in accordance with FTR, a conscious effort to use only basic vocabulary and, moreover, to use it with utmost economy, accompanies the selection of lexical items. Also the fact that idiomatic expressions are commonly paraphrased or substituted in samples of speech directed to foreign students, implies that the speakers actively control their vocabulary; however, because of the limitations of the samples in the present study, I am hesitant to draw the conclusion that a native speaker is fully aware of the intrinsic idioms of his speech.

The initial hypothesis of this paper, apart from the assertion that FLCR will incorporate features of simplified speech, posited that speech addressed to foreign students, furthermore, will be modeled also in such a manner as to comply with the variety of the language which is used as the medium of the classroom instruction, which was Standard Literary Czech in this experiment.

It is a well-known fact that educational programs do take advantage of the uniforming and integrative potential of a standardized variety of language all over the world, though there are large differences in the conditions and social contexts that define its status and influence the users' attitudes towards it. These factors are necessarily reflected in the degree to which the Standard language interferes with the FLCR. Literary Czech as a Standard which is not directly connected to speech of any social or regional community, is defined strictly functionally. In such a case a native speaker respects the rules for the appropriate usage of SLC in a classroom setting, and, subsequently, when talking to foreign students, he will simplify his speech only to the point where the simplification is permitted by rules of SLC.

Conclusion

The results of the study, though limited in scope and confined to one language, Czech, demonstrate that the original set of hypotheses, which aimed to define a Foreign Language Classroom Register in terms of (1) simplified speech as it is found in Foreigner Talk and Baby Talk, and (2) the language of classroom instruction, constitute a feasible guideline for the description of such a linguistic register, or, in an extended sense, for the description of various forms of Foreigner Talk constrained by specific social conditions. For the general understanding of linguistic simplification, or the overall tensions of linguistic systems, the identification of the competing forces in language is of some importance, as, for example, the existence of SLC rules in the study prevented an analysis of a mere Czech version of Foreigner Talk. Returning to Ferguson's hypothesis (1971) that relates a simplifying register and the process of pidginization, we can view the interactions observed in the present experiment, as one of the possible natural processes that block the advance of linguistic change by which Foreigner Talk may, under favorable social conditions, become an incipient pidgin.

410   RELATED ASPECTS

Notes

I wish to express my gratitude to Professor Charles A. Ferguson, whose interest initiated this study, and whose invaluable comments and suggestions helped in its completion.

1. In the Czech linguistic terminology the standardized code of Czech is referred to as *spisovný jazyk* (literary language) or *spisovná čeština* (literary Czech). Thus, the present term Standard Literary Czech should be taken as a compromise between the English and the Czech linguistic conventions.
2. The official description of the SLC code is published and from time to time revised by the Academy (see *Pravidla českého pravopisu* 1968); the prescribed pronunciation of SLC is provided for by special manuals (see Hála 1955).
3. By and large, spoken Czech is a sporadically described and vaguely defined unit. In linguistic literature, the terminology referring to this variety of Czech ranges from a "Spoken Form of Literary Czech" or "All-National Common Czech" to "Common Czech" and "Colloquial Czech." The terms overlap from one analysis to another; therefore, specific qualifications by each author are needed (cf. Havránek 1942; Kopečný 1949; Bělič 1958; Trávníček 1958). Systematic work on colloquial Czech has been done by Kučera (1961, 1973), and especially by Kovtun (1972) who is currently preparing an exhaustive description of CC for publication in the United States.
4. The vocabulary reduction in FLCR is carried out only to the point where it does not conflict with grammatical rules of SLC. For example, in Czech, the equivalent for the English word "I know" is either a transitive verb *znám* or an intransitive verb *vím*. Though we have seen the verb *vím* used in both meanings in our CC data—which is in agreement with its common application in carefree speech—this type of "lexical simplification" was not carried over to the FLCR speech (See no. 3-1A: *víš jméno* 'do you know the name' versus no. 3-1B: *znáš jméno* 'Do you know the name.').
5. For a detailed description of the domains of morphological and phonological differences between Colloquial Czech and Standard Literary Czech see Kovtun (1972) and Kučera (1973).
6. Occasionally, a vowel was dropped completely, as in no. 5-1A: *ňáký* 'some' versus no. 5-1B: *nějaký* 'some'.

References

Agheyisi, Rebecca N. "West African Pidgin English: Simplification and Simplicity." Ph.D. dissertation, Stanford University, 1971.

Bělič, Jaromí. "Vznik hovorové češtiny a její poměr k češtině spisovné" [The origin of colloquial Czech and its relation to literary Czech]. Československé přednášky pro IV. Mezinárodní sjezd slavistů v Moskvě, pp. 59–71. Praha: Československá akademie věd, 1958.

Bellack, Arno A., et al. *The Language of the Classroom.* New York: Teachers College Press, 1966.

Broen, Patricia Ann. *The Verbal Environment of the Language-Learning Child.* ASHA Monograph no. 17. Washington: American Speech and Hearing Association, 1972.

Cazden, Courtney B., et al. *Functions of Language in the Classroom.* New York: Teachers College Press, 1972.

Clyne, Michael. "Zum Pidgin-Deutsch der Gastarbeiter." *Z.f. Mundartforschung* 34 (1968):130–39.

Ferguson, Charles A. "Baby Talk in Six Languages." *American Anthropologist* 66, special issue (1964): pt. 2, pp. 103–14.

———. "Absence of Copula and the Notion of Simplicity: A Study of Normal Speech, Baby Talk, Foreigner Talk, and Pidgins." *Pidginization and Creolization in Language,* edited by Dell Hymes, 141–50. Cambridge: At the University Press, 1971.

———. "Toward a Characterization of English Foreigner Talk." Paper read at the Third International Congress of Applied Linguistics; August 1972, Copenhagen. Printed in *Anthropological Linguistics* 17, no. 1 (1975):1–14.

Gleason, Jean Berko. "Code Switching in Children's Language." Unpublished. 1971.

Goldman-Eisler, F. *Psycholinguistics. Experiments in Spontaneous Speech.* London: Academic Press, 1968.

Hála, Bohuslav, ed. *Výslovnost spisovné češtiny, její zaklady a pravidla I* [The pronunciation of literary Czech: Its principles and rules I]. Praha: Československá akademie věd, 1955.

Halliday, Michael A. K. "The Users and Uses of Language." *Readings in the Sociology of Language,* edited by Joshua A. Fishman. 2d ed. The Hague: Mouton, 1970.

Havránek, Bohuslav. "K funkčnímu rozřstvenú spisovného jazyka." [On functional stratification of the literary language]. *Časopis pro moderní filologii* 28 (1942):409–16.

———. *Studie o spisovném jazyce* [A study of the literary language]. Praha: Nakladetelství Československé akademie věd, 1963.

Henzl, Vera M. "Foreigner Talk in the Classroom." *IRAL* 17, no. 2 (1979):159–67.

Hronek, Jiří. *Obecná čeština* [Common Czech]. Praha: Universita Karlova, 1972.

Kisseberth, Charles W. "The Interaction of Phonological Rules and the Polarity of Language." Paper presented at the Indiana University Conference on Rule Ordering, Bloomington, Indiana, April, 1973.

Kopečný, František. "Spisovný jazyk a jeho forma hovorová." [The literary language and its colloquial form]. *Naše řeč* 33 (1949):14–22.

Kovtun, Emil and Micklesen, Lew R. *Textbook for Beginning Czech with an Appendix on Colloquial Czech.* Seattle: University of Washington, 1972.

Kučera, Henry. "Phonemic Variations of Spoken Czech." *Word* 11 (1955):575–602.

————. *The Phonology of Czech*. The Hague: Mouton, 1961.

————. "Language Variability, Rule Interdependency and the Grammar of Czech." *Language Inquiry* 4 (1973):499–521.

Marvan, Jiří. "K některým morfologickým otázkám diftongu ej v obecné češtině v konfrontaci se stavem staročeským" [On some morphological aspects of the diphthong ej in common Czech in relation to its position in old Czech]. *Listy filologické* 87 (1964):76–85.

Phillips, Juliet R. "Formal Characteristics of Speech which Mothers Address to Their Young Children." Ph.D. dissertation, Johns Hopkins University, 1970.

————. "Mothers' Speech to Young Children: Syntax and Vocabulary." Unpublished. 1972.

Poldauf, Ivan, and Šprunk, Karel. *Čeština jazyk cizí* [Czech as a foreign language]. Praha: Státní pedagogické nakladatelství, 1968.

Pravidla českého pravopisu [The orthographic dictionary of Czech]. Praha: Nakladatelství Československé akademie věd, 1968.

Snow, Catherine E. "Mothers' Speech to Children Learning Language." *Child Development* 43 (1972):549–65.

Trávníček, František. *Úvod do českého jazyka* [Introduction to the Czech language]. Praha: Státní pedagogické nakladatelství, 1958.

Ure, Jean and Ellis, Jeffrey. "Register in Descriptive Linguistics and Linguistic Sociology." Unpublished. 1971.

Wilkins, D. A. *Linguistics in Language Teaching*. Cambridge, Mass.: MIT Press, 1972.

Foreigner Talk and Conversational Interaction

Barbara F. Freed

At a recent learned conference, so the story goes, a distinguished group of scientists was seated at dinner, prior to the post prandial presentation of scientific papers. One of the group. an American, turned to his Oriental dinner partner and politely asked "Likee soupee?" The Oriental nodded assent. When dinner was over, the Oriental left the table to give the first paper of the evening. It was delivered in perfect English. Following his presentation, he returned to his seat, turned to his American partner and politely asked: "Likee speechee?"

Foreigner Talk as defined by Ferguson (1975, p. 1) is a register of simplified speech used by speakers of a language to outsiders who are felt to have very limited command of the language or no knowledge of it at all. It may vary in terms of its realization from slight to full depending on the speakers' assessment of the addressees' status and level of competence in the language. (Ferguson and DeBose 1976, p. 8)

It has been assumed that the characteristics of Foreigner Talk result from the linguistic limitations of the foreign listener. While this is in large part true, linguistic limitations are only one of the attributes of the foreign listener to which native speakers respond. If this were not the case, the features of all speech registers used with different categories of limited listeners would show little or no variation. However, as I and others have reported elsewhere (Freed 1978a, 1978c, 1980, 1981), speech to at least two categories of limited listeners, young children and foreign adults, is not totally overlapping. As Roger Brown has postulated, there appear to be distinctions made by native speakers in clusters of simplifying/clarifying features and expressive/affective features used in speech to different categories of listeners. Foreign adults and native adults, despite differences in linguistic competence may share the attributes of relatively equal status and presumably equal cognitive sophistication. By contrast, young children and foreign adults differ on just these dimensions. Conse-

This article is a slightly revised version of a paper presented at the March, 1979 TESOL Convention, Boston, Massachusetts. Reprinted by permission of the author.

quently Foreigner Talk has been shown to approximate caretaker speech syntactically but not functionally.

The purposes of this article are twofold. First to describe the characteristics of Foreigner Talk which have emerged from my recent study of conversational interaction between native speakers of English and foreign listeners, and secondly, to demonstrate that the features of this register emerge through a complex set of factors which include the functional meaning of utterances within a conversational context as well as perceptions of the foreigner's proficiency in English.

The study compares the speech adjustment made by eleven native speakers of English when in conversation with eleven nonnative speakers (each of varying proficiency in English) to their speech when in casual conversation with a native speaker of English.

Both native and foreign speakers were graduate or undergraduate students who had volunteered to participate in a culture and conversation program which related in no way to the study. The conversational pairs subsequently agreed, however, to let me tape some of their conversations. Each pair met at least twice. Their meetings took place in a variety of settings, all of their own choosing. Despite some cultural variation, all were from roughly equivalent social backgrounds and had similar status as students.

Approximately 150 utterances of speech to both foreign and native listeners were coded and analyzed, thereby establishing the properties of Foreigner Talk and what I have termed "Native Talk"—casual conversation between native speakers (Freed 1978a). The respective adjustments in each corpus were then compared syntactically and functionally.

Syntactic Analyses

Independent analyses of the Foreigner Talk and Native Talk corpora yielded results which on some measures were strikingly similar, while on others significantly different.

As shown in table 1, speech to two categories of foreign listeners, beginner and advanced speakers, as well as to native listeners is characteristically well formed.[1] The most striking finding is that there are no ungrammatical utterances (i.e., structurally or semantically anomalous) and almost none so slurred or garbled that they are unanalyzable. (Statistical comparisons between speech to foreign listeners and native listeners apply in tables 1–4.)

Within the tolerance granted to colloquial speech, over one-half of all utterances directed to all listener types are well-formed, grammatically

Freed 415

TABLE 1. Analysis of Well-Formedness (in mean percentage)

Utterance	Native Speaker to Beginner Foreigner	Native Speaker to Advanced Foreigner	Native Speaker to Native Speaker
Uanalyzable	.01	.01	.01
Ungrammatical	.00	.00	.00
Grammatically acceptable	.60	.57	.70**
Stock expressions	.16	.18	.12*
Fragments	.24	.25	.17**

* p < .05
** p < .01

acceptable utterances, containing at least one (and sometimes more than one) complete English sentence. However, as table 1 shows, significantly more utterances of this type are addressed to the native listener than to either group of foreign listeners. On the average, 58 percent of all Foreigner Talk utterances as compared to 70 percent of Native Talk utterances are of this type. This is so whether the foreigners are beginner or advanced speakers. Compared another way, significantly more stereotyped stock expressions—"mmm," "uhuh," "really?" and fragments, isolated sentence constituents such as "for three years," or "the what?" are used in conversation with foreign listeners than with native adults. The importance of this distinction will be made clear when the speech samples are compared functionally.

In addition to analysis of well-formedness, each well-formed, grammatically acceptable sentence was analyzed for syntactic complexity. As shown in table 2, sentences addressed to native listeners are, on every measure, more complex syntactically than those addressed to foreign listeners. Moreover, not only are there significant differences between speech to native listeners and to foreigners listeners, but there are also significant differences between a native speaker's speech to beginner and advanced foreigners.

The average sentence addressed to all foreign listeners is shorter both lexically and propositionally than that addressed to a native listener. For example, when beginner and advanced groups are averaged, there are roughly 1.5 S-nodes or main verbs in the average Foreigner Talk sentence, compared to somewhat more than 2 S-nodes in the average Native Talk sentence. There are roughly eight words per sentence in the average Foreigner Talk sentence and approximately twelve in the average sentence directed to native listeners. Not only are Foreigner Talk sentences shorter and propositionally less complex, but more simple sentences (that is sentences with only 1 main verb) are addressed to foreign listeners than to native listeners. When the percentage of sentences with only 1 S-node is compared, significantly more are addressed to both beginner and advanced foreigners than to native listeners. It can be concluded that native speakers not only reduce the number of propositions and words in the average sentence when talking to foreigners, but they also significantly limit the number of multiclausal sentences.

TABLE 2. Analysis of Syntactic Complexity (in mean percentage)

Sentence Complexity	Native Speaker to Beginner Foreigner	Native Speaker to Advanced Foreigner	Native Speaker to Native Speaker
% S-nodes/average sentence	1.38	1.81‡†	2.24***
MLSW (mean length of sentence in words)	6.74	9.66‡	12.13***
% of sentences with 1 S-node	.71	.55†	.41***
MLSW of 1 S-node sentences	5.34	6.10	6.90*

Note: Statistical comparisons of the difference between natives' speech to beginner foreigners and advanced foreigners
  † p < .05   * p < .05
  ‡ p < .01   ***p < .001
  ‡† p < .001

As table 2 shows, the less proficient the foreign listener (the beginner group) the greater the syntactic reductions. As the foreigners' proficiency in English increases, the characteristic properties of Foreigner Talk diminish. These findings suggest that despite the opening anecdote, linguistic adjustments are not solely attributable to a foreigner's "foreignness," but rather they are fine-tuned to perceived linguistic sophistication.

In addition to analyses of syntactic complexity, each well-formed sentence in both corpora was analyzed according to surface sentence type as displayed in table 3.

While the declarative sentence was the most frequently used sentence type in Foreigner Talk and Native Talk, there was a significant difference in the relative proportions of each. Column 1 of table 3 represents the means of the first and second meeting of the conversational pairs. When considered together, 69 percent of all Foreigner Talk sentences were declarative, compared to an overwhelming 97 percent of Native Talk sentences. By contrast, interrogatives (yes-no and *wh-* questions) occurred with greater frequency in Foreigner Talk than in Native Talk. Again in column one, 25 percent of all Foreigner Talk sentences, but only 2 percent of all Native Talk sentences were questions. When the first and second meetings are considered together, the relative proportion of *wh-* and yes-no questions are roughly equivalent. Note, however, when data for the second meeting alone are considered, as in columns two and three, the relative proportion of *wh*-questions diminishes. Independent comparisons of the first and second meetings has shown that for *wh*-questions there is a significant difference between the first and second meeting. On all other measures there was no reliable difference in the properties of Foreigner Talk between the first and second meeting (Freed 1978*a*).

TABLE 3. Analysis of Surface Sentence Type (in mean percentage)

Sentence Type	Native Speaker to Foreign Speakers (1st and 2d)[a] meetings)	Native Speaker to Beginner Foreigner (2d meeting)	Native Speaker to Advanced Foreigner (2d meeting)	Native Speaker to Native Speaker
Declarative	.68	.71	.73	.97***
Wh-question	.11	.07	.07	.01**
Yes-no question	.14	.11	.15	.01**
Imperative	.03	.03	.01	.01
Deixis	.02	.03	.01	.00
Wh deixis	.01	.01	.00	.00

** p < .01
*** p < .001
a. Since data for speech to beginner and advanced foreign speakers are from the second meeting of the pair they will not necessarily equal the means for both meetings grouped together as presented in column 1.

In contrast to declaratives and questions, the proportions of imperative and deictic sentences used in conversation with all groups of listeners were almost identical. Furthermore, as will be clear when examined functionally, even these slight differences decrease. Interestingly, unlike indices of syntactic complexity, measures of surface sentence type do not vary as a function of the foreign listener's ability in English.

Discussion of Foreigner Talk inevitably raises the question of simplicity. Therefore, an effort was made to compare the transformational complexity of several surface sentence types in each corpus. As just described, the vast majority of all sentences in both Foreigner Talk and Native Talk were declarative in form and retained in their surface structure a relatively close representation of base structure form with standard subject, verb, object order. While this was the case, the declarative sentences exchanged between native speakers did display more stylistic transformations such as dative and particle movement. There was also more passivization in Native Talk. Furthermore, as previously stated, Native Talk sentences were more commonly multiclausal.

Deformations from canonical shape appeared in both corpora in the imperative formation where the subject *you* and the auxiliary *will* were obligatorily deleted. Note though, there were a few instances in Foreigner Talk where the subject *you* was retained before the imperative: "*You* call me tonight!" This phenomenon did not appear in Native Talk.

Other deformations occurred as a result of obligatory subject-auxiliary inversion and *wh*-replacement and preposing in question formation as shown in table 4.

TABLE 4. Analysis of Transformational Complexity of Yes-no and
Wh-Questions (in mean percentage)

Question Type	Native Speaker to Foreign Speaker (1st and 2d meetings)	Native Speaker to Native Speaker
Wh-Question	.11	.01**
% *Wh*-Questions with no fronting of *Wh*-particle	.01	.002
Yes-no questions	.14	.01**
% of yes-no questions with no subject-aux inversion and *do* and/or *you* deletion	.05	.01**

** p < .01

The 2 percent of Native Talk questions almost always exhibited subject-auxiliary inversion as well as *wh*-replacement and preposing ("Were you in France for a long time?" or "Where can I buy a tape recorder?"). By contrast a significant portion of the yes-no questions and a nonsignificant but noticeable portion of *wh*-questions in Foreigner Talk did not exhibit standard question formation.

As table 4 shows, 1 percent of Foreigner Talk *wh*-questions compared to a mere .0002 of the Native Talk questions did not prepose the *wh* particle. Canonical form was thus retained by keeping the *wh* particle at the end of the sentence ("You're studying what?" "You were afraid of what?" "You will return to your country when?").

While such instances were not significantly different between the two speech samples the tendency deserves comment. It is possible that native speakers unconsciously notice the deformation caused by moving the *wh* particle to the front of the sentence and monitor this by sometimes avoiding preposing the *wh* particle.

This claim is reinforced by the fact that native speakers occasionally monitor their use of *wh*-questions by following them immediately with yes-no questions: "How is the food there? Is the food very good?" Sometimes this change takes place mid-utterance; "How much. . .Did you pay a lot?"

While this tendency to change from *wh* to yes-no questions was also not reliably different in the two corpora, the slight inclination to do so supports the above hypotheses that native speakers do notice the complexity of *wh*-questions and monitor it by failing to prepose the *wh* particle. Another explanation for this tendency has been offered by Hatch (1976) who suggests that the change is a function of the native speaker's effort to limit the demand placed on the foreigner's response. That is, it is easier to answer a yes-no question than a *wh*-question.

Yes-no question formation was significantly different in the two corpora. Five percent of all yes-no questions in Foreigner Talk but only .01 percent of yes-no Native Talk questions preserved canonical shape and signalled the question by a final rising intonation. ("You are studying English here?" "It's too loud to sleep?"). In addition to ignoring obligatory subject-auxiliary inversion, there was sometimes no insertion of the dummy auxiliary *do* when the sentence had no auxiliary. Furthermore the subject *you* was sometimes deleted altogether. That is, the question, "Do you want to come to my house?" was realized as "Want to come to my house?"[2]

To summarize, on many of the measures thus far considered, speech to foreign listeners differs significantly from that to another native listener. In addition to reduced syntactic complexity, native speakers distinguish between conversations with native and foreign listeners in their selection of surface sentence types. They use more declaratives with natives and more questions when in conversation with foreigners. When analyzed functionally, however, these distinctions take on another light and are clarified on the basis of conversational constraints.

Functional Analysis

A gross functional analysis of the conversational meaning in context of various utterance and sentence types was also carried out. Since syntactic descriptions cannot detect relationships between utterances within the communicative context, we decided to look, as far as possible, for the functional intent of an utterance as distinguished from its surface form. Since no technical description of functional use presently exists, this was an inferential interpretation of the data based on audio tapes alone. No quantative analysis was computed.

There emerged from this method of analysis ten functional categories to which an utterance could potentially be assigned. These have been reported elsewhere (Freed 1978a, 1981) and are listed in the appendix. For purposes of this article only the major categories will be discussed: information exchange, conversation continuation, and clarification.

Information exchange, a broad category including facts, ideas and opinions, was identified as the primary communicative intent in conversations between both groups of adults: native and foreign alike. In neither case were conversations topically constrained, but rather, they pertained to a wide range of topics to which both participants could contribute equally. Despite the foreign listener's limitations in English, conversations were not characterized by "here and nowness" as is partially evidenced by the vanishingly small proportions of deictic utterances. Moreover, unlike much child-directed speech, there were essentially no action-directives, either direct commands realized as imperatives or indirect requests in the form of questions or declaratives.

While the declarative sentence was the most common vehicle for sharing information, questions, which occurred with greater frequency in Foreigner Talk, assumed the functional role of "information elicitors." They served to nominate topics and solicit information from reticent speakers. Imperatives, while few in number in both corpora, were not, when analyzed for functional meaning in context, direct commands at all. They served rather to supply information as to procedures to follow ("Cover the bread, then let it rise for three hours"; "Walk down Spruce Street. Turn right and look for the big white house."). No response to these imperative forms was anticipated; indeed, such responses would have been bizarre and inappropriate.

As has been previously noted by Hatch and her colleagues (Gough and Hatch 1975; Hatch, Shapira, and Gough 1978), conversation between Americans and foreign adults, as in conversations between native speakers, covers a wide range of topics. There were a small number of explicitly referential forms referring to the immediate environment, but again, when analyzed for meaning in context the few deictic utterances made appropriate contributions to the exchange of information. ("That's the bathroom." "That's a picture of my mom."). In this respect, native speakers relate conversationally to foreigners as they do to other natives. By focusing on the sharing of information they reveal an attitude or relationship to the foreign listener that cannot be inferred by the reduced syntactic complexity of their utterances.

In addition to sharing information, two other major functional intents were identified: conversation continuation and clarification. Both categories facilitated the primary intent of information exchange.

In principle, the responsibility of maintaining a conversation is shared equally by both participants in that conversation. In Foreigner Talk, however, it appears that many of the native speakers' utterances were motivated by the need to keep the conversation going. Stock expressions, which were shown in table 1 to be more characteristic of Foreigner Talk than Native Talk, were interpreted as serving this function. These *conversation continuers* conveyed attention and interest as the foreign speakers, sometimes laboriously, constructed a phrase. Questions, too, conveyed interest at the same time as they helped to keep conversation alive. They served to elicit a new bit of information that might not otherwise be forthcoming from the foreign speakers. Questions thus served simultaneously and often indistinguishably to maintain two roles. They were both information elicitors and conversation continuers.

Native speakers in conversation with each other are sometimes called upon to clarify their speech. Such *clarifications* are often expansions. Syntactic analysis revealed that there were significantly more fragments in Foreigner Talk than Native Talk. Functional analysis showed why. Analysis of functional meaning in context revealed that many of these fragments were motivated by a need to clarify speech. A lack of comprehension clue—a puzzled expression, blank stare, or direct question—frequently resulted in fragments which were partial repetitions of a previous misunderstood utterance; there were often synonyms of analytic paraphrases. For example,

Native Speaker (NS): "Do you go to the bookstore a lot?"
Foreign Speaker (FS): "Bookstore?"
NS: "Bookstore. Books. The place to buy books. Do you go there?"

Misunderstanding was not always on the part of the foreign speaker. Sometimes a native speaker did not understand a foreign speaker's utterance. Such misunderstandings were often signaled by the native speaker's imitating some portion of the foreigner's utterance which the native speaker had not understood. In a conversation concerning American television cartoons the following exchange occurred:

FS: "I like White Snow and Shop Men."
NS: "White Snow and Shop Men?"
FS: "Yes, Seven Shop Men."
NS: "Shop Men? Shop Men?"
FS: "White Snow and Seven Shop Men."
NS: "Oh, White Snow, I mean, Snow White and the Seven Short, and the Seven Dwarfs!"

A functional comparison of Native Talk and Foreigner Talk has led us to conclude that native speakers relate conversationally to foreign speakers in many of the same ways they do with any other native speaker. This is so regardless of the foreigner's proficiency in English. The primary intent of all conversation is to exchange information. This is accomplished primarily through the declarative commentary form. Beyond information exchange, native speakers in their conversations with foreign speakers have two other concerns: comprehension and the continued flow of conversation. There are thus many questions which function to express interest and to elicit information. Conversation with foreigners is also punctuated by the frequent use of fragments and stock expressions which are less common in conversation with other native speakers. These forms complement the exchange of information by expressing interest and attention, and by clarifying misunderstood speech. Declaratives, questions, and fragments are thus closely related when analyzed for meaning in context. All three contribute to the exchange of information in Foreigner Talk. This motive is identical to that of Native Talk; only the means are different.

Such inferential analysis of the speaker's intent suggests that conversational intent might be as responsible for the features of Foreigner Talk as are the linguistic deficiencies of the listener. By comparing syntactic and functional analyses, it is possible to see that native speakers' adjustments are motivated by an interacting set of evaluations of their listeners. Unconscious judgments appear to be made and speech is adjusted in different ways to the different characteristics of the listener. While listener fluency determines to some extent the nature of linguistic adjustments, both attributes influence the communicative devices selected in speaking with different categories of listeners.

Syntactic analysis suggests that native speakers modify their speech in response to the linguistic limitations of the foreign listener. Syntactic analysis does not, however, totally account for the properties of Foreigner Talk, for it does not consider the relationship of the Foreigner Talk utterance to the total communicative situation. By contrast, a functional description of Foreigner Talk and Native Talk suggests that despite limitations of syntactic complexity, native speakers relate to foreign speakers much as they do to other adults. The foreign speaker is treated as a conversational peer with whom one engages in conversation for the purpose of exchanging ideas. To achieve the goal of information exchange, native speakers will, when conversing with foreigners, resort to clarification and continuation devices not needed in talk with most native speakers of a language. Functionally, though, these devices are directed to the major purpose of the conversational interchange: the sharing of thoughts, ideas, and attitudes.

In sum, it can be concluded that despite adjustments native speakers make to the foreigners' linguistic limitations, on a social level conversational interaction leads them to respond to the foreign listener as an adult with cognitive and social presence.

Appendix: Functional Categories

1. *Information exchange*—utterances which serve to communicate information in the broadest sense: facts, opinions, ideas. This category incorporates a wide range of potential statements that have been defined elsewhere as assertions, modulations, expressions of mental state, and descriptions.

2. *Conversation continuers*—utterances utilized to signify attention and interest or to maintain the flow of conversation.

3. *Clarification*—utterances used to elaborate or explain the meaning of a previous utterance. Clarifications appear in the form of repetitions, imitations, synonyms and analytic paraphrases. They are frequently prompted by a verbal or nonverbal lack of comprehension clue.

4. *Correction*—utterances which repair another's incorrect fact or form. They often, but not always, occur in "correction-invitation formats" (Schegloff, Jefferson, and Sacks 1977). They are distinguished from clarifications to the extent that clarifications were contextually analyzed to be motivated by a need to isolate or establish meaning; correction was then a secondary result. Corrections are also distinguished from word search responses.

5. *Contribution*—utterances which supply an unknown lexical item or grammatical form. Contributions are usually provided in response to direct or indirect requests (obvious word searches), but sometimes they are predictions or foreshadowings prompted by a pause or hesitation.

6. *Conversation support*—empathetic utterances which convey understanding or support for the partner's state or situation.

7. *Action-directive*—utterances which serve as direct or indirect requests for behavior or verbalization.

8. *Reported speech*—utterances which convey a third party's speech. Such utterances are always in the indirect discourse.

9. *Self-directed speech*—utterances which are self-directed and which call for no response from the conversational partner.

10. *Language instruction*—utterances which serve an explicitly instructive function. That is, where it is clear that the speaker is trying to "teach." Indirectly corrections, clarifications, and contributions serve an instructional function, but their primary intent is interpreted otherwise.

Notes

1. The distinction between beginner and advanced foreigners is based on an analysis of the foreign subjects' speech. This consisted primarily of a measure

of mean length of utterance in words (MLUW) of twenty-five of their utterances. The MLUW was based only on those utterances which were at least one complete sentence in length and excluded imitations and repetitions.

2. It may be the case as Zobl (1977) points out that yes-no questions which exhibit no subject-auxiliary inversion and are signalled by rising intonation might be, when addressed to native speakers, sociolinguistically marked. That is, the informality of a situation may elicit such terms. Such is probably not the case in conversation between natives and foreigners, even in this study where the conversations were not chance encounters on the street. Thus, it is possible that the yes-no questions which display no subject-auxiliary inversion and deletion of *do* and/or *you* cannot be compared at all because the motivation for their use is different: reduced complexity in one case and informality in the other.

References

Brown, R. Introduction to *Talking to Children*, edited by C. E. Snow and C. A. Ferguson. Cambridge: At the University Press, 1977.

———. *Speech Register Grant Proposal*. Cambridge, Mass.: Harvard University Press, 1978.

Campbell, C.; Gaskill, W.; and Brook, S. V. "Some Aspects of Foreigner Talk." In *Proceedings of the Los Angeles Second Language Forum*, edited by C. A. Henning. Los Angeles: University of California at Los Angeles, 1977.

Chaudron, Craig. "A Descriptive Model of Discourse in the Corrective Treatment of Learners' Errors." *Language Learning* 27, no 1. (1977):29–46.

Ferguson, C. A. "Absence of Copula and the Notion of Simplicity. In *Pidginization and Creolization of Language*, edited by D. Hymes. Cambridge: At the University Press, 1971.

———. "Toward a Characterization of English Foreigner Talk." *Anthropological Linguistics* 17 (1975):1–14.

———. "Simplified Registers, Broken Language and Gastarbeiterdeutsch." In *German in Contact with Other Languages*, edited by C. Molony et al. Kronberg Lts.: Scripton Verlag, 1977*a*.

———. "Baby Talk as a Simplified Register." In *Talking to Children*, edited by C. E. Snow and C. A. Ferguson. Cambridge: At the University Press, 1977*b*.

Ferguson, C. A., and DeBose, C. "Simplified Registers, Broken Language and Pidginization." In *Pidgin and Creole Linguistics*, edited by A. Valdman. Bloomington: Indiana University Press, 1976.

Freed, B. "Foreigner Talk: A Study of Speech Adjustments Made by Native Speakers of English in Conversation with Non-Native Speakers." Ph.D. dissertation, University of Pennsylvania, 1978*a*.

———. "Functional Use of Language and the Second Language Classroom." Paper presented at the Meeting of the American Association of Applied Linguistics, Boston, Massachusetts, December, 1978*b*.

———. "Speech Adjustments to Perceived Listener Attributes." Paper presented at the winter meeting of the Linguistic Society of America, Boston, Massachusetts, 1978*c*.

———. "Talking to Foreigners Versus Talking to Children, Similarities and Differences." In *Research in Second Language Acquisition*, edited by R. C. Scarcella and S. D. Krashen. Rowley, Mass.: Newbury House Publishers, 1980.

———. "Foreigner Talk, Baby Talk, Native Talk." *International Journal of Sociology of Language*, 28 (1981):19–39.

Gaies, S. J. "'The Syntax of ESL Teachers' Classroom Language: A Preliminary Report Paper." Presented at the Summer Conference on Second Language Learning, Oswego, New York, July 16, 1976.

Gaskill, W. "Correction in Adult Native Speaker, Non-Native Speaker Conversation." Paper presented at the TESOL Conference, Mexico City, April 1978.

Gough, J., and Hatch, E. "The Importance of Input Data in Second Language Acquisition Studies." *Language Learning* 25 (1975):297–338.

Hatch, E. "Discourse Analysis and Second Language Acquisition." Paper presented at NAFSA Convention, San Diego, California, 1976.

Hatch, E.; Shapira, R.; and Gough, J. "Foreigner Talk Discourse." *ITL: Review of Applied Linguistics*, 39–40 (1978):39–60.

Hatch, E., and Wagner-Gough, J. "Explaining Sequence and Variation in Second Language Acquisition." In *Papers in Second Language Acquisition*, edited by H. D. Brown. *Language Learning;* special issue no. 4 (January 1976).

Henzel, V. M. "Linguistic Register of Foreign Language Instruction." *Language Learning* 23 (1974):207–22.

Hymes, D. "Models of the Interaction of Language and Social Life." In *Directions in Sociolinguistics: The Ethnography of Communication*, edited by J. J. Gumperz and D. Hymes. New York: Holt, Rinehart, and Winston, 1972.

Labov, W. *Sociolinguistic Patterns*. Philadelphia: University of Pennsylvania Press, 1977.

Long, M. H. "Input, Interaction, and Second Language Acquisition." Paper presented at the New York Academy of Sciences Conference on Native Language and Foreign Language Acquisition, New York, January 15–16, 1981*a*.

———. "Questions in Foreigner Talk Discourse." *Language Learning* 31 no. 1, June 1981*b*.

Molony, C.; Zobl, H.; and Stölting, W. (HRSG). *Deutsch in Kontakt mit anderen Sprachen* [Germany in contact with other languages]. Kronberg Lts.: Scriptor Verlag, 1977.

Newport, E.; Gleitman, H.; and Gleitman, L. "Mother, I'd Rather do it Myself:

Some Effects and Noneffects of Maternal Speech Style." In *Talking to Children,* edited by C. E. Snow and C. A. Ferguson. Cambridge: At the University Press, 1977.

Sachs, H.; Schegloff, E.; and Jefferson, G. A. "Simplest Systematics for the Organization of Turn-taking for Conversation." *Language* 50 (1974):696–785.

Schegloff, E.; Jefferson, G. A.; and Sachs, H. "The preference for Self-correction in the Organization of Repair in Conversation." *Language* 53 (1977):361–82.

Snow, C. E., and Ferguson, C. A., eds. *Talking to Children: Language Input and Acquisition.* Cambridge: At the University Press, 1977.

Zobl, M. "The Forms of Interference. Some Evidence for a Complexity Metric in Foreign Language Learning." In *German in Contact with Other Languages,* edited by C. Molony, H. Zobl, and W. Stölting. Kronbert Lts.: Scriptor Verlag, 1977.

A Descriptive Model of Discourse in the Corrective Treatment of Learners' Errors

Craig Chaudron

A number of recent studies (Allwright 1975; Fanselow 1974; Holley and King 1971) have brought attention to the role of oral corrections of learners' errors in second language instruction. The opposing positions in regard to the source of learners' errors—the interlanguage–developmental–hypothesis-testing position (Corder 1967; Selinker 1972; Dulay and Burt 1974*a*, 1974*b*, and many others), and the earlier habit-formation position (described in Rivers 1964; Politzer 1965; and discussion in Dulay and Burt 1974*b*)—have both largely avoided the analysis or description of the target language input during second language learning.

For either position, it should be clear that the specific reactions of the target language speaker to the learner's correct and incorrect utterances, that is, the ways in which the learner's utterances are rejected or reformulated, can contribute to the individual learner's rate and manner of learning. While discussing general learning tasks, Annett (1969) describes three dimensions or functions of feedback, or "knowledge of results": (1) incentive—stimulating increased effort (motivating), (2) reinforcement—promoting maintenance of the learner's responses, and (3) information—contributing to changes in responses. Rarely will corrective feedback fulfill only one of these dimensions. The habit-formation position has concentrated, however, on reinforcement alone; the developmental position has, in contrast, virtually disregarded the role of feedback, sometimes merely suggesting that the teacher should provide more information.

Although some investigators (Cohen 1975; George 1972; and Paulston and Bruder 1976) have entertained the possibility of withholding correction altogether under certain conditions, it is not likely that this approach can be maintained through all instruction. The form of corrective feedback and the ways in which teachers' corrections can play a role

Reprinted by permission of the publisher and the author from *Language Learning* 27, no. 1 (1977): 29–46.

in instruction have especially been investigated by researchers outside the field of language instruction (Zahorik 1968, 1970*a,* 1970*b;* Hughes 1973). But language teachers, more so than many, are likely to benefit from a better understanding of when and how to correct learners' errors. An adequate *description* of the options available to the teacher/speaker of the target language at the "crisis points" (Allwright 1975) when errors are "corrected" would aid the further study of which corrective treatments are most likely to be motivating, reinforcing, and/or informative.

With the goal of such a description in mind, a study was undertaken in three teachers' grade eight and nine French immersion classrooms (for English-speaking students), in which all instruction (in French, science, mathematics, history, and geography) is conducted in French. (For details on this "late immersion" program, see Barik and Swain 1976*a,* 1976*b.*) It was believed that this context would provide an opportunity to observe both the discursive form of, the priorities among, and the effectiveness of the teachers' corrections—not only for linguistic errors, but for various other classroom behaviors, such as subject matter knowledge and other discursive interaction. Tape recordings were made of six lessons early in the year and again late in the year. These were transcribed and coded for the different types of teacher corrective reactions. The model to be presented below was derived through analysis of the coded transcripts.

In order to determine what is in fact a correction, *errors* must be located, for which some criteria are discussed below, and criteria for isolating teachers' *corrective reactions* need to be clarified. Strictly speaking, one might consider as corrections only those treatments which, after correction of a given item, succeeded in establishing the learner's consistent correct performance and his autonomous ability to correct himself on the item. The identification of such treatments is obviously nearly impossible within any one period of instruction. A second conception of correction permits detection during normal classroom interaction: a correction occurs when the teacher is able to elicit a corrected response from the committer of the error or from one or more of his classmates. This conception is henceforth named "successful correction." None of the empirical studies reviewed by this author has discussed such a measure or its correlation with corrective reactions. In his L_1 study, Mehan (1974) did not analyze the *form* of the teacher's reactions; rather, he categorized the criteria for judging the learner's error that were implicit in the teacher's reaction.

A third conception of correction simply includes any reaction of the teacher which clearly transforms, disapprovingly refers to, or demands improvement of the learner's utterance. This is the common conception employed by most recent investigators, and it includes both parts of the common distinction between "explicit" corrections and "implicit" corrections. This distinction is mainly based on judgments about the psychological reality of the correction for the teacher or for the student; the present study has attempted to describe the linguistic, discursive interaction first, prior to making such judgments.

There is a fourth, very narrow and excluding concept of correction, namely, positive or negative reinforcement. Since such a concept either restricts investigation to words of "approval" and "disapproval," or to post hoc definition of "reinforcing" reactions, it was not useful in developing an adequate description. It will be seen that the third conception of correction allows the most inclusive study of teachers' reactions, while the second conception, "successful corrections," can be used to isolate apparently effective corrective treatments. (For the sake of simplicity, peer correction is not being considered, although it can easily be incorporated in this present model.)

In the present study, furthermore, the location of errors has been determined by the teachers' reactions according to the third concept of correction above, by their own expressed criteria,[1] and/or by objective linguistic judgments (cf. Fanselow 1974, for a similar approach). Some errors go unnoticed by the teacher, some are intentionally left uncorrected, and some are actually erroneously repeated by the teacher. A given error is rarely corrected all the time. This variation in teachers' reactions makes the location of errors a tedious task; the complications for the students' learning are possibly more complex (cf. Mehan 1974 and Chaudron 1977).

Categories of errors range from the strictly "linguistic" (*phonological, morphological, syntactic*), to subject matter "content" (factual and conceptual knowledge) and *lexical* items, to errors of classroom *interaction and discourse*—insofar as these last ones are orally manifested, as in speaking out of turn, taking up the wrong question in the lesson, using English in the immersion context, on occasion failing to speak, and not speaking in complete sentences (regarding this last category, cf. Mehan 1974).

Numerous investigators who have attempted to describe corrective reactions in relation to learners' errors, have employed fairly gross descriptive categories for the types of reaction, such as "repetition," "reproof," "correct model," "present alternatives," "location indicated," and so on (e.g., Fanselow 1974; Zahorik 1970a; Cathcart and Olsen 1976; and Allwright 1975). Almost invariably, the codes that have been suggested are either "molar" or gross "molecular" descriptions of the teachers' reactions, an approach which risks overlooking "elemental" features and types of corrective discourse, not to mention overlooking the potential effects of special combinations of elements in the larger classroom interaction. Fanselow (1975), Zahorik, and Allwright have implied larger combinations without developing a more explicitly structured description of their form.

Furthermore, by not dealing more explicitly with the various types of errors suggested above, these descriptions have not recognized the ways in which, say, a content error, a phonological error, and a lexical error may be "corrected" all at once (or one ignored while another is corrected). The model to be explained here helps describe such a phenomenon as simultaneous correction of different errors, as well as combinations of types of reaction and recursive corrective interaction.

A skeleton structure, upon which a more precise, expanded description will be made below, is suggested by a synthesis of the descriptive system for classroom discourse developed by Sinclair and Coulthard (1975), and of Allwright's (1975) suggestions for the basic options open to the teacher in corrective reactions (fig. 1). The boxes in figure 1 are adapted from Allwright; parentheses enclose steps that are only implied in his description.

In figure 1, Sinclair and Coulthard's classroom *moves* (only their described opening, answering, and follow-up moves are relevant for the present purposes) are indicated along the left side. The particular "acts" that constitute these moves and that are pertinent to corrections are shown in quotation marks. Allwright's suggested options fit within this structure in a rough way, as shown by the boxes connected by optional or mandatory flow arrows.

It will be noticed from the flow of correction in figure 1 that a simple "correction" can involve at least three moves after the student's initial error.

1. The teacher can react in an initial follow-up move, which consists of some sort of treatment (containing types and features to be described below) that optionally accepts, evaluates, and/or comments on the error. Ignoring an error, or "exiting," may occur simultaneously with the treatment of a second error in the same student utterance—that is, the model must already be seen to have the third dimension of depth.

2. Some opening move, or elicitation, will be necessary to get the student or transferred students, to respond again, whether or not any initial follow-up treatment has been provided. Lacking a follow-up move, the opening move may convey information regarding the error in some implicit way, or even explicitly if the elicitation focuses on the error.

3. The student(s) will then reply again.

Sinclair and Coulthard's *Moves* and "Acts"	Discursive Options

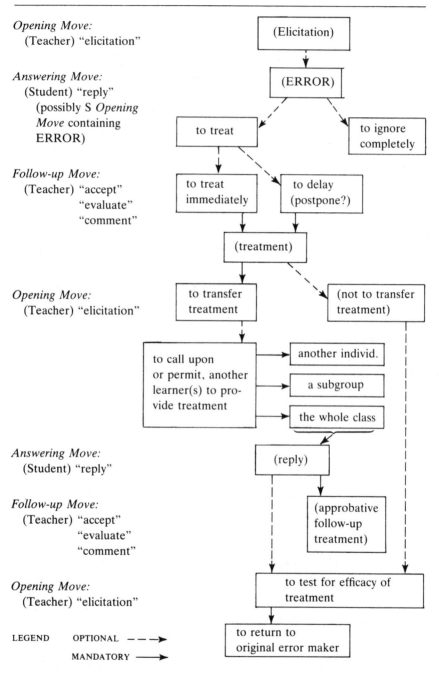

Sinclair and Coulthard's *Moves* and "Acts":

Opening Move:
(Teacher) "elicitation"

Answering Move:
(Student) "reply"
(possibly S *Opening Move* containing ERROR)

Follow-up Move:
(Teacher) "accept"
"evaluate"
"comment"

Opening Move:
(Teacher) "elicitation"

Answering Move:
(Student) "reply"

Follow-up Move:
(Teacher) "accept"
"evaluate"
"comment"

Opening Move:
(Teacher) "elicitation"

LEGEND OPTIONAL – – →
        MANDATORY ——→

Discursive Options:

(Elicitation)

(ERROR)

to treat

to ignore completely

to treat immediately

to delay (postpone?)

(treatment)

to transfer treatment

(not to transfer treatment)

to call upon or permit, another learner(s) to provide treatment

another individ.

a subgroup

the whole class

(reply)

(approbative follow-up treatment)

to test for efficacy of treatment

to return to original error maker

Fig. 1. Sinclair and Coulthard's moves and "acts" with discursive options.
(Adapted from Sinclair and Coulthard 1975 and Allwright 1975.)

Not shown in figure 1 is the fact that further errors would automatically reenter the flow at the top of the diagram as a student's answering move (this results in a new corrective treatment cycle). Correct replies may optionally be followed by two further moves as indicated: (1) a teacher follow-up move offering approbation (again accepting, evaluating, and/or commenting, although positively only), and then (2) an opening move intended to verify the understanding of the correction. (This last move is intimated by Allwright's "test for efficacy" or "return to original error maker.")

The reader will recognize that many "corrections" may fail to go past the teacher's initial follow-up move, or if the teacher elicits a new reply, there may have been little information provided to the learner as to the nature of the error or its proper rectification. Other corrections may continue through numerous cycles (which, taken all together, might collectively be considered as the teacher's "treatment") until correct responses occur. In Sinclair and Coulthard's terms, the basic series of moves (follow-up, opening, answering) described would constitute a correcting exchange; the cyclic series of which would make up a transaction.

A major premise of the present study is that a given utterance in the teacher's corrective reaction, however it is typified formally, will have meaning only in reaction to its place in the flow through the model. Furthermore, the structure of classroom interaction is such that different formal types or features of utterances are more likely to occur at certain points than at others, thus establishing expectancies in the learner that help in his interpretation of the meaning of any utterance. An approbative follow-up may, although not always, differ in certain ways from a corrective follow-up (e.g., in intonation). But the fact that the two are often very similar may create ambiguities that the learners will not decipher (Chaudron 1976).

A careful analysis of the transcripts of the French immersion lessons revealed numerous highly regular patterns in teachers' oral reactions. These were isolated largely on the basis of their regular appearance in instruction, their potential information content, and their clear relationship to the surrounding discourse. A fairly clear distinction exists between *features* and *types* of reactions. *Features* are those linguistic or discursive markers which are either "bound" to larger utterances (e.g., stress and some attention-getters, like "mais"), or which exist *only* by the fact that two adjacent utterances bear a relation to each other (e.g., *interruption*, *reduction* of the utterance in error, and *ignor*ing, see table 1). Thus, features cannot stand alone.

Types, on the other hand, are self-standing, unbound utterances;

TABLE 1. Features and Types of Corrective Reactions in the Model of Discourse

Feature or Type of "Act" (F and/or T)	Description	Example of Exponent of Expression
Ignore (F)	Teacher (T) ignores Student's (S) *error*, goes on to other topic, or shows *acceptance** of content.	
Interrupt (F)	T interrupts S utterance (ut.) following *error*, or before S has completed.	
Delay (F)	T waits to complete ut. before correcting. (Usually not coded, *interrupt* is "marked")	
Acceptance (T)	Simple approving or accepting word (usually as sign of reception of ut.), but T may immediately correct a linguistic *error*.	Bon, oui, bien, d'accord
Attention (T-F)	Attention-getter; probably quickly learned by Ss.	Euhh, regarde, attention, allez, mais
Negation (T-F)	T shows rejection of part or all of S ut.	Non, ne . . . pas.
Provide (T)	T provides the correct answer when S has been unable or when no response is offered.	S: Cinquante, uh . . . T: Pour cent.
Reduction (F) (red.)	T ut. employs only a segment of S. ut.	S: Vee, eee . . . (spelling) T:Vé . . .
Expansion (F) (exp.)	T adds more linguistic material to S ut., possibly making more complete.	S: Et c'est bien. T: Ils ont pensé que c'était bien?
Emphasis (F) (emph.)	T uses stress, iterative repetition, or question intonation, to mark area or fact of incorrectness	S: Mille. T: Mille?
Repetition with no change (T) (optional exp. and red.)	T repeats S ut. with no change of *error*, or omission of *error*.	T: (les auto-routes) n'a pas de feux de circulation.
Repetition with no change and emph. (T) (F) (optional exp. and red.)	T repeats S ut. with no change of *error*, but *emph.* locates or indicates fact of *error*.	S: Mille. T: Mille?
Repetition with change (T) (optional exp. and red.)	Usually T simply adds correction and continues to other topics. Normally only when *emph.* is added will T attempt to correcting *change* become clear, or will T attempt to	S: Le maison est jaune. T: La maison est jaune.

Term	Description	Example
and emphasis (T) (F) (optional exp. and red.)	formulation.	T: *Du* tout. (stress)
Explanation (T) (optional exp and red.)	T provides information as to cause or type of *error*.	S: Uh, E. (spelling *grand*) T: D. Non, il n'y a pas de E. de E.
Complex explanation (T)	Combination of *negation*, *repetitions*, and/or *explanation*.	
Repeat (T)	T requests S to repeat ut., with intent to have S self-correct.	S: Petit. Grande.
Repeat (implicit)	Procedures are understood that by pointing or otherwise signaling, T can have S repeat.	T: Petit . . .
Loop (T)	T honestly needs a replay of S ut., due to lack of clarity or certainty of its form.	S: Les stations-services sont rares.
Prompt (T)	T uses a lead-in cue to get S to repeat ut., possibly at point of *error*; possible slight rising intonation.	T: *Sont* rares? Au présent?
Clue (T)	T reaction provides S with isolation of type of *error* or of the nature of its immediate correction, without providing correction.	
Original question (T)	T repeats the original question that led to response.	
Altered question (T)	T alters original question syntactically, but not semantically.	
Questions (T) (optional red., exp., emph.)	Numerous ways of asking for new response, often with *clues*, etc.	
Transfer (T)	T asks another S or several, or class to provide correction.	
Acceptance* (T)	T shows approval of S ut.	
Repetitions* (T)	Where T attempts reinforcement of correct response.	
Explanation* (T)	T explains why response is correct.	
Return (T)	T returns to original error-maker for another attempt, after *transfer*. A type of *verification*.	
Verification (T-F)	T attempts to assure understanding of correction; a new elicitation is implicit or made more explicit.	
Exit (F)	At any stage in the exchange T may drop correction of the *error*, though usually not after explicit *negation*, *emph.*, etc.	

their relationship to surrounding utterances will, however, determine their specific nature and information potential. Often, certain features serve to distinguish between the common types. (For example, repeating the student's utterance with question intonation can never be regarded as an approbative "reinforcing" follow-up.) Some of the codes to be discussed can actually be either features or types, such as *negation;* where "Non!" is a type, but "ne . . . pas" is a feature. Together, the features and types are the set of elemental "acts" of corrective discourse. Some actual "expressive exponents" of these acts are very frequent. They are likely to be important aids from the learner in decoding the teacher's reaction.

Figure 2 presents the expanded model for the flow of corrective discourse, and table 1 describes the codes which are indicated.

The dashed arrows in figure 2 indicate options proceeding in the direction of the arrows from the emitting boxes. The separate boxes, representing acts or conglomerates of acts, constitute the major alternative pathways through the model. Within any conglomerate box the types or features separated by dashed lines can occur alone or combine optionally in a variety of indeterminate ways, as far as the present analysis has been able to discern. However, there seems to be a tendency for combinations (and for the flow through the entire model) to occur in a downward and possibly clockwise movement. (The lower part of the diagram is excepted from this movement, mainly for graphic reasons.)

Some hypothetical examples should make the flow clear. Assume a student has uttered: S: "Le maison est jaune." The teacher may react: T: "Oui. Jaune. Et de quelle couleur est la chemise?" This follows the flow: (Morpheme) *error* ("Le")—*ignore—exit—acceptance*—repetition** with *reduction—exit.* That is, the teacher has accepted and approved the student's communication without correcting.

An alternative is for the teacher to react:

	(*error*)
T: La Maison est jaune.	(*delay*) *repetition* with *change*
Et de quelle couleur est	("La") *exit²*
la chemise?	

Another alternative is for the teacher to react:

	(*error*)
T: Non!	(*delay*) *negation*
Attention!	*attention* (flow to opening move)
De quelle couleur est	*original question* with
la maison?	*emphasis* (stress)

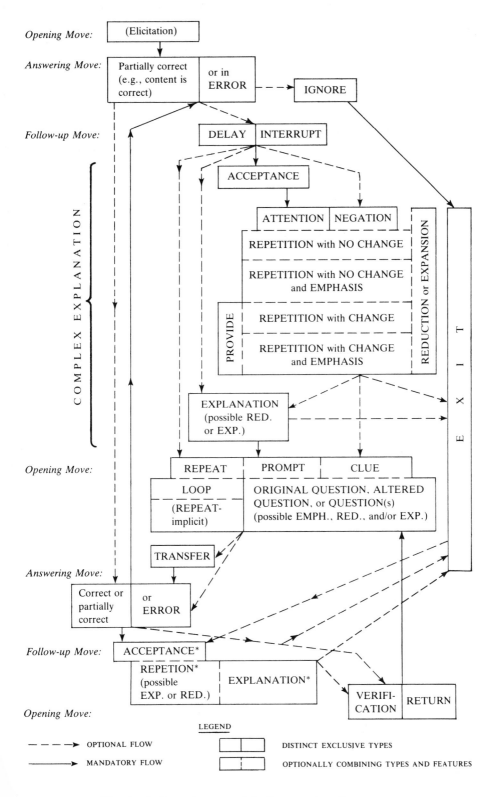

Fig. 2. A flow chart model of corrective discourse

Another:

		(error)
T:	*Le* maison est jaune?	(delay) *repetition* with *no change* and *emphasis* (stress and question)
	C'est une erreur de genre	*explanation*
	qu'on ne devrait pas faire.	(negation)
	Essaie une fois,	*repeat*
	Michael (Another student)	*transfer*
S$_2$:	La maison est jaune.	(transferee)(correct response)
T:	Très bien, Michael.	*acceptance**
	Alors, David,	*return*
	la réponse encore,	*repeat*
	et le genre correct cette fois-ci.	*clue*

Another possibility; assume the student has only managed to say:

S:	Le maison est . . .	(morpheme *error*)
T:	On ne dit *pas* en français,	(interrupt) *negation*
	"Le maison,"	*repetition* with *no change*
	on dit "*la* maison."	*repetition* with *change* and *emphasis* (stress) (this constitutes a *complex explanation*)
	Marie,	*repeat*
	. . .maison . .	*prompt*
S:	La maison est jaune.	(correct response)

There are clearly a large number of possibilities for paths through the model. Rhetorical questions, which Sinclair and Coulthard noted as part of "comment" acts, serve as *explanations* or *complex explanations*, in that they do not serve to elicit further replies. Several of the present codes, in particular *explanations*, *clues*, and *questions*, have so many possible exponents of expression that they may likely be analyzed in their own right. The present study has not attempted any more detailed breakdown of these types.

The present model permits a more precise description of several important factors in corrective discourse than previous schema have provided. This description is then a basis for analysis of the reasons for failure or success of a given reaction. For example, in a case cited by Fanselow (1974), the following dialogue took place:

S:	He holding hat.	(*error*—omission of *is* morpheme)
T:	Again	*repeat*
S:	She holding hat.	(*errors*—omission, and change in pronoun)
T:	She?	*repetition* with *no change*,
S:	. . holding . .	*reduction*, and *emphasis* (question)

The *repetition* with *no change* and question *emphasis* is a surprisingly common reaction among the teachers in the present study, and possibly a common reaction elsewhere. As a relatively common reaction to content or communicative errors and frequently to phonological errors, it also appears to be an effective spur to the student to reformulate a correct response (successful correction). With grammatical errors however, it may be misread by the student as applying to the semantic content in the utterance.

In the above example from Fanselow's study, in fact, the *repetition* with *no change* appears to have been mistaken for *prompt*, the intonation of which seems to be only slightly less rising than a question. The meaning of a *prompt* is itself ambiguous, in that it may either be a location of an error or just a way for the teacher to effect a *loop* (or a *repeat*) at a desired point.

The problem for the teacher of clearly locating the error for his student is particularly clarified by this model and its isolation of certain special features. The degree of explicitness of corrections has previously been evaluated without precise linguistic criteria, and appeal has normally been made to contextual features. The present model may help to distinguish the effective linguistic/discursive features from semantic/contextual ones. There appear to be, for example, some rather clear discursive markers of the *fact* of correction, while information in the corrective reaction as to the nature of the error and of its correct reformulation, may involve more semantic/contextual elements.

Taking the case of *repetitions* of various kinds, which are perhaps the most frequent of any one kind of reaction to errors, their effectiveness appears to be dependent on their incorporation of the features of *emphasis, reduction*, and *negation* (question *emphasis* and *negation* additionally help to distinguish corrective *repetitions* from approbative *repetitions**). These features, along with *interrupt*, help to locate and amplify the nature of the error.

Previous studies have failed to recognize at one time the four basic types of *repetition* (with and without *change*, and with and without *emphasis*, as shown in fig. 2). *Repetition* with *change* alone is especially weak in helping to locate the error. Its failure has perhaps led to mistrust of this type of *repetition*—"response modeling"—as a corrective technique in language teaching. Besides failing clearly to isolate the nature of the error, in many cases the teacher assumes that his correct model is automatically perceived, and he neglects to insure its "intake" by the learner with new elicitative acts.

Repetition with *no change* might also be mistrusted, in part due to fears that it would model the incorrect utterance, but the potential negative and contrasting information it can provide demands that it be considered as a viable type of feedback. This possibility has been recognized by several investigators (Paulston and Bruder 1976; Corder 1973; Fanselow 1974), and is conditionally supported by results presented later.

The two features, *reduction* and *expansion*, also regularly occur with *repetitions*. Studies in first language acquisition (Cazden 1965 and Ervin-Tripp 1973) have suggested that *repetitions* with *expansion* are liable not to improve the learner's syntactic progress. Their effectiveness would seem to depend on the nature of the information added in the *expansion*. It is evident in many such *expansions* that the new information distracts the learner from the point of the correction. The *expansion* is ambiguous as to whether the new information is necessary for syntactic (or phonological) correctness, whether it is merely a coincidental addition, or whether it was the semantic/grammatical cause of whatever changes occurred in the repeated portion of the learner's utterance. (The difference between such first language studies and the present L_2 study, in their exact definitions for such *expansions* or for certain of the *repetitions*, does not seriously alter the point being made here.)

In the discussion of conceptions of correction earlier, it was suggested that the main immediate measurement of effectiveness of any type of corrective reaction would be a frequency count of the students' correct responses following each type. This would establish only an associative link between a specific type and the successes following it. Results from the present study, on the proportion of occurrences of types of *repetitions* to their successes for different types of error, and in total, are shown in table 2.

These totals are suggestive of: a positive relationship between *repetitions* with *reduction* and success, somewhat of a positive relationship between success and *repetitions* that are *unaltered* in length (i.e., neither *reductions* nor *expansions*), and a very low success ratio for *repetitions*

Type of Corrections

Type of Error and Frequency of Correction and Success	Repetition with Change			Repetition with Change and Emphasis			Repetition with No Change			Repetition with No Change and Emphasis		
	Unaltered	Exp.	Red.	Unaltered	Exp.	Red.	Unaltered	Exp.	Red.	Unaltered	Exp.	Red.
Phonological:												
# corrections	52	14	28	18	3	14	2	0	0	1	0	2
# successes	15	1	11	7	1	10	1	1	—	1	—	2
% success ratio[a]	29%	7%	39%	39%	33%	71%	50%	—	—	100%	—	100%
Morphological:												
# corrections	57	36	14	8	1	3	9	0	0	5	0	0
# successes	10	1	5	5	0	0	1	—	—	1	—	—
% success ratio[a]	17%	3%	36%	63%	0%	0%	11%	—	—	20%	—	—
Syntactic:												
# corrections	6	5	0	2	1	0	0	0	2	2	0	0
# successes	1	0	—	1	0	—	—	—	2	0	—	—
% success ratio[a]	17%	0%	—	50%	0%	—	—	—	100%	0%	—	—
Lexical:												
# corrections	11	4	3	2	1	0	4	0	2	2	0	0
# successes	3	0	1	0	1	—	0	—	1	0	—	—
% success ratio[a]	27%	0%	33%	0%	100%	—	0%	—	50%	0%	—	—
Content:												
# corrections	7	4	4	1	3	0	26	0	3	19	7	6
# successes	0	0	0	0	0	—	4	—	1	12	1	4
% success ratio[a]	0%	0%	0%	0%	0%	—	15%	—	33%	63%	14%	67%
Totals:												
# corrections	133	63	49	31	9	17	41	0	7	29	7	8
# successes	29	2	17	13	2	10	6	—	4	14	1	6
% successes ratio[a]	20%	3%	35%	42%	22%	59%	15%	—	57%	48%	14%	75%

a. success ratio $= \dfrac{\text{\# successes}}{\text{\# corrections}}$

with *expansion*. It will also be noted that the use of *emphasis* increases chances of success (an approximate ratio of 46 percent success for *repetitions* with *emphasis*, compared to 20 percent without *emphasis*).

However, taking into account the entire model in figure 2, the results shown must be interpreted cautiously. The student will respond to the teacher's treatment for other reasons than the effectiveness and clarity of the *repetition* alone. Very often, elicitative acts or other types of treatment are used in conjunction with the *repetition*. As noted earlier, many *repetitions* with *change* and *expansion* are not followed by a teacher elicitation, and the occurrence of reduction or *emphasis* appears to be an indication of the teacher's greater insistence on correctness. This would more normally be followed by a persistent follow-up and elicitation.

But the frequencies of correct responses (number of successes) were determined by counting every student reply within one exchange cycle. The success ratio is therefore not too distorted by the effect of complex intervening treatments.

A similar, or more complex, analysis could be attempted with other prominent types of reaction, and then for combined types (such as the *complex explanation,* which Fanselow 1974, and Cathcart and Olsen 1976, among others, have cited as potentially mroe successful reactions). The differences between teachers can readily be observed, and variations for any one teacher will also be recognized. This is to say that any use of the present model in actual observation will have to take into account individual teachers' "basal" features or types of corrections, so that special intonation and uses of stress would be evaluated relative to each other and to the teacher's "unmarked" reactions. This point was made in regard to teachers' positive and negative reactions by Naiman et al. (1975).

The present three teachers' priorities among corrections are indicated in a generally greater rate of corrections for subject matter, "content" errors than for linguistic errors (Chaudron 1977 and Swain, in press). A similar measure needs to be taken of more teachers in different educational contexts and correlated with measures of the learners' linguistic and subject matter achievement.

A further use of the model may also turn out to be the most fruitful one. Cathcart and Olsen (1976), Holley and King (1971), Zahorik (1970a), and, in an interesting suggestion, Mehan (1974), have pointed out the usefulness of the learner(s) awareness of and productive involvement in the corrective exchange/transaction. Far from being a manipulative process with the teacher directing and reinforcing students' "automatic" responses, the corrective discourse usually demands an active concentration by the learner, and sometimes group-dependent cooperation.

(Mehan cites "cohort production" and pupil-initiated "searching," which serves to clarify the teacher's expectations.)

L_2 learners could be sensitized to the types of teacher corrective reactions, to the function they fulfill, and to what each type expects of them in return. Such an approach could enhance all three functions of feedback (incentive, reinforcement, and information) and take much of the guesswork out of teaching and learning.

Notes

The present article is a significantly revised portion of a Qualifying Research Paper, prepared for entrance into a doctoral program at the Ontario Institute for Studies in Education (OISE). The empirical study on which it is based was conducted by the author in 1975–1976 as a pilot study of the Bilingual Education Project of OISE, which is funded by a grant-in-aid from the Ministry of Education, Province of Ontario, to Merrill Swain. The author wishes to acknowledge the constant helpful comments and encouragement, during the study and the writing of this paper, offered by the Project Director, Merrill Swain. In addition, the suggestions of H. H. Stern, Maria Fröhlich, and Marjatta Turenius are gratefully acknowledged.

1. The teachers in this study were asked, following a second series of observations, to listen to the tape recordings of their lessons, to isolate their corrections, and/or students' errors left uncorrected, and to indicate their reasons for judging incorrectness. Prior to this, they had simply been informed that the investigator was interested in the learning processes taking place in immersion classrooms. For more details, see Chaudron (1977).

2. *Repetition** and *exit* also occur, in the sense that the correct content is probably being approved more than the error is being corrected; this is indicated by the optional arrows from the student's initial reply to his second reply, in figure 2. Being what may be called an "implicit" correction, it illustrates the simultaneity of flow through several depth layers of the model—possibly one corresponding to each class of errors.

References

Allwright, Richard L. "Problems in the Study of the Language Teacher's Treatment of Learner Error." In *New Directions in Second Language Learning, Teaching and Bilingual Education,* edited by Marina Burt and Heidi Dulay. Washington, D.C.: TESOL, 1975.

Annett, John. *Feedback and Human Behaviour.* Harmondsworth: Penguin Books, 1969.

Barik, Henri C., and Swain, Merrill. "A Canadian Experiment in Bilingual Education at the Grade Eight and Nine Levels: The Peel Study." *Foreign
Language Annals* 9 (1976a):465–79.

———. "A Canadian Experiment in Bilingual Schooling in the Senior Grades:
The Peel Study Through Grade Ten." *International Review of Applied Psychology* 25 (1976b):99–113.

Cathcart, Ruth L., and Olsen, Judy E. W. B. "Teachers' and Students' Preferences for Correction of Classroom Conversation Errors." Paper presented
at TESOL Conference, New York, March, 1976.

Cazden, Courtney B. "Environmental Assistance to the Child's Acquisition of
Grammar." Ph.D. dissertation, Harvard University, 1965.

Chaudron, Craig. "Teacher Strategies in Handling Student Errors in French Immersion Classes." Paper delivered at the Linguistic Circle of Ontario, Toronto, March 6, 1976.

———. "Teachers' Priorities in Correcting Learners' Errors in French Immersion
Classes." *Working papers on Bilingualism/Travaux de recherches sur le bilinguisme,* no. 12. Toronto: Ontario Institute for Studies in Education,
1977.

Cohen, Andrew D. "Error Correction and the Training of Language Teachers."
Modern Language Journal 59 (1975):414–22.

Corder, S. P. "The Significance of Learners' Errors." In *Error Analysis,* edited
by Jack C. Richards. London: Longman Group, 1974. Reprinted from
IRAL 5, no. 4 (1967):161–70.

———. *Introducing Applied Linguistics.* Harmondsworth: Penguin Books, 1973.

Dulay, Heidi C., and Burt, Marina K. "Natural Sequences in Child Second
Language Learning." *Working Papers on Bilingualism, no. 3.* Toronto:
Ontario Institute for Studies in Education 1974a. Reprinted from *Language
Learning* 24 (1974):37–53.

———. "You Can't Learn without Goofing: An Analysis of Children's Language
Errors." In *Error Analysis,* edited by Jack C. Richards. London: Longman
Group, 1974.

Ervin-Tripp, Susan. "Some Strategies for the First Two Years." In *Cognitive
Development and the Acquisition of Language,* edited by Timothy E.
Moore. New York: Academic Press, 1973.

Fanselow, John. "The Treatment of Error in Oral Work." Paper presented at
Eighth Annual TESOL Convention, Denver, 1974. *Foreign Language Annals* 10, no. 5 (October, 1977):583–93.

———. "Beyond Rashomon." *TESOL Quarterly* 11 (1975):17–39.

George, H. V. *Common Errors in Language Learning: Insights from English.*
Rowley, Mass.: Newbury House Publishers, 1972.

Holley, Freda M., and King, Janet K. "Imitation and Correction in Foreign
Language Learning." *Modern Language Journal* 55 (1971):494–98.

Hughes, David C. "An Experimental Investigation of the Effects of Pupil Responding and Teacher Reacting on Pupil Achievement." *American Educational Research Journal* 10 (1973):21–37.

Mehan, Hugh. "Accomplishing Classroom Lessons." In *Language Use and School Performance,* edited by Cicourel et al. New York: Academic Press, 1974.

Naiman, Neil; Fröhlich, Maria; and Stern, H. H. *The Good Language Learner.* Toronto: Ontario Institute for Studies in Education, Modern Language Centre, 1975.

Paulston, Christina B., and Bruder, Mary Newton. *Teaching English as a Second Language: Techniques and Procedures.* Cambridge, Mass.: Winthrop Publishers, 1976.

Politzer, Robert L. *Teaching French: An Introduction to Applied Linguistics.* Waltham, Mass.: Blaisdell Publishing Co., 1965.

Richards, Jack C., ed. *Error Analysis: Perspectives on Second Language Acquisition.* London: Longman Group, 1974.

Rivers, Wilga M. *The Psychologist and the Foreign-Language Teacher.* Chicago: University of Chicago Press, 1964.

Selinker, Larry. "Interlanguage." In *Error Analysis,* edited by Jack C. Richards. London: Longman Group, 1974. Reprinted from *IRAL* 10, no. 3 (1972): 209–31.

Sinclair, J. McH., and Coulthard, R. M. *Towards an Analysis of Discourse: The English Used by Teachers and Pupils.* London: Oxford University Press, 1975.

Swain, Merrill. "L2 and Content Learning: A Canadian Bilingual Education Program at the Secondary Grade Levels. In *Language Development in a Bilingual Setting,* edited by Briéve. In press.

Zahorik, John A. "Classroom Feedback Behavior of Teachers." *Journal of Educational Research* 62 (1968):147–50.

———. "Pupils' Perception of Teachers' Verbal Feedback." *Elementary School Journal* 71 (1970a):105–14.

———. "Teacher Verbal Feedback and Content Development." *Journal of Educational Research* 63 (1970b):410–23.

Teacher Feedback and Learner Error: Mapping Cognitions

Michael H. Long

The purpose of this article is briefly to consider the importance of the role of feedback in any cognitive theory of second language learning, and then to review some recent descriptive studies of the classroom behaviors of teachers following learner error, in an attempt to ascertain what the teachers studied currently do when providing feedback. I will then set out what I see as the basic options open to teachers when giving feedback on error and describe some of the factors affecting decisions when choosing among the options presented. In the absence of any studies of the effect of different forms of feedback on student learning, I will, clearly, be unable to recommend one decision or series of decisions over another; I will, however, question the status commonly attributed to so-called teacher "correction" of error as an essential characteristic of successful classroom foreign/second language instruction.

The Role of Feedback

In order to learn how to perform even the simplest task people require information on the success or failure of their attempts at performance. The form of that feedback can vary greatly. Thus, an infant may learn to coordinate the movements needed to stretch out its arm in order to pick up an object by seeing its hand touch the object and by feeling and perhaps hearing the contact made between object and hand. The function of knowledge of results (KR), too, can vary. Annett (1969) has observed that its effect on the learner may be primarily that it provides him or her with (a) information and/or (b) reinforcement, and/or (c) some form of incentive.

As language teachers we give tacit recognition to the importance of KR both by the amount of time we spend informing our students of when, where and (sometimes) why they have gone wrong, and by the wide range of techniques we have developed for doing so. Krashen and Seliger (1975) found that the possibility of some sort of feedback, error detection (by the learner) or correction (by the teacher), was one of only two characteristics common to all language teaching methods known to be successful. By implication, feedback on error[1] by the teacher or some teacher surrogate is potentially one of the necessary and sufficient conditions for successful foreign/second language learning. This and the universality of the practice makes it a subject worthy of careful study; one would like to know whether we achieve by it what we *think* we do and if there are any ways of making the process more efficient.

We are interested in error detection, i.e., KR, rather than the narrower error correction alone, for we are all familiar with the ability of some of our students obstinately to repeat the wrong answer despite our dogged provision of the correct one. It would boost our confidence to know that, even if a learner could not get an utterance right as a result of our provision of feedback, he at least knew when he was wrong. For present purposes error "correction" is too limited a term for other reasons, describing as it does the (hoped for) *result* of feedback on error, not the feedback itself. This underlines the importance of viewing feedback in its proper context, that is, following error and prior to further attempts at correct student performance. What is sometimes described in the literature as "a correcting move" should be seen for what it is: behavior by the teacher which allows the learner to obtain KR, on the basis of which, hopefully, it will be the *learner* who makes a correcting move. Feedback is designed to promote correction but is not itself correction. Correction occurs, according to the hypothesis-testing model of language learning (see later), when the learner modifies a rule in his or her interim grammar of the language being learned.

The study of feedback on error is of theoretical as well as practical interest. Increasingly, the learner of a first or second language is believed to progress by the formulation of hypotheses about the target language grammar, based on the input data received, the use of feedback to test those hypotheses, and their subsequent rejection or modification. Language learning has not always been viewed in these terms.

Due largely to the predominant influence of neo-behaviorist theories of learning on foreign language education in many (but not all) parts of the world during the 1950s and 1960s, the importance attributed to KR was for some time limited to its perceived role in reinforcing emergent (correct) second language habits. However, with the reevaluation of the language learner's intellect by Corder, Nemser, Dulay and Burt, Se-

linker, Richards, Taylor, and others, the role of errors and of feedback
on error has taken on a new significance. Of errors, for example, Corder
wrote in his classic 1967 paper:

> Errors are indispensable to the learner himself, because we can
> regard the making of errors as a device the learner uses in order to
> learn. It is a way the learner has of testing his hypotheses about the
> nature of the language he is learning. [Corder 1967, p. 167]

And of feedback, eight years later:

> In order to test this hypothesis of his—this is in no sense, of course,
> a conscious process—he makes utterances which are generated by
> his particular interlanguage grammar at a particular moment. *The
> behavior of the teacher or other speakers of the target language en-
> ables him to decide whether any particular hypothesis he has devel-
> oped is valid or not.* [Corder 1975, p. 411. Emphasis added]

At first sight, far from undervaluing the learner's potential cognitive contribution to the learning process, the above statement would seem to
attribute to him or her part of the ability of the professional linguist.
Corder and others are careful to emphasize, however, that the hypothesis
testing is in no sense a conscious process. Nonetheless, it is clear that the
way in which language teachers behave following their students' commission of error is potentially of interest for any cognitive theory of the
second language learning process aided by formal instruction.

Teacher Feedback on Learner Error

Several writers on child language development in the sixties reported the
focus of mothers on the communicative effectiveness rather than on the
formal accuracy of what their children said. (See, e.g., Brown, Cazden,
and Bellugi 1969.) They were observed to expand child utterances, adding missing functors. but seemed to do so to confirm that communication
had taken place rather than to provide specific language instruction.
Some more recent studies, (e.g., Nelson, Carskaddon, and Bonvillian
1973; Moerk 1976), suggest that deliberate "teaching activities" can play
a role in first language acquisition. In spontaneous mother-child interactions in the home, Moerk observed such activities as mothers modelling
little question and answer sequences for the child, and what Moerk calls
"prodding," where the mother urges the child to make some improve-

ment with "Say X" or "Can you say X?", where X is the model of the construction she wants the child to imitate. These data appear to argue against an outright dismissal of negative feedback on formal inaccuracies as a factor in successful L_1 acquisition—and, by implication, in L_2 learning with formal instruction. However, even with Moerk's data one is struck by the presence of a message clarification element often lacking in second language classrooms. Further, what appear to be "language teaching" sequences may not have this function but again that of establishing (lack of) communication. Also, showing that mothers do this kind of "teaching" does not prove that children learn by it, unless, that is, one is prepared to accept apparent improvement of some kind in the child's next utterance as evidence of learning. This would seem unjustified given what longitudinal L_1 acquisition studies show about the gradual emergence of nativelike forms, errors co-occuring with correct production over periods of several months. (See, e.g., Slobin 1971.)

In the last few years there have been a number of participant observational studies of teacher behavior following errors by second language learners. They have mostly described the feedback practices of experienced teachers working with students of differing ages and levels of language proficiency, often in relatively small groups, and with English or French as the second language being taught. Some of the findings of these studies are reported and discussed below. Descriptive studies only are considered here as it would seem reasonable to suppose that the value of the provision of feedback on error, like any other teaching behavior, will only be measurable once we have identified what teachers actually do in classrooms, and can distinguish this from what they are sometimes imagined to do or are urged to do by textbook writers, teacher-trainers or the authors of methods books.

Teacher reacting moves following learner error have been observed by several investigators to lack clarity. In a pioneering study of teacher feedback on error in oral work, Fanselow (1977*b*) videotaped eleven experienced teachers giving the same lesson on adjective order, ("He's wearing a grey plastic raincoat," etc.). Verbal and nonverbal behaviors were analyzed. It was found that, following student errors, teachers often gave more than one form of feedback simultaneously, e.g., gesturing "no," rubbing one item of clothing (to indicate the material from which it was made) and pointing to another object to be described, or saying "fine" while shaking the head sideways. As Fanselow points out, even if students *were* able to interpret the intended message correctly, (factually correct answer but with one or more errors of form), they would be no wiser as to what was wrong with their utterance. Subtle shakings of the head and "Again" might have meant "I didn't hear you—please repeat" or "You made a mistake." Such messages were often given while students were looking at fellow students, at the learner who had just committed the error, at materials, or anywhere but at the teacher. Thus, they can have meant nothing to the learner for being unseen.

Fanselow also found clarity to suffer due to the teachers' frequent use of the same overt behavior for two or more purposes, a phenomenon noted by several investigators. Typical is the provision by the teacher of the model response desired immediately after an unsuccessful student attempt at production. Fanselow offers the following example:

A. 1 T : It's blue. (*Sample*)
    2 Sl : It blue.
    3 T : It's blue. (*Model for comparison*)
    4 S2 : It's blue.
    5 T : It's blue. (*Confirmation*)
    6 S1 : It blue.
    7 T : It's blue. (*Model for comparison*)
    8 S1 : It blue.

The same teacher utterance sometimes serves as (1) a sample of the target language data to be imitated by the student, (line 1), as (2) a model with which the learner is supposed to compare his own imperfect response, and, by implication, an indication that an error has been made, (lines 3 and 7), and as (3) confirmation and (some people would say) "reinforcement" of a correct response, (line 5). In fact, as Allwright (1976) has noted, function (1) characterizes everything a teacher says in the target language, "guidance" as to its nature simultaneously constituting a further language sample. Teachers sometimes attempt to distinguish overtly identical but multifunctional utterances of "It's blue" variety by changes in intonation, e.g., the use of a rising "question" tone or the addition of emphasis for case (2) above, (model for comparison), and/or by accompanying nonverbal cues. From the point of view of lack of clarity, however, a learner's inadequate grasp of English intonation may often prevent him from making the same (or any) distinction. Further, even if interpretation (2), i.e., "Wrong—listen to what you should have said," is correctly understood, the learner may again be unclear as to which part of what he said was wrong. Neither the source, nor location nor identity of error has been indicated—simply its presence.

Here is another example,[2] this time from an elementary level ESL class for ten-year-olds during practice of adverbs of frequency:

B. 1 T   : All together.
    2 T & SS: Yes, I always use a toothbrush to brush my teeth.
    3 T   : OK. David, can you repeat?
    4 S1   : It's brush eh-
    5 T   : Yes, I always use a toothbrush to brush my teeth.
    6 S1   : It's always toothbrush and it's my teeth.
    7 T   : I always use a toothbrush to brush my teeth. Marie?

David's possible belief that his second attempt (line 6) was correct will have been strengthened if he interpreted either his teacher's third statement of the correct form (line 7) or the transfer of attention to another student as confirmation/"reinforcement." Even if he interpreted the feedback correctly, the obvious disparity between what he is currently capable of and what he is being asked to produce makes it extremely unlikely that he was able (*a*) to remember what he said, (*b*) to do so long enough to compare it with what his teacher said, in order (*c*) to spot the differences and (*d*) to modify his future attempts at production. (See Allwright 1975*a*, for a discussion of these and related problems.) That is, the teacher's feedback may not have been very informative, even if interpreted by the student as having this purpose at all.

Another often reported source of ambiguity concerns teachers' use of positive feedback, usually in the form of praise markers. The next example, concerning feedback on a pronunciation error, is from a corpus of data from four classes at the University of Essex, where experienced ESL teachers were working with adult Venezuelan students. It is quoted by Stokes (1975):

C.   1 T : Again.
    2 SS : The fifth of January, nineteen seventy-four.
    3 T : I think, Eulyces, I heard something else here. Will you
           say it alone?
           The . . .
    4 S2 : The . . .
    5 T : The first.
    6 S2 : No, the [fɪf]
    7 T : Fifth?
    8 S2 : [fɪf]
    9 T : It's very hard to say . . . fifth.
   10 S2 : The [fɪs] of January, nineteen seventy-four.
   11 T : Good.

Notice the redundancy (at least in terms of feedback on the error the teacher supposes s/he has heard) of lines 3 to 5. The teacher's communication of the existence of error (line 3) is, in effect, an invitation for the student to commit it again, and is lacking in information as to its location or identity. Of the teacher's use of "Good" in line 11, Stokes comments:

> One suspects the approval in line 11 is a measure of desperation on the part of the teacher. However, the word was used on a number of occasions when the response was incorrect. One might suggest that "Good" at times simply signalled a boundary marker and did not carry any meaning of commendation. But how does the student interpret the word? If he knows that his answer was really not correct, is his confidence in his teacher weakened? If he believes that "Good" indicates a correct response, will the student continue with the error? [Stokes 1975, p. 61]

Loftus writes of the use of the "praise markers," "Good," "Fine," "OK" in more of the Essex data:

> The word "praise" is really a misnomer for these words, as very often it is really a question of encouragement, conciliation, or simply use as a boundary marker. [Loftus 1975, p. 81]

In our own data, the same ambiguity occurs with "Yes" and "Mm hm," which are sometimes used to interrupt a student, (see, for example, extract B, line 5), sometimes to confirm correctness and sometimes to indicate the existence of error, then usually accompanied by changes in intonation, voice quality, gestures, facial expressions, or combinations of these.

Another source of lack of clarity is, of course, the sheer linguistic or conceptual complexity of some of the feedback teachers give. This has already been alluded to in the previous discussion of the teacher reacting moves in extract B, lines 5 and 7, and extract C, line 3. Most of us are familiar, too, with "explanations" of points of grammar that can be conceptually taxing even for a linguistically unsophisticated native speaker. Both teachers and textbook writers occasionally add to the student's burden by couching the ideas in metalanguage more complex than the point of grammar under discussion.

The lack of clarity of individual feedback moves is often compounded by the inconsistency in a series of such moves. (It may be, of course, that the inconsistency is well-motivated, as we shall see later.) In some of the lessons studied, *what* is treated as erroneous, *who* is so treated and *how* that message is transmitted sometimes appear, superficially at least, somewhat arbitrary. Fanselow (1977*b*) found teachers focusing students' attention on the omission of articles or auxiliaries in one part of a lesson but ignoring the same errors in other parts. Stokes (1975) cites this example concerning the definite article:

D.   1 S3 : When did you leave Venezuela?
    2 S2 : I left Venezuela eh eleventh of January.
    3T : Good.

followed later in the same lesson by:

    4 T : When was he born?
    5 S2 : Twenty . . . twenty-first of January, nineteen sixty-three.
    6 T : Come on, Eulyces, you missed something here. Just say it over again.
    7 S2 : Twenty . . .
    8 T : The twenty-first.
    9 S2 : Twenty-first of February, nineteen sixty-three.
    10 T : Good.

Stokes wonders what hypotheses the student can be forming. The first article omission was praised (lines 2 and 3), the second reprimanded (lines 5 and 6), and the third approved again (lines 9 and 10).

The same inconsistency as to what is treated as error and also as to who is treated as having made an error was found by Mehan (1974) in his study of two "orientation lessons" for early primary-school-age children. Mehan reports the teacher's insistence on complete sentences for children's responses on some occasions, her acceptance of incomplete sentences on others, even from the same children, and her rejection of the complete correct response on others.

The following exchange occurred in an ESL class for ten and eleven year olds.

E.   1 T : What are you looking at? . . . The T.V.
    2 S1 : I'm looking at oranges flowers.
    3 T : OK. I'm looking at oranges flowers.
    4 S1 : I'm looking at oranges flowers.
    5 T : What is he looking at? Yes eh Peter?
    6 S2 : He's looking at oranges flowers.

7 T : Flowers. Orange flowers. OK. David.

8 S3 : He's looking at orange he's looking at orange flowers.

9 T : OK. Good. Marie.

10 S4 : He's eh looking at eh oranges flowers.

11 T : Orange flowers.

12 S4 : Orange flowers.

13 T : OK. Orange flowers.

15 T : OK. All together. Orange flowers.

16 SS : Orange flowers.

17 T : He's looking at orange flowers.

18 SS : He's looking at orange flowers.

19 T : OK. Very good. You can go back to your place.

The whole sequence lasted 58 seconds. Student one's erroneous "oranges flowers" is accepted (line 3) and repeated by the teacher, a nonnative speaker, who temporarily adopts the wrong form herself, followed (in line 4) by a second production of the erroneous version by student one. This, too, is tacitly approved (line 5) by the teacher's transfer of attention to another student, Peter, who dutifully proceeds to perfom the desired I'm→He's transformation and copy the rest of the model sentence (line 6) complete with error. Whether student two, the teacher or anyone else in the class notices the difference between Peter's answer and the teacher's echoed acceptance (line 7) is unclear. The teacher has now reverted to the correct form and (line 8) student three proceeds to get it right, too. Marie, student four, does not. Her "oranges flowers" is the same as two efforts by student one and one by student two which have been accepted by the teacher as well as modelled by her once; however, perhaps because of her hesitant rendition, it is now rejected by the teacher (line 11). Marie is obliged to repeat the correct version twice, alone, before treatment is transferred to the whole class.

It is interesting to note that, prior to Marie's first attempt at production, there had been four incorrect models (lines 2, 3, 4, and 6) and two and a half right ones (lines 7 and 8). A linguist working with the same data from an unknown language would perhaps like Marie, have hypothesized that "orange" and "oranges" were free variants or that the pluralized adjective was the correct form because it was the more frequent one. Of course, extract E is (perhaps) atypical because of the teacher's momentary lapse. Nonetheless, the presence of grammatical errors in the classroom learner's input data, due to the presence in this of his fellow students' interlingual speech, is the rule rather than the exception, and has been noted (e.g., by Allwright 1975a, and in some studies of immersion programs, e.g., Plann 1977) occasionally to be adopted in preference to the teacher's error-free production. In the same article, Allwright has discussed the multitude of conflicting hypotheses a learner may construe when erroneous forms are accepted from some students but not from others. Similar cases have been noted by Stokes (1975) and Mehan (1974). Loftus (1975) found differential use of the praise markers, "OK," "Good," and "Fine," in accordance with his (the teacher's) perceptions of students' abilities and personalities.

The variety of ways in which feedback is transmitted is perhaps less likely to cause confusion than some of the other factors noted. Zahorik's study (Zahorik 1968) of positive and negative feedback by teachers in fifteen "content" subject classrooms revealed 175 different types, but only 16 of these occurred with any frequency. Also, the kind of feedback given was not found to vary randomly but with grade level, lesson purpose, the kind of learning tasks set, and the quality of student response. The kinds of options taken up by second language teachers—remodeling the correct response, with or without emphasis of some elements, resetting the task, setting a simpler one, and so on—are reflected in the various category systems and fragments thereof, found in Fanselow (1977a), Allwright (1975a), Cathcart and Olsen (1976) and others. Such systems do not show, however, that individual teachers may actually use a fairly narrow range of the options listed in category form in instruments purporting to provide exhaustive coverage of all teacher feedback behaviors observed during their creation.

Fanselow (1977b) found that teachers entirely avoided some possible categories of feedback and that other forms categorized by him were employed by just a few of the teachers he observed. There was variation, however; only one form, presenting the right answer or part of it after an error, was found to be common to all the teachers studied. This coincides with Cathcart and Olsen's finding, in their survey of twenty-one teachers of ESL in California, that (re)modeling the correct responses was the most used option (Cathcart and Olsen 1976). The *consistency* shown here needs to be interpreted cautiously, however, in view of the findings concerning the multifaceted use of this and other overt teaching behaviors. Also, in many ESL programs, students move from one teacher to another with a change of course and/or receive instruction from more than one teacher within a given course. They have to learn how and when each teacher gives feedback and to interpret accordingly. Nevertheless, there is some evidence that groups of teachers, however vaguely defined, may share characteristics. In her study of ten female ESL teachers in Israeli secondary schools, Lucas (1975) found variations in the quantity and type

of errors treated. Native speakers of English treated more lexical errors
than any other kind; nonnative speakers treated more pronunciation errors. In general, native speakers tended to ignore more, to treat less and
to disapprove less than did the nonnative speakers. In a study of a total of
twelve half hour lessons in grades eight and nine by three teachers in
French immersion programmes in Canada, Chaudron (1977b) also found
consistency in the (greater) relative importance attached by teachers, as
reflected in their feedback moves, to the learning of lesson content (science, math, geography, and history) over errors in the students' French,
except in French classes, where there was relatively more equal treatment
of grammar and content errors. In this respect the content subject
teachers were behaving more like mothers interacting with children acquiring their L_1.

The data presented need to be viewed in perspective. Both the
numbers of teachers studied and the periods of observation have been
small, and so the extracts cited are not necessarily representative samples
of most teachers' feedback practices or even of *these* teachers' normal,
i.e., unobserved styles. Such generalizations as have been made, must be
interpreted cautiously and should be understood only as testable hypotheses about classroom language teaching in general, not as facts about
what teachers everywhere do. Further, as discussed in the section below,
much of the apparent lack of clarity and consistency may be just that—
apparent—and attributable to sound pedagogical practice.

Options and Decisions

Short stretches of recorded verbal classroom interaction like those examined lose much by being taken out of the context not only of the lessons
from which they come but of the whole history of the relationships established prior to those lessons between the teacher and students concerned.
When an error occurs and is noticed by the teacher, he or she is faced
with several complex decisions the making of which require the careful
weighing of many factors often not apparent in the transcripts even of
complete lessons. Just some of these are the teacher's awareness of his or
her usual (previous) feedback practices with these students, and beliefs as
to the students' familiarity with them, his/her beliefs as to their success so
far (particularly with the student who has just committed an error) and
perception of the measures' popularity among the students in the class,
(including, again, the error-making student). Other factors considered
include the objectives of this lesson and the course as a whole, the pedagogic focus at the moment of error commission and the teacher's percep-

tion of the likely outcome of treatment in terms of the error-making student's aptitude, personality, ability, and sociometric status.

To take just one of these considerations as an example, it is a rare teacher indeed who is blessed with a class of students of equal proficiency in the target language and equal ability for learning more of it. Mixed ability groups are taken into account (among a lot of other ways) by the distribution among the students of questions of different complexity and by the acceptance of different standards of performance from them. Student X rarely seems to get anything right and, so that he does not give up altogether, he is set simpler performance tasks and given encouragement for almost anything he produces. Student Y, on the other hand, has a superior command of English, picks up new pieces of it as fast as they are presented to him and can easily become bored if not set demanding learning tasks. His aims and the teacher's for him are higher; thus, when he commits an error—any error—amid an otherwise near-perfect performance, he is informed of the fact in the knowledge that he will (and will want to) attain a still higher standard of accuracy. This example of well-intentioned differential treatment, (resulting from teacher perceptions of just one kind of individual differences among learners), is one of many potential explanations of the inconsistencies in the teacher feedback in, for example, extracts C, D and E.

Figure 1 is a model of the major steps in the decision-making process teachers go through prior to performing some overt (and so directly observable) behavior following learner error. The remainder of this section is devoted to a discussion of these steps and an attempt to show how various factors can influence the making of the decisions.

Teachers do not provide feedback on all errors that are committed. For a variety of reasons many errors go unnoticed; it is only those perceived by the teacher which serve as input to the decision-making process. Having noticed an error, the first (and, I would argue, crucial) decision the teacher makes is whether or not to treat it at all. In order to make the decision the teacher may have recourse to factors with immediate, temporary bearing, such as the importance of the error to the current pedagogic focus of the lesson, the teacher's perception of the chance of eliciting correct performance from the student if negative feedback is given, and so on. Consideration of these ephemeral factors may be preempted, however, by the teacher's beliefs (conscious or unconscious) as to what a language is and how a new one is learned. These beliefs may have been formed years before the lesson in question.

If the teacher decides to ignore the error and, for example, to set the same or a new learning task, notice that the overt teaching behavior

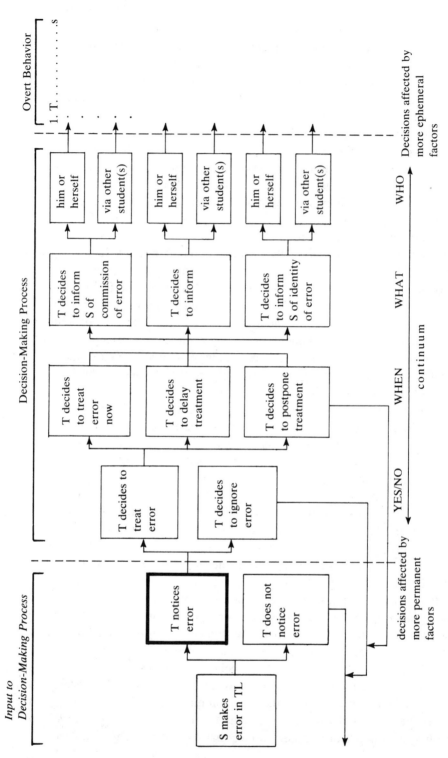

Fig. 1. Model of the decision-making process prior to the teacher feedback move

can be the same as that if he or she failed to notice the error at all or noticed but decided to postpone treatment until a later lesson or part of the current lesson. An observer will not be able to tell the difference, except indirectly through a subsequent interview with the teacher. Note, too, how teachers favoring broadly inductive or deductive teaching strategies could weigh such factors as pessimism about the likelihood of improved student performance over the importance they attach to their general approaches to teaching languages, and opt for the same reacting move, e.g., resetting the same task for another student. That is, the same overt teaching behavior could be appropriate at a given moment for either, despite the different quantity or quality of feedback one might expect under either basic approach.

Assuming the teacher decides to treat the error in some way, the next decision concerns *when*. Here the options appear to be (*a*) immediately, which often involves interrupting the student, (*b*) after the (apparent) completion of the student's utterance, or (*c*) at some future time, including, for example, in the course of a future lesson. Chaudron (1977*a*) calls (*b*) and (*c*) "delayed" and "postponed" feedback, respectively. There is some evidence in the psychology literature that the value of feedback decreases the greater the time lapse between performance and KR, and that KR given verbally by an experimenter after each response or failure to respond is effective in preventing the normally observed decline in vigilance over time, (Mackworth 1950). There is, however, the important question of the inhibiting effect of interruptions, and their inevitable communication to the student of the greater value placed by the teacher on the form as opposed to the content of what he or she says.

In favor of choosing to delay or postpone treatment, there is also some evidence of the positive effects of what is known as "wait time." Hoetker (1968) found that in classes of above average ability English teachers allowed more time for students to begin their responses to soliciting moves than they gave students in below average classes. Rowe (1969), studying science lessons, reported that if average wait time was prolonged to five seconds or more, the length of student responses increased, as did the number of complete sentences produced, the confidence of those utterances as judged by their tone, the amount of speculative thinking verbalized by the children, and the number of children who engaged in that kind of talk.

In the second language classroom, Holley and King (1971) have described some innovations they made in the provision of feedback in the teaching of German to graduate students. Feedback was given on students' success in communicating "content" in the foreign language rather than on the grammatical accuracy of the forms used to do so. Specifically, teachers were told not to interrupt students trying to answer questions, and when they hesitated in answering, to say and do nothing (except wait) for from five to ten seconds. Only then were they to (a) rephrase the question, reducing where possible the number of words while consciously emphasizing content words over functors, or (b) cue the correct answer using grammatical variations of a key content word, or (c) encourage other students in the class to "generate" simple sentences from the faltering students' incomplete utterances. They were also urged to expand ungrammatical but meaningful answers in the manner observed in parents interacting with young children, but not to demand repetitions of such expansions. Holley and King report that in over 50 percent of the instances they filmed, no "corrective measure" (rephrasing, cueing, sentence generating) was needed. Simply allowing students sufficient time to reformulate their responses led to improved performance.

Having made the decision as to *when* to treat errors the teacher then has three basic options, (a) to inform the student of the existence of error, (b) to inform the student of the location of error, or (c) to inform the student of the identity of error. Choice (b) will entail (a); (c) will entail (a) and (b). Examples of overt behaviors realizing these options might be:

> S : He go to the park on Saturdays.
> (a) T : No.
> or   T : He go to the park on Saturdays? (i.e., the student's utterance repeated with rising intonation, probably accompanied by some nonverbal cue, such as raising eyebrows.)
> (b) T : He *go* to the park on Saturdays?
> or   T : He *what* to the park?
> (c) T : *Go* or *goes?*
> or   T : You missed the third person *s* off *goes.*

There then follows a decision as to whether (a), (b), or (c) will be carried out by the teacher or by another student or students (col. 4—*who*—in fig. 1). There is no obviously recommendable path through columns 3 or 4, even for specific types of learners. Given the abundant possibilities for lack of clarity of feedback, however, other things being equal, there may be a case for more attention to be paid to option (c), with, where appropriate, an explanation of the source of error. Evidence as to the desirability of peer feedback is attractive, but this is but one of a variety of considerations affecting choice among the options in column 4. It might be outweighed, for example, by knowledge that other students are making the same error, or that the student concerned is unlikely/unwilling, e.g., for cultural reasons, to listen to his peers in a case like this.

Allwright (1976) has presented an "inductive model incorporating cognitions" of the conditions necessary for successful learner production of the *response* part of the (teacher) initiation—(student) response—(teacher) feedback sequence in classroom discourse. He showed how, following a teacher soliciting move and prior to the student response, (two overt behaviors), the learner must be attending, must believe he has heard the teacher's "question" correctly, that he remembers and understands the soliciting move, and so on. All of these factors are covert, unobservable, the result of a logical analysis of what the learning situation described must demand of any learner in cognitive terms. In the second part of this paper I have followed a similar approach in suggesting what I believe to be the basic decisions a teacher takes prior to the observable act of providing feedback on learner error, and have indicated a few of the factors bearing on those decisions. I have not argued the case for any particular decisions or series of decisions for the simple reason that, like so much of what we do as teachers in classrooms, there is little or no empirical evidence relating some form(s) of feedback with student learning.

Some studies *have* talked of the success of various forms of feedback in terms of the extent to which, following them, the learner is observed to incorporate some immediate improvement into his next utterance. This seems a questionable yardstick by which to judge efficacy. It does not fit with what, as teachers, we know to happen in classrooms. Students' errors do not by and large change in such a decisive manner from one moment to the next. Incorrect forms disappear gradually, and then often reemerge later, much as they do in first language development; they are not there one moment and gone the next. Temporary correct (improved) performance of what Krashen et al. (1977) call "easy" grammatical items, e.g., third person singular *s*, is understandable following feedback because such items are easily monitorable. At the second attempt, having got this message across the first time he spoke, the learner is concentrating (and specifically being asked by the teacher to concentrate) on formal accuracy, so improvement should be expected. But what of "hard" areas of grammar, such as article usage? A missing or wrongly chosen article is easily incorporated in an adult learner's speech when he is focusing on formal accuracy, immediately after feedback. It seems unreasonable to suppose, however, that the learner has mastered this complex syntactic domain due to his attention having been drawn (explicitly or implicitly in the teacher's feedback move) to one more instance of correct usage after so many previous examples have failed. There seems to exist a danger of confusing the efficacy of various forms of feedback in terms of their effect on monitored linguistic performance with their usefulness in terms of bringing about a lasting modification of the learner's interim hypotheses about rules in the target language grammar.

Conclusion

Intuitively, the hypothesis-testing model makes sense in terms of adult learners seeking positive confirmation of hypotheses about the target language grammar, and this interpretation is supported by work on simplification and generalization strategies by Taylor, Richards and others. Richards (1974), on the other hand, has pointed out that taking the model to suggest that learners seek out negative instances in order to test (in the sense of *falsify*) their hypotheses is counterintuitive. People like to discover they are right about things, not mistaken. Setting out to elicit negative feedback in this way would be an emotionally unrewarding task, one that was of low productivity in communicative terms and a very inefficient manner of achieving anything of use. (As Richards observes, learners could, instead, simply ask whether a given sentence was not in fact wrong.) Given the unclear, inconsistent, and complex nature of much teacher feedback on error, as illustrated in this article, it would also be unlikely to work. Yet the falsification idea seems to be the interpretation one would have to hold in order to suggest, as one or two writers have done recently, that teachers should encourage learners to make errors.

The role of teacher feedback, whether errors are in any sense committed intentionally or not, is clearly vital, but it may be that not all forms of feedback are as vital as we sometimes think. We know that, like children, adults can and do acquire second languages outside classrooms simply by exposure to their use in situations involving verbal interaction for communicative purposes, i.e., with the aid of little or no formal "teaching" of any kind, including the "correction" of ungrammatical forms. What adult acquirers do undoubtedly have access to is information as to the success or otherwise in communicative terms of their attempts at using the new language; that is, they are able to find out whether or not they are succeeding in transmitting or understanding a message and, on the basis of this knowledge (in some as yet unknown way) to work out where improvement is needed. I would suggest that the case for what Krashen and Seliger call error correction (as opposed to detection) as one of the necessary conditions for successful second language learning is unproven and will remain so until longitudinal studies are undertaken of the second language acquisition process aided by formal instruction with differing feedback conditions.

Elsewhere (Long 1976), I have drawn attention to the deleterious effects on the naturalness of classroom discourse of, among other practices, the so-called correction of errors. The greater *efficiency* (if any) of language instruction which includes various kinds of feedback on formal accuracy needs to be tested, but meanwhile can probably be improved by teachers reconsidering the options available to them and the decisions they make following learner error. Greater clarity and consistency of feedback, at least, must be desirable, if only on the grounds that if a job is worth doing, it is worth doing properly. Hopefully, further research will show whether the job is really worth doing at all.

Notes

At various stages in the preparation of this article I received valuable comments from Richard Allwright, Fernando Castaños, Craig Chaudron, Alison d'Anglejan, Patsy Lightbown, and Brian Smith. The opinions expressed do not necessarily reflect theirs, and all errors are, of course, my own.

1. In this article an "error" will refer to (1) any phonological, morphological, syntactic, or lexical deviance in the form of what students say from a standard variety of English which is attributable to the application by the learner of incorrect grammatical rules, (2) recognizable misconstrual of or lack of factual information, (3) a breach of rules of classroom discourse, and (4) a bit of student language behavior treated as an example of (1), (2), or (3) by the teacher.
2. Extracts from transcripts not attributed to other sources are from preliminary data gathered by the author and Brian Smith of the TESL Centre, Concordia University.

References

Allwright, R. L. "Problems in the Study of Teachers' Treatment of Learner Error." In *New Directions in Second Language Learning, Teaching and Bilingual Education: On TESOL '75*, edited by M. Burt and H. Dulay. Washington, D.C.: TESOL, 1975a.

———. ed. *Working Papers: Language Teaching Classroom Research*. Essex:

University of Essex, Department of Language and Linguistics, September, 1975*b*.

———. "Putting Cognitions on the Map: An Attempt to Model the Role of Cognitions in Language Learning." Paper presented at the Fourth AILA Congress, Stuttgart, August, 1975. In *Workpapers in TESL 9*, June, 1976, University of California, Los Angeles.

Annett, J. *Feedback and Human Behavior*. Harmondsworth: Penguin, 1969.

Brown, R.; Cazden, C.; and Bellugi, U. "The Child's Grammar from I to III." In *Minnesota Symposium on Child Psychology*, edited by J. P. Hill, 1969.

Cathcart, R., and Olsen, J. "Teachers' and Students' Preferences for Correction of Classroom Conversation Errors." In *On TESOL '76*, edited by J. Fanselow and R. Crymes. Washington, D.C.: TESOL, 1976.

Chaudron, C. "The Context and Method of Oral Error Correction in Second Language Learning." Unpublished. 1977*a*.

Chaudron, C. "Teacher Priorities in Correcting Learning Errors in French Immersion Classes." *Working Papers on Bilingualism*, no. 12, 1977*b*.

Chaudron, C. "A Descriptive Model of Discourse in the Corrective Treatment of Learners' Errors." *Language Learning* 27, no. 1 (1977):29–46.

Corder, S. P. "The Significance of Learner's Errors." *IRAL* 5, no. 4 (1967):161–70.

———. "The Language of Second Language Learners: The Broader Issues." *Modern Language Journal* 59, no. 8 (1975):409–13.

Fanselow, J. "Beyond *Rashomon*—conceptualizing the teaching act." *TESOL Quarterly* 11, no. 1 (1977*a*):17–39.

———. "The Treatment of Error in Oral Work." *Foreign Language Annals* 10, no. 5 (October, 1977*b*):583–93.

Holley, F., and King, J. "Imitation and Correction in Foreign Language Learning." *Modern Language Journal* 55, no. 8 (1971).

Krashen, S., and Seliger, H. "The Essential Contributions of Formal Instruction in Adult Second Language Learning." *TESOL Quarterly* 9, no. 2 (1975):173–83.

Krashen, S.; Butler, J.; Birnbaum, R.; and Robertson, J. "Two Studies in Language Acquisition and Language Learning." Paper presented at the First Annual Second Language Research Forum, Los Angeles, February, 1977.

Loftus, G. "A Study of Four Teachers' Lessons." In *Working Papers: Language Teaching Classroom Research*, edited by R. L. Allwright. University of Essex, Department of Language and Linguistics, September, 1975.

Long, M. H. "Encouraging Language Acquisition by Adults in a Formal Instructional Setting." *ELT Documents* 3 (1976) British Council, London.

Lucas, E. "Teachers' Reacting Moves Following Errors Made by Pupils in Post-Primary English-as-a-second Language Classes in Israel." Master's thesis, Tel Aviv University, 1975.

Mackworth, N. H. "Researches on the Measurement of Human Performance." *Med. Res. Council Special Report*, no. 268, 1950.

Mehan, H. "Accomplishing Classroom Lessons." In *Language Use and School Performance*, edited by A. Cicourel *et al.*, pp. 76–142. New York: Academic Press; 1974.

Moerk, E. "Processes of Language Teaching and Training in the Interactions of Mother-Child Dyads." *Child Development* 47, no. 4 (December 1976): 1064–78.

Nelson, K. E.; Carskaddon, G.; and Bonvillian, J. D. "Syntax Acquisition: Impact of Experimental Variation in Adult Verbal Interaction with the Child." *Child Development* 44 (1973):497–504.

Plann, S. "Second Language Acquisition in the Spanish Immersion Program: Towards Native-Like Proficiency or a Classroom Dialect?" Paper presented at the Eleventh Annual TESOL Convention, Miami Beach, Florida, April, 1977.

Richards, D. R. "On Communicative Efficiency and the Treatment of Error." Unpublished paper, University of Essex, Department of Language and Linguistics, 1974.

Rowe, M. B. "Science, Silence and Sanctions." *Science and Children* 6, no. 6 (1969):11–13.

Slobin, D. *"Psycholinguistics.* Glenview, Ill.: Scott, Foresman, 1971.

Stokes, A. "Errors and Teacher-Student Interaction." In *Working Papers: Language Teaching Classroom Research*, edited by R. L. Allwright. Essex: University of Essex, Department of Language and Linguistics, September, 1975.

Zahorik, J. A. "Classroom Feedback Behaviour of Teachers." *Journal of Educational Research* 62, no. 4 (1968):147–50.

Questions

1. Ferguson, Henzl, and Freed show that we native speakers modify our speech to learners, probably without thinking about it very much. The question is, should we as teachers consciously manipulate our classroom speech? And if so, in what areas? Clear pronunciation and simple grammatical structures are areas where we do this naturally. But what if we want to teach elisions and contractions in speech, or complex grammatical structures?

2. Chaudron very cautiously suggests, on the basis of his findings, that certain correction types may be more beneficial, since they have relatively good success ratios. Long, on the other hand, seems to think that teacher corrections may do more harm than good because of inconsistency and ambiguity in their use. What is your conclusion regarding this matter? On what do you base your conclusion? If you have decided against correction, in what ways can you provide the incentive, reinforcement, and information function that such feedback is said to provide? If you decide for correction, how do you deal with the consistency and ambiguity problems?

3. The Bailey, Madden, and Krashen article and the Schachter article were published in the same year, 1974. Using different data bases, they came to opposite conclusions regarding the strong (a priori) version of the CA hypothesis. Why did they reach such different conclusions? How can this apparent conflict be resolved? Does the Larsen-Freeman article help to resolve the conflict or does it create further confusion?

4. Celce-Murcia enumerates three kinds of comparative constructions among the world's languages: the *degree* comparative, the *limited universe* comparative, and the *surpass* comparative. Which of these comparative constructions would the Schachter and Rutherford article lead you to predict that Igbo, Japanese, and Mandarin learners would overproduce in English? Which would they be likely to underproduce?

Problems

A. If you have access to a classroom, tape record three to five hours of class time and then record the correcting behaviors of the teacher during those hours and their effects on the learners, if any. What regularities do you find? And what advice would you give the teacher, given Chaudron's claims of effectiveness and your analysis of the teacher's and students' behavior? A word of caution: be sure to record the same kinds of activities over the three to five hours.

B. Schachter and Hart* have claimed, on the basis of cross-sectional data, that Persian learners of English avoid producing infinitival complements on nouns (as in "the ability to sing well") and that Persian and Japanese learners avoid producing infinitival complements on verbs (as in "I want to go" or "I told him to go"). How would you test these claims? Be as explicit as possible.

C. English Morphology/Arabic Learners (data from a study done by Jacquelyn Schachter and Beverly Hart in 1979)

Intermediate Arabic learners of English produce a good deal of variation in pronoun use. See if you can make sense of this variation. Hints: first divide the sentences below into grammatical and ungrammatical groups and compare the sentence type in the grammatical group with that of the ungrammatical group. Are there exceptions? What group do they fit into best? Then divide the ungrammatical sentences according to error type. What generalizations can you arrive at?

In terms of simple percentages, what is the accuracy order of the three clause types you identified earlier? Do you think the acquisition order was the same? Explain.

1. As the years have passed more and more cars have come to Saudi Arabia for people to use them.
2. The relations between the parents and their sons it not strong enough such as in the past.
3. The ladies in some parts of my country are not allowed to work.
4. But when oil discovered in 1948. . .everything in Kuwait changed.

*In a study done by Jacquelyn Schachter and Beverly Hart in 1979.

467

5. Any job like this it should be very important.
6. The people of Sharjah are divided into two groups.
7. They put up their tents when find water.
8. In every evening there will be a party where can go dancing.
9. Foreign teachers they might face a lot of problems.
10. Now we got what need.
11. The future of young men and women now it not clear.
12. They spend a lot of time until give us a report.
13. Some of the students they graduated and did not find work.
14. The village was completely destroyed.
15. The young people in my country they want to change.
16. Every year more than five hundred thousand of Muslim people come to Saudi Arabia to visit the Islamic places.

Name Index

Italicized numerals indicate page numbers of article(s) in this text by the author named in the entry.

Subject Index

Accent, 10, 18, 29, 98, 243; rating scale, 245, 248, 249
Accuracy order. *See* Order of acquisition
Acquisition order. *See* Order of acquisition
Affective variables, 374, 375. *See also* Motivation
Anglo children, 121–34
Aphasia, 323, 325
Approximative system, 334. *See also* Interlanguage
Arabic, 33–35, 39, 187, 240, 263, 279, 304, 356–60, 364–66, 369–74, 467; classical, 34; Egyptian, 3, 32, 33, 141
Articles, use of, 148, 151, 201, 217, 219–22, 231, 232, 265, 278, 311, 312, 335, 341, 346, 350, 382, 453, 461
Australian languages, 342
Avoidance phenomenon, 279, 291, 292, 359, 360, 363–75

Bantu languages, 280, 297, 299
Behaviorism, 164, 273, 329, 331, 447
Bilingualism, 95, 114, 174, 175, 197
Burmese, 198, 201

Chadic languages, 111
Chinese, 4, 21, 96, 97, 100–104, 148, 198, 277, 279, 304, 305, 308–11, 326, 336, 350, 356–61, 364
Cognitive model, 329–31
Cognitive processes, 4, 6, 109
Cognitive theory of language learning, 446, 448
Complexity, syntactic, 415–23
Consonant clusters, 30, 34, 48–53, 55, 59–62, 64, 71, 141, 408; simplification of, 403
Contrastive analysis: a posteriori (explanatory or weak version), 3, 7–13, 354–61; a priori (predictive or strong version), 3, 4, 7–13, 89, 354–62
Correction, 169, 257, 268, 269, 275,
293, 428–33, 439–43, 446, 447, 462, 463, 466; correcting moves, 432, 438, 447; self-correction, 160
Creole, 387
Culture, 4, 5, 7, 120, 133; cultural-rhetorical difference, 5
Czech, 89, 90, 140, 141, 146–54, 198, 215, 219–32

Deep structure, 11–13, 90, 91, 270, 295
Developmental errors. *See* Errors
Dialect, 22, 23, 27, 31, 36, 61, 65, 90, 94, 132, 396; idiosyncratic, 265
Difficulty in language learning, 6–12, 18–21, 27–29, 363; order of, 52–55, 317, 319, 322, 331; prediction of, 4, 163, 197, 215, 272, 354, 357, 363, 366
Discourse, 5, 120–21, 131, 303–15, 428; "corrective," 431, 436–38, 442. *See also* Narrative
Dutch, 148

Ease in language learning, 12, 27, 363
Errors: classification of, 215–19, 276, 278; developmental, 198, 199, 203, 206, 274, 279, 316, 350, 428; fossilized, 146; induced, 146, 256–71; interlingual, 274, 299; intralingual, 198, 199, 203, 206, 268, 280, 285, 323; morphological, 219, 222–26, 229, 230

Farsi, 5, 116
Feedback, 160, 161, 428, 440, 443, 446–63, 466
Finnish, 96
Foreigner talk, 292, 378–92, 399, 408, 409, 413–23
Fossilization, 177–86, 189–92
French, 4, 9, 11, 12, 63, 72, 73, 76, 82, 91, 96, 105–7, 146, 151, 154, 177, 178, 187, 198, 203, 223, 228, 282, 294, 348, 364, 386–89, 429, 433, 449, 456; Canadian, 241, 243, 246

475

Variability, phonetic and phonological, 146, 240, 243, 250, 251
Variation in language acquisition data, 335, 336, 341–48
Vietnamese, 63, 96, 187
Vocabulary, 20, 108, 179; errors in, 256; lack of, 364, 365; order of introducing, 152. *See also* Lexical elements

Vowels, reduction in length of, 403, 404

Warm Spring Indians, 122, 124
Word order, 15–19, 148, 151, 152, 220, 231, 306, 309, 347; errors in, 219, 231; typology, 340

Yakima Indians, 120–34